FREUD AND FREUDIANS ON RELIGION

Freud
and
Freudians
on
Religion

A Reader

EDITED BY

DONALD CAPPS

Yale University Press   New Haven & London

Published with assistance from the foundation
established in memory of Philip Hamilton
McMillan of the Class of 1894, Yale College.

Designed by James J. Johnson and set in New Aster
type by dix! Quality Graphics and Information
Processing, Syracuse, New York.

Printed in the United States of America

Library of Congress Cataloging-in-Publication Data

Freud and Freudians on religion : a reader /
edited by Donald Capps.
p. cm.
Includes bibliographical references and index.

ISBN: 978-0-300-08201-2

1. Psychoanalysis and religion. 2. Freud,
Sigmund, 1856–1939. I. Capps, Donald.
II. Title.
BF175.4.R44 F74 2001
200'.1'9—dc21
00–011921

Contents

Acknowledgments

I especially want to thank Otto Bohlmann, editor at Yale University Press, who provided timely guidance throughout the process of conceiving, refining, and bringing this project to completion. I also want to express my appreciation to James W. Jones of Rutgers University and John McDargh of Boston College for their insightful reviews of the project at an early stage of its development. Princeton Theological Seminary provided valuable assistance through its faculty research fund. Joan Blyth-Lovell typed the manuscript with consummate skill. Tom Ireland, copy editor, and Margaret Otzel, production editor, made the process of making the manuscript into a book seem easy. I would also like to express my appreciation to James E. Dittes, who introduced me to psychoanalysis; to Peter Homans, who encouraged a close reading of Freud's texts; to David Bakan, who stimulated my interest in the psychoanalysis of the Bible; and to Paul W. Pruyser with whom I formed an invaluable collegial relationship during our mutual involvement in the Society for the Scientific Study of Religion. It seemed that we were the Society's lone defenders of psychoanalysis, a fact we lamented over leisurely dinners in otherwise barren surroundings.

Introduction

Sigmund Freud's classic text *The Interpretation of Dreams* was originally published in 1899. A century later, his views are still being discussed, and his positions on various issues continue to stimulate
controversy and germinate ideas in fields well beyond their original
locus in psychology. In an age in which concepts and ideas have brief
life spans, judged obsolete in a matter of years, even months, the dura-
bility of Freud's theories is all the more remarkable. When his "dream
book" saw the light of day in 1899, few, including Freud himself,
would have predicted that his work would have such staying power. In
a letter to his friend, Wilhelm Fliess, Freud described a later visit to
the house where he had the dream that led to his theory of dreams as
wish-fulfillments, and mused, "Do you suppose that some day a marble tablet will be placed on the house, inscribed with these words, 'In
This House—on July 24th, 1895, the Secret of Dreams was Revealed to
Dr. Sigm. Freud'? At the moment there seems little prospect of it." [1]

This book of readings focuses on a subject—religion—which
Freud wrote about throughout his psychoanalytic career, beginning
with "Obsessive Actions and Religious Practices," originally published
in 1907, and concluding with *Moses and Monotheism: Three Essays*,
published in 1939, the year he died. The fact that his publications on
religion increased as he grew older has itself been a matter of some
controversy within psychoanalytic circles. Some have viewed his interest in the subject as something of an embarrassment for the psychoanalytic movement itself, arguing that his writings on religion are
peripheral to psychoanalysis and were in fact detrimental to it, as they
provoked unnecessary controversy reflecting negatively on psychoanalysis itself. Freud himself worried that they might have this effect
and sometimes took measures to distance himself from them (for ex-

ample, by publishing them anonymously or intending to publish them posthumously).

Others have argued, however, that his writings on religion are not only revealing of his own personality, reflective (whether directly or indirectly) of his efforts to come to terms with his Jewish heritage, but also inseparable from the rest of his corpus. Viewed thus, there is no discontinuity between his writings on religion and his other writings, including, for example, *The Interpretation of Dreams*, a subject that has deep roots in the biblical tradition itself.

The premise behind this book is that Freud's writings on religion are, in fact, inseparable from his work as a whole, but that they may also be read as a subgenre within the larger corpus, as this is essentially how Freud himself viewed them. When he wrote on religion, he was keenly aware that he was engaging in applied psychoanalysis, using insights derived from concepts and theories developed in his clinical work with patients to illumine various aspects of religion, especially those that seemed impenetrable by other methods of inquiry. To say that they were applied psychoanalysis is not, however, to denigrate them, or to imply that they are to be viewed as "second-class." For one thing, they make up a very substantial portion of his corpus, as examination of the twenty-four volume *Standard Edition* of his work attests.[2] For another, they reflect Freud's desire that psychoanalysis be viewed not only as a clinical enterprise, but a theory of culture as well. His writings on religion, together with those on art, played a vital role in substantiating this more expansive view of psychoanalysis.

Thus, while some members of the psychoanalytic community viewed his writings on religion, especially in his later years, as indicative of his declining mental acuity, for Freud himself, they were precisely the opposite, as they constituted a return to the broader cultural issues that had interested him prior to his decision to enter the medical profession.

Another premise behind this book is that, for all the innovative power of Freud's own writings on religion, this aspect of psychoanalysis could not have survived on the strength of his writings alone. In a sense, psychoanalytic interpretation of religion is much like religious traditions themselves, for if religious traditions usually have founders who stand at the headwaters of the tradition, their survival is dependent on successors, not merely persons with organizational skills, but more important, successors who are able to think through various conceptual problems that the founder recognized but was unable to resolve.

While several of Freud's own contemporaries, such as Otto Rank, Ernest Jones, Theodor Reik, and Oskar Pfister, made original contributions to the psychoanalytic study of religion, I have chosen to include in this volume a later generation of authors, ones whose writings reflect the preoccupations of the latter half of the twentieth century. A useful reference point in this regard is Erik H. Erikson's *Childhood and Society,* his first major publication, which originally appeared in 1950.[3] With its emphasis on the psychosocial features of psychoanalytic theory, *Childhood and Society* was not a radical departure from Freud's own work (anticipated, for example, by Freud's *Group Psychology and the Analysis of the Ego),*[4] but Erikson's own interest in religion throughout his career did much to sustain this aspect of psychoanalytic reflection through the latter half of twentieth century. In recent years, the writings of Julia Kristeva have played a similar role and are destined to shape its contours to an even greater extent in the early decades of the twenty-first century.

This collection, then, provides an introduction, first, to Freud's own writings on religion, and second, to psychoanalytic writings on religion by several major contributors in the latter half of the twentieth century. While this is by no means a complete roster of significant authors, those included here are not only representative of the field but also original thinkers in their own right. None is simply an expositor of Freud's work; all take their cues from Freud but plow their own ground. As the reader will readily discern, some of these authors (notably David Bakan, Erikson, and Kristeva) address the subject of religion directly, while others (D. W. Winnicott and Heinz Kohut) approach it more indirectly, whether through brief allusions to religion, through clinical cases where religion is a factor in a patient's psychopathology, or through exploration of universal human conflicts and aspirations. As my introductions to the individual authors will indicate, however, all make a distinctive contribution to the ongoing tradition of the psychoanalysis of religion, and all have contributed to a vital legacy to which subsequent generations will make their own unique contributions.

Thus far in these introductory comments, I have used the word *religion* without taking time to indicate how it is being used in this context. Religion is notoriously elastic and multifarious, and attempts to define it, or to say what its "essence" is, invariably result in the exclusion of one or more of its most salient features, or to acknowledgments that there are exceptional cases that the definition fails to encompass. In earlier writings, I have endorsed the view of those who focus on its multidimensionality,[5] noting, for example, cultural anthropologist Clifford Geertz's proposal that religion be construed in terms of "socially available 'systems of significance'—beliefs, rites, meaningful objects—in terms of which subjective life is ordered and outward behavior guided."[6] But how does one begin to identify these systems of significance? Geertz suggests that one does not begin with the task of defining religion, sorting out religion from superstition, magic, philosophy, custom, folklore, myth, ceremony, and so forth. Rather, the task is more akin to beginning in a fog and trying to clear it:

> One can begin with an assortment of phenomena almost everyone but the professionally contrary will regard as having something vaguely to do with "religion" and seek for what it is that leads us to think so, what it is that leads us to think that these rather singular things certain people do, believe, feel, or say somehow belong together with sufficient intimacy to submit to a common name. . . . We look not for a universal property— "sacredness" or "belief in the supernatural," for example—that divides religious phenomena off from nonreligious ones with Cartesian sharpness, but for a system of concepts that can sum up a set of inexact similarities, which are yet genuine similarities, we sense to inhere in a given body of material. We are attempting to articulate a way of looking at the world, not to describe an unusual object.[7]

Here, Geertz proposes that we think about and perceive religion as a system or structure of meaning that is based not on the dichotomization of religion and nonreligion but on the pattern that religion, in spite of its diffuseness and multiplicity, presents to the observer as the fog begins to clear. Some distinctions must of course be made as one begins to discern the system of significance. The various dimensions or facets of the system come into focus, and these appear to constitute the shape of the total configuration. These dimensions are not exclusive but inclusive; they give texture to an otherwise undifferentiated though related mass of experiences, sensations, thoughts, attitudes, activities.

I have no particular investment in the attempts of historians of religion to isolate and name the various dimensions (for example, Ninian Smart's six-dimensional model, including ritual, mythological, doctrinal, ethical, social, and experiential),[8] but they are illustrative of Geertz's point that there are rather singular things that certain people do, believe, feel, or say which somehow belong together with sufficient intimacy to submit to a common name. By and large, the authors included in this text would not be uncomfortable with this more inclusive view of religion, though each has written more about some aspects than others. Also, while one might have expected that they, being psychologists, would be especially attentive to what people "feel" (or to the "experiential" dimension), this is clearly not the case. Freud, for example, is at least as interested in what people do and believe as in what they feel or experience.

In the course of developing this collection of readings, I became aware of two issues of special concern to Freud that are also manifest in the work of his successors. One is the relationship between religion and art, which, in Freud's writings, almost invariably comes out in favor of art over religion. There are, however, some borderline cases, as when the art is concerned with religious subject matter. I have included excerpts from three of his writings—"The Moses of Michelangelo," his monograph on Leonardo da Vinci, and *Civilization and Its Discontents*—which have direct bearing on this issue. Excerpts from the writings of Erik H. Erikson and Julia Kristeva reflect the continuing interest of psychoanalytic authors in this intriguing issue, leading us to ask whether religion filtered through art evokes from the psychoanalytically inclined a more positive response than other religious expressions, such as doctrinal or ethical formulations and practices.

A second issue is the central role that the Bible plays in psychoanalytic interpretations of religion. Here, as well, Freud's employment of psychoanalytic concepts in his interpretation of biblical texts, as in his *Moses and Monotheism*, is carried forward by virtually all the authors included in this volume. This, in my view, is evidence of their own identification with (if qualified endorsement of) the Judaeo-Christian tradition itself. Kristeva's essay "Reading the Bible" is especially explicit about what is to be gained from reading biblical texts psychoanalytically, while David Bakan's essay on Job and Erikson's essay on Jesus may be viewed as direct descendants of Freud's writings on Moses.

The selections included here represent a mere sample of psychoanalytic writings on religion in general, and by these authors in particular. Readers who are familiar with the writings of one or more of them may justifiably contend that other selections would have been preferable, or that I have omitted an essay or chapter that surely ought to have been included. The most difficult decisions occurred in relation to Erik H. Erikson's and Julia Kristeva's writings, as virtually everything in their published works has bearing—directly or indirectly—on religion. Freud also presented difficulties, but of a somewhat different nature. I wanted, of course, to include material from his writings on religion, which are extensive in themselves. Other writings, however, while less directly related to religion in a formal or topical way, not only place his writings on religion in context but also present a different side of Freud as far as religion itself is concerned. I have in mind here his essays "Mourning and Melancholia," "The 'Uncanny,'" "The Theme of the Three Caskets," "Humor," and sections of *Beyond the Pleasure Principle* and *The Interpretation of Dreams*. A book similar to this one, but exclusively devoted to Freud, would enable an even more complex picture of his understanding of religion to emerge.

By the same token, I believe that much is to be gained from placing several authors together in a single volume, as their work can be profitably read intertextually, that is, by recognizing common themes between two or more of the authors. Several of the selections in this volume were chosen for this very reason. Thus, authors writing in the latter half of the twentieth century are not only reflecting on what Freud himself wrote but are also concerned, directly or indirectly, with issues that have attracted the attention of others. This is a further indication that the psychoanalytic study of religion is comparable to a religious tradition, as such traditions not only involve elaborations on the views of their founders, but also reflect cross-fertilizations among the founder's successors. In sociological terms, the authors included here (excepting, of course, Freud himself) constitute a cohort group, that is, they are a group of scholars who share common experiences and who, for all their individual differences, have rather similar outlooks on the world of religion.

I want to say a concluding word about the manner in which the individual selections were constructed. In the interests of space and readability, I have often deleted material from the original essay or book chapter included here. In some instances, I have taken material from two or more sections of a book and spliced them together into what I hope is an integral, coherent whole. In every instance, I have retained the core points or themes of the original and made every effort not to distort the author's original meanings or to undermine the complexities and subtleties of the author's views. In all cases, I have made an effort to select material that is accessible to the general reader and therefore favored material that is free from psychoanalytic technicalities or was written with the professional analyst primarily in mind. In some instances, I have supplied connecting language and headings in order to enhance the intelligibility of the final piece. I have also, in many cases, deleted footnote material, while retaining direct references to other publications. I have not employed ellipses, either because the sheer number of them would be needlessly distracting, or because they would be misleading, as a hundred or more pages might be signified by a single ellipsis. This, therefore, is a text not for research scholars but for general readers who seek an introduction to the psychoanalytic study of religion.

NOTES

1. Sigmund Freud, *The Interpretation of Dreams*, vol. 4 of *The Standard Edition of the Complete Psychological Works of Sigmund Freud*, ed. James Strachey (London: Hogarth Press, 1953), 1.

2. Ibid.

3. Erik H. Erikson, *Childhood and Society* (New York: W. W. Norton, 1950, 1963).

4. Sigmund Freud, *Group Psychology and the Analysis of the Ego*, vol. 18 of *The Standard Edition of the Complete Psychological Works of Sigmund Freud*, ed. James Strachey (London: Hogarth Press, 1955).

5. See Donald Capps, "Contemporary Psychology of Religion: The Task of Theoretical Reconstruction," *Social Research* 41 (1974): 362–83.

6. Clifford Geertz, *Islam Observed* (New Haven: Yale University Press, 1968), 95.

7. Ibid., 95–96.

8. Ninian Smart, *The Religious Experience of Mankind* (New York: Charles Scribner's Sons, 1969), 6–12.

Sigmund Freud

The selections in this section, arranged chronologically, reflect three decades of Freud's writings on religion. Born May 6, 1856, in the small town of Freiburg in Moravia, Freud was fifty-one years old when "Obsessive Actions and Religious Practices" appeared and eighty-three years old, living in London, when *Moses and Monotheism* was published.

The issue of Freud's personal identification with the religion of his forebears had been a matter of continuing controversy, ranging from suggestions that psychoanalysis was deeply imbedded in the Jewish mystical tradition and was a sort of secularized version of this subversive movement within Judaism, to claims that his self-identification as a "godless" or "infidel" Jew are accurate self-appraisals.[1] What is beyond controversy, as his own writings on religion make clear, is Philip Rieff's observation that Freud had the same "analytic attitude" toward religion as toward his patients and other cultural phenomena (art, literature, philosophy, and so forth). This means that Freud approached religion as a realist, Rieff says, for "to be analytical is to be a realist. It is not required of a realist to be hopeful or hopeless, but only truthful."[2] Rieff adds that among Freud's first and most important followers "there were those who considered his realism therapeutically limiting; nor did they find that the dynamics of the transference supplied an adequate substitute."[3] Thus, they "refused to approach reality in Freud's neutralist terms. Faith reappeared, understood in terms of therapy. This was done rather easily, for religion has always had a therapeutic aspect," either in the sense of "a therapeutic control of everyday life or a therapeutic respite from that very control."[4]

Freud's writings collected here bear out the truth of Rieff's claim that Freud approached religious subjects with an "analytic attitude." This necessarily means that the orientation of an observer of religion from the outside predominates. On the other hand, even a determined realist is prone to moments when the object of observation exerts a certain attraction (or repulsion), resisting his best efforts to maintain a studied neutrality.[5] There are occasional instances of such departures from neutrality in the following essays. The complexity of this attraction/repulsion dynamic is perhaps most evident in Freud's essays on works of religious art, especially Michelangelo's Moses and da Vinci's *Mona Lisa* and *St. Anne with Virgin and Child*.

A strategy that Freud employs in his analytical approach to religion is to draw an analogy between a religious phenomenon and what he has discovered in the clinical setting. He disclaims any perfect correspondence between the two but suggests that the similarities are often so striking that the fact someone had not drawn attention to them before is rather surprising. Thus, the first essay, "Obsessive Actions and Religious Practices," makes a connection between the "ceremonials" of obsessive compulsives and religious rituals. As in other analogies, his concern is not to center merely on surface resemblances but to discover the deeper, emotional basis for their similarity. In this particular case, the connection is in the guilt one believes one will experience if the action or practice is not carried out, which helps to explain why religious practices are so resistant to extinction. This feature of the analytic attitude is designed to rebut those who point to obvious differences between the two phenomena, such as the fact that obsessive actions are private (having meanings significant only to the individual who carries them out), whereas religious rites are public and involve shared meanings. That Freud never abandoned this analogical strategy is attested by his use of it in *Moses and Monotheism*, where he employs his theory of the "return of the repressed" among individuals to account for the reemergence of Moses (and monotheism) in Jewish religious life after a prolonged absence. As desires and experiences repressed in early childhood reemerge in adolescence after the latency period of later childhood, so Moses and the monotheism he promoted, repressed by the people of Israel for several centuries, were reinstated in the postexilic period.

The selection from Freud's monograph on Leonardo da Vinci does not include its most discussed and controversial feature (to which Julia Kristeva alludes in "The Wheel of Smiles"), involving his interpretation of a childhood memory of Leonardo's. As it is now well established that this interpretation was misguided, based on a poor English translation of the original Italian, it seemed more appropriate to select material that has stood the test of time, namely, his analysis of Leonardo's paintings of maternal figures in light of the circumstances of the artist's parental relationships.[6] This selection illustrates my earlier point that Freud viewed religious art more favorably than religious beliefs, in part because it reflected the artist's unconventional insights into religion, but also because art (like science) tends to reflect the son's triumph over the father, and not, as in religion, a submission to the father. In psychoanalytic language, art reflects the triumph of the ego over the superego.

"The Moses of Michelangelo" essay has attracted considerable critical attention because it offers insights into Freud's commitment to psychoanalysis and his personal attitudes toward his religious heritage. The former was noted early on by Ernest Jones, who suggested that Freud may have been drawn into making this analysis of the feelings depicted in Michelangelo's statue by his own attitudes toward the dissident movements of Alfred Adler and C. G. Jung, these splits having occurred just prior to his writing of the essay.[7] The latter is explored in detail by David Bakan, who suggests that Moses, for Freud, is representative of the superego. Because the force behind the superego is the fear of punishment, Freud's suggestion that the feared punishment will never eventuate is a veiled assertion of freedom against the severe restrictions of thought and action which had been the life strategy of eastern European Jews.[8]

The essay on a seventeenth-century demonological neurosis is especially noteworthy for the connection it perceives between the ambivalent reaction of an aspiring Bavarian painter, Christoph Haizmann, to his father's death and his subsequent pact with the Devil as father-substitute. This essay is precursor to several of Freud's critical writings concerning the Father-God of the Judaeo-Christian tradition. It illustrates his theoretical points in "Mourning and Melancholia" (1917), where he emphasizes the ambivalence felt toward the lost object in the case of melancholia.[9] From this perspective, Haizmann's neurosis is symptomatic of the Judaeo-Christian tradition's tendency to split the father image, with God and the Devil representing the two sides of the son's ambivalence. Thus, it exemplifies but does not resolve the conflicts of melancholia. In contrast to the painter in this essay, Freud views Leonardo da Vinci as one who triumphed over his father through his art, whereas Haizmann, a much less able individual, is forced to take refuge in the religious community of "the pious Fathers."

The *Future of an Illusion,* published in 1927, and from which the selection on the psychological significance of religious ideas derives, is the second of Freud's major writings on religion. It was preceded by *Totem and Taboo* in 1913. *The Future of an Illusion* is probably the best known of Freud's writings on religion and the most responsible for his controversial public image as an opponent of religion. In it, Freud puts forward his view of religion as illusion. In recent years, however, a reevaluation of this view of religion as "illusion" has been under way, prompted by Winnicottians and others who have noted that "illusion," if viewed as the imaginative capacity of humankind, may well have positive meanings and significance. Erikson's association of religion with hope, which is based on future projections, has similar implications. In this sense, religion has much in common with art and many forms of literature. On the collective level, it has much in common with utopian visions. Freud, however, did not hold such a sanguine view of religious "illusions," in part because they appeal (unlike art) to the masses and also reflect an immature understanding of reality.

The brief essay "A Religious Experience" nicely illustrates Rieff's point about Freud's analytical attitude. It is also reflective of the negative reception that Freud's views on religion have been accorded in America. While psychoanalysis gained considerable acceptance in the psychiatric community in the United States, Freud's application of psychoanalytic methods of analysis to religion has been widely rejected. This essay is also a rare instance of Freud's recognition that the son's ambivalence regarding the lost object may be directed as much to the mother as to the father. He cannot resist commenting on the incongruousness of his correspondent's assurances that Freud's Jewishness "was not an obstacle in the pathway to true faith." He responds to the implied condescension in this remark with ironic humor, observing that his correspondent's prayers in behalf of this "infidel Jew" have not had any noticeable results.

The selection from *Civilization and Its Discontents* reflects Freud's view that the religion of the common person—the only religion that deserves the name—is based on the "figure of an enormously exalted father." This not only confines the believer to an infantile view of reality but also places undue restrictions on the human imagination. This chapter may be read in the light of his conviction, stated most force-fully in *The Ego and the Id*, that monotheistic religion is based on a deeply imprinted image of a "father of personal prehistory," who is historically and developmentally prior to identification with the fa-ther of the child's everyday experiences.[10] This chapter also reflects Freud's view that life in the civilized world is more painful than pleas-urable; this fact, together with the inevitability of death, creates the need for various palliatives to soften or dull the pain. Among these, re-ligion is less effective than either art or science.

The final selection, from *Moses and Monotheism*, reflects Freud's own sense of a progression in his thinking on religion. In his autobio-graphical study, published in 1935, he acknowledged: "In *The Future of an Illusion* I expressed an essentially negative valuation of religion. Later, I found a formula which did better justice to it; while granting that its power lies in the truth which it contains, I showed that the truth was not a material but a historical truth."[11] The selection from *Moses and Monotheism* focuses, therefore, on what Freud considered to be the historical truth of religion. It especially concerns the fact that, among the Jewish people, monotheism, which Moses (an Egyptian prince) adopted from the Pharaoh Amenhotep IV (or Ikhnaton), has been enormously resistant to extinction. While the source of Jewish claims to special status with God, monotheism has also been a major factor in its sufferings, especially with regard to antisemitism, but also its burden of internalized guilt. In this selection, Freud reprises his basic argument in *Totem and Taboo* about the murder of the primitive father and the ensuing guilt among his surviving sons, applying it to Moses himself. He relates this to clinical evidence of the return of re-pressed memories after a period of latency. Egyptologist Jan Assmann considers Freud's use of latency theory to explain Moses' revival in Jewish history to be his most important contribution to the subject:

> In the long history of the discourse on Moses and Egypt, from Hecataeus to Freud, a displacement of antagonism can be ascer-tained which proceeds from the outer to the inner. We start with rev-olution and expulsion, then proceed to secrecy and mystery, in which the antagonism takes place within one society, and end up with la-tency, where the antagonism resides in the individual as well as the collective soul. Latency as a third model of religious antagonism and tension is the discovery of Sigmund Freud and constitutes his most important contribution to the discourse on Moses and Egypt. . . . The concepts of latency and the return of the repressed are indispensable for any adequate theory of cultural memory.[12]

Assmann concludes that, since Freud, no cultural theory can afford not to take "cultural forgetting" or "repression" into consideration.

Readers will undoubtedly want to ask what evidence Freud offers in behalf of his theory that Moses was murdered by his followers. In support, he cites Ernst Sellin's groundbreaking study of the meaning of Moses for the religious history of Israelites. This study, published in 1922, finds in the book of the prophet Hosea "unmistakable traces of a tradition to the effect that the founder of their religion, Moses, met a violent end in a rebellion of his stubborn and refractory people. The religion he had instituted was at the same time abandoned." This tradition is not restricted to Hosea but recurs in the writings of most of the later prophets. The account in Numbers 16 of Moses' retaliation against the rebel Korah and his men, leading to murmurings against Moses for having "killed the people of the Lord," invites speculation that a subsequent rebellion against Moses may have been more successful and is consistent with the tradition that Moses was not permitted by the Lord to enter the promised land.

The selection concludes with Freud's comments about the dynamic relationship between Judaism and Christianity. He notes that Christianity, with its concept of original sin (emphasized by Paul), introduces another chapter in the effort of sons to expiate guilt for wrongs allegedly committed against God the Father. Through such expiation— the sacrifice of one of their own— the son is accorded divine status. In Freud's view, this is another form of the effort to displace the father.

NOTES

1. David Bakan makes the former argument in *Sigmund Freud and the Jewish Mystical Tradition* (New York: Schocken Books, 1965), while Peter Gay makes the latter in *A Godless Jew: Freud, Atheism, and the Making of Psychoanalysis* (New Haven and London: Yale University Press, 1987).

2. Philip Rieff, *The Triumph of the Therapeutic: Uses of Faith after Freud* (New York: Harper & Row, 1966), 34.

3. Ibid., 34.

4. See James Elkins, *The Object Stares Back: On the Nature of Seeing* (San Diego: Harcourt Brace, 1996).

5. Bradley I. Collins, *Leonardo, Psychoanalysis, and Art History: A Critical Study of Psychobiographical Approaches to Leonardo da Vinci* (Evanston: Northwestern University Press, 1997).

6. See Sigmund Freud, "The Moses of Michelangelo," in vol. 13 of *The Standard Edition of the Complete Psychological Works of Sigmund Freud*, ed. James Strachey (London: Hogarth Press, 1955), 230.

7. Bakan, *Sigmund Freud*, 128.

8. Sigmund Freud, "Mourning and Melancholia," in vol. 14 of *The Standard*

Edition of the Complete Psychological Works of Sigmund Freud, ed. James Strachey (London: Hogarth Press, 1957), 239–58.

9. Sigmund Freud, *The Ego and the Id,* vol. 19 of *The Standard Edition of the Complete Psychological Works of Sigmund Freud,* ed. James Strachey (London: Hogarth Press, 1961), 31.

10. Sigmund Freud, *An Autobiographical Study,* vol. 20 of *The Standard Edition of the Complete Psychological Works of Sigmund Freud,* ed. James Strachey (London: Hogarth Press, 1959), 72.

11. Jan Assmann, *Moses the Egyptian: The Memory of Egypt in Western Monotheism* (Cambridge and London: Harvard University Press, 1997), 215.

12. Sigmund Freud, *Moses and Monotheism: Three Essays,* vol. 23 of *The Standard Edition of the Complete Psychological Works of Sigmund Freud,* ed. James Strachey (London: Hogarth Press, 1964), 36.

CHAPTER 1

Obsessive Actions and Religious Practices

SIGMUND FREUD

I am certainly not the first person to have been struck by the resemblance between what are called obsessive actions in sufferers from nervous affections and the observance by means of which believers give expression to their piety. The term "ceremonial," which has been applied to some of these obsessive actions is evidence of this. The resemblance, however, seems to me to be more than a superficial one, so that an insight into the origin of neurotic ceremonial may embolden us to draw inferences by analogy about the psychological processes of religious life.

People who carry out obsessive actions or ceremonials belong to the same class as those who suffer from obsessive thinking, obsessive ideas, obsessive impulses and the like. Taken together, these form a particular clinical entity, to which the name of "obsessional neurosis" is customarily applied. But one should not attempt to deduce the character of the illness from its name; for, strictly speaking, other kinds of morbid mental phenomena have an equal claim to possessing what are spoken of as "obsessional" characteristics. In place of a definition we must for the time being be content with obtaining a detailed knowledge of these states, since we have not yet been able to arrive at a criterion of obsessional neuroses; it probably lies very deep, although we seem to sense its presence everywhere in the manifestations of the illness.

Neurotic ceremonials consist in making small adjustments to particular everyday actions, small additions or restrictions or arrangements, which have always to be carried out in the same, or in a methodically varied, manner. These activities give the impression of being mere formalities, and they seem quite meaningless to us. Nor do they appear otherwise to the patient himself; yet he is incapable of giving them up, for any deviation from the ceremonial is visited by intolerable anxiety, which obliges him at once to make his omission good. Just as trivial as the ceremonial actions themselves are the occasions and activities which are embellished, encumbered and in any case prolonged by the ceremonial—for instance, dressing and undressing, going to bed or satisfying bodily needs. The performance of a ceremonial can be described by replacing it, as it were, by a series of unwritten laws. For instance, to take the case of the bed ceremonial: the chair must stand in a particular place beside the bed; the clothes must lie upon it folded in a particular order; the blanket must be tucked in at the bottom and the sheet smoothed out; the pillows must be arranged in such and such a manner, and the subject's own body must lie in a precisely defined position. Only after all this may he go to sleep. Thus in slight cases the ceremonial seems to be no more than an exaggeration of an orderly procedure that is customary and justifiable; but the special conscientiousness with which it is carried out and the anxiety which follows upon its neglect stamp the ceremonial as a "sacred act." Any interruption of it is for the most part badly tolerated, and the presence of other people during its performance is almost always ruled out.

Any activities whatever may become obsessive actions in the wider sense of the term if they are elaborated by small additions or given a rhythmic character by means of pauses and repetitions. We shall not expect to find a sharp distinction between "ceremonials" and "obsessive actions." As a rule obsessive actions have grown out of ceremonials. Besides these two, prohibitions and hindrances (abulias) make up the content of the disorder; these, in fact, only continue the work of the obsessive actions, inasmuch as some things are completely forbidden to the patient and others only allowed subject to his following a prescribed ceremonial.

It is remarkable that both compulsions and prohibitions (having to do something and having *not* to do something) apply in the first instance only to the subject's solitary activities and for a long time leave his social behaviour unaffected. Sufferers from this illness are consequently able to treat their affliction as a private matter and keep it concealed for many years. And, indeed, many more people suffer from these forms of obsessional neurosis than doctors hear of. For many sufferers, too, concealment is made easier from the fact that they are quite well able to fulfil their social duties during a part of the day, once they have devoted a number of hours to their secret doings, hidden from view like Mélusine.[1]

It is easy to see where the resemblances lie between neurotic ceremonials and the sacred acts of religious ritual: in the qualms of conscience brought on by their neglect, in their complete isolation from
all other actions (shown in the prohibition against interruption) and
in the conscientiousness with which they are carried out in every detail. But the differences are equally obvious, and a few of them are so
glaring that they make a comparison a sacrilege: the greater individual variability of [neurotic] ceremonial actions in contrast to the
stereotyped character of rituals (prayer, turning to the East, etc.), their
private nature as opposed to the public and communal character of
religious observances, above all, however, the fact that, while the
minutiae of religious ceremonial are full of significance and have a
symbolic meaning, those of neurotics seem foolish and senseless. In
this respect an obsessional neurosis presents a travesty, half comic
and half tragic, of a private religion. But it is precisely this sharpest
difference between neurotic and religious ceremonial which disappears when, with the help of the psycho-analytic technique of investigation, one penetrates to the true meaning of obsessive actions. In the
course of such an investigation the appearance which obsessive actions afford of being foolish and senseless is completely effaced, and
the reason for their having that appearance is explained. It is found
that the obsessive actions are perfectly significant in every detail, that
they serve important interests of the personality and that they give expression to experiences that are still operative and to thoughts that are
cathected with affect. They do this in two ways, either by direct or by
symbolic representation; and they are consequently to be interpreted
either historically or symbolically.

I must give a few examples to illustrate my point. Those who are
familiar with the findings of psycho-analytic investigation into the
psychoneuroses will not be surprised to learn that what is being represented in obsessive actions or in ceremonials is derived from the
most intimate, and for the most part from the sexual, experiences of
the patient.

> (a) A girl whom I was able to observe was under a compulsion to
> rinse round her wash-basin several times after washing. The signifi-
> cance of this ceremonial action lay in the proverbial saying: "Don't
> throw away dirty water till you have clean." Her action was intended
> to give a warning to her sister, of whom she was very fond, and to re-
> strain her from getting divorced from her unsatisfactory husband
> until she had established a relationship with a better man.
> (b) A woman who was living apart from her husband was subject

to a compulsion, whenever she ate anything, to leave what was the best of it behind: for example, she would only take the outside of a piece of roast meat. This renunciation was explained by the date of its origin. It appeared on the day after she had refused marital relations with her husband—that is to say, after she had given up what was the best.

(c) The same patient could only sit on one particular chair and could only get up from it with difficulty. In regard to certain details of her married life, the chair symbolized her husband, to whom she remained faithful. She found an explanation of her compulsion in this sentence: "It is so hard to part from anything (a husband, a chair) upon which one has once settled."

(d) Over a period of time she used to repeat an especially noticeable and senseless obsessive action. She would run out of her room into another room in the middle of which there was a table. She would straighten the table-cloth on it in a particular manner and ring for the housemaid. The latter had to come up to the table, and the patient would then dismiss her on some indifferent errand. In the attempt to explain this compulsion, it occurred to her that at one place on the table-cloth there was a stain, and that she always arranged the cloth in such a way that the housemaid was bound to see the stain. The whole scene proved to be a reproduction of an experience in her married life which had later on given her thoughts a problem to solve. On the wedding-night her husband had met with a not unusual mishap. He found himself impotent, and "many times in the course of the night he came hurrying from his room into hers" to try once more whether he could succeed. In the morning he said he would feel ashamed in front of the hotel housemaid who made the beds, and he took a bottle of red ink and poured its contents over the sheet; but he did it so clumsily that the red stain came in a place that was very unsuitable for his purpose. With her obsessive action, therefore, she was representing the wedding-night. "Bed and board" between them make up marriage.

(e) Another compulsion which she started—of writing down the number of every bank-note before parting with it—had also to be interpreted historically. At a time when she was still intending to leave her husband if she could find another more trustworthy man, she allowed herself to receive advances from a man whom she met at a watering-place, but she was in doubt as to whether his intentions were serious. One day, being short of small change, she asked him to change a five-kronen [2] piece for her. He did so, pocketed the large coin and declared with a gallant air that he would never part with it, since it had passed through her hands. At their later meetings she was frequently tempted to challenge him to show her the five-kronen piece, as though she wanted to convince herself that she could believe in his intentions. But she refrained, for the good reason that it is impossible to distinguish between coins of the same value. Thus her doubt remained unresolved; and it left her with the compulsion to write down the number of each bank-note, by which it *can* be distinguished from all others of the same value.

These few examples, selected from the great number I have met with, are merely intended to illustrate my assertion that in obsessive actions everything has its meaning and can be interpreted. The same is true of ceremonials in the strict sense, only that the evidence for this would require a more circumstantial presentation. I am quite aware of how far our explanations of obsessive actions are apparently taking us from the sphere of religious thought.

It is one of the conditions of the illness that the person who is obeying a compulsion carries it out without understanding its meaning—or at any rate its chief meaning. It is only thanks to the efforts of psycho-analytic treatment that he becomes conscious of the meaning of his obsessive action and, with it, of the motives that are impelling him to it. We express this important fact by saying that the obsessive action serves to express *unconscious* motives and ideas. In this, we seem to find a further departure from religious practices; but we must remember that as a rule the ordinary pious individual, too, performs a ceremonial without concerning himself with its significance, although priests and scientific investigators may be familiar with the—mostly symbolic—meaning of the ritual. In all believers, however, the motives which impel them to religious practices are unknown to them or are represented in consciousness by others which are advanced in their place.

Analysis of obsessive actions has already given us some sort of an insight into their causes and into the chain of motives which bring them into effect. We may say that the sufferer from compulsions and prohibitions behaves as if he were dominated by a sense of guilt, of which, however, he knows nothing, so that we must call it an unconscious sense of guilt, in spite of the apparent contradiction in terms. This sense of guilt has its source in certain early mental events, but it is constantly being revived by renewed temptations which arise whenever there is a contemporary provocation. Moreover, it occasions a lurking sense of expectant anxiety, an expectation of misfortune, which is linked, through the idea of punishment, with the internal perception of the temptation. When the ceremonial is first being constructed, the patient is still conscious that he must do this or that lest some ill should befall, and as a rule the nature of the ill that is to be expected is still known to his consciousness. But what is already hidden from him is the connection—which is always demonstrable—between the occasion on which this expectant anxiety arises and the danger which it conjures up. Thus a ceremonial starts as an *action for defense or insurance, a protective measure.*

The sense of guilt of obsessional neurotics finds its counterpart in the protestations of pious people that they know that at heart they are miserable sinners; and the pious observances (such as prayers, invocations, etc.,) with which such people preface every daily act, and in especial every unusual undertaking, seem to have the value of defensive or protective measures.

A deeper insight into the mechanism of obsessional neurosis is gained if we take into account the primary fact which lies at the bottom of it. This is always the repression of an instinctual *impulse* (a component of the sexual instinct) which was present in the subject's constitution and which was allowed to find expression for a while during his childhood but later succumbed to suppression. In the course of the repression of this instinct a special *conscientiousness* is created which is directed against the instinct's aims; but this psychical reaction-formation feels insecure and constantly threatened by the instinct which is lurking in the unconscious. The influence of the repressed instinct is felt as a temptation, and during the process of repression itself anxiety is generated, which gains control over the future in the form of *expectant* anxiety. The process of repression which leads to obsessional neurosis must be considered as one which is only partly successful and which increasingly threatens to fail. It may thus be compared to an unending conflict; fresh psychical efforts are continually required to counterbalance the forward pressure of the instinct.

Thus the ceremonial and obsessive actions arise partly as a defense against the temptation and partly as a protection against the ill which is expected. Against the temptation the protective measures seem soon to become inadequate; then the prohibitions come into play, with the purpose of keeping at a distance situations that give rise to temptation. Prohibitions take the place of obsessive actions, it will be seen, just as a phobia is designed to avert a hysterical attack. Again, a ceremonial represents the sum of the conditions subject to which something that is not yet absolutely forbidden is permitted, just as the Church's marriage ceremony signifies for the believer a sanctioning of sexual enjoyment which would otherwise be sinful. A further characteristic of obsessional neurosis, as of all similar affections, is that its manifestations (its symptoms, including the obsessive actions) fulfil the condition of being a compromise between the warring forces of the mind. They thus always reproduce something of the pleasure which they are designed to prevent; they serve the repressed instinct no less than the agencies which are repressing it. As the illness progresses, indeed, actions which were originally mostly concerned with maintaining the defense come to approximate more and more to the proscribed actions through which the instinct was able to find expression in childhood.

Some features of this state of affairs may be seen in the sphere of religious life as well. The formation of a religion, too, seems to be based on the suppression, the renunciation of certain instinctual impulses. These impulses, however, are not, as in the neuroses, exclusively components of the sexual instinct; they are self-seeking, socially harmful instincts, though, even so, they are usually not without a sexual component. A sense of guilt following upon continual temptation and an expectant anxiety in the form of fear of divine punishment have, after all, been familiar to us in the field of religion longer than in that of neurosis. Perhaps because of the admixture of sexual components, perhaps because of some general characteristics of the instincts, the suppression of instinct proves to be an inadequate and interminable process in religious life also. Indeed, complete backslidings into sin are more common among pious people than among neurotics and these give rise to a new form of religious activity, namely acts of penance, which have their counterpart in obsessional neurosis.

We have noted as a curious and derogatory characteristic of obsessional neurosis that its ceremonials are concerned with the small actions of daily life and are expressed in foolish regulations and restrictions in connection with them. We cannot understand this remarkable feature of the clinical picture until we have realized that the mechanism of psychical *displacement*, which was first discovered by me in the construction of dreams, dominates the mental processes of obsessional neurosis. It is already clear from the few examples of obsessive actions given above that their symbolism and the details of their execution are brought about by a displacement from the actual, important thing on to a small one which takes its place—for instance, from a husband on to a chair. It is this tendency to displacement which progressively changes the clinical picture and eventually succeeds in turning what is apparently the most trivial matter into something of the utmost importance and urgency. It cannot be denied that in the religious field as well there is a similar tendency to a displacement of psychical values, and in the same direction, so that the petty ceremonials of religious practice gradually become the essential thing and push aside the underlying thoughts. That is why religions are subject to reforms which work retroactively and aim at a re-establishment of the original balance of values.

The character of compromise which obsessive actions possess in their capacity as neurotic symptoms is the character least easily detected in corresponding religious observances. Yet here, too, one is reminded of this feature of neuroses when one remembers how commonly all the acts which religion forbids—the expressions of the instincts it has suppressed—are committed precisely in the name of, and ostensibly for the sake of, religion.

In view of these similarities and analogies one might venture to regard obsessional neurosis as a pathological counterpart of the formation of a religion, and to describe that neurosis as an individual religiosity and religion as a universal obsessional neurosis. The most essential similarity would reside in the underlying renunciation of the activation of instincts that are constitutionally present; and the chief difference would lie in the nature of those instincts, which in the neurosis are exclusively sexual in their origin, while in religion they spring from egoistic sources.

A progressive renunciation of constitutional instincts, whose activation might afford the ego primary pleasure, appears to be one of the foundations of the development of human civilization. Some part of this instinctual repression is effected by its religions, in that they require the individual to sacrifice his instinctual pleasure to the Deity: "Vengeance is mine, saith the Lord." In the development of the ancient religions one seems to discern that many things which mankind had renounced as 'iniquities' had been surrendered to the Deity and were still permitted in his name, so that the handing over to him of bad and socially harmful instincts was the means by which man freed himself from their domination. For this reason, it is surely no accident that all the attributes of man, along with the misdeeds that follow from them, were to an unlimited amount ascribed to the ancient gods. Nor is it a contradiction of this that nevertheless man was not permitted to justify his own iniquities by appealing to divine example.

NOTES

1. A beautiful woman in mediaeval legend, who led a secret existence as a water-nymph.
2. Equivalent at that time to four shillings or a dollar.

CHAPTER 2

From *Leonardo da Vinci and a Memory of His Childhood*

SIGMUND FREUD

Anyone who thinks of Leonardo's paintings will be reminded of a remarkable smile, at once fascinating and puzzling, which he conjured up on the lips of his female subjects. It is an unchanging smile, on long, curved lips; it has become a mark of his style and the name "Leonardesque" has been chosen for it. In the strangely beautiful face of the Florentine Mona Lisa del Giocondo it has produced the most powerful and confusing effect on whoever looks at it. This smile has called for an interpretation, and it has met with many of the most varied kinds, none of which has been satisfactory. Gruyer comments: "For almost four centuries now Mona Lisa has caused all who talk of her, after having gazed on her for long, to lose their heads." Muther writes: "What especially casts a spell on the spectator is the daemonic magic of this smile. Hundreds of poets and authors have written about this woman who now appears to smile on us so seductively, and now to stare coldly and without soul into space; and no one has solved the riddle of her smile, no one has read the meaning of her thoughts. Everything, even the landscape, is mysteriously dream-like, and seems to be trembling in a kind of sultry sensuality."

The idea that two distinct elements are combined in Mona Lisa's smile is one that has struck several critics. They accordingly find in the beautiful Florentine's expression the most perfect representation of the contrasts which dominate the erotic life of women; the contrast between reserve and seduction, and between the most devoted tenderness and a sensuality that is ruthlessly demanding—consuming men as if they were alien beings. This is the view of Müntz: "We know what an insoluble and enthralling enigma Mona Lisa Gioconda has never ceased through nearly four centuries to pose to the admirers that throng in front of her. No artist (I borrow the words from the sensitive writer who conceals himself behind the pseudonym of Pierre de Corlay) 'has ever expressed so well the very essence of femininity: tenderness and coquetry, modesty and secret sensuous joy, all the mystery of a heart that holds aloof, a brain that meditates, a personality that holds back and yields nothing of itself save its radiance.' " The Italian writer Angelo Conti saw the picture in the Louvre brought to life by a ray of sunshine: "The lady smiled in regal calm: her instincts of conquest, of ferocity, all the heredity of the species, the will to seduce and to ensnare, the charm of deceit, the kindness that conceals a cruel purpose,—all this appeared and disappeared by turns behind the laughing veil and buried itself in the poem of her smile . . . Good and wicked, cruel and compassionate, graceful and feline, she laughed . . ."

Leonardo spent four years painting at this picture, perhaps from 1503 to 1507, during his second period of residence in Florence, when he was over fifty. According to Vasari he employed the most elaborate artifices to keep the lady amused during the sittings and to retain the famous smile on her features. In its present condition the picture has preserved but little of all the delicate details which his brush reproduced on the canvas at that time; while it was being painted it was considered to be the highest that art could achieve, but it is certain that Leonardo himself was not satisfied with it, declaring it to be incomplete, and did not deliver it to the person who had commissioned it, but took it to France with him, where his patron, Francis I, acquired it from him for the Louvre.

Let us leave unsolved the riddle of the expression on Mona Lisa's face, and note the indisputable fact that her smile exercised no less powerful a fascination on the artist than on those who have looked at it for the last four hundred years. From that date the captivating smile reappears in all his pictures and in those of his pupils. As Leonardo's Mona Lisa is a portrait, we cannot assume that he added on his own account such an expressive feature to her face—a feature that she did not herself possess. The conclusion seems hardly to be avoided that he found this smile in his model and fell so strongly under its spell that from then on he bestowed it on the free creations of his phantasy. This interpretation, which cannot be called far-fetched, is put forward, for example, by Konstantinowa: "During the long period in which the artist was occupied with the portrait of Mona Lisa del Giocondo, he had entered into the subtle details of the features on this lady's face with such sympathetic feeling that he transferred its traits—in partic-

Leonardo da Vinci. *Madonna and Child with St. Anne,* ca. 1508–1518, oil on panel, 168 x 130 cm (Musée du Louvre, Paris)

ular the mysterious smile and the strange gaze—to all the faces that he painted or drew afterwards. The Gioconda's peculiar facial expression can even be perceived in the picture of John the Baptist in the Louvre; but above all it may be clearly recognized in the expression on Mary's face in the 'Madonna and Child with St. Anne'."

Yet this situation may also have come about in another way. The need for a deeper reason behind the attraction of La Gioconda's smile, which so moved the artist that he was never again free from it, has been felt by more than one of his biographers. Walter Pater, who sees in the picture of Mona Lisa a "presence . . . expressive of what in the ways of a thousand years men had come to desire," and who writes very sensitively of "the unfathomable smile, always with a touch of something sinister in it, which plays over all Leonardo's work," leads us to another clue when he declares: "Besides, the picture is a portrait. From childhood we see this image defining itself on the fabric of his dreams; and but for express historical testimony, we might fancy that this was but his ideal lady, embodied and beheld at last . . ."

Marie Herzfeld has no doubt something very similar in mind when she declares that in the Mona Lisa Leonardo encountered his own self and for this reason was able to put so much of his own nature into the picture "whose features had lain all along in mysterious sympathy within Leonardo's mind."

Let us attempt to clarify what is suggested here. It may very well have been that Leonardo was fascinated by Mona Lisa's smile for the reason that it awoke something in him which had for long lain dormant in his mind—probably an old memory. This memory was of sufficient importance for him never to get free of it when it had once been aroused; he was continually forced to give it new expression. Pater's confident assertion that we can see, from childhood, a face like Mona Lisa's defining itself on the fabric of his dreams, seems convincing and deserves to be taken literally.

The painting of Leonardo's which stands nearest to the Mona Lisa in point of time is the so-called "St. Anne with Two Others," St. Anne with the Madonna and child. In it the Leonardesque smile is most beautifully and markedly portrayed on both the women's faces. It is not possible to discover how long before or after the painting of the Mona Lisa Leonardo began to paint this picture. As both works extended over years, it may, I think, be assumed that the artist was engaged on them at the same time. It would best agree with our expectations if it was the intensity of Leonardo's preoccupation with the features of Mona Lisa which stimulated him to create the composition of St. Anne out of his phantasy. For if the Gioconda's smile called up in his mind the memory of his mother, it is easy to understand how it drove him at once to create a glorification of motherhood, and to give back to his mother the smile he had found in the noble lady. We may therefore permit our interest to pass from Mona Lisa's portrait to this other picture—one which is hardly less beautiful, and which today also hangs in the Louvre.

St. Anne with her daughter and her grandchild is a subject that is rarely handled in Italian painting. At all events Leonardo's treatment of it differs widely from all other known versions. Muther writes: "Some artists, like Hans Fries, the elder Holbein and Girolamo dai Libri, made Anne sit beside Mary and put the child between them. Others, like Jakob Cornelisz in his Berlin picture, painted what was truly a 'St. Anne with Two Others'; in other words, they represented her as holding in her arms the small figure of Mary upon which the still smaller figure of the child Christ is sitting." In Leonardo's picture Mary is sitting on her mother's lap, leaning forward, and is stretching out both arms towards the boy, who is playing with a young lamb and perhaps treating it a little unkindly. The grandmother rests on her hip the arm that is not concealed and gazes down on the pair with blissful smile. The grouping is certainly not entirely unconstrained. But although the smile that plays on the lips of the two women is unmistakably the same as that in the picture of Mona Lisa, it has lost its uncanny and mysterious character; what it expresses is inward feeling and quiet blissfulness.

After we have studied this picture for some time, it suddenly dawns on us that only Leonardo could have painted it. The picture contains the synthesis of the history of his childhood: its details are to be explained by reference to the most personal impressions in Leonardo's life. In his father's house he found not only his kind stepmother, Donna Albiera, but also his grandmother, his father's mother, Monna Lucia, who—so we will assume—was no less tender to him than grandmothers usually are. These circumstances might well suggest to him a picture representing childhood watched over by mother and grandmother. Another striking feature of the picture assumes even greater significance. St. Anne, Mary's mother and the boy's grandmother, who must have been a matron, is here portrayed as being perhaps a little more mature and serious than the Virgin Mary, but as still being a young woman of unfaded beauty. In point of fact Leonardo has given the boy two mothers, one who stretches her arms out to him, and another in the background; and both are endowed with the blissful smile of the joy of motherhood. This peculiarity of the picture has not failed to surprise those who have written about it: Muther, for example, is of the opinion that Leonardo could not bring himself to paint old age, lines and wrinkles, and for this reason made Anne too into a woman of radiant beauty. But can we be satisfied with this explanation? Others have had recourse to denying that there is any similarity in age between the mother and daughter. But Muther's attempt at an explanation is surely enough to prove that the impression that St. Anne has been made more youthful derives from the picture and is not an invention for an ulterior purpose.

Leonardo's childhood was remarkable in precisely the same way as this picture. He had had two mothers: first, his true mother Caterina, from whom he was torn away when he was between three and five, and then a young and tender stepmother, his father's wife, Donna Albiera. By his combining this fact about his childhood with the one mentioned above (the presence of his mother and grandmother) and by his condensing them into a composite unity, the design of "St. Anne with Two Others" took shape for him. The maternal figure that is further away from the boy—the grandmother—corresponds to the earlier and true mother, Caterina, in its appearance and in its special relation to the boy. The artist seems to have used the blissful smile of St. Anne to disavow and to cloak the envy which the unfortunate woman felt when she was forced to give up her son to her better-born rival, as she had once given up his father as well.[1]

We thus find a confirmation in another of Leonardo's works of our suspicion that the smile of Mona Lisa del Giocondo had awakened in him as a grown man the memory of the mother of his earliest childhood. From that time onward, madonnas and aristocratic ladies were depicted in Italian painting humbly bowing their heads and smiling the strange, blissful smile of Caterina, the poor peasant girl who had brought into the world the splendid son who was destined to paint, to search and to suffer. In her love for her child the poor forsaken mother had to give vent to all her memories of the caresses she had enjoyed as well as her longing for new ones; and she was forced to do so not only to compensate herself for having no husband, but also to compensate her child for having no father to fondle him. So, like all unsatisfied mothers, she took her little son in place of her husband, and by the too early maturing of his erotism robbed him of a part of his masculinity. A mother's love for the infant she suckles and cares for is something far more profound than her later affection for the growing child. It is in the nature of a completely satisfying love-relation, which not only fulfils every mental wish but also every physical need; and if it represents one of the forms of attainable human happiness, that is in no little measure due to the possibility it offers of satisfying, without reproach, wishful impulses which have long been repressed and which must be called perverse. In the happiest young marriage the father is aware that the baby, especially if he is a baby son, has become his rival, and this is the starting-point of an antagonism towards the favourite which is deeply rooted in the unconscious.

When, in the prime of life, Leonardo once more encountered the smile of bliss and rapture which had once played on his mother's lips as she fondled him, he had for long been under the dominance of an inhibition which forbade him ever again to desire such caresses from the lips of women. But he had become a painter, and therefore he strove to reproduce the smile with his brush, giving it to all his pictures (whether he in fact executed them himself or had them done by his pupils under his direction)—to Leda, to John the Baptist and to Bacchus. These pictures breathe a mystical air into whose secret one dares not penetrate; at the very most one can attempt to establish their connections with Leonardo's earlier creations. The figures are still androgynous, but they are beautiful youths of feminine delicacy and with effeminate forms; they do not cast their eyes down, but gaze in mysterious triumph, as if they knew of a great achievement of happiness, about which silence must be kept. The familiar smile of fascination leads one to guess that it is a secret of love. It is possible that in these figures Leonardo has denied the unhappiness of his erotic life and has triumphed over it in his art, by representing the wishes of the boy, infatuated with his mother, as fulfilled in this blissful union of the male and female natures.

NOTE

1. [Freud added the following note in 1919.] If an attempt is made to separate the figures of Anne and Mary in this picture and to trace the outline of each, it will not be found altogether easy. One is inclined to say that they are fused with each other like badly condensed dream-figures, so that in some places it is hard to say where Anne ends and where Mary begins. But what appears to an artist's eye as a fault, as a defect in composition, is vindicated in the eyes of analysis by reference to its secret meaning. It seems that for the artist the two mothers of his childhood were melted into a single form.

CHAPTER 3

The Moses of Michelangelo

SIGMUND FREUD

O ne of the inscrutable and wonderful works of art is the marble status of Moses, by Michelangelo, in the church of S. Pietro in Vincoli in Rome. As we know, it was only a fragment of the gigantic tomb which the artist was to have erected for the powerful Pope Julius II. It always delights me to read an appreciative sentence about this statue, such as that it is "the crown of modern sculpture" (Grimm). For no piece of statuary has ever made a stronger impression on me than this. How often have I mounted the steep steps from the unlovely Corso Cavour to the lonely piazza where the deserted church stands, and have essayed to support the angry scorn of the hero's glance! Sometimes I have crept cautiously out of the half-gloom of the interior as though I myself belonged to the mob upon whom his eye is turned— the mob which can hold fast no conviction, which has neither faith nor patience, and which rejoices when it has regained its illusory idols.

Did Michelangelo intend to create a "timeless study of character and mood" in this Moses, or did he portray him at a particular moment of his life and, if so, at a highly significant one? The majority of judges have decided in the latter sense and are able to tell us what episode in his life it is which the artist has immortalized in stone. It is the descent from Mount Sinai, where Moses has received the Tables from God, and it is the moment when he perceives that the people have meanwhile made themselves a Golden Calf and are dancing around it and rejoicing. This is the scene upon which his eyes are turned, this is the spectacle which calls out the feelings depicted in his countenance—feelings which in the next instant will launch his great frame into violent action. Michelangelo has chosen this last moment

Michelangelo, *Moses*, 1513–1516, St. Peter in Chains, Rome (Archivi Alinari, Florence)

of hesitation, of calm before the storm, for his representation. In the next instant Moses will spring to his feet—his left foot is already raised from the ground—dash the Tables to the earth, and let loose his rage upon his faithless people.

Long before I had any opportunity of hearing about psychoanalysis,[1] I learnt that a Russian art-connoisseur, Ivan Lermolieff, had
caused a revolution in the art galleries of Europe by questioning the
authorship of many pictures, showing how to distinguish copies from
originals with certainty, and constructing hypothetical artists for
those works whose former supposed authorship had been discredited.
He achieved this by insisting that attention should be diverted from
the general impression and main features of a picture, and by laying
stress on the significance of minor details, of things like the drawing
of the fingernails, of the lobe of an ear, of halos and such unconsidered
trifles which the copyist neglects to imitate and yet which every artist
executes in his own characteristic way. I was then greatly interested
to learn that the Russian pseudonym concealed the identity of an
Italian physician called Morelli, who died in 1891 with the rank of
Senator of the Kingdom of Italy. It seems to me that his method of
inquiry is closely related to the technique of psycho-analysis. It,
too, is accustomed to divine secret and concealed things from de-
spised or unnoticed features, from the rubbish-heap, as it were, of our
observations.

Now in two places in the figure of Moses there are certain details
which have hitherto not only escaped notice but, in fact, have not even
been properly described. These are the attitude of his right hand and
the position of the two Tables of the Law. We may say that this hand
forms a very singular, unnatural link, and one which calls for explanation, between the Tables and the wrathful hero's beard. He has been
described as running his fingers through his beard and playing with
its locks, while the outer edge of his hand rests on the Tables. But this
is plainly not so. It is worth while examining more closely what those
fingers of the right hand are doing, and describing more minutely the
mighty beard with which they are in contact.

We now quite clearly perceive the following things: the thumb of
the hand is concealed and the index finger alone is in effective contact
with the beard. It is pressed so deeply against the soft masses of hair
that they bulge out beyond it both above and below, that is, both towards the head and towards the abdomen. The other three fingers are
propped upon the wall of his chest and are bent at the upper joints;
they are barely touched by the extreme right-hand lock of the beard
which falls past them. They have, as it were, withdrawn from the
beard. It is therefore not correct to say that the right hand is playing
with the beard or plunged in it; the simple truth is that the index finger
is laid over a part of the beard and makes a deep trough in it. It cannot

be denied that to press one's beard with one finger is an extraordinary gesture and one not easy to understand.

The much admired beard of Moses flows from his cheeks, chin and upper lip in a number of waving strands which are kept distinct from one another all the way down. One of the strands on his extreme right, growing from the cheek, falls down to the inward-pressing index finger, by which it is retained. We may assume that it resumes its course between that finger and the concealed thumb. The corresponding strand on his left side falls practically unimpeded far down over his breast. What has received the most unusual treatment is the thick mass of hair on the inside of this latter strand, the part between it and the middle line. It is not suffered to follow the turn of the head to the left; it is forced to roll over loosely and form part of a kind of scroll which lies across and over the strands on the inner right side of the beard. This is because it is held fast by the pressure of the right index finger, although it grows from the left side of the face and is, in fact, the main portion of the whole left side of the beard. Thus, the main mass of the beard is thrown to the right of the figure, whereas the head is sharply turned to the left. At the place where the right index finger is pressed in, a kind of whorl of hairs is formed; strands of hair coming from the left lie over strands coming from the right, both caught in by that despotic finger. It is only beyond this place that the masses of hair, deflected from their course, flow freely once more, and now they fall vertically until their ends are gathered up in Moses' left hand as it lies open on his lap.

I have no illusions as to the clarity of my description, and venture no opinion whether the sculptor really does invite us to solve the riddle of that knot in the beard of his statue. But apart from this, the fact remains that the pressure of the *right* index finger affects mainly the strands of hair from the *left* side; and that this oblique hold prevents the beard from accompanying the turn of the head and eyes to the left. Now we may be allowed to ask what this arrangement means and to what motives it owes its existence. If it was indeed considerations of linear and spatial design which caused the sculptor to draw the downward-streaming wealth of hair across to the right of the figure which is looking to its left, how strangely unsuitable as a means does the pressure of a single finger appear to be! And what man who, for some reason or other, has drawn his beard over to the other side, would take it into his head to hold down the one half across the other by the pressure of one finger? Yet may not these minute particulars mean nothing in reality, and may we not be racking our brains about things which were of no moment to their creator?

But let us proceed on the assumption that even these details have significance. There is a solution which will remove our difficulties and afford a glimpse of a new meaning. If the left side of Moses' beard lies under the pressure of his right finger, we may perhaps take this pose as the last stage of some connection between his right hand and the left half of his beard, a connection which was a much more intimate one at some moment before that chosen for representation. Perhaps his hand had seized his beard with far more energy, had reached across to its left edge, and in returning to that position in which the statue shows it, had been followed by a part of his beard which now testifies to the movement which has just taken place. The loop of the beard would thus be an indication of the path taken by his hand.

Thus we shall have inferred that there had been a retreating motion of the right hand. This one assumption necessarily brings others with it. In imagination we complete the scene of which this movement, established by the evidence of the beard, is a part; and we are brought back quite naturally to the hypothesis according to which the resting Moses is startled by the clamour of the people and the spectacle of the Golden Calf. He was sitting there calmly, we will suppose, his head with its flowing beard facing forward, and his hand in all probability not near it at all. Suddenly the clamour strikes his ear; he turns his head and eyes in the direction from which the disturbance comes, sees the scene and takes it in. Now wrath and indignation lay hold of him; and he would fain leap up and punish the wrongdoers, annihilate them. His rage, distant as yet from its object, is meanwhile directed in a gesture against his own body. His impatient hand, ready to act, clutches at his beard which has moved with the turn of his head, and presses it between his thumb and palm in the iron grasp of his closing fingers. It is a gesture whose power and vehemence remind us of other creations of Michelangelo's. But now an alteration takes place, as yet we do not know how or why. The hand that had been put forward and had sunk into his beard is hastily withdrawn and unclasped, and the fingers let go their hold; but so deeply have they been plunged in that in their withdrawal they drag a great piece of the left side of the beard across to the right, and this piece remains lodged over the hair of the right under the weight of one finger, the longest and uppermost one of the hand. And this new position, which can only be understood with reference to the former one, is now retained.

It is time now to pause and reflect. We have assumed that the right hand was, to begin with, away from the beard; that then it reached across to the left of the figure in a moment of great emotional tension and seized the beard; and that it was finally drawn back again, taking a part of the beard with it. We have disposed of this right hand as though we had the free use of it. But may we do this? Is the hand indeed so free? Must it not hold or support the Tables? Are not such mimetic evolutions as these prohibited by its important function? And furthermore, what could have occasioned its withdrawal if the motive which made it leave its original position was such a strong one?

We begin to suspect that the Tables too have arrived at their present position as the result of a previous movement; that this movement was a consequence of the change of place of the right hand that we have postulated, and in its turn compelled that hand to make its subsequent retreat. The movements of the hand and of the Tables can be co-ordinated in this way: at first the figure of Moses, while it was still sitting quietly, carried the Tables perpendicularly under its right arm. Its right hand grasped their lower edge and found a hold in the projection on their front part. (The fact that this made them easier to carry sufficiently accounts for the upside-down position in which the Tables were held.) Then came the moment when Moses' calm was broken by the disturbance. He turned his head in its direction, and when he saw the spectacle he lifted his foot preparatory to starting up, let go the Tables with his hand and plunged it to the left and upwards into his beard, as though to turn his violence against his own body. The Tables were now consigned to the pressure of his arm, which had to squeeze them against his side. But this support was not sufficient and the Tables began to slip in a forward and downward direction. The upper edge, which had been held horizontally, now began to face forwards and downwards; and the lower edge, deprived of its stay, was nearing the stone seat with its front corner. Another instant and the Tables would have pivoted upon this new point of support, have hit the ground with the upper edge foremost, and been shattered to pieces. It is to prevent this that the right hand retreated, let go the beard, a part of which was drawn back with it unintentionally, came against the upper edge of the Tables in time and held them near the hind corner, which had now come uppermost. Thus the singularly contained air of the whole—beard, hand and tilted Tables—can be traced to that one passionate movement of the hand and its natural consequences. If we wish to reverse the effects of those stormy movements, we must raise the upper front corner of the Tables and push it back, thus lifting their lower front corner (the one with the protuberance) from the stone seat; and then lower the right hand and bring it under the now horizontal lower edge of the Tables.

We may now, I believe, permit ourselves to reap the fruits of our endeavours. What we see before us is not the inception of a violent action but the remains of a movement that has already taken place. In his first transport of fury, Moses desired to act, to spring up and take vengeance and forget the Tables; but he has overcome the temptation, and he will now remain seated and still, in his frozen wrath and in his pain mingled with contempt. Nor will he throw away the Tables so that they will break on the stones, for it is on their especial account that he has controlled his anger; it was to preserve them that he kept his passions in check. In giving way to his rage and indignation, he had to neglect the Tables, and the hand which upheld them was withdrawn. They began to slide down and were in danger of being broken. This brought him to himself. He remembered his mission and for its sake renounced an indulgence of his feelings. His hand returned and saved the unsupported Tables before they had actually fallen to the ground. In this attitude he remained immobilized, and in this attitude Michelangelo has portrayed him as the guardian of the tomb.

As our eyes travel down it the figure exhibits three distinct emotional strata. The lines of the face reflect the feelings which have won the ascendancy; the middle of the figure shows the traces of suppressed movement; and the foot still retains the attitude of the projected action. It is as though the controlling influence had proceeded downwards from above. No mention has been made so far of the left arm, and it seems to claim a share in our interpretation. The hand is laid in the lap in a mild gesture and holds as though in a caress the end of the flowing beard. It seems as if it is meant to counteract the violence with which the other hand had misused the beard a few moments ago.

But here it will be objected that after all this is not the Moses of the Bible. For that Moses did actually fall into a fit of rage and did throw away the Tables and break them. This Moses must be a quite different man, a new Moses of the artist's conception; so that Michelangelo must have had the presumption to emend the sacred text and to falsify the character of that holy man. Can we think him capable of a boldness which might almost be said to approach an act of blasphemy? According to the Scriptures Moses was already instructed about the idolatry of his people and had ranged himself on the side of mildness and forgiveness; nevertheless, when he saw the Golden Calf and the dancing crowd, he was overcome by a sudden frenzy of rage. It would therefore not surprise us to find that the artist, in depicting the reaction of his hero to that painful surprise, had deviated from the text from inner motives. Moreover, such deviations from the scriptural text on a much slighter pretext were by no means unusual or disallowed to artists. A celebrated picture by Parmigiano possessed by his native town depicts Moses sitting on the top of a mountain and dashing the Tables to the ground, although the Bible expressly says that he broke them "beneath the mount." Even the representation of a seated Moses finds no support in the text and seems rather to bear out those critics who maintain that Michelangelo's statue is not meant to record any particular moment in the prophet's life.

More important than his infidelity to the text of the Scriptures is the alteration which Michelangelo has, in our supposition, made in the character of Moses. The Moses of legend and tradition had a hasty temper and was subject to fits of passion. It was in a transport of divine wrath of this kind that he slew an Egyptian who was maltreating an Israelite, and had to flee out of the land into the wilderness; and it was in a similar passion that he broke the Tables of the Law, inscribed by God Himself. Tradition, in recording such a characteristic, is unbiased, and preserves the impression of a great personality who once lived. But Michelangelo has placed a different Moses on the tomb of the Pope, one superior to the historical or traditional Moses. He has modified the theme of the broken Tables; he does not let Moses break them in his wrath, but makes him be influenced by the danger that they will be broken and makes him calm that wrath, or at any rate prevent it from becoming an act. In this way he has added something new and more than human to the figure of Moses; so that the giant frame with its tremendous physical power becomes only a concrete expression of the highest mental achievement that is possible in a man, that of struggling successfully against an inward passion for the sake of a cause to which he has devoted himself.

NOTE

1. Editor's note: This essay was originally published anonymously in *Imago*, a psychoanalytic journal, with the following editorial comment: "Although this paper does not, strictly speaking, conform to the conditions under which contributions are accepted for publication in this journal, the editors have decided to print it, since the author, who is personally known to them, belongs to psychoanalytic circles, and since his mode of thought has in point of fact a certain resemblance to the methodology of psychoanalysis."

CHAPTER 4

A Seventeenth-Century Demonological Neurosis

SIGMUND FREUD

The neuroses of childhood have taught us that a number of things can easily be seen in them with the naked eye which at a later age are only to be discovered after a thorough investigation. We may expect that the same will turn out to be true of neurotic illnesses in earlier centuries, provided that we are prepared to recognize them under names other than those of our present-day neuroses. We need not be surprised to find that, whereas the neuroses of our unpsychological modern days take on a hypochrondriacal aspect and appear disguised as organic illnesses, the neuroses of those early times emerge in demonological trappings. Several authors, foremost among them Charcot, have, as we know, identified the manifestations of hysteria in the portrayals of possession and ecstasy that have been preserved for us in the productions of art. If more attention had been paid to the histories of such cases at the time, it would not have been difficult to retrace in them the subject-matter of a neurosis.

The demonological theory of those dark times has won in the end against all the somatic views of the period of "exact" science. The states of possession correspond to our neuroses, for the explanation of which we once more have recourse to psychical powers. In our eyes, the demons are bad and reprehensible wishes, derivatives of instinctual impulses that have been repudiated and repressed. We merely eliminate the projection of these mental entities into the external world which the middle ages carried out; instead, we regard them as having arisen in the patient's internal life, where they have their abode.

I am indebted to the friendly interest of Dr. Payer-Thurn for the opportunity of studying a seventeenth-century demonological neurosis of this kind. Payer-Thurn had discovered a manuscript which originated from the shrine of Mariazell and in which there was a detailed account of a miraculous redemption from a pact with the Devil through the grace of the Blessed Virgin Mary. His interest was aroused by the resemblance of this story to the legend of Faust, and has led him to undertake the exhaustive publication and editing of the material. Finding, however, that the person whose redemption was described had been subject to convulsive seizures and visions he approached me for a medical opinion on the case. We came to an agreement to publish our investigations independently and separately. I should like to take this opportunity of thanking him for his original suggestion and for the many ways in which he has assisted me in the study of the manuscript.

The manuscript, an exact copy of which lies before me, falls into two quite distinct sections. One is a report, written in Latin, by a monastic scribe or compiler; the other is a fragment from the patient's diary, written in German. The first section contains a preface and a description of the actual miraculous cure. The second can scarcely have been of any significance for the reverend Fathers but so much the more is it of value for us. It serves in large part to confirm our judgement of the case, which might otherwise have been hesitant, and we have good cause to be grateful to the clergy for having preserved the document although it added nothing to support the tenor of their views and, indeed, may rather have weakened it.

But before going further into the composition of this little manuscript brochure, which bears the title *Trophaeum Mariano-Cellense*, I must relate a part of its contents, which I take from the preface.

On September 5, 1677, the painter Christoph Haizmann, a Bavarian, was brought to Mariazell, with a letter of introduction from the village priest of Pottenbrunn (in lower Austria) not far away. The letter states that the man had been staying in Pottenbrunn for some months, pursuing his occupation of painting. On August 29, while in the church there, he had been seized with frightful convulsions. As these convulsions recurred during the following days, he had been examined by the *Praefectus Dominii Pottenbrunnensis* with a view to discovering what it was that was oppressing him and whether perhaps he had entered into illicit traffic with the Evil Spirit. Upon this, the man had admitted that nine years before, when he was in a state of despondency about his art and doubtful whether he could support himself, he had yielded to the Devil, who had tempted him nine times, and that he had given him his bond in writing to belong to him in body and soul after a period of nine years. This period would expire on the twenty-fourth day of the current month. The letter went on to say that the unfortunate man had repented and was convinced that only the grace of the Mother of God at Mariazell could save him, by compelling the Evil One to deliver up the bond, which had been written in blood. After he had undergone a prolonged period of penance and prayer at Mariazell, the Devil appeared to him in the sacred Chapel at midnight, on September 8, the Nativity of the Virgin, in the form of a winged dragon, and gave him back the pact, which was written in blood.

The miracle was great, and the victory of the Holy Mother over Satan without question; but unfortunately the cure was not a lasting one. It is once more to the credit of the clergy that they have not concealed this. After a short time the painter left Mariazell in the best of health and went to Vienna, where he lived with a married sister. On October 11 fresh attacks began, some of them very severe, and these are reported in the diary until January 13. They consisted in visions and "*absences*," in which he saw and experienced every kind of thing, in convulsive seizures accompanied by the most painful sensations, on one occasion in paralysis of the legs, and so on. This time, however, it was not the Devil who tormented him; it was by sacred figures that he was vexed—by Christ and by the Blessed Virgin herself. It is remarkable that he suffered no less through these heavenly manifestations and the punishments they inflicted on him than he had formerly through his traffic with the Devil. In his diary, indeed, he included these fresh experiences too as manifestations of the Devil; and when, in May, 1678, he returned to Mariazell, he complained of "manifestations of the Evil Spirit."

He told the reverend Fathers that his reason for returning was that he had to require the Devil to give him back another, earlier bond, which had been written in ink. This bond had been signed in September, 1668, and by May, 1678, nine and half years later, it would long since have fallen due. This time once more the Blessed Virgin and the pious Fathers helped him to obtain the fulfilment of his request. As to how this came about, however, the report is silent. He prayed once again and received the pact back. After this he felt quite free and entered the Order of the Brother Hospitallers.

The Motive for the Pact with the Devil

If we look at this bond with the Devil as if it were the case history of a neurotic, our interest will turn in the first instance to the question of its motivation, which is, of course, intimately connected with its exciting cause. Why does anyone sign a bond with the Devil? Faust, it is true, asked contemptuously: "What hast thou to give, poor Devil?" But he was wrong. In return for an immortal soul, the Devil has many things to offer which are highly prized by men: wealth, security from danger, power over mankind and the forces of nature, even magical arts, and, above all else, enjoyment—the enjoyment of beautiful women. These services performed or undertakings made by the Devil are usually mentioned specifically in the agreement made with him. What, then, was the motive which induced Christoph Haizmann to make his pact?

Curiously enough, it was none of these very natural wishes. To put the matter beyond doubt, one has only to read the short remarks attached by the painter to his illustrations of the apparitions of the Devil. For example, the caption of the third vision runs: "On the third occasion within a year and a half, he appeared to me in this loathsome shape, with a book in his hand which was full of magic and black arts . . ." But from the legend attached to a later apparition we learn that the Devil reproached him violently for having "burnt his beforementioned book," and threatened to tear him to pieces if he did not give it back.

At his fourth appearance the Devil showed him a large yellow money-bag and a great ducat and promised to give him as many of these as he wanted at any time. But the painter is able to boast that he "had taken nothing whatever of the kind."

Another time the Devil asked him to turn to enjoyment and entertainment, and the painter remarks that "this indeed came to pass at his desire; but I did not continue for more than three days and it was then brought to an end."

Since he rejected magical arts, money and pleasures when they were offered him by the Devil, and still less made them conditions of the pact, it becomes really imperative to know what the painter in fact wanted from the Devil when he signed a bond with him. *Some* motive he must have had for his dealings with the Devil.

On this point, too, the *Trophaeum* provides us with reliable information. He had become low-spirited, was unable or unwilling to work properly and was worried about making a livelihood; that is to say, he was suffering from melancholic depression, with an inhibition in his work and (justified) fears about his future. We can see that what we are dealing with really is a case history. We learn, too, the exciting cause of the illness, which the painter himself, in the caption to one of his pictures of the Devil, actually calls a melancholia ("that I should seek diversion and banish melancholy"). The first of our three sources of information, the village priest's letter of introduction, speaks, it is true, only of the state of depression, but the second source, the Abbot Franciscus's report, tells us the cause of this despondency or depression as well. His father had died and he had in consequence fallen into a state of melancholia; whereupon the Devil had approached him and asked him why he was so downcast and sad, and had promised "to help him in every way and to give him support."

Here was a person, therefore, who signed a bond with the Devil in order to be freed from a state of depression. Undoubtedly an excellent motive, as anyone will agree who can have an understanding sense of the torments of such a state and who knows as well how little medicine can do to alleviate this ailment. Yet no one who has followed the story so far as this would be able to guess what the wording of this bond (or rather, of these two bonds) with the Devil actually was.

These bonds bring us two great surprises. In the first place, they mention no *undertaking* given by the Devil in return for whose fulfilment the painter pledges his eternal bliss, but only a *demand* made by the Devil which the painter must satisfy. It strikes us as quite illogical and absurd that this man should give up his soul, not for something he is to *get* from the Devil but for something he is to *do* for him. But the undertaking given by the *painter* seems even stranger. The first 'syngrapha' [bond], written in ink, runs as follows: "I, Christoph Haizmann, subscribe myself to this Lord as his bounden son till the ninth year, Year 1669." The second, written in blood, runs: "Christoph Haizmann. I sign a bond with this Satan, to be his bounden son and in the ninth year to belong to him body and soul." All our astonishment vanishes, however, if we read the text of the bonds in the sense that what is represented in them as a demand made by the Devil is, on the contrary, a service performed by him—that is to say, it is a demand made by the *painter.* The incomprehensible pact would in that case have a straightforward meaning and could be paraphrased thus. The Devil undertakes to replace the painter's lost father for nine years. At the end of that time the painter becomes the property, body and soul, of the Devil, as was the usual custom in such bargains. The train of thought which motivated the painter in making the pact seems to have been this: his father's death had made him lose his spirits and his capacity to work; if he could only obtain a father-substitute he might hope to regain what he had lost.

A man who has fallen into a melancholia on account of his father's death must really have been fond of him. But, if so, it is very strange that such a man should have hit upon the idea of taking the Devil as a substitute for the father whom he loved.

The Devil as a Father-Substitute

I fear that the sober critics will not be prepared to admit that this fresh interpretation has made the meaning of this pact with the Devil clear. They will have two objections to make to it. In the first place they will say that it is not necessary to regard the bond as a contract in which the undertakings of both parties have been set out. On the contrary, they will argue, it contains only the painter's undertaking; the Devil's is omitted from the text, and is, as it were, *sousentendu:* the painter gives *two* undertakings—firstly to be the Devil's son for nine years, and secondly to belong to him entirely after death. In this way one of the premises on which our conclusion is built would be disposed of.

The second objection will be that we are not justified in attaching any special importance to the expression "the Devil's bounden son"; that this is no more than a common figure of speech, which anyone could interpret in the same way as the reverend Fathers may have done. For in their Latin translation they did not mention the relationship of son promised in the bonds, but merely say that the painter *'mancipavit'* himself—made himself a bondslave—to the Evil One and had undertaken to lead a sinful life and to deny God and the Holy Trinity. Why depart from this obvious and natural view of the matter? The position would simply be that a man, in the torment and perplexity of a melancholic depression, signs a bond with the Devil, to whom he ascribes the greatest therapeutic power. That the depression was occasioned by his father's death would then be irrelevant; the occasion might quite as well have been something else.

All this sounds convincing and reasonable. Psycho-analysis has once more to meet the reproach that it makes hair-splitting complications in the simplest things and sees mysteries and problems where none exist, and that it does this by laying undue stress on insignificant and irrelevant details, such as occur everywhere, and making them the basis of the most far-reaching and strangest conclusions. It would be useless for us to point out that this rejection of our interpretation would do away with many striking analogies and break a number of subtle connections which we are able to demonstrate in this case. Our opponents will say that those analogies and connections do not in fact exist, but have been imported into the case by us with quite uncalled-for ingenuity.

If we are right in regarding our painter's bond with the Devil as a neurotic phantasy, there is no need for any further apology for considering it psycho-analytically. Even small indications have a meaning and importance, and quite specially when they are related to the conditions under which a neurosis originates. To be sure, it is as possible to overvalue as to undervalue them, and it is a matter of judgment how far one should go in exploiting them. But anyone who does not believe in psycho-analysis—or, for the matter of that, even in the Devil—must be left to what he can of the painter's case, whether he is able to furnish an explanation of his own or whether he sees nothing in it that needs explaining.

We therefore come back to our hypothesis that the Devil with whom the painter signed the bond was a direct substitute for his father. And this is borne out by the shape in which the Devil first appeared to him—as an honest elderly citizen with a brown beard, dressed in a red cloak and leaning with his right hand on a stick, with a black dog beside him. Later on his appearance grows more and more terrifying—more mythological, one might say. He is equipped with horns, eagle's claws and bat's wings. Finally he appears in the chapel as a flying dragon. We shall have to come back later to a particular detail of his bodily shape.

It does indeed sound strange that the Devil should be chosen as a substitute for a loved father. But this is only so at first sight, for we know a good many things which lessen our surprise. To begin with, we know that God is a father-substitute; or, more correctly, that he is an exalted father; or, yet again, that he is a copy of a father as he is seen and experienced in childhood—by individuals in their own childhood and by mankind in its prehistory as the father of the primitive and primal horde. Later on in life the individual sees his father as something different and lesser. But the ideational image belonging to his childhood is preserved and becomes merged with the inherited memory-traces of the primal father to form the individual's idea of God. We also know, from the secret life of the individual which analysis uncovers, that his relation to his father was perhaps ambivalent from the outset, or, at any rate, soon became so. That is to say, it contained two sets of emotional impulses that were opposed to each other: it contained not only impulses of an affectionate and submissive nature, but also hostile and defiant ones. It is our view that the same ambivalence governs the relations of mankind to its Deity. The unresolved conflict between, on the one hand, a longing for the father and, on the other, a fear of him and a son's defiance of him, has furnished us with an explanation of important characteristics of religion and decisive vicissitudes in it.

Concerning the Evil Demon, we know that he is regarded as the antithesis of God and yet is very close to him in his nature. His history has not been so well studied as that of God; not all religions have adopted the Evil Spirit, the opponent of God, and his prototype in the life of the individual has so far remained obscure. One thing, however, is certain: gods can turn into evil demons when new gods oust them. When one people has been conquered by another, their fallen gods not seldom turn into demons in the eyes of the conquerors. The evil demon of the Christian faith—the Devil of the Middle Ages—was, according to Christian mythology, himself a fallen angel and of a godlike nature. It does not need much analytic perspicacity to guess that God and the Devil were originally identical—were a single figure which was later split into two figures with opposite attributes. In the earliest ages of religion God himself still possessed all the terrifying features which were afterwards combined to form a counterpart of him.

We have here an example of the process, with which we are familiar, by which an idea that has a contradictory—an ambivalent—content becomes divided into two sharply contrasted opposites. The contradictions in the original nature of God are, however, a reflection of the ambivalence which governs the relation of the individual to his personal father. If the benevolent and righteous God is a substitute for his father, it is not to be wondered at that his hostile attitude to his father, too, which is one of hating and fearing him and of making complaints against him, should have come to expression in the creation of Satan. Thus the father, it seems, is the individual prototype of both God and the Devil. But we should expect religions to bear ineffaceable marks of the fact that the primitive primal father was a being of unlimited evil—a being less like God than the Devil.

It is true that it is by no means easy to demonstrate the traces of this satanic view of the father in the mental life of the individual. When a boy draws grotesque faces and caricatures, we may no doubt be able to show that he is jeering at his father in them; and when a person of either sex is afraid of robbers and burglars at night, it is not hard to recognize these as split-off portions of the father. The animals, too, which appear in children's animal phobias are most often father-substitutes, as were the totem animals of primaeval times. But that the Devil is a duplicate of the father and can act as a substitute for him has not been shown so clearly elsewhere as in the demonological neurosis of this seventeenth-century painter. That is why, at the beginning of this paper, I foretold that a demonological case history of this kind would yield in the form of pure metal material which, in the neuroses of a later epoch (no longer superstitious but hypochrondriacal instead) has to be laboriously extracted by analytic work from the ore of free associations and symptoms.[1] A deeper penetration into the analysis of our painter's illness will probably bring stronger conviction. It is no unusual thing for a man to acquire a melancholic depression and an inhibition in his work as a result of his father's death. When this happens, we conclude that the man had been attached to his father with an especially strong love, and we remember how often a severe melancholia appears as a neurotic form of mourning.

In this we are undoubtedly right. But we are not right if we conclude further that this relation has been merely one of love. On the contrary, his mourning over the loss of his father is the more likely to turn into melancholia, the more his attitude to him bore the stamp of ambivalence. This emphasis on ambivalence, however, prepares us for the possibility of the father being subjected to a debasement, as we see happening in the painter's demonological neurosis. If we were able to learn as much about Christoph Haizmann as about a patient undergoing an analysis with us, it would be an easy matter to elicit this ambivalence, to get him to remember when and under what provocations he was given cause to fear and hate his father; and, above all, to discover what were the accidental factors that were added to the typical motives for a hatred of the father which are necessarily inherent in the natural relationship of son to father. Perhaps we might then find a special explanation for the painter's inhibition in work. It is possible that his father had opposed his wish to become a painter. If that was so, his inability to practise his art after his father's death would on the one hand be an expression of the familiar phenomenon of "deferred obedience"; and, on the other hand, by making him incapable of earning a livelihood, it would be bound to increase his longing for his father as a protector from the cares of life. In its aspect as deferred obedience it would also be an expression of remorse and a successful self-punishment.

Reading the diary, we gain insight into another part of the story. It will be remembered that the painter signed a bond with the Devil because after his father's death, feeling depressed and unable to work, he was worried about making a livelihood. These factors of depression, inhibition in his work and mourning for his father are somehow connected with one another, whether in a simple or a complicated way. Perhaps the reason why the apparitions of the Devil were so overgenerously furnished with breasts was that the Evil One was meant to become his foster-father. This hope was not fulfilled, and the painter continued to be in a bad state. He could not work properly, or he was out of luck and could not find enough employment. He was thus not only in moral straits but was suffering material want. In the account [in his diary] of his later visions, we find remarks here and there indicating—as do the contents of the scenes described—that even after the successful first exorcism, nothing had been changed in his situation. We come to know him as a man who fails in everything and who is therefore trusted by no one. In his first vision the cavalier asked him "what he is going to do, since he has no one to stand by him." The first series of visions in Vienna tallied completely with the wishful phantasies of a poor man, who had come down in the world and who hungered for enjoyment: magnificent halls, high living, a silver dinner-service and beautiful women. Here we find what was missing in his relations with the Devil made good. At that time he had been in a melancholia which made him unable to enjoy anything and obliged him to reject the most attractive offers. After the exorcism the melancholia seems to have been overcome and all his worldly-minded desires had once more become active.

In one of the ascetic visions he complained to his guide (Christ) that nobody had any faith in him, so that he was unable to carry out the commands laid upon him. The reply he was given is, unfortunately, obscure to us: "Although they will not believe me, yet I know well what has happened, but I am not able to declare it." Especially illuminating, however, are the experiences which his heavenly Guide made him have among the anchorites. He came to a cave in which an old man had been sitting for the last sixty years, and in answer to a question he learnt that this old man had been fed every day by God's angels. And then he saw for himself how an angel brought the old man food: "Three dishes with food, a loaf, a dumpling and some drink." After the anchorite had eaten, the angel collected everything and carried it away. We can see what the temptation was which the pious visions offered the painter: they were meant to induce him to adopt a mode of existence in which he need no longer worry about sustenance. The utterances of Christ in the last vision are also worthy of note. After threatening that, if he did not prove amenable, something would happen which would oblige him and the people to believe in it, Christ gave him a direct warning that "I should not heed the people; even if they were to persecute me or give me no help, God would not abandon me."

Christoph Haizmann was enough of an artist and a child of the world to find it difficult to renounce this sinful world. Nevertheless, in view of his helpless position, he did so in the end. He entered a Holy Order. With this, both his internal struggle and his material need came to an end. In his neurosis, this outcome was reflected in the fact of his seizures and visions being brought to an end by the return of an alleged first bond. Actually, both portions of his demonological illness had the same meaning. He wanted all along simply to make his life secure. He tried first to achieve this with the help of the Devil at the cost of his salvation; and when this failed and had to be given up, he tried to achieve it with the help of the clergy at the cost of his freedom and most of the possibilities of enjoyment in life. Perhaps he himself was only a poor devil who simply had no luck; perhaps he was too ineffective or untalented to make a living, and was one of those types of people who are known as "eternal sucklings"—who cannot tear themselves away from the blissful situation at the mother's breast, and who, all through their lives, persist in a demand to be nourished by someone else.—And so it was that, in this history of his illness, he followed the path which led from his father, by way of the Devil as a father- substitute, to the pious Fathers of the Church.

NOTE

1. The fact that in our analyses we so seldom succeed in finding the Devil as a father-substitute may be an indication that for those who come to us for analysis this figure from medieval mythology has long since played out its part. For the pious Christian of earlier centuries belief in the Devil was no less a duty than belief in God. In point of fact, he needed the Devil in order to be able to keep hold of God. The later decrease in faith has, for various reasons, first and foremost affected the figure of the Devil.

CHAPTER 5

From *The Future of an Illusion*

SIGMUND FREUD

What, then, is the psychological significance of religious ideas and under what heading are we to classify them? The question is not at all easy to answer immediately. After rejecting a number of formulations, we will take our stand on the following one. Religious ideas are teachings and assertions about facts and conditions of external (or internal) reality which tell one something one has not discovered for oneself and which lay claim to one's belief. Since they give us information about what is most important and interesting to us in life, they are particularly highly prized. Anyone who knows nothing of them is very ignorant; and anyone who has added them to his knowledge may consider himself much the richer.

There are, of course, many such teachings about the most various things in the world. Every school lesson is full of them. Let us take geography. We are told that the town of Constance lies on the Bodensee. A student song adds: "if you don't believe it, go and see." I happen to have been there and can confirm the fact that the lovely town lies on the shore of a wide stretch of water which all those who live round it call the Bodensee; and I am now completely convinced of the correctness of this geographical assertion. In this connection I am reminded of another, very remarkable, experience. I was already a man of mature years when I stood for the first time on the hill of the Acropolis in Athens, between the temple ruins, looking out over the blue sea. A feeling of astonishment mingled with my joy. It seemed to say: 'So it really *is* true, just as we learnt at school!' How shallow and weak must have been the relief I then acquired in the real truth of what I heard, if I could be so astonished now! But I will not lay too much stress on the significance of this experience; for my astonishment could have had another explanation, which did not occur to me at the time and which is of a wholly subjective nature and has to do with the special character of the place.

All teachings like these, then, demand belief in their contents, but not without producing grounds for their claim. They are put forward as the epitomized result of a longer process of thought based on observation and certainly also on inferences. If anyone wants to go through this process himself instead of accepting its result, they show him how to set about it. Moreover, we are always in addition given the source of the knowledge conveyed by them, where that source is not self-evident, as it is in the case of geographical assertions. For instance, the earth is shaped like a sphere; the proofs adduced for this are Foucault's pendulum experiment,[1] the behavior of the horizon and the possibility of circumnavigating the earth. Since it is impracticable, as everyone concerned realizes, to send every schoolchild on a voyage round the world, we are satisfied with letting what is taught at school be taken on trust; but we know that the path to acquiring a personal conviction remains open.

Let us try to apply the same test to the teachings of religion. When we ask on what their claim to be believed is founded, we are met with three answers, which harmonize remarkably badly with one another. Firstly, these teachings deserve to be believed because they were already believed by our primal ancestors; secondly, we possess proofs which have been handed down to us from those same primaeval times; and thirdly, it is forbidden to raise the question of their authentication at all. In former days anything so presumptuous was visited with the severest penalties, and even today society looks askance at any attempt to raise the question again.

This third point is bound to rouse our strongest suspicions. After all, a prohibition like this can only be for one reason—that society is very well aware of the insecurity of the claim it makes on behalf of its religious doctrines. Otherwise it would certainly be very ready to put the necessary data at the disposal of anyone who wanted to arrive at conviction. This being so, it is with a feeling of mistrust which it is hard to allay that we pass on to an examination of the other two grounds of proof. We ought to believe because our forefathers believed. But these ancestors of ours were far more ignorant than we are. They believed in things we could not possibly accept today; and the possibility occurs to us that the doctrines of religion may belong to that class too. The proofs they have left us are set down in writings which themselves bear every mark of untrustworthiness. They are full of contradictions, revisions and falsifications, and where they speak of factual confirmations they are themselves unconfirmed. It does not help much to have it asserted that their wording, or even their content only, originates from divine revelation; for this assertion is itself one of the doctrines whose authenticity is under examination, and no proposition can be a proof of itself.

Thus we arrive at the singular conclusion that of all the information provided by our cultural assets it is precisely the elements which might be of the greatest importance to us and which have the task of solving the riddles of the universe and of reconciling us to the sufferings of life—it is precisely those elements that are the least well authenticated of any. We should not be able to bring ourselves to accept anything of so little concern to us as the fact that whales bear young instead of laying eggs, if it were not capable of better proof than this.

This state of affairs is in itself a very remarkable psychological problem. And let no one suppose that what I have said about the impossibility of proving the truth of religious doctrines contains anything new. It has been felt at all times—undoubtedly, too, by the ancestors who bequeathed us this legacy. Many of them probably nourished the same doubts as ours, but the pressure imposed on them was too strong for them to have dared to utter them. And since then countless people have been tormented by similar doubts, and have striven to suppress them, because they thought it was their duty to believe; many brilliant intellects have broken down over this conflict, and many characters have been impaired by the compromises with which they have tried to find a way out of it.

If all the evidence put forward for the authenticity of religious teachings originates in the past, it is natural to look round and see whether the present, about which it is easier to form judgements, may not also be able to furnish evidence of the sort. If by this means we could succeed in clearing even a single portion of the religious system from doubt, the whole of it would gain enormously in credibility. The proceedings of the spiritualists meet us at this point; they are convinced of the survival of the individual soul and they seek to demonstrate to us beyond doubt the truth of this one religious doctrine. Unfortunately they cannot succeed in refuting the fact that the appearance and utterances of their spirits are merely the products of their own mental activity. They have called up the spirits of the greatest men and of the most eminent thinkers, but all the pronouncements and information which they have received from them have been so

foolish and so wretchedly meaningless that one can find nothing credible in them but the capacity of the spirits to adapt themselves to the
circle of people who have conjured them up.

I must now mention two attempts that have been made—both of
which convey the impression of being desperate efforts—to evade the
problem. One, of a violent nature, is ancient; the other is subtle and
modern. The first is the *"Credo quia absurdum"* of the early Father of
the Church. ["I believe because it is absurd," attributed to Tertullian.]
It maintains that religious doctrines are outside the jurisdiction of
reason—are above reason. Their truth must be felt inwardly, and they
need not be comprehended. But this Credo is only of interest as a self-
confession. As an authoritative statement it has no binding force. Am
I to be obliged to believe *every* absurdity? And if not, why this one in
particular? There is no appeal to a court above that of reason. If the
truth of religious doctrines is dependent on an inner experience which
bears witness to that truth, what is one to do about the many people
who do not have this rare experience? One may require every man to
use the gift of reason which he possesses, but one cannot erect, on the
basis of a motive that exists only for a very few, an obligation that shall
apply to everyone. If one man has gained an unshakable conviction of
the true reality of religious doctrines from a state of ecstasy which has
deeply moved him, of what significance is that to others?

The second attempt is the one made by the philosophy of "As if."
This asserts that our thought-activity includes a great number of hypotheses whose groundlessness and even absurdity we fully realize.
They are called "fictions," but for a variety of practical reasons we
have to behave "as if" we believed in these fictions. This is the case
with religious doctrines because of their incomparable importance
for the maintenance of human society. This line of argument is not far
removed from the *"Credo quia absurdum."* But I think the demand
made by the "As if" argument is one that only a philosopher could put
forward. A man whose thinking is not influenced by the artifices of
philosophy will never be able to accept it; in such a man's view, the admission that something is absurd or contrary to reason leaves no more
to be said. It cannot be expected of him that precisely in treating his
most important interests he shall forgo the guarantees he requires for
all his ordinary activities. I am reminded of one of my children who
was distinguished at an early age by a peculiarly marked matter-of-
factness. When the children were being told a fairy story and were listening to it with rapt attention, he would come up and ask: "Is that a
true story?" When he was told it was not, he would turn away with a

look of disdain. We may expect that people will soon behave in the same way towards the fairy tales of religion, in spite of the advocacy of "As if."

But at present they still behave quite differently; and in past times religious ideas, in spite of their incontrovertible lack of authentication, have exercised the strongest possible influence on mankind. This is a fresh psychological problem. We must ask where the inner force of those doctrines lies and to what it is that they owe their efficacy, independent as it is of recognition by reason.

I think we have prepared the way sufficiently for an answer to both these questions. It will be found if we turn our attention to the psychical origin of religious ideas. These, which are given out as teachings, are not precipitates of experience or end-results of thinking: they are illusions, fulfillment of the oldest, strongest and most urgent wishes of mankind. The secret of their strength lies in the strength of those wishes. As we already know, the terrifying impression of helplessness in childhood aroused the need for protection—for protection through love—which was provided by the father; and the recognition that this helplessness lasts throughout life made it necessary to cling to the existence of a father, but this time a more powerful one. Thus the benevolent rule of a divine Providence allays our fear of the dangers of life; the establishment of a moral world-order ensures the fulfillment of the demands of justice, which have so often remained unfulfilled in human civilization; and the prolongation of earthly existence in a future life provides the local and temporal framework in which these wish-fulfillments shall take place. Answers to the riddles that tempt the curiosity of man, such as how the universe began or what the relation is between body and mind, are developed in conformity with the underlying assumptions of this system. It is an enormous relief to the individual psyche if the conflicts of its childhood arising from the father-complex—conflicts which it has never wholly overcome—are removed from it and brought to a solution which is universally accepted.

When I say that these things are all illusions, I must define the meaning of the word. An illusion is not the same thing as an error; nor is it necessarily an error. Aristotle's belief that vermin are developed out of dung (a belief to which ignorant people still cling) was an error; so was the belief of a former generation of doctors that *tabes dorsalis* [a chronic disease of the nervous system] is the result of sexual excess. It would be incorrect to call these errors illusions. On the other hand, it was an illusion of Columbus's that he discovered a new sea-route to the

Indies. The part played by his wish in this error is very clear. One may describe as an illusion the assertion made by certain nationalists that the Indo-Germanic race is the only one capable of civilization; or the belief, which was only destroyed by psycho-analysis, that children are creatures without sexuality. What is characteristic of illusions is that they are derived from human wishes. In this respect they come near to psychiatric delusions. But they differ from them, too, apart from the more complicated structure of delusions. In the case of delusions, we emphasize as essential their being in contradiction with reality. Illusions need not necessarily be false—that is to say, unrealizable or in contradiction to reality. For instance, a middle-class girl may have the illusion that a prince will come and marry her. This is possible; and a few such cases have occurred. That the Messiah will come and found a golden age is much less likely. Whether one classifies this belief as an illusion or as something analogous to a delusion will depend on one's personal attitude. Examples of illusions which have proved true are not easy to find, but the illusion of the alchemists that all metals can be turned into gold might be one of them. The wish to have a great deal of gold, as much gold as possible, has, it is true, been a good deal dampened by our present-day knowledge of the determinants of wealth, but chemistry no longer regards the transmutation of metals into gold as impossible. Thus we call a belief an illusion when a wish-fulfillment is a prominent factor in its motivation, and in doing so we disregard its relations to reality, just as the illusion itself sets no store by verification.

Having thus taken our bearings, let us return once more to the question of religious doctrines. We can now repeat that all of them are illusions and insusceptible of proof. No one can be compelled to think them true, to believe in them. Some of them are so improbable, so incompatible with everything we have laboriously discovered about the reality of the world, that we may compare them—if we pay proper regard to the psychological differences—to delusions. Of the reality value of most of them we cannot judge; just as they cannot be proved, so they cannot be refuted. We still know too little to make a critical approach to them. The riddles of the universe reveal themselves only slowly to our investigation; there are many questions to which science today can give no answer. But scientific work is the only road which can lead us to a knowledge of reality outside ourselves. It is once again merely an illusion to expect anything from intuition and introspection; they can give us nothing but particulars about our own mental life, which are hard to interpret, never any information about the questions which religious doctrine finds it so easy to answer. It would be insolent to let one's own arbitrary will step into the breach and, according to one's personal estimate, declare this or that part of the religious system to be less or more acceptable. Such questions are too momentous for that; they might be called too sacred.

To assess the truth-value of religious doctrines does not lie within the scope of the present enquiry. It is enough for us that we have recognized them as being, in their psychological nature, illusions. But we do not have to conceal the fact that this discovery also strongly influences our attitude to the question which must appear to many to be the most important of all. We know approximately at what periods and by what kind of men religious doctrines were created. If in addition we discover the motives which led to this, our attitude to the problem of religion will undergo a marked displacement. We shall tell ourselves that it would be very nice if there were a God who created the world and was a benevolent Providence, and if there were a moral order in the universe and an after-life; but it is a very striking fact that all this is exactly as we are bound to wish it to be. And it would be more remarkable still if our wretched, ignorant and downtrodden ancestors had succeeded in solving all these difficult riddles of the universe.

NOTE

1. J. B. L. Foucault demonstrated the diurnal motion of the earth by means of a pendulum in 1851.

CHAPTER 6

A Religious Experience

SIGMUND FREUD

In the autumn of 1927, G. S. Viereck, a German-American journalist who had paid me a welcome visit, published an account of a conversation with me, in the course of which he mentioned my lack of religious faith and my indifference on the subject of survival after death. This "interview," as it was called, was widely read and brought me, among others, the following letter from an American physician:

"What struck me most was your answer to the question whether you believe in a survival of personality after death. You are reported as having said: 'I give no thought to the matter.'

I am writing now to tell you of an experience that I had in the year I graduated at the University of X. One afternoon while I was passing through the dissecting-room my attention was attracted to a sweet-faced dear old woman who was being carried to a dissecting-table. This sweet-faced woman made such an impression on me that a thought flashed up in my mind: 'There is no God: if there were a God he would not have allowed this dear old woman to be brought into the dissecting room.'

When I got home that afternoon the feeling I had had at the sight in the dissecting-room had determined me to discontinue going to church. The doctrines of Christianity had before this been the subject of doubts in my mind.

While I was meditating on this matter a voice spoke to my soul that 'I should consider the step I was about to take.' My spirit replied to this inner voice by saying, 'If I knew of a certainty that Christianity was truth and the Bible was the Word of God, then I would accept it.'

In the course of the next few days God made it clear to my soul that the Bible was His Word, that the teachings about Jesus Christ were true, and that Jesus was our only hope. After such a clear revelation I accepted the Bible as God's Word and Jesus Christ as my personal Saviour. Since then God has revealed Himself to me by many infallible proofs.

I beg you as a brother physician to give thought to this most important matter, and I can assure you, if you look into this subject with an open mind, God will reveal the *truth* to your soul, the same as he did to me and to multitudes of others."

I sent a polite answer, saying that I was glad to hear that this experience had enabled him to retain his faith. As for myself, God had not done so much for me. He had never allowed me to hear an inner voice; and if, in view of my age, he did not make haste, it would not be my fault if I remained to the end of my life what I now was—"an infidel Jew."

In the course of a friendly reply, my colleague gave me an assurance that being a Jew was not an obstacle in the pathway to true faith and proved this by several instances. His letter culminated in the information that prayers were being earnestly addressed to God that he might grant me "faith to believe."

I am still awaiting the outcome of this intercession. In the meantime, my colleague's religious experience provides food for thought. It seems to me to demand some attempt at an interpretation based upon emotional motives; for his experience is puzzling in itself and is based on particularly bad logic. God, as we know, allows horrors to take place of a kind very different from the removal to a dissecting-room of the dead body of a pleasant looking old woman. This has been true at all times, and it must have been so while my American colleague was pursuing his studies. Nor, as a medical student, can he have been so sheltered from the world as to have known nothing of such evils. Why was it, then, that his indignation against God broke out precisely when he received this particular impression in the dissecting-room?

For anyone who is accustomed to regard men's internal experiences and actions analytically the explanation is very obvious—so obvious that it actually crept into my recollections of the facts themselves. Once, when I was referring to my pious colleague's letter in the course of a discussion, I spoke of his having written that the dead woman's face had reminded him of his own mother. In fact these words were not in his letter, and a moment's reflection will show that they could not possibly have been. But that is the explanation irresistibly forced on us by his affectionately phrased description of the "sweet-faced dear old woman." Thus the weakness of judgement displayed by the young doctor is to be accounted for by the emotion roused in him by the memory of his mother. It is difficult to escape from the bad psycho-analytic habit of bringing forward as evidence details which also allow of more superficial explanations—and I am tempted to recall the fact that my colleague addressed me later as a "brother physician."

We may suppose, therefore, that this was the way in which things happened. The sight of a woman's dead body, naked or on the point of being stripped, reminded the young man of his mother. It roused in him a longing for his mother which sprang from his Oedipus complex, and this was immediately completed by a feeling of indignation against his father. His ideas of "father" and "God" had not yet become widely separated; so that his desire to destroy his father could become conscious as doubt in the existence of God and could seek to justify itself in the eyes of reason as indignation about the ill-treatment of a mother-object. It is of course typical for a child to regard what his father does to his mother in sexual intercourse as ill-treatment. The new impulse, which was displaced into the sphere of religion, was only a repetition of the Oedipus situation and consequently soon met with a similar fate. It succumbed to a powerful opposing current. During the actual conflict the level of displacement was not maintained: there is no mention of arguments in justification of God, nor are we told what the infallible signs were by which God proved his existence to the doubter. The conflict seems to have been unfolded in the form of a hallucinatory psychosis: inner voices were heard which uttered warnings against resistance to God. But the outcome of the struggle was displayed once again in the sphere of religion and it was a kind predetermined by the fate of the Oedipus complex: complete submission to the will of God the Father. The young man became a believer and accepted everything he had been taught since his childhood about God and Jesus Christ. He had had a religious experience and had undergone a conversion.

All of this is so simple and straightforward that we cannot but ask ourselves whether by understanding this case we have thrown any light at all on the psychology of conversion in general. I may refer the reader to an admirable volume on the subject by Sante de Sanctis (1924), which incidentally takes all the findings of psycho-analysis into account. Study of this work confirms our expectation that by no means every case of conversion can be understood so easily as this one. In no respect, however, does our case contradict the views arrived at on the subject by modern research. The point which our present observation throws into relief is the manner in which the conversion was attached to a particular determining event, which caused the subject's scepticism to flare up for a last time before being finally extinguished.

CHAPTER 7

From *Civilization and Its Discontents*

SIGMUND FREUD

In my *Future of an Illusion* I was concerned much less with the deepest sources of the religious feeling than with what the common man understands by his religion—with the system of doctrines and promises which on the one hand explains to him the riddles of this world with enviable completeness, and, on the other, assures him that a careful Providence will watch over his life and will compensate him in a future existence for any frustrations he suffers here. The common man cannot imagine this Providence otherwise than in the figure of an enormously exalted father. Only such a being can understand the needs of the children of men and be softened by their prayers and placated by the signs of their remorse. The whole thing is so patently infantile, so foreign to reality, that to anyone with a friendly attitude to humanity it is painful to think that the great majority of mortals will never be able to rise above this view of life. It is still more humiliating to discover how large a number of people living today, who cannot but see that this religion is not tenable, nevertheless try to defend it piece by piece in a series of pitiful rearguard actions. One would like to mix among the ranks of the believers in order to meet these philosophers, who think they can rescue the God of religion by replacing him by an impersonal, shadowy and abstract principle, and to address them with the warning words: "Thou shalt not take the name of the Lord thy God in vain!" And if some of the great men of the past acted in the same way, no appeal can be made to their example: we know why they were obliged to.

Let us return to the common man and to his religion—the only religion which ought to bear that name. The first thing that we think of is the well-known saying of one of our great poets and thinkers concerning the relation of religion to art and science: "He who possesses science and art also has religion; but he who possesses neither of those two, let him have religion!" (Goethe).

This saying on the one hand draws an antithesis between religion and the two highest achievements of man, and on the other, asserts that, as regards their value in life, those achievements and religion can represent or replace each other. If we also set out to deprive the common man [who has neither science nor art] of his religion, we shall clearly not have the poet's authority on our side. We will choose a particular path to bring us nearer an appreciation of his words. Life, as we find it, is too hard for us; it brings us too many pains, disappointments and impossible tasks. In order to bear it we cannot dispense with palliative measures. "We cannot do without auxiliary constructions," as Theodor Fontane tells us. There are perhaps three such measures: powerful deflections, which cause us to make light of our misery; substitutive satisfactions, which diminish it; and intoxicating substances, which make us insensitive to it. Something of the kind is indispensable. Voltaire has deflections in mind when he ends *Candide* with the advice to cultivate one's garden; and scientific activity is a deflection of this kind, too. The substitutive satisfactions, as offered by art, are illusions in contrast with reality, but they are none the less psychically effective, thanks to the role which phantasy has assumed in mental life. The intoxicating substances influence our body and alter its chemistry. It is no simple matter to see where religion has its place in this series. We must look further afield.

The question of the purpose of human life has been raised countless times; it has never yet received a satisfactory answer and perhaps does not admit of one. Some of those who have asked it have added that if it should turn out that life has no purpose, it would lose all value for them. But this threat alters nothing. It looks, on the contrary, as though one had a right to dismiss the question, for it seems to derive from the human presumptuousness, many other manifestations of which are already familiar to us. Nobody talks about the purpose of the life of animals, unless, perhaps, it may be supposed to lie in being of service to man. But this view is not tenable either, for there are many animals of which man can make nothing, except to describe, classify and study them; and innumerable species of animals have escaped even this use, since they existed and became extinct before man set eyes on them. Once again, only religion can answer the question of the purpose of life. One can hardly be wrong in concluding that the idea of life having a purpose stands and falls with the religious system.

We will therefore turn to the less ambitious question of what men themselves show by their behavior to be the purpose and intention of their lives. What do they demand of life and wish to achieve in it? The answer to this can hardly be in doubt. They strive after happiness; they want to become happy and to remain so. This endeavour has two sides, a positive and a negative aim. It aims, on the one hand, at an absence of pain and unpleasure, and, on the other, at the experiencing of strong feelings of pleasure. In its narrower sense the word "happiness" only relates to the last. In conformity with this dichotomy in his aims, man's activity develops in two directions, according as it seeks to realize—in the main, or even exclusively—the one or the other of these aims.

As we see, what decides the purpose of life is simply the program of the pleasure principle. This principle dominates the operation of the mental apparatus from the start. There can be no doubt about its efficacy, and yet its program is at loggerheads with the whole world, with the macrocosm as much as with the microcosm. There is no possibility at all of its being carried through; all the regulations of the universe run counter to it. One feels inclined to say that the intention that man should be "happy" is not included in the plan of "Creation." What we call happiness in the strictest sense comes from the (preferably sudden) satisfaction of needs which have been dammed up to a high degree, and it is from its nature only possible as an episodic phenomenon. When any situation that is desired by the pleasure principle is prolonged, it only produces a feeling of mild contentment. We are so made that we can derive intense enjoyment only from a contrast and very little from a state of things.[1] Thus our possibilities of happiness are already restricted by our constitution. Unhappiness is much less difficult to experience. We are threatened with suffering from three directions: from our own body, which is doomed to decay and dissolution and which cannot even do without pain and anxiety as warning signals; from the external world, which may rage against us with overwhelming and merciless forces of destruction; and finally from our relations to other men. The suffering which comes from this last source is perhaps more painful to us than any other. We tend to regard it as a kind of gratuitous addition, although it cannot be any less fatefully inevitable than the suffering which comes from elsewhere.

It is no wonder if, under the pressure of these possibilities of suffering, men are accustomed to moderate their claims to happiness—

just as the pleasure principle itself, indeed, under the influence of the external world, changed into the more modest reality principle—, if a man thinks himself happy merely to have escaped unhappiness or to have survived his suffering, and if in general the task of avoiding suffering pushes that of obtaining pleasure into the background. Reflection shows that the accomplishment of this task can be attempted along very different paths; and all these paths have been recommended by the various schools of worldly wisdom and put into practice by men. An unrestricted satisfaction of every need presents itself as the most enticing method of conducting one's life, but it means putting enjoyment before caution, and soon brings its own punishment. The other methods, in which avoidance of unpleasure is the main purpose, are differentiated according to the source of unpleasure to which their attention is chiefly turned. Some of these methods are extreme and some moderate; some are one-sided and some attack the problem simultaneously at several points. Against the suffering which may come upon one from human relationships the readiest safeguard is voluntary isolation, keeping oneself aloof from other people. The happiness which can be achieved along this path is, as we see, the happiness of quiet. Against the dreaded external world one can only defend oneself by some kind of turning away from it, if one intends to solve the task by oneself. There is, indeed, another and better path: that of becoming a member of the human community, and, with the help of a technique guided by science, going over to the attack against nature and subjecting her to the human will. Then one is working with all for the good of all. But the most interesting methods of averting suffering are those which seek to influence our own organism. In the last analysis, all suffering is nothing else than sensation; it only exists in so far as we feel it, and we only feel it in consequence of certain ways in which our organism is regulated.

The crudest, but also the most effective among these methods of influence is the chemical one—intoxication. I do not think that anyone completely understands its mechanism, but it is a fact that there are foreign substances which, when present in the blood or tissues, directly cause us pleasurable sensations; and they also so alter the conditions governing our sensibility that we become incapable of receiving unpleasurable impulses. The two effects not only occur simultaneously, but seem to be intimately bound up with each other. But there must be substances in the chemistry of our own bodies which have similar effects, for we know at least one pathological state, mania, in which a condition similar to intoxication arises without the administration of any intoxicating drug. Besides this, our normal mental life exhibits oscillations between a comparatively easy liberation of pleasure and a comparatively difficult one, parallel with which there goes a diminished or an increased receptivity to unpleasure. It is greatly to be regretted that this toxic side of mental processes has so far escaped scientific examination. The service rendered by intoxicating media in the struggle for happiness and in keeping misery at a distance is so highly prized as a benefit that individuals and people alike have given them an established place in the economics of their libido. We owe to such media not merely the immediate yield of pleasure, but also a greatly desired degree of independence from the external world. For one knows that, with the help of this "drowner of cares" one can at any time withdraw from the pressure of reality and find refuge in a world of one's own with better conditions of sensibility. As is well known, it is precisely this property of intoxicants which also determines their danger and their injuriousness. They are responsible, in certain circumstances, for the useless waste of a large quota of energy which might have been employed for the improvement of the human lot.

The complicated structure of our mental apparatus admits, however, of a whole number of other influences. Just as a satisfaction of instinct spells happiness for us, so severe suffering is caused us if the external world lets us starve, if it refuses to sate our needs. One may therefore hope to be freed from a part of one's sufferings by influencing the instinctual impulses. This type of defense against suffering is no longer brought to bear on the sensory apparatus; it seeks to master the internal sources of our needs. The extreme form of this is brought about by killing off the instincts, as is prescribed by the worldly wisdom of the East and practiced by Yoga. If it succeeds, then the subject has, it is true, given up all other activities as well—he has sacrificed his life; and, by another path, he has once more only achieved the happiness of quietness. We follow the same path when our aims are less extreme and we merely attempt to control our instinctual life. In that case, the controlling elements are the higher psychical agencies, which have subjected themselves to the reality principle. Here the aim of satisfaction is not by any means relinquished; but a certain amount of protection against suffering is secured, in that non-satisfaction is not so painfully felt in the case of instincts kept in dependence as in the case of uninhibited ones. As against this, there is an undeniable diminution in the potentialities of enjoyment. The feeling of happiness derived from the satisfaction of a wild instinctual impulse untamed by the ego is incomparably more intense than that derived from sating an instinct that has been tamed. The irresistibility of perverse instincts, and perhaps the attraction in general of forbidden things finds an economic explanation here.

Another technique for fending off suffering is the employment of the displacements of libido which our mental apparatus permits of and through which its function gains so much in flexibility. The task here is that of shifting the instinctual aims in such a way that they cannot come up against frustration from the external world. In this, sublimation of the instincts lends its assistance. One gains the most if one can sufficiently heighten the yield of pleasure from the sources of psychical and intellectual work. When that is so, fate can do little against one. A satisfaction of this kind, such as an artist's joy in creating, in giving his phantasies body, or a scientist's in solving problems or discovering truths, has a special quality which we shall certainly one day be able to characterize in metapsychological terms. At present we can only say figuratively that such satisfactions seem "finer and higher." But their intensity is mild as compared with that derived from the sating of crude and primary instinctual impulses; it does not convulse our physical being. And the weak point of this method is that it is not applicable generally: it is accessible to only a few people. It presupposes the possession of special dispositions and gifts which are far from being common to any practical degree. And even to the few who do possess them, this method cannot give complete protection from suffering. It creates no impenetrable armor against the arrows of fortune, and it habitually fails when the source of suffering is a person's own body.

While this procedure already clearly shows an intention of making oneself independent of the external world by seeking satisfaction in internal, psychical processes, the next procedure brings out those features yet more strongly. In it, the connection with reality is still further loosened; satisfaction is obtained from illusions, which are recognized as such without the discrepancy between them and reality being allowed to interfere with enjoyment. The region from which these illusions arise is the life of the imagination; at the time when the development of the sense of reality took place, this region was expressly exempted from the demands of reality-testing and was set apart for the purpose of fulfilling wishes which were difficult to carry out. At the head of these satisfactions through phantasy stands the enjoyment of works of art—an enjoyment which, by the agency of the artist, is made accessible even to those who are not themselves creative. People who are receptive to the influence of art cannot set too high a value on it as a source of pleasure and consolation in life. Nevertheless the mild narcosis induced in us by art can do no more than bring about a transient withdrawal from the pressure of vital needs, and it is not strong enough to make us forget real misery.

Another procedure operates more energetically and more thoroughly. It regards reality as the sole enemy and as the source of all suffering, with which it is impossible to live, so that one must break off all relations with it if one is to be in any way happy. The hermit turns his back on the world and will have no truck with it. But one can do more than that; one can try to re-create the world, to build up in its stead another world in which its most unbearable features are eliminated and replaced by others that are in conformity with one's own wishes. But whoever, in desperate defiance, sets out upon this path to happiness will as a rule attain nothing. Reality is too strong for him. He becomes a madman, who for the most part finds no one to help him in carrying through his delusion. It is asserted, however, that each one of us behaves in some one respect like a paranoic, corrects some aspect of the world which is unbearable to him by the construction of a wish and introduces this delusion into reality. A special importance attaches to the case in which this attempt to procure a certainty of happiness and a protection against suffering through a delusional remolding of reality is made by a considerable number of people in common. The religions of mankind must be classed among the mass-delusions of this kind. No one, needless to say, who shares a delusion ever recognizes it as such.

I do not think that I have made a complete enumeration of the methods by which men strive to gain happiness and keep suffering away and I know, too, that the material might have been differently arranged. One procedure I have not yet mentioned—not because I have forgotten it but because it will concern us later in another connection. And how could one possibly forget, of all others, this technique in the art of living? It is conspicuous for a most remarkable combination of characteristic features. It, too, aims of course at making the subject independent of Fate (as it is best to call it), and to that end it locates satisfaction in internal mental processes, making use, in so doing, of the displaceability of the libido. But it does not turn away from the external world; on the contrary, it clings to the objects belonging to that world and obtains happiness from an emotional relationship to them. Nor is it content to aim at an avoidance of unpleasure—a goal, as we might call it, of weary resignation; it passes this by without heed and holds fast to the original, passionate striving for a positive fulfilment of happiness. And perhaps it does in fact come nearer to this goal than any other method. I am, of course, speaking of the way of life which makes love the center of everything, which looks for all satisfaction in loving and being loved. A psychical attitude of this sort comes naturally enough to all of us; one of the forms in which love manifests itself—sexual love—has given us our most intense experience of an overwhelming sensation of pleasure and has thus furnished us with a pattern for our search for happiness. What is more natural than that we should persist in looking for happiness along the path on which we first encountered it? The weak side of this technique of living is easy to see; otherwise no human being would have thought of abandoning this path to happiness for any other. It is that we are never so defenseless against suffering as when we love, never so helplessly unhappy as when we have lost our loved object or its love. But this does not dispose of the technique of living based on the value of love as a means of happiness. There is much more to be said about it.

We may go on from here to consider the interesting case in which happiness in life is predominantly sought in the enjoyment of beauty, whatever beauty presents itself to our senses and our judgement—the beauty of human forms and gestures, of natural objects and landscapes and of artistic and even scientific creations. This aesthetic attitude to the goal of life offers little protection against the threat of suffering, but it can compensate for a great deal. The enjoyment of beauty has a peculiar, mildly intoxicating quality of feeling. Beauty has no obvious use; nor is there any clear cultural necessity for it. Yet civilization could not do without it. The science of aesthetics investigates the conditions under which things are felt as beautiful, but it has been unable to give any explanation of the nature and origin of beauty, and as usually happens, lack of success is concealed beneath a flood of resounding and empty words. Psychoanalysis, unfortunately, has scarcely anything to say about beauty either. All that seems certain is its derivation from the field of sexual feeling. The love of beauty seems a perfect example of an impulse inhibited in its aim. "Beauty" and "attraction" are originally attributes of the sexual object. It is worth remarking that the genitals themselves, the sight of which is always exciting, are nevertheless hardly ever judged to be beautiful; the quality of beauty seems, instead, to attach to certain secondary sexual characters.

In spite of the incompleteness of my enumeration, I will venture on a few remarks as a conclusion to our enquiry. The program of becoming happy, which the pleasure principle imposes on us, cannot be fulfilled; yet we must not—indeed, we cannot—give up our efforts to bring it nearer to fulfillment by some means or other. Very different paths may be taken in that direction, and we may give priority either to the positive aspect of the aim, that of gaining pleasure, or to its negative one, that of avoiding unpleasure. By none of these paths can we attain all that we desire. Happiness, in the reduced sense in which we recognize it as possible, is a problem of the economics of the individual's libido. There is no golden rule which applies to everyone: every man must find out for himself in what particular fashion he can be saved. All kinds of different factors will operate to direct his choice. It is a question of how much real satisfaction he can expect to get from the external world, how far he is led to make himself independent of it, and, finally, how much strength he feels he has for altering the world to suit his wishes. In this, his physical constitution will play a decisive part, irrespectively of the external circumstances. The man who is predominantly erotic will give first preference to his emotional relationships to other people; the narcissistic man, who inclines to be self-sufficient, will seek his main satisfactions in his internal mental processes; the man of action will never give up the external world on which he can try out his strength. As regards the second of these types, the nature of his talents and the amount of instinctual sublimation open to him will decide where he shall locate his interests. Any choice that is pushed to an extreme will be penalized by exposing the individual to the dangers which arise if a technique of living that has been chosen as an exclusive one should prove inadequate. Just as a cautious businessman avoids tying up all his capital in one concern, so, perhaps, worldly wisdom will advise us not to look for the whole of our satisfaction from a single aspiration. Its success is never certain, for that depends on the convergence of many factors, perhaps on none more than on the capacity of the psychical constitution to adapt its function to the environment and then to exploit that environment for a yield of pleasure. A person who is born with a specially unfavorable instinctual constitution, and who has not properly undergone the transformation and rearrangement of his libidinal components which is indispensable for later achievements, will find it hard to obtain happiness from his external situation, especially if he is faced with tasks of some difficulty. As a last technique of living, which will at least bring him substitutive satisfactions, he is offered that of a flight into neurotic illness—a flight which he usually accomplishes when he is still young. The man who sees his pursuit of happiness come to nothing in later years can still find consolation in the yield of pleasure of chronic intoxication; or he can embark on the desperate attempt at rebellion seen in a psychosis.

Religion restricts this play of choice and adaptation, since it imposes equally on everyone its own path to the acquisition of happiness and protection from suffering. Its technique consists in depressing the value of life and distorting the picture of the real world in a delusional manner—which presupposes an intimidation of the intelligence. At this price, by forcibly fixing them in a state of psychical infantilism and by drawing them into a mass-delusion, religion succeeds in sparing many people an individual neurosis. But hardly anything more. There are, as we have said, many paths which *may* lead to such happiness as is attainable by men, but there is none which does so for certain. Even religion cannot keep its promise. If the believer finally sees himself obliged to speak of God's "inscrutable decrees," he is admitting that all that is left to him as a last possible consolation and source of pleasure in his suffering is an unconditional submission. And if he is prepared for that, he could probably have spared himself the *détour* he has made.

NOTE

1. Goethe, indeed, warns us that "nothing is harder to bear than a succession of fair days." But this may be an exaggeration.

CHAPTER 8

From *Moses and Monotheism*

SIGMUND FREUD

In 1922 Ernst Sellin made a discovery of decisive importance. He found in the book of the Prophet Hosea (second half of the eighth century) unmistakable traces of a tradition to the effect that the founder of their religion, Moses, met a violent end in a rebellion of his stubborn and refractory people. The religion he had instituted [based on the monotheism of the Egyptian Pharoah Ikhnaton] was at the same time abandoned. This tradition is not restricted to Hosea; it recurs in the writings of most of the later Prophets; indeed, according to Sellin, it was the basis of all the later expectations of the Messiah. Towards the end of the Babylonian exile the hope arose among the Jewish people that the man they had so callously murdered would return from the realm of the dead and lead his contrite people—and perhaps not only his people—into the land of eternal bliss.

Naturally, I am not in a position to decide whether Sellin has correctly interpreted the relevant passages in the Prophets. If he is right, however, we may regard as historically credible the tradition he recognized; for such things are not readily invented—there is no tangible motive for doing so. And if they have really happened, the wish to forget them is easily understood. We need not accept every detail of the tradition.

Let us adopt from Sellin the surmise that the Egyptian Moses was killed by the Jews, and the religion he instituted abandoned. It allows us to spin our thread further without contradicting the trustworthy results of historical research. But we venture to be independent of the historians in other respects and to blaze our own trail. The Exodus from Egypt remains our starting-point. It must have been a considerable number that left the country with Moses; a small crowd would not have been worth the while of that ambitious man, with his great schemes. The immigrants had probably been in the country long enough to develop into a numerous people. We shall certainly not go astray, however, if we suppose with the majority of research workers that only a part of those who later became the Jewish people had undergone the fate of bondage in Egypt. In other words, the tribe returning from Egypt combined later in the country between Egypt and Canaan with other related tribes that had been settled there for some time. This union, from which was born the people of Israel, expressed itself in the adoption of a new religion, common to all the tribes, the religion of Jahve.

It is certain that many very diverse elements contributed to the building up of the Jewish people, but the greatest difference among them must have depended on whether they had experienced the sojourn in Egypt and what followed it, or not. From this point of view we may say that the nation was made up by the union of two constituents, and it accords with this fact that, after a short period of political unity, it broke asunder into two parts—the Kingdom of Israel and the Kingdom of Judah. History loves such restorations, in which later fusions are redissolved and former separations become once more apparent. The most impressive example—a very well-known one—was provided by the Reformation, when, after an interval of more than a thousand years, it brought to light again the frontier between the Germania that had been Roman and the part that had always remained independent. With the Jewish people we cannot verify such a faithful reproduction of the former state of affairs. Our knowledge of those times is too uncertain to permit the assumption that the northern Kingdom had absorbed the original settlers, the southern those returning from Egypt; but the later dissolution, in this case also, could not have been unconnected with the earlier union. The former Egyptians were probably fewer than the others, but they proved to be on a higher level culturally. They exercised a more important influence on the later development of the people because they brought with them a tradition the others lacked.

Perhaps they brought something else, something more tangible than a tradition. Among the greatest riddles of Jewish prehistoric times is that concerning the antecedents of the Levites. They are said to have been derived from one of the twelve tribes of Israel, the tribe of Levi, but no tradition has ever ventured to pronounce on where that tribe originally dwelt or what portion of the conquered country of

Canaan had been allotted to it. They occupied the most important priestly positions, but yet they were distinguished from the priests. A Levite is not necessarily a priest; it is not the name of a caste. Our supposition about the person of Moses suggests an explanation. It is not credible that a great gentleman like the Egyptian Moses approached a people strange to him without an escort. He must have brought his retinue with him, his nearest adherents, his scribes, his servants. These were the original Levites. Tradition maintains that Moses was a Levite. This seems a transparent distortion of the actual state of affairs: the Levites were Moses' people. This solution is supported by what I mentioned in my previous essay: that in later times we find Egyptian names only among the Levites. We may suppose that a fair number of these Moses people escaped the fate that overtook him and his religion. They increased in the following generations and fused with the people among whom they lived, but they remained faithful to their master, honoured his memory, and retained the tradition of his teaching. At the time of the union with the followers of Jahve they formed an influential minority, culturally superior to the rest.

The Return of the Repressed

It has long since become common knowledge that the experiences of a person's first five years exercise a determining effect on his life, which nothing later can withstand. Much that deserves knowing might be said about the way in which these early impressions maintain themselves against any influences in more mature periods of life—but it would not be relevant here. It may, however, be less well known that the strongest compulsive influence arises from impressions which impinge upon a child at a time when we would have to regard his psychical apparatus as not yet completely receptive. The fact itself cannot be doubted; but it is so puzzling that we may make it more comprehensible by comparing it with a photographic exposure which can be developed after any interval of time and transformed into a picture. I am nevertheless glad to point out that this uncomfortable discovery of ours has been anticipated by an imaginative writer, with the boldness that is permitted to poets. E. T. A. Hoffman used to trace back the wealth of figures that put themselves at his disposal for his creative writings to the changing images and impressions which he had experienced during a journey of some weeks in a post-chaise while he was still an infant at his mother's breast. What children have experienced at the age of two and have not understood, need never be remembered by them except in dreams; they may only come to know of it through psycho-analytic treatment. But at some later time it will break into their life with obsessional impulses, it will govern their actions, it will decide their sympathies and antipathies and will quite often determine their choice of a love-object, for which it is so frequently impossible to find a rational basis. The two points at which these facts touch upon our problem cannot be mistaken.

First, there is the remoteness of the period concerned, which is recognized here as the truly determining factor—in the special state of the memory, for instance, which in the case of these childhood experiences we classify as "unconscious." We expect to find an analogy in this with the state which we are seeking to attribute to tradition in the mental life of the people. It was not easy, to be sure, to introduce the idea of the unconscious into group psychology.

Secondly, regular contributions are made to the phenomena we are in search of by the mechanisms which lead to the formation of neuroses. Here again the determining events occur in early childhood times, but here the stress is not upon the time but upon the process by which the event is met, the reaction to it. We can describe it schematically thus. As a result of the experience, an instinctual demand arises which calls for satisfaction. The ego refuses that satisfaction, either because it is paralyzed by the magnitude of the demand or because it recognizes it as a danger. The former of these grounds is the more primary one; both of them amount to the avoidance of a situation of danger. The ego fends off the danger by the process of repression. The instinctual impulse is in some way inhibited, its precipitating cause, with its attendant perceptions and ideas, is forgotten. This, however, is not the end of the process: the instinct has either retained its forces, or collects them again, or it is reawakened by some new precipitating cause. Thereupon it renews its demand, and, since the path to normal satisfaction remains closed to it by what we may call the scar of repression, somewhere, at a weak spot, it opens another path for itself to what is known as a substitutive satisfaction, which comes to light as a symptom, without the acquiescence of the ego, but also without its understanding. All the phenomena of the formation of symptoms may justly be described as the "return of the repressed." Their distinguishing characteristic, however, is the far-reaching distortion to which the returning material has been subjected as compared with the original. It will perhaps be thought that this last group of facts has carried us too far away from the similarity with tradition. But we ought not to regret it if it has brought us close to the problems of the renunciation of instinct.

Historical Truth

We have undertaken all these psychological diversions in order to make it more credible to us that the religion of Moses only carried through its effect on the Jewish people as a tradition. It is likely that we have not achieved more than a certain degree of probability. Let us suppose, however, that we have succeeded in completely proving it. Even so the impression would remain that we have merely satisfied the qualitative factor of what was demanded, but not the quantitative one as well. There is an element of grandeur about everything to do with the origin of a religion, certainly including the Jewish one, and this is not matched by the explanations we have hitherto given. Some other factor must be involved to which there is little that is analogous and nothing that is of the same kind, something unique and something of the same order of magnitude as what has come out of it, as religion itself.

Let us try to approach the subject from the opposite direction. We understand how a primitive man is in need of a god as creator of the universe, as chief of his clan, as personal protector. This god takes his position behind the dead fathers [of the clan], about whom tradition still has something to say. A man of later days, of our own day, behaves in the same way. He, too, remains childish and in need of protection, even when he is grown up; he thinks he cannot do without support from his god. That much is undisputed. But it is less easy to understand why there may only be a *single* god, why precisely the advance from henotheism[1] to monotheism acquires an overwhelming significance. No doubt it is true, that the believer has a share in the greatness of his god; and the greater the god the more reliable is the protection which he can offer. But a god's power does not necessarily presuppose that he is the only one. Many peoples regarded it only as a glorification of their chief god if he ruled over other deities who were inferior to him, and they did not think it diminished his greatness if there were other gods besides him. No doubt, if this god became a universal one and had all countries and peoples as his concern, it meant a sacrifice of intimacy, too. It was as though one were sharing one's god with the foreigners and one had to make up for this by the proviso that one was preferred by him. We can make the further point that the idea of a single god means in itself an advance in intellectuality, but it is impossible to rate this point so highly.

Pious believers, however, know how to fill this obvious gap in motivation adequately. They say that the idea of a single god produced such an overwhelming effect on men because it is a portion of the eternal *truth* which, long concealed, came to light at last and was then bound to carry everyone along with it. We must admit that a factor of this kind is at last something that matches the magnitude both of the subject and of its effect.

We too would like to accept this solution. But we are brought up by a doubt. The pious argument rests on an optimistic and idealistic premise. It has not been possible to demonstrate in other connections that the human intellect has a particularly fine flair for the truth or that the human mind shows any special inclination for recognizing the truth. We have rather found, on the contrary, that our intellect very easily goes astray without any warning, and that nothing is more easily believed by us than what, without reference to the truth, comes to meet our wishful illusions. We must for that reason add a reservation to our agreement. We too believe that the pious solution contains the truth—but the *historical* truth and not the *material* truth. And we assume the right to correct a certain distortion to which this truth has been subjected on its return. That is to say, we do not believe that there is a single great god today, but that in primaeval times there was a single person who was bound to appear huge at that time and who afterwards returned in men's memory elevated to divinity.

We had assumed that the religion of Moses was to begin with rejected and half-forgotten and afterwards broke through as a tradition. We are now assuming that this process was being repeated then for the second time. When Moses brought the people the idea of a single god, it was not a novelty but signified the revival of an experience in the primaeval ages of the human family which had long vanished from men's conscious memory. But it had been so important and had produced or paved the way for such deeply penetrating changes in men's life that we cannot avoid believing that it had left behind it in the human mind some permanent traces, which can be compared to a tradition.

We have learnt from the psycho-analyses of individuals that their earliest impressions, received at a time when the child was scarcely yet capable of speaking, produce at some time or another effects of a compulsive character without themselves being consciously remembered. We believe we have a right to make the same assumption about the earliest experiences of the whole of humanity. One of these effects would be the emergence of the idea of a single great god—an idea which must be recognized as a completely justified memory, though, it is true, one that has been distorted. An idea such as this has a compulsive character: it *must* be believed. To the extent to which it is distorted, it may be described as a *delusion;* in so far as it brings a return of the past, it must be called the *truth.* Psychiatric delusions, too, contain a small fragment of truth and the patient's conviction extends over from this truth on to its delusional wrappings.

In 1912 I attempted, in my *Totem and Taboo,* to reconstruct the ancient situation from which these consequences followed. In doing so, I made use of some theoretical ideas put forward by Darwin, Atkinson and particularly by Robertson Smith, and combined them with the findings and indications derived from psycho-analysis. From Darwin I borrowed the hypothesis that human beings originally lived in small hordes, each of which was under the despotic rule of an older male who appropriated all the females and castigated or disposed of the younger males, including his sons. From Atkinson I took, in continuation of this account, the idea that this patriarchal system ended in a rebellion by the sons, who banded together against their father, overcame him and devoured him in common. Basing myself on Robertson Smith's totem theory, I assumed that subsequently the father-horde gave place to the totemic brother-clan. In order to be able to live in peace with one another, the victorious brothers renounced the woman on whose account they had, after all, killed their father, and instituted exogamy. The power of fathers was broken and the families were organized as a matriarchy. The ambivalent emotional attitude of the sons to their father remained in force during the whole of later development. A particular animal was set up in the father's place as a totem. It was regarded as ancestor and protective spirit and might not be injured or killed. But once a year the whole male community came together to a ceremonial meal at which the totem animal (worshiped at all other times) was torn to pieces and devoured in common. No one might absent himself from this meal: it was the ceremonial repetition of the killing of the father, with which social order, moral laws and religion had taken their start. The conformity between Robertson Smith's totem meal and the Christian Lord's Supper had struck a number of writers before me.

The Historical Development

I cannot here repeat the contents of *Totem and Taboo* in greater detail. But I must undertake to fill up the long stretch between that hypothetical primaeval period and the victory of monotheism in historical times. After the institution of the combination of brother-clan, matriarchy, exogamy and totemism, a development began which must be described as a slow "return of the repressed." Here I am not using the term "the repressed" in its proper sense. What is in question is something in a people's life which is past, lost to view, superseded and which we venture to compare with what is repressed in the mental life of an individual. We cannot at first sight say in what form this past existed during the time of its eclipse. It is not easy for us to carry over the concepts of individual psychology into group psychology; and I do not think we gain anything by introducing the concept of a "collective" unconscious. The content of the unconscious, indeed, is in any case a collective, universal property of mankind. For the moment, then, we will make shift with the use of analogies. The processes in the life of peoples which we are studying here are very similar to those familiar to us in psychopathology, but nevertheless not quite the same. We must finally make up our minds to adopt the hypothesis that the psychical precipitates of the primaeval period became inherited property which, in each fresh generation, called not for acquisition but only for awakening. In this we have in mind the example of what is certainly the "innate" symbolism which derives from the period of the development of speech, which is familiar to all children without their being instructed, and which is the same among all peoples despite their different languages. What we may perhaps still lack in certainty here is made good by other products of psycho-analytic research. We find that in a number of important relations our children react, not in a manner corresponding to their own experience, but instinctively, like the animals, in a manner that is only explicable as phylogenetic acquisition.

The return of the repressed took place slowly and certainly not spontaneously but under the influence of all the changes in conditions of life which fill the history of human civilization. I cannot give a survey here of these determinants nor more than a fragmentary enumeration of the stages of this return. The father once more became the head of the family, but was not by any means so absolute as the father of the primal horde had been. The totem animal was replaced by a god in a series of transitions which are still very plain. To begin with, the god in human form still bore an animal's head; later he turned himself by preference into that particular animal, and afterwards it became sacred to him and was his favorite attendant; or he killed the animal and himself bore its name as an epithet. Between the totem animal and the god, the hero emerged, often as a preliminary step towards deification.

The idea of a supreme deity seems to have started early, at first only in a shadowy manner without intruding into men's daily interests. As tribes and peoples came together into larger unities, the gods too organized themselves into families and into hierarchies. One of them was often elevated into being supreme lord over gods and men. After this, the further step was hesitatingly taken of paying respect to only one god, and finally the decision was taken of giving all power to a single god and of tolerating no other gods beside him. Only thus was it that the supremacy of the father of the primal horde was re-established and that the emotions relating to him could be repeated.

The first effect of meeting the being who had so long been missed and longed for was overwhelming and was like the traditional description of the law-giving from Mount Sinai. Admiration, awe and thankfulness for having found grace in his eyes—the religion of Moses knew none but these positive feelings towards the father-god. The conviction of his irresistibility, the submission to his will, could not have been more unquestioning in the helpless and intimidated son of the father of the horde—indeed those feelings only become fully intelligible when they are transposed into the primitive and infantile setting. A child's emotional impulses are intensely and inexhaustibly deep to a degree quite other than those of an adult; only religious ecstasy can bring them back. A rapture of devotion to God was thus the first reaction to the return of the great father.

The direction to be taken by this father-religion was in this way laid down for all time. Yet this did not bring its development to an end. Ambivalence is a part of the essence of the relation to the father: in the course of time the hostility too could not fail to stir, which had once driven the sons into killing their admired and dreaded father. There was no place in the framework of the religion of Moses for a direct expression of the murderous hatred of the father. All that could come to light was a mighty reaction against it—a sense of guilt on account of that hostility, a bad conscience for having sinned against God and for not ceasing to sin. This sense of guilt, which was uninterruptedly kept awake by the Prophets, and which soon formed an essential part of the religious system, had yet another superficial motivation, which neatly disguised its true origin. Things were going badly for the people; the hopes resting on the favor of God failed in fulfilment; it was not easy to maintain the illusion, loved above all else, of being God's chosen people. If they wished to avoid renouncing that happiness, a sense of guilt on account of their own sinfulness offered a welcome means of exculpating God: they deserved no better than to be punished by him since they had not obeyed his commandments. And, driven by the need to satisfy this sense of guilt, which was insatiable and came from sources so much deeper, they must make those commandments grow ever stricter, more meticulous and even more trivial. In a fresh rapture of moral asceticism they imposed more and more new instinctual renunciations on themselves and in that way reached—in doctrine and precept, at least—ethical heights which had remained inaccessible to the other peoples of antiquity. Many Jews regard this attainment of ethical heights as the second main characteristic and the second great achievement of their religion. The way in which it was connected with the first one—the idea of a single god—should be plain from our remarks. These ethical ideas cannot, however, disavow their origin from the sense of guilt felt on account of a suppressed hostility to God. They possess the characteristic—uncompleted and incapable of completion—of obsessional neurotic reaction-formations; we can guess, too, that they serve the secret purposes of punishment.

The further development takes us beyond Judaism. The remainder of what returned from the tragic drama of the primal father was no longer reconcilable in any way with the religion of Moses. The sense of guilt of those days was very far from being any longer restricted to the Jewish people; it had caught hold of all the Mediterranean peoples as a dull *malaise,* a premonition of calamity for which no one could suggest a reason. Historians of our day speak of an aging of ancient civilization, but I suspect that they have only grasped accidental and contributory causes of this depressed mood of the peoples. The elucidation of this situation of depression sprang from Jewry. Irrespectively of all the approximations and preparations in the surrounding world, it was after all a Jewish man, Saul of Tarsus (who, as a Roman citizen, called himself Paul), in whose spirit the realization first emerged: "The reason we are so unhappy is that we have killed God the father." And it is entirely understandable that he could only grasp this piece of truth in the delusional disguise of the glad tidings: "We are freed from all guilt since one of us has sacrificed his life to absolve us." In this formula the killing of God was of course not mentioned, but a crime that had to be atoned by the sacrifice of a victim could only have been a murder. And the intermediate step between the delusion and the historical truth was provided by the assurance that the victim of the sacrifice had been God's son. With the strength which it derived from the source of historical truth, this new faith overthrew every obstacle. The blissful sense of being chosen was replaced by the

liberating sense of redemption. But the fact of the parricide, in returning to the memory of mankind, had to overcome greater resistances
than the other fact, which had constituted the subject-matter of
monotheism; it was also obliged to submit to a more powerful distortion. The unnameable crime was replaced by the hypothesis of what
must be described as a shadowy "original sin."

Original sin and redemption by the sacrifice of a victim became
the foundation stones of the new religion founded by Paul. It must remain uncertain whether there was a ringleader and instigator to the
murder among the band of brothers who rebelled against their primal
father, or whether such a figure was created later by the imagination
of creative artists in order to turn themselves into heroes, and was
then introduced into the tradition. After the Christian doctrine had
burst the framework of Judaism, it took up components from many
other sources, renounced a number of characteristics of pure
monotheism and adapted itself in many details to the rituals of the
other Mediterranean peoples. It is worth noticing how the new religion dealt with the ancient ambivalence in the relation to the father.
Its main content was, it is true, reconciliation with God the Father,
atonement for the crime committed against him; but the other side of
the emotional relation showed itself in the fact that the son, who had
taken the atonement on himself, became a god himself beside the father and, actually, in place of the father. Christianity, having arisen out
of a father-religion, became a son-religion. It has not escaped the fate
of having to get rid of the father.

Only a portion of the Jewish people accepted the new doctrine.
Those who refused to are still called Jews today. Owing to this cleav-
age, they have become even more sharply divided from other peoples
than before. They were obliged to hear the new religious community
(which, besides Jews, included Egyptians, Greeks, Syrians, Romans
and eventually Germans) reproach them with having murdered God.
In full, this reproach would run as follows: "They will not accept it as
true that they murdered God, whereas we admit it and have been
cleansed of that guilt." It is easy therefore to see how much truth lies
behind this approach. A special enquiry would be called for to discover why it has been impossible for the Jews to join in this forward
step which was implied, in spite of all its distortions, by the admission
of having murdered God. In a certain sense they have in that way
taken a tragic load of guilt on themselves; they have been made to pay
heavy penance for it.

Our investigations may perhaps have thrown a little light on the question of how the Jewish people have acquired the characteristics which distinguish them. Less light has been thrown on the problem of how it is that they have been able to retain their individuality till the present day. But exhaustive answers to such riddles cannot in fairness be either demanded or expected. A contribution, to be judged in view of the limitations which I mentioned at the start, is all that I can offer.

NOTE

1. The word has not been very clearly defined. It is used to mean the belief of a community in one particular god of its own, and also to mean the belief in the dominance of one particular god over a hierarchy of other gods. In neither case does the belief imply that the god in question is the *only* god.

PART II

David Bakan

D avid Bakan, who is perhaps closest of all the authors in this volume to Freud in terms of background, temperament, and methods of interpretation, taught in the psychology departments of several American universities, including the University of Chicago, before moving to York University in Canada in 1968. Besides the books represented here, he has written on methods of psychological investigation, abuse of children, and a more recent book on Maimonides and prophecy.

The first selection is from Bakan's book on Freud and the Jewish mystical tradition, which centers on Freud's own writings, especially on religious subjects, to make the case that psychoanalysis has deep roots in the mystical tradition of Judaism. At one point in the book, Bakan describes psychoanalysis as a "secularized" form of Jewish mysticism, thereby emphasizing that Freud was not attempting to create a new religion but was employing certain religious ideas and methods in the service of his scientific project. The mystical tradition, especially in its Chassidic form, was familiar to Freud as a boy growing up in Freiberg. The material I have chosen for inclusion here is from the section entitled "The Devil as Suspended Superego." It centers on his interpretation of Freud's essay on Christoph Haizmann, the struggling painter who made a pact with Satan. Bakan contends that Freud recognized similarities between himself and Haizmann, for Freud was also depressed over his father's death and concerned about earning a living. While Freud viewed the Devil as a metaphor, not a supernatural being, psychoanalysis may be viewed as his own "pact" with the Devil, one that offered a cure for his own depression and a means of making a living. In Bakan's view, Freud's formulation of this new healer role for himself resonated with the tradition of Chassidic wonder workers. Thus, while this selection centers primarily on Freud, it exemplifies Bakan's own project, that of showing ways in which psychoanalysis derived its inspiration from a radical movement within Judaism.

The second selection, excerpted from *The Duality of Human Existence*, centers on a pervasive theme in the Bible, that of the biological role of the adult male in the conception of children. This theme lies behind assertions in the Bible of male supremacy (reflected in monotheistic religion itself) and male mistrust (of women and other males), leading to conflict, both personally and collectively, over what to do about illegitimate offspring. Such conflict, in Bakan's view, gives rise to the infanticidal impulse and to substitutionary rituals designed to counteract this impulse. In this excerpt from a much longer chapter encompassing the whole sweep of the biblical tradition—including the victimization of Jesus—Bakan focuses on the Abraham and Isaac story as exemplary of the illegitimacy problem and efforts of the Jewish community to address it via religious rituals. His psychoanalytic interpretation has gained indirect support from Jon D. Levenson's book on the transformation of child sacrifice in Judaism and Christianity.[1]

Levenson argues that although the practice of child sacrifice was eradicated during the late seventh and sixth centuries B.C.E., the idea of sacrificing the first-born son (or the later-born son whose preferential treatment promotes him to this exalted status) remained potent in religious literature. He, too, notes that tales of the son handed over to death by his loving father in the Hebrew Bible influenced Christianity's identification of Jesus as sacrificial victim. What Bakan uniquely offers, however, is a psychological explanation for the motivation to kill the first-born based on doubts regarding paternity. In addition, he considers the other side of Freud's analysis of the father's ambivalence toward the son, noting that there is more than love in the father's handing of the son over to death. In other writings, Bakan has pointed out that while Freud emphasizes the son's murderous impulses toward the father in his Oedipal theory, the original story of Oedipus begins with Oedipus's abandonment by his parents in response to the oracle that he would someday murder his father and marry his mother.[2]

Thus, paternal abandonment precipitated the son's impulse to kill his father.

The third selection is from the third chapter of *Disease, Pain, and Sacrifice.* Here Bakan uses the Book of Job to explore the relationship of the infanticidal impulse to religious sacrifice, enlarging his earlier analysis to include parental fantasies of destroying their children for reasons other than illegitimacy. In this essay, he focuses on such extenuating circumstances in parent-child relations as the younger generation's disregard for their elders, and environmental conditions (such as drought) that turn children from valued property as workers into hungry mouths to feed. Bakan shows that in these cases as well, resort is taken to sacrificial rituals to control the infanticidal impulse. He also suggests, however, that the ritual was becoming less effective at the time the Book of Job was written. An important feature of his interpretation of Job is his use of the psychoanalytic theory of projection, for the text not only attributes to God the infanticidal impulses originating in human parents, but also portrays Job as attempting to claim victimhood for himself, affirming his innocence by locating himself within the chorus of victims.

Throughout this essay, Bakan employs Freud's own distinction between "manifest" and "latent" content in his textual interpretation. In his earlier book on Freud and the Jewish mystical tradition, he had argued that techniques of interpretation developed in Freud's work with his patients' and his own dreams were derived to a considerable degree from methods of textual interpretation in the rabbinic and Jewish mystical literature. He makes the further suggestion that Freud's famous case of Dora (a pseudonym) bears an association with the Torah, and that Freud therefore made implicit use of the idea in Jewish mysticism that the same methods employed with texts may be applied to analysis of individuals.[3] In the final analysis, Bakan offers a psychoanalytic explanation for why the rabbinical tradition treated the Book of Job as canonically marginal, thus disavowing the human motivations that lie beneath the surface of the text. His interpretation is comparable to that of Rene Girard, who also seeks to penetrate beneath its surface to discern the communal mechanism of scapegoating.[4]

NOTES

1. Jon D. Levenson, *The Death and Resurrection of the Beloved Son: The Transformation of Child Sacrifice in Judaism and Christianity* (New Haven and London: Yale University Press, 1993).

2. For example, *The Duality of Human Existence* (Chicago: Rand McNally, 1966), 200–201.

3. David Bakan, *Sigmund Freud and the Jewish Mystical Tradition* (New York: Schocken Books, 1965), ch. 32.

4. Rene Girard, *Job: The Victim of His People*, trans. Yvonne Freccero (Stanford: Stanford University Press, 1987).

CHAPTER 9

Freud's Paper on Demonological Possession

DAVID BAKAN

Freud begins his paper "A Neurosis of Demonological Possession in the Seventeenth Century" by telling us that neuroses which may now appear in a "hypochondriacal guise" would formerly masquerade in "demonological shape." Then he writes, "Despite the somatic ideology of the ear of 'exact' science, the demonological theory of these dark ages has in the long run justified itself." The paper is an analysis of a man by the name of Christoph Haizmann, a painter who is supposed to have entered into a contract with the Devil. Documents associated with the events surrounding the contract were brought to Freud's attention. The paper attempts to discover the underlying psychological factors involved in such a contract. Early in the paper Freud says:

> What in those days were thought to be evil spirits to us are base and evil wishes, the derivatives of impulses which have been rejected and repressed. In one respect only do we not subscribe to the explanation of these phenomena current in mediaeval times; we have abandoned the projection of them into the outer world, attributing their origin instead to the inner life of the patient in whom they manifest themselves.

With this proviso Freud enters into the spirit of the documents. On the basis of his detailed analysis, he tells us that the essential conditions for making such a contract are (1) *that the man was depressed*, (2) *that the depression resulted from the death of his father;* and (3) *that he was concerned with earning a livelihood.* From the Fliess correspondence we know that these conditions actually coincide exactly with

Freud's own state at the time that *The Interpretation of Dreams* was
being written.

The question of the *seriousness* of Freud's entry into the Satanic
Pact may well be raised. Freud was a modern man who did not believe
in supernatural beings. Indeed Freud himself, in this essay on a medieval document, questions the seriousness of the Satanic Pact *even at
that time.* He suggests, on the basis of a somewhat tenuous interpretation of the internal features of the document, that some deception
may have been involved: "But then it would all have been a ruse rather
than a neurosis, the painter a malingerer and a cheat instead of a man
sick of demoniacal possession! But the transition-stages between neurosis and malingering are, as we know, very elastic." If, in his conception, Christoph Haizmann may not have been serious about all of this,
we can hardly expect Freud to have been fully taken by the metaphor.
Yet what Freud is saying is, in effect, that the full acceptance of the supernatural reality of the Devil is not an essential feature of the motivation of the Satanic Pact.

Concerning the motivation of the Satanic Pact, Freud asks, "Why
does one sell oneself to the Devil?" He enumerates the possibilities:
"Wealth, immunity from dangers, power over mankind and over the
forces of Nature, but above all these, pleasure, the enjoyment of beautiful women." Then he says, "Remarkable to relate, it was not for any
one of these very natural desires." He cites offers of the Devil to the
painter which the painter refuses. Rather, "This man sold himself to
the Devil, therefore, in order to be freed from a state of depression.
Truly an excellent motive, in the judgment of those who can understand the torment of these states and who appreciate, moreover, how
little the art of medicine can do to alleviate the malady." Freud's allusion to the art of medicine is odd. As comment on the art of medicine
in the nineteenth century, particularly in contrast with psychoanalysis, it might have some meaning. Thus this remark again suggests the
contemporaneous reference of this paper for Freud.

He cites some additional supporting material from the document,
indicating Haizmann's sense of himself as a son of the body of the
Devil, and specifying the term of the Pact as nine years. In the preface
to the second edition of *The Interpretation of Dreams*, written in the
summer of 1908, Freud writes, "For this book has a further subjective
significance for me personally—a significance which I only grasped
after I had completed it. It was, I found, a portion of my own self-
analysis, my reaction to my father's death—that is to say, to the most
important event, the most poignant loss, of a man's life." [1] It should be

noted that *The Interpretation of Dreams* was brought to completion in the summer of 1899, from May to September. Thus this preface, indicating the emotional significance of the death of his father, was written almost exactly nine years after the completion of the book!

Having introduced the idea of the Devil "as a substitute for the loved parent," Freud starts a new section which he entitles *The Devil as a Father-Substitute*, and spends over two pages presenting and refuting arguments by imagined "sober-minded critics." He argues for his imagined critic,

> Why should we hold aloof from this obvious and natural explanation? The state of affairs would then simply be that someone in a helpless state, tortured with melancholic depression, sells himself to the Devil, in whose healing powers he reposes the greatest confidence. That the depression was caused by the father's demise would then be quite irrelevant: it could conceivably have been due to some other cause. This seems a forceful and reasonable objection. We hear once more the familiar criticism of psycho-analysis that it regards the simplest affairs in an unduly subtle and complicated way, discovers secrets and problems where none exist, and that it achieves this by magnifying the most insignificant trifles to support far-reaching and bizarre conclusions.

Freud goes on to argue, in reply, for the general soundness of the psychoanalytic mode of thought. This protest in the midst of his discussion again suggests his personal involvement in conceiving of the Pact with the Devil as a reaction to the father's death, although we must add that this in no way detracts from the validity of what he says. Perhaps precisely because Freud did not accept the supernatural reality of the Devil, he could permit himself the full exploitation of the metaphor. We may imagine that at times the sense of possession became quite strong; and it is this feeling of possession that Freud is analyzing in his paper.

The Curative Power Inherent in the Devil

The Devil notion has associated with it a feature which we might call that of aid-in-deep-despair. The Devil is supposed to have great powers and is characteristically called upon *when all else has failed*. He is a terrible cure, but a powerful one nonetheless. Characteristically the Devil is approached, to use the expression Freud used of writing the third part of his *Moses and Monotheism*, "with the audacity of one who has little or nothing to lose."[2]

From a psychological point of view we envisage, on the basis of what Freud has taught us, the individual, in his development, as entering into a kind of social contract, in which the individual agrees to abide by the demands of society in return for certain basic satisfactions and protections. When one's life situation grows too bad, the question arises as to whether the other party is abiding by his part of the contract. If this doubt crosses the line and becomes a conclusion, that the other party has broken the contract, then the individual feels free to do as he pleases. This is the conflict of Job, and the conflict the Jews have experienced over and over again as they were persecuted. The notion of the Covenant is psychologically the idea of the social contract, that the Jews would accept the yoke of the Law in return for God's favor. The idea of the contract with the Devil is of course consistent with the contractual feature of both the Covenant and the social contract, but is a new one in its details. The new contract is entered into because, with the loss of hope, the anguish turns into despair; for despair is exactly anguish without hope of relief.

The Devil is then a cure for despair. He is called upon as an assertive act when all hope is gone. And in this sense also, the Devil is always the Tempter. The essential message of the Tempter is that the anticipated rewards associated with resistance to temptation will not be forthcoming, that faith is groundless. The Devil presents the new hope, and supports his promise by *immediate* tokens of his favor. But since these tokens themselves bring so much relief, one permits oneself, in his relationship to the Devil, to be thus taken in (by the Devil), since he feels that he has already been taken in (by God).

In more secular terms, Freud suffered from acute depressions. His self-analysis, and his development of psychoanalysis, were the cure for his depression. His practice had already provided him with ample evidence that diseases which other people were suffering from, for which there was no other hope, could be cured by such means. In his despair over making a living, and in his despair over anti-Semitism, he had "little or nothing to lose" by his "audacity." Furthermore, this new set of methods which he was producing held out the promise of bringing patients to him and so solving at least the problem of making a living.

In thus becoming involved in the metaphor of the Devil, Freud certainly risked great sin (or its psychological equivalent, guilt) himself. But in this he had the support of the tradition of the Chassidic healers, who, since the 1700s, were in serious competition with the physicians in Eastern European Jewish communities. These wonder-workers repeatedly risked themselves by invoking God's name in their efforts to cure other people. In order to help people it was necessary for them to thus invoke the Ineffable Name, which was always a possible violation of the third commandment, that "Thou shalt not take the name of the Lord thy God in vain; for the Lord will not hold him guiltless that taketh His name in vain" (Exodus 20:7).

NOTES

1. Sigmund Freud (1900), *The Interpretation of Dreams, The Standard Edition of the Complete Psychological Works of Sigmund Freud,* vol. 4, James Strachey (ed.). (London: Hogarth Press, (1953), p. 3.

2. Sigmund Freud, *Moses and Monotheism: Three Essays* (1939), *The Standard Edition of the Complete Psychological Works of Sigmund Freud*, vol. 23, James Strachey (ed.). (London: Hogarth Press), p. 4.

CHAPTER 10

From *The Duality of Human Existence*

DAVID BAKAN

One of the pervasive themes that runs through the Bible is that there is *a biological role for the male in conception.* We may presume that there was a time in history prior to Biblical times in which this was not known. It is certainly not "obvious." Sexual intercourse can take place without conception. The interval between conception and either the signs of pregnancy or the birth of a child is considerable. And whether a particular woman has had intercourse or not often remains her "secret." If we consider a two-way table with pregnancy-no pregnancy on one axis and intercourse-no intercourse on the other, observation would show that there are instances of pregnancy and no pregnancy with intercourse; and definitive data in the no intercourse cells are hard to come by. We can presume that there was an early "scientist" who made the discovery of the relationship between sexuality and pregnancy. Furthermore, as I have already indicated, the natural development of the male ego does not usually encompass the ejaculated semen; and we might presume that there may have been a good deal of resistance to the acceptance of the validity of this "scientific discovery." In contrast, there was probably no time in human history in which the biological connectedness of the mother to the child was ever in question, the act of childbearing being too prominent a part of experience. In the same way that more recent scientific discoveries have shocked mankind with their implications, so must there have been a time in history when mankind was similarly shocked by this particular "scientific discovery," and its implications. I take it that the Bible is a document which expresses man's efforts to come to grips with the problems presented by the fact that the male has a biological role in conception.

The Bible expresses man's effort to extend the boundary of his ego to include his "seed." This particular metaphor for semen is interesting in that it not only suggests property and food, but also tends to make the male even more important than the female, as seed is the determining factor of the nature of the plant, with the soil, water, and sun playing only enabling roles. The very conception of semen as "seed" which is deposited in the ground is suggestive that the ego has moved to include the semen.

The major personages of the Old Testament are presented principally in their role as fathers to their children. This is particularly evident in the patriarchs Abraham, Isaac, and Jacob. Even the sonhoods which are represented are transitionary to fatherhood. The very name "Abraham" means father. Jacob has two names, Jacob, largely for his sonhood, and Israel, characteristically used to designate his fatherhood. In these figures, there is evident not only the extension of the ego to their "seed" but to the children themselves. Their principal preoccupations are with their children. We can, in fact, interpret the image of the father as presented in the Bible as a kind of "motherization" of the male. These are males who provide for their children. The Biblical patriarchs are affluent; they have flocks and servants and position. It is through their property that they can provide for children; and the economic conditions of their lives are such that by the increase of their children they themselves increase in wealth and power.

The Infanticidal Impulse

The integration [of fatherhood] in the Bible is an uneasy one, reflecting the difficulties of making it. It is manifested in providing abiding care for children, and its failure is manifested in infanticide. Freud had made killing the father central in his various discussions of religion. This feature may be important in psychological development. However, I believe that close examination of the Biblical text indicates that, in addition to the Old Testament being much more patrocentric than filiocentric, the killing of children as a psychological impulse is highly significant. If there was some original holocaust of the kind that Freud envisaged, it appears less likely that it was the killing of the father by the son than the killing of the children by the father. The allusions to the killing of children in the Bible are numerous, and the injunction against it is repeated so often as to indicate that this was not only a psychological tendency, but one which was at least sometimes "acted out." If the characteristics attributed to God come from man himself, we may note an infanticidal tendency in the numerous references to God killing people, his children, throughout the Old Testament, as exemplified in the Flood and in his killing of the Sodomites, the Egyptians, and so on. God is tempted to kill all of the Children of Israel but is dissuaded by Moses (Exodus 32:9ff.), who then goes down from the mountain and himself kills about three thousand men (Exodus 32:28).

The story of Abraham's move to sacrifice Isaac is indicative not only of the infanticidal impulse, but also of ambivalence about infanticide. God enjoins Abraham to sacrifice Isaac as a burnt offering. Psychologically, Abraham has projected his infanticidal tendency on to God. When he is about to slay Isaac, his arm is restrained (Genesis 22:1ff.). The infanticidal impulse in Abraham is also evident in his treatment of Ishmael, whom he banishes to the wilderness with only bread and a bottle of water for himself and his mother (Genesis 21:14). Abraham is told, after demonstrating his readiness to kill Isaac, "because thou hast done this thing, and hast not withheld thy son, thine only son: That in blessing I will bless thee, and in multiplying I will multiply thy seed as the stars of the heaven, and as the sand which is upon the sea shore" (Genesis 22:16–17). This may be interpreted as a reaction to the infanticidal impulse. God of the Bible is deeply ambivalent about this tendency within him. Its "neurotic" character is indicated by his tendency to kill and then make promises not to do it again (Genesis 9:9ff.). The story of Abraham and Isaac is, as has often been pointed out, a harbinger of the crucifixion of Jesus, in which the arm that would kill the son, referred to as "thine only son," is not restrained.

We can identify two sets of motives for the infanticidal impulse. The first is that the necessities of child care threaten the separatistic tendencies of the male. The second is that, where the ego boundary has extended to include the semen of the male, the authenticity of paternity of children becomes very important. Doubt over this authenticity provokes the tendency to kill the child of doubtful paternity.

Doubt concerning Paternity and Infanticide

My interpretation suggests a reason for the special importance of the first-born in the Bible. It is of interest that the Bible should manifest great ambivalence toward the first-born particularly.

On the one hand, the first-born is favored. The first-born is entitled to the "birth-right" and "blessing" (Genesis 25:29–34; 27:1ff.). The first-born is to inherit twice as much as the other children and is protected against arbitrary action which would take this away from him (Deuteronomy 21:15–17; II Kings 2:9). The right of succession to rule is given to the first-born (II Chronicles 21:3). Pharaoh, who yields to nothing else, yields to the slaying of the first-born (Exodus 12:31). The favor of God to the Israelites is shown by his so referring to them: "Israel is my son, even my first-born" (Exodus 4:22). Even firstlings among animals are not to be eaten (Deuteronomy 12:17).

On the other hand, there are several instances in the Bible which indicate that the first-born is not favored. God favors the younger Abel over Cain, which is Cain's reason for killing Abel (Genesis 4:3–5). Abraham favors Isaac over Ishmael. Isaac gives the birthright to the younger Jacob. Jacob curses his first-born (Genesis 49:4). Jacob favors Joseph's younger son (Genesis 48:13–20). Er, Judah's first-born, is killed by God (Genesis 38:7). Jephthah kills his oldest daughter (Judges 11:34ff.). The king of Moab kills his first-born (II Kings 3:27). Hosah makes a younger son the chief instead of the first-born (I Chronicles 26:10). And Jesus is a first-born!

The profound ambivalence is shown by making the first-born belong to God. To give the first-born to God entails removing it from one's self. Thus, the Biblical writers attributed to God such things as: "Sanctify unto me all the first-born, whatsoever openeth the womb among the children of Israel, both of man and of beast: it is mine" (Exodus 13:2). And "Thou shalt not delay to offer the first of thy ripe fruits, and of thy liquors: the firstborn of thy sons shalt thou give unto me. Likewise shalt thou do with thine oxen, and with thy sheep: seven days it shall be with his dam; on the eighth day thou shalt give it me" (Exodus 22:29–30). There is little ambiguity throughout the Bible of what it means to "give" a living thing to God. "Giving" to God is a euphemism for killing, with what appears to be divine permission.

The male prior to the birth of the first child, has tenuously moved toward self-integration in his relations with his wife. The first-born is the critical test of this integration. With respect to the child, he needs to be a motherized father. The communion of the mother, which has been directed toward him, tends to turn in the direction of the child, and he regresses toward his earlier separatistic condition. His impulse to say, "You are not my son," is then particularly strong with respect to the first-born.

The way in which the Biblical story of Sarah's conception of Isaac is told raises questions concerning the authenticity of the paternity of Isaac and throws some light on Abraham's temptation to kill him. The

Biblical text has several "difficulties." These allow for an interpretation of dubious paternity of Isaac, if they do not suggest it. (It should
be made clear at this point that I am making no effort to attempt to
find out what "really happened." It is rather that I am seeking to understand the nature of the Biblical text as a document which renders a
state of mind for our understanding.) On two occasions Abraham conceals the fact that Sarah is his wife, allowing her to be married to
someone else. This happens once before the visit of the angels, and
once afterward. In the first instance, she enters the house of Pharaoh.
The text has Pharaoh saying, "I took her to me for a wife," although
the Biblical text is sufficiently ambiguous to make it possible for the
King James version to render it as "so I might have taken her to me to
wife" (Genesis 12:19). Whether she actually has sexual relations with
Pharaoh is not so important as is the fact that the Hebrew text would
allow one to think so. In the second instance, she is taken into the
house of Abimelech, who has a dream which prevents him from having sexual relations with her (Genesis 20:1ff.).

The possibility of Abraham not being the biological father seems
to have been enough on the mind of the distinguished commentator
Rashi for him to deal with it and deny it. The proof is, according to
Rashi, that the text reads, "And these are the generations of Isaac,
Abraham's son; Abraham begot Isaac."[1] Why does the Biblical text de-
viate from its usual pattern here? If these are the "generations of
Isaac," why does the Biblical writer go backward to mention Abraham? And why is it necessary to say it twice? Rashi's commentary is:
Since the text wrote "Isaac, the son of Abraham," it became necessary
to state, "Abraham begot Isaac"; for the scorners of the generation
were saying "From Abimelech did Sarah conceive, since for many
years she tarried with Abraham and did not conceive from him." What
did the Holy One Blessed Be He do? He formed the features of Isaac's
face similar to Abraham, and there attested everyone, "Abraham
begot Isaac." And that is why it is written here, "Isaac was the son of
Abraham," for there is testimony that "Abraham begot Isaac." Needless to say, Rashi and his sources in the *Midrash* had neither photo-
graphs nor testimonials. Having to add a facial similarity between
Abraham and Isaac would indicate that doubt was suggested by the
text.[2]

Chapter 18 of Genesis, which deals with the visit of the angels, has
difficulties. In this chapter it is foretold that Sarah will have a son. In
the sixth verse, Abraham instructs Sarah to bake cakes for the guests,
while in the seventh verse, he runs off to get and prepare a calf. But in

the eighth verse, where the meal is served, a meal of "butter, and milk, and the calf which he had dressed," there is no mention of the cakes. The text here allows a period of time in which Sarah was supposed to have been baking cakes while Abraham was away, and yet there are no cakes!

This chapter begins with three angels. Then the next chapter begins with only two angels, and there is no indication of what happened to the third angel. The ninth verse is "And they said unto him, Where is Sarah thy wife? And he said, Behold, in the tent." According to Biblical scholars, the next six verses, verses 10 through 15, are a substitution by the J2 author for something which had been put there earlier by the J1 author. These six verses are the critical ones in connection with the birth of Isaac, and one can only speculate that perhaps what is now only hinted at in the text might have been more explicit in the earlier version. The tenth verse is as follows: "And he said, I will certainly return unto thee according to the time of life; and, lo, Sarah thy wife shall have a son. And Sarah heard it in the tent door, *v'hoo acharav.*" I have simply transliterated the Hebrew at this point, rather than rendering the usual translation, "which was behind him." Rashi made it that the door was behind the angel, which probably was the basis for the translation in this manner. It can, however, be translated equally well as "and he behind it," suggesting that the angel was in the tent with Sarah. In one commentary, *Sifte Hakhamin,* it is explicitly suggested that the angel was in the tent and Abraham was outside. Tradition has it that the message was delivered to Sarah secretly. And tradition also has it that Sarah was radiant and that a beam of her beauty struck one of the angels.[3]

Isaac's name, which can mean "one laughs," the laughter of Sarah, and her denial of it, are also suggestive. Sarah laughs at the prediction that she will have a child, presumably at the irony of it. But it would appear that if she were laughing at the irony of it, she could certainly share this with her husband, who himself laughs at it (Genesis 17:17). The fifteenth verse is "Then Sarah denied, saying, I laughed not; for she was afraid. And he said, Nay; but thou didst laugh." Certainly the irony could provoke laughter. But then why is she afraid? Because she does not want to offend her guests by laughing at their outlandish prediction? The laughter and the denial might also be at Abraham's cuckoldry, with Isaac, "one laughs," the incarnation of the joke.

It is indicated that the angels will appear at the time of the birth of the child. Yet they do not reappear in the Old Testament. It is not until several hundred years later that the men, the wise men from the east

of the New Testament, can be considered to appear again, at the birth
of Jesus, "the son of Abraham," as Jesus is described in Matthew (1:1),
for whom the delayed fate of Isaac is in store.

What we may presume is that Abraham is a man who, in spite of
tendencies and provocation to infanticide, would restrain his arm
from killing. The Biblical text at this point provides some further illumination of the conflict and Abraham's handling of it in his personality. The Bible blends the story of the angels' visitation with the story of
the destruction of Sodom. It would appear from the Biblical narrative
that they stopped off to visit with Abraham on their way to Sodom.
Fused here are the two tendencies I have been speaking of, the extension of the ego to include children and the tendency to destroy. The remainder of the chapter contains an interesting dialogue between
Abraham and God, God bent on destroying the people of Sodom, and
Abraham trying to dissuade him. Within this chapter is an explicit description of Abraham as the "good father." "For I know him, that he
will command his children and his household after him, and they
shall keep the way of the Lord, to do justice and judgment" (Genesis
18:19). We are now in a position to understand the symbolic significance of circumcision in terms of the conflict within Abraham. By circumcising his children, he puts "his" mark upon them. Thus, even if
doubt exists in his mind concerning his paternity, he makes them "his"
by putting a mark upon them as he has upon himself and seeks to
arrange it so that his offspring will carry this mark indefinitely from
generation to generation.

But what is equally important is that the act of circumcising the
male child takes place on the eighth day, the day when children are to
be "given" to God. The circumcision may be interpreted as a symbolic
infanticide, whereby, instead of putting the child to death by the knife,
only the foreskin is removed. By this ritual, while making the child
"his," he symbolically expresses the infanticidal impulse in a partial
"acting out." Later in the Bible, we find that Moses has not circum-
cised his child. His wife Zipporah performs a hurried circumcision.
She "cut off the foreskin of her son, and cast it at his feet, and said,
Surely a bloody husband art thou to me. So he let him go: then she
said, A bloody husband thou art, because of the circumcision" (Exodus 4:25–26). In this text the association of circumcision and infanticide is strongly suggested.

One cannot hope to plumb the meaning of the Old Testament by
any single interpretation. Yet its significance as a document which
tells of the crisis involved in becoming a good father to children can-

not be overlooked. I have presumed that there must have been some time in history when the biological role of the male in pregnancy was unknown, and that there must have been some historical period in which this particular fact was discovered and integrated into the social structure. Yet this is not only historical, but must be repeated in the life of the individual male. Abraham, presented as the father of nations, is a paradigmatic figure in whom is formed a transgenerational ego identity.

NOTES

1. The Pentateuch and Rashi's Commentary, trans. Abraham ben Isaiah and Benjamin Sharfman (S. S. & R. Publishers, 1949), Vol. 1, Genesis 25:19.

2. That such doubt may even have been on Paul's mind is suggested by "Neither, because they are the seed of Abraham, are they all children: but, in Isaac shall thy seed be called" (Romans 9:7).

3. Louis Ginzberg, *The Legends of the Jews* (Jewish Publication Society, 1913), Vol. 1, p. 244.

CHAPTER 11

Sacrifice and the Book of Job

DAVID BAKAN

The Book of Job especially commends itself to our attention. It deals with suffering, the psychological suffering associated with the loss of children and property, and physical suffering in the form of boils. It arises from and directs our attention to both the crisis in life of man, the crisis that in some way must take place in the life of each individual who lives into adulthood, and a historical crisis in the Judeo-Christian tradition, the crisis associated with the transition from Judaism to Christianity. The Book of Job also commends itself to our attention because of a particular insight I believe it contains: that there is an intrinsic relationship among separation-estrangement, physical disease, and the psychological condition associated with sacrifice.

Let us consider the manifest level of the Book of Job. It begins with a double disaster occurring to a seemingly righteous man. The protagonist of this drama, a victim of tragic occurrences, is visited by three friends, and, for most of the text, there is discussion relevant to the tragedies. The book, it seems, raises doubts about the justice of God who would make a righteous man suffer. The rhetoric of the book presumes, as does so much of the Bible, the independent existence of a God, creator and overseer of the world, and raises the question how such a God might allow or even cause this suffering.

Let us bring to bear the modern discovery, basic to psychoanalytic thought, that the fantastic creations of man's mind arise out of the deepest parts of his psyche and that these fantastic creations are of man himself. If there is a question for us of God's goodness or justice in the Book of Job, then we have to inquire about the nature of man who thus conceives of God. Indeed, the very ascription of evil to the divine, as such a hint exists in the Book of Job, is a hint to us of the nature of the psychological processes associated with suffering.

I have indicated that the canonical quality itself of the Bible is to be taken into account in using the Bible to understand those whose collective mind it somehow expresses. We must take equal cognizance of the fact that there are special characteristics of the Book of Job affecting its canonical authenticity. The Book of Job stands, as it were, on the canonical margin. It is sometimes true that marginal instances may best help us to understand phenomena. The very characteristics of the Book of Job which provoke questions of its canonical authenticity are, I believe, significant for understanding the meaning of the book. I believe further that the Book of Job is distinguished both because it deals rather directly with the profoundest problems in the biblical mind and because its latent content is only thinly disguised. The former demands that it be regarded as part of the canon; the latter, that it be rejected. Allowing it to stay in the canon while it carries earmarks suggestive of canonical inauthenticity is a way of handling those problems.

The canonical marginality of the Book of Job is evident in the rough handling it received by the rabbis of the Talmud. They suggest that Job never existed; that he was not an Israelite; that his name is a disguised form of the word meaning "enemy,"[1] and that he and the other personages of the Book of Job were prophets for heathens rather than for Israel. The latter suggests that the Book of Job might not properly belong in the Old Testament at all.

The book has characteristics that invite the reader to wonder about its authenticity. Theodore of Mopsuestia (d. 428) omitted it from his canon of the Bible, regarding it as a work of fiction. It consists of at least two radically different parts, one being in prose and the other in poetry. Because of this, scholars have maintained that there must have been at least two authors. The prose part, comprising the beginning and the end, chapters 1 and 2, and chapter 42:7–17, is regarded as having been composed by a considerably less skilled and experienced writer than the other. The long poetic part, which begins with 3:2, is manifestly the work of a talented and accomplished author. The substantive problem presented by the text is never quite resolved. The book closes with a *deus ex machina* type of ending, all things set to rights, giving the tragedy a simple but very contrived "happy ending," as it were. And even here there are some peculiarities. Although the Book of Job closes with the rhetoric of a happy ending,

Job dies with its final sentence. Death is, of course, usually associated with tragedy. Furthermore, simple replacements are provided for the children who were killed at the beginning of the book, as though this could compensate for the death of the others. Kallen has cogently argued that the book is really quite marginal to the Jewish tradition, that it is a Hebraized version of a Greek tragedy after the style of Euripides, and that it reflects the crisis in Jewish history and thought when it was confronted by Greek civilization.[2] Kallen shows how by simple rearrangement of the lines the Book of Job may readily take on the appearance of an authentic Greek drama, demonstrating that it could thus have been an original form of the drama. It may be that the rabbis also sensed the to them odious Greek influence.

The book has been rather unimportant in Jewish history. As one reviewer of this history has put it, "All in all, it appears that Job has made a far greater impression upon the Christian than the Jewish group." Its reading among Jews, he maintains, has been with "solemnity, but inattention."[3] From the point of view of traditional Judaism there is considerable substance in the assertion by one scholar that "it is clear that Job's words were generally less in agreement with religious principles than were those of his three comforters."[4] The doubt which forms much of the substance of the book is somehow echoed in doubt concerning the canonical authenticity of the book.

The very artfulness of the Book of Job is also relevant. It has a self-consciously literary quality. It strongly urges the reader to look at it as a book. The poetic form of the central portion invites the reader to consider it a deliberate work of art rather than a narrative report of events. Indeed, certain lines in the book point to a literary awareness, as in "Oh that my words were now written! oh that they were printed in a book!" (19:23), and, "Oh that one would hear me! behold, my desire is, that the Almighty would answer me, and that mine adversary had written a book!" (31:35).

But what is a book? Among other things a book demands of the reader that he classify it as fiction or non-fiction, as fantasy or fact, as modern librarians characteristically do for us. The Book of Job seems somehow more fictional than perhaps any other book of the Bible. The ancients presumably did not draw the line between fact and fiction as firmly as we do, but the decision that the Book of Job should be part of the canon was undoubtedly informed by a decision that it should be regarded as non-fiction, as based on fact.

The hints of canonical inauthenticity, as well as the literary qualities which suggest that it is fiction, may be interpreted as serving psychologically to defend against the manifestation of the latent content of the book. They make it possible to reject the book should the latent content break through. The problem with which the text is grappling is so profound that the psychological defense of its possibly being outside of the canon or being fictional, combined with the characteristic strengthening of faith associated with doubt, have played their role in making it a significant expression of Western civilization. Fiction allows the reader to consider in detail the deepest psychological and existential questions without having to face the danger of a concrete threatening reality. In the entertainment of fiction, no matter what cognitive or affective or fantasied volitional activities one may engage in, there is always the defense that, after all, it is only fiction. Learning that the unbelievable is to be believed creates doubt. At the same time, overcoming doubt gives faith a tenacity which is otherwise unattainable. The psychological mechanism expressed by *credo quia absurdum est* against a background of doubt has long been associated with religious belief and is the reason why some religions have thrived on miracles. No one has ever thought about a reported miracle without at least a shadow of doubt crossing his mind. In overcoming that doubt, faith becomes a hard alloy.

What then is the latent content in the Book of Job that led the biblical mind to defend against its manifestation? At this point we need to consider the infanticidal impulse, picking up a line of thought I have discussed elsewhere.[5] Freud's notion of the Oedipus complex certainly recognized the psychological significance of the identifications and conflicts in the father-son relationship. I believe, however, that Freud did not carry this sufficiently far to recognize that the Oedipus complex might itself be a reaction of the child to the infanticidal impulse in the father—Laius leaving Oedipus to die as a child—and a defensive response of the child against aggression. The infanticidal impulse in the male is associated, in Western civilization, with patrilineality and the assumption by the male of the responsibility of caring for the children. The infanticidal impulse is the reverse of this assumption of responsibility. Various regulations of traditional Judaism, such as the redemption of the first-born and the wearing of phylacteries, may be interpreted as efforts to counteract the infanticidal impulse. Christianity may also be interpreted as an effort to counteract this infanticidal impulse, having arisen against a background in which the then classical Jewish modes of dealing with this impulse were faltering, as witness especially the holocaust of infant slaughter under Herod from which Jesus was saved. Christianity provided new devices for handling the impulse, especially in the sacrifice of the Mass.

That the Book of Job opens with the death of Job's children, and that the death of the children is a critical part of Job's tragedy and fate, suggests the same problem, the management of the infanticidal impulse. The book may therefore provide the appearance of fictionality and canonical inauthenticity in order to defend against this latent content. It is thus rendered ostensibly as a "story," which ought perhaps not to have been made part of the canon.

The Book of Job is continuous with the story of Abraham; and one might well assume that the story of Job is highly conditioned by the story of Abraham. Abraham is the major figure in the Old Testament representing the shift of the adult male into a position of accepting biological bondage of the father to the child. The story of Abraham's move to sacrifice Isaac is indicative of the infanticidal impulse. The fact that Abraham's arm is restrained is indicative of the effectiveness of the contra-infanticidal tendencies.

The relationship of the Job story to the story of Abraham was evidently quite taken for granted by the rabbis of the Talmud. In their commentary on the opening to the Book of Job they ascribe the following words to Satan: "Sovereign of the Universe, I have traversed the whole world and found none so faithful as thy servant Abraham."[6] Job and Abraham are presented to the reader principally as fathers. Both have relationships with God in which the major concern is with offspring. Their names are similar. Abraham's names in the Old Testament are first AVRM (Abram) and then AVRHM (Abraham), with AV meaning father. Job's name is AYOV, with the first and last letters also being AV.[7] As Abraham is visited by three men (Gen. 18), so is Job. (Three men also appear at the birth of the infant Jesus.) As Abraham is described as righteous, so is Job. As God concocted a test of Abraham entailing the death of his offspring, so does he do with Job. As Abraham is described as dying in great age, so is Job (Gen. 25:8; Job 42:17).

But the Book of Job differs dramatically from the story of Abraham in the following respect: whereas, in the story of Abraham the child is not killed, in the Book of Job the children *are* killed. Although in both instances there is a test of righteousness involved, the test for Abraham is whether he would kill Isaac; but the test for Job is his response to the killing of his children. The story of the children's being killed is a fantasy in the biblical mind of their being killed. And a fantasy of their being killed suggests a wish that they be killed. The Book of Job begins with God and Satan involved in a plot to kill Job's children. The attribution of the infanticidal activity to God and Satan is a thin disguise. In spite of the fact that the killing of the children is attributed to these supernatural beings, the fact is that the Book of Job was written by men and constitutes their fantasy.

Let us again consider the possibility that the fictional quality of the Book of Job is a defense against making manifest that which it contains latently. As I have already indicated, the first two chapters of the Book of Job and the last differ radically from the remainder. Indeed, modern translations use different type styles for them. This stylistic feature seems to convey to the reader that the central poetic portion is the substantive part of the book and that the substantially shorter beginning and the end are merely rhetorically introductory and concluding material. Many critics, in point of fact, responded to the book of Job by directing their attention principally to the central poetic portion and paying little or no attention to the beginning and the end. If there is an infanticidal theme in the Book of Job, however, it is far more evident in the beginning and the end than in the central longer poetic part. The radically different and more insistent style of that much larger portion of the book tends thus to obscure the infanticidal theme, which is closer to being manifest in the shorter prose part.

Even within the central poetic portion, however, there is at least one indication of the infanticidal impulse, and this too is made to appear extraneous to the text. The "Poem of the Ostrich" describes how the ostrich jeopardizes her eggs:

> Gavest thou the goodly wings unto the peacocks!
>   or wings and feathers unto the ostrich?
> Which leaveth her eggs in the earth, and warmeth
>   them in the dust,
> And forgetteth that the foot may crush them, or
>   that the wild beast may break them.
> She is hardened against her young ones, as
>   though they were not hers: her labor is in vain
>   without fear;
> Because God hath deprived her of wisdom,
>   neither hath he imparted to her understanding.
> What time she lifteth up herself on high, she
>   scorneth the horse and his rider. [Job 39:13–18]

Stevenson, in his textual analysis of the Book of Job, points out that the "Poem of the Ostrich" is not only substantively different from the context but is also different in poetic form. It consists of a six-line stanza, whereas the other stanzas in the text are of either four or eight lines.[8] He is, furthermore, of the opinion that the "Poem of the Ostrich" is best kept apart from the rest of the poem. It is impossible to exclude it from the Book of Job. It is simply there. But this critic's response means that the reader must recognize that there are features of this particular poem which suggest the possibility that it might be considered apart from the rest. It is particularly interesting that this very stanza, poetically different from its context, should be one in which the infanticidal impulse is so clearly depicted; in which it is indicated that God creates infanticidal creatures.

It is rather interesting that the rabbis of the Talmud also gave an infanticidal interpretation to a line very close, in the same chapter, as the "Poem of the Ostrich." This is the line: "Knowest thou the time when the wild goats of the rock bring forth?" (39:1). The interpretation of this line is: "This wild goat is heartless toward her young. When she crouches for delivery, she goes up to the top of a mountain so that the young shall fall down and be killed, and I prepare an eagle to catch it in his wings and set it before her, and if he were one second too soon or too late it would be killed."[9] Thus the Talmud could attribute an infanticidal interpretation to a line even more obscure than the "Poem of the Ostrich."

Aside from such considerations suggesting an infanticidal theme latently contained in the Book of Job, the book also ascribes to Job a certain coldness toward his children. Job's ten children are counted with the number of his sheep, camels, oxen, and she-asses, as though they too were livestock and property. The loss of the children is recited among the losses of the livestock. At the end of the story, when all things appear to be rectified, he is granted children and livestock together, as though dead children were simply replaceable by live ones as were animals. Furthermore, Job does not mourn for *them*. His distress is hardly mourning in the sense of being possessed with the tragedy of *their* death. His distress, quite the contrary, is over *his* losses and the anguish of his body. Nowhere in the text is there any indication that he bewails the fate of his dead children. Indeed, upon learning of the loss of his livestock and children he comments: "Naked came I out of my mother's womb, and naked shall I return thither: the Lord gave, and the Lord hath taken away; blessed be the name of the Lord" (1:21). His first comment to his friends is equally egocentric: "Let the day perish wherein I was born, and the night in which it was said, There is a man child conceived" (3:3).

The text indicates that it was the custom of Job's children to engage in feasts together, but that Job himself was not among them. Job is said to have occupied himself differently: "And it was

so, when the days of their feasting were gone about, that Job sent
and sanctified them, and rose up early in the morning, and offered
burnt offerings according to the number of them all: for Job said, It
may be that my sons have sinned, and cursed God in their hearts.
Thus did Job continually" [1:5]. We have here the suggestion of
Job's alienation from his children in not being companion to their
drinking and feasting, his clearly indicated suspicion of them, and his
clearly indicated sacrifice on their behalf. I take it that, as in the story
of Abraham, Job's sacrifices are central to our understanding of the
Book of Job.

The Voices of the Victims

Let us assume that behind the biblical text there is a latent myth that
the victims of infanticidal acts, the slain children, are "Sons of God."
Thus, if the Book of Job is critically based on a latent infanticidal impulse, and if it constitutes an effort to come to terms with the impulse,
it is appropriate that the story should begin with a gathering of the
"Sons of God," come seeking justice. "Now there was a day when the
sons of God came to present themselves before the Lord, and Satan
came also among them" (Job 1:6). Satan, as I have suggested elsewhere, should be thought of as among "whatsoever openeth the
womb" (Exod. 13:2) and as victim.[10]

There is a sequence of two challenges of Job at Satan's instigation.
Job first loses his livestock and children. Since Job, evidently, does not
sin as a result of this, Satan makes the second challenge: "Skin for
skin, yea, all that a man hath will he give for his life. But put forth
thine hand now, and touch his bone and his flesh, and he will curse
thee to thy face" (2:4–5). If we interpret Satan to be himself one of the
victimized, and spokesman for all of them, he is, in effect, charging
that certainly justice for the crime of infanticide has not been done by
depriving Job of his livestock and especially his children; and justice
remains to be done by injuring Job's body directly.

Thus, one way of interpreting the Book of Job is as a story of the
"Sons of God" coming back to haunt the child-killer or, at least, as an
expression of the state of mind haunted by that complex in which the
infanticidal impulse is the nucleus. Job's speeches just before the appearance of Elihu contain protestations of how well he took care of
the young and the needy (30, 31). It is immediately following these
speeches that Elihu, the youth and possible victim, is introduced,
speaking angrily in reply to Job's self-justifications (32:2).

The appearance of Elihu in the Book of Job constitutes a further literary peculiarity. His appearance is extraneous to the manifest structure of the book. Job, it would seem, has been the victim of tragedy and three friends properly come to console him. The dialogue goes on among Job and his three friends. And then, quite out of nowhere, the speech of Elihu appears. In some respects the literary device is similar to the one pointed out in connection with the "Poem of the Ostrich," in which material is presented that allows and even invites itself to be put apart from the rest of the text. Elihu, too, should be thought of as a possible target of the infanticidal impulse; he is, in this respect, a transitional figure between Isaac and Jesus, between Isaac, who was spared, and Jesus, who was not. Indeed, there is a traditional view that Elihu really is Isaac.[11] The text takes great pains to have the reader understand that Elihu is young. Although there is no prior mention of him, his earlier presence is taken for granted in the text, since his remarks indicate that he has been listening to what has been said by the others. He challenges the elders, contending that they are not always wise or understanding, in much the same way that Jesus does when he proclaims that that which is hidden from the wise and the prudent is revealed to the babes (Matt. 11:25; Luke 10:21). I have earlier suggested that what Jesus was referring to was the existence of the infanticidal impulse in adults.[12]

Elihu's position on the issue differs dramatically from the positions of the three friends, Eliphaz, Bildad, and Zophar. They tend to conceive of the relationship between man and God as rational, even contractual, with God being the dispenser of the rewards and punishments. It is from this perspective that they seek somehow to find reason for Job's suffering. Elihu's comments, however, are not legalistic in this sense but are rather like those of a child who has no alternative but to trust—the voice of the child who is in the hands of the father. The father is his creator: "The Spirit of God hath made me, and the breath of the Almighty hath given me life" (33:4). God "giveth not account of any of his matters" (33:13). "Touching the Almighty, we cannot find him out: he is excellent in power, and in judgment, and in plenty of justice: he will not afflict" (37:23).

A Son, Not a Father

Psychologically the Book of Job may be regarded as expressing a transition from the state of mind of father to the state of mind of son, the change coming about as a defense against the guilt associated with the infanticidal impulse. This change is important for understanding the emergence of Christianity. In it the many varieties of suffering to which the human being is subject are reinterpreted in the model of a child as victim of the father. The infanticidal impulse is apparently got rid of by projecting it. Guilt is reduced because one appears to one's self as the victim rather than as the infanticidal father. At the same time, however, it conceptualizes suffering and especially death as being under the will, albeit someone else's will, and thus allows the logical possibility of immortality as a function of will. If death comes only at the will of God, and if God could be persuaded to decide in one's favor, then one might live forever. If there is any guilt associated with audaciously willing to live forever, this guilt is removed by ascribing it to God. It is of note that nowhere in the whole of the Book of Job is there even a suggestion that Job's suffering might have natural causes independent of God's will. There is only one cause for all of Job's suffering, the will of God. The book is an attempt to take on the voice of trust of the child in his father, who is conceived of as all-powerful, and who is in the first instance the very creator of being.

These considerations help us to appreciate the important difference between Job and Abraham. Abraham contracted with God to care for his children after he was gone. Job, in contrast, having psychologically engaged in infanticide, as it were, strains to identify himself with the victim, subject to injury only by God. This identification is the fusion of the one who kills with the one who is killed, which Freud conceptualized as the internalizing of the father into the psyche as the superego.

If death is only through the will of a God who can grant eternal life, and he spares not even one, then one who may be caught in the whirlpool of this construction is brought to the point of reproaching God. Indeed one piece of liturgy which, I believe, is illuminated by interpreting it as a reproach, is the Kaddish said by Jewish mourners. It is little more than praise of God. But it appears to have the implicit meaning, in addition, that if God is so great, why has he allowed or caused this? Job's initial reaction, that "the Lord gave, and the Lord hath taken away; blessed be the name of the Lord" (1:21) may also be interpreted as the victim justifying the infanticidal act of the father. It is the father who made being in the first place, and therefore it is his right to undo it. But justification is always built on reproach, explicit or implicit. If this first response is only a veiled reproach, the second response is less veiled: "Let the day perish wherein I was born, and the night in which it was said, There is a man child conceived" (3:3). This is the Freudian Oedipus complex reproach, the reproach against the father for having engaged in the act which led to one's creation. It is a reproach against the father for having created him if he was to kill him later; a reproach against the sexuality of the father out of which the child was conceived; and a reproach against one's self insofar as one is thus the lustful and infanticidal father.

The Christian idea of the virgin birth, succeeding as it does the story of Job, carries the reproach even further; for it even denies the relationship to the father, and denies him his procreative role. Against a background of a culture engaged in a struggle to maintain the dominance of the patrilineal idea, a culture struggling to make men identify with their children as their "seed," the idea of the virgin birth also defends against the guilt of the father for killing the child; for in the major infanticide in history the victim is said to have had no human biological father. Paradoxically, of course, the New Testament still endows Jesus with a completely patrilineal genealogy (Matt. 1:1–17). We need thus to recognize that Job's denunciation of his own conception is a reproach against the father for his infanticidal tendencies; and that one psychological solution to the problem of the guilt of infanticide is to move from the role of the father to the role of son. Job's answer to tragedy is to announce that he is to be understood as a child, as a son and not as a father. In effect, Job, psychologically the slayer of children, is depicted as attempting to hide among the children, adding his voice to the children's chorus. Yet in so doing, living or dying becomes a prerogative of will, even if it has to be God's will.

Sacrifice as Righteousness

The Book of Job explicitly indicates that Job is righteous, but, at the same time, it contains allusions suggesting that he is involved in the deepest of sins. How can one be both simultaneously? I suggest that by answering this riddle we may understand suffering better; and that, furthermore, we can answer this riddle by considering that one activity, sacrifice, which, according to the text, Job is said to have engaged in with great conscientiousness.

There is a clue in a statement attributed to Job's wife in the text: "Dost thou still retain thine integrity? curse God, and die" (2:9). In order to appreciate its significance we must return to the Hebrew. The word translated as "curse" is not curse at all, but "bless." The context is such, however, that the translator is quite correct in interpreting "bless" as a euphemism for "curse." The suggestion is very strong that "bless" and "curse" are deeply intertwined, that they are, in some sense, one. The principal act of righteousness is sacrifice. It is precisely in sacrifice that "bless" and "curse" coalesce. If this is how Job expresses his righteousness, it is both "bless" and "curse."

Consider again the story of Abraham and Isaac, the paradigmatic sacrifice tale. That story is indicative of profound ambivalence. On the one hand, there is Abraham's wish for many children and for God to provide them with land and eternal protection. On the other hand, there is the wish to kill Isaac, although the latter wish is projected onto God also, appearing as God's command to Abraham. When a human being inflicts pain upon another human being, he characteristically believes that he does so out of necessity. In the case of Abraham it is out of obedience to God. But one can reasonably ask about the locus of the necessity. A common psychodynamic mechanism is to convert desire so that it appears as external necessity. It is thus an open question in each instance whether what appears to be external necessity really is that, or is simply a facade concealing some internal pressure. The appearance of the ram at the last moment indicates the possibility of substituting an animal for Abraham's son. Psychologically, however, the sacrifice of an animal is then also symbolic of killing the son. Since if A is a substitute for B, then A is also symbolic of B, killing an animal instead of a son is a symbolic way of killing the son. In the story of Abraham, the substitution of an animal appears to resolve the conflict. The ram is killed, and Isaac is spared.

In contrast to the Abraham and Isaac story, the Book of Job is indicative of a state of mind for which the use of animals as a way of appeasing the infanticidal impulse has lost its effectiveness. By the time the Book of Job was composed, the strong distinction between animals and children had become considerably blurred in the biblical mind. All of Job's sacrificing of animals has been to no avail. He is said to have lost animals and children simultaneously. If the distinction between children and animals is drawn either very sharply, or if the distinction is very blurred, then the sacrifice of animals gives little satisfaction to the infanticidal impulse. If it is the former, the distinction between child and animal makes it impossible to feel that the child is being killed in the killing of the animal. If it is the latter, then one moves to killing the children with the same impunity as one kills animals. It is this second situation that we encounter in the Book of Job.

Wherein, then, lies Job's righteousness? In the biblical mind righteousness consists in part in making sacrifices; and this Job has clearly done. It is not only in action that righteousness consists, however, but also in a certain condition of mind. Righteousness would also consist in being able to maintain a balanced distinction between children and animals so that, as in the case of the righteous Abraham, a ram could substitute for Isaac. The question of the Book of Job really is, as indeed the rabbis of the Talmud took it to be, whether Job was as righteous as Abraham. For in the Book of Job it is not at all clear. Job is said to have sacrificed, but the children died. Abraham sacrificed but Isaac lived on that account. Genuine righteousness should at least consist in being able to maintain a piety that does its psychological work. In the Book of Job the problem is whether piety does the work it is supposed to do. The book rather bespeaks a state of mind in which the distinction between children and animals was not maintained, a state of mind going toward an acted-out infanticidal impulse. Had the state of the biblical mind been such as to win a sense of satisfaction for the infanticidal impulse from the sacrifice of animals, it is unlikely that the Book of Job would have been composed or written down.

The child who may be killed by the father is ambiguously both someone else and the father himself. The substitution of familial immortality for individual immortality is among the important psychological efforts represented in the Old Testament. There is hardly a page in the Bible on which it is not asserted in one way or another that the male can have children. There is an overlay of one conflict upon another in the biblical mind, for which sacrifice was such a significant act. There is an initial conflict between individual survival and survival through one's offspring. If one opts for individual survival rather than survival through one's offspring, another conflict arises. Shall one survive by being an adult and killing the child or by being a child to the "father," deferring to him so that he will not kill one as the "child?" Taking the child's role spares one from the temptations of infanticide. Taking the child's role also opens up the possibility of endless life, since the termination of life has been converted into something dependent only on the sufferance of the "father." If he can be appeased, one might live forever. But taking the role of the child means surrendering sexuality, reproduction, and one's own fatherhood—which, indeed, developed into an ideal of Christianity—and thus not having available the possibility of immortality through one's offspring. One is left only with personal immortality; and personal mortality is inexorable.

The conflicts posed by the Abraham and Isaac story are between the two ways of surviving as an individual: between killing the child so that one will survive one's self and infantile deference to the father so that one will not be killed by him. Whichever of these means is taken would remove the possibility of survival through one's offspring. In the Abraham and Isaac story the way out of the conflict was symbolic: an animal was sacrificed instead of a child. By sacrificing an animal one does not kill the child and is therefore not "cut off" by the act. One also defers to the "father" by sacrificing to him and thus preventing him from killing one, thereby opening the possibility of personal immortality. And one satisfies the infanticidal impulse at least symbolically.

In contrast, Job, for all his sacrificing, is "cut off," at least until the restoration at the end of the book. The biblical expression "cut off" means to be killed, to be socially ostracized, and, in particular, to be childless. It might be pointed out parenthetically that Freud's use of the notion of "castration" as a concretization of the most drastic punishment was perhaps conditioned by the biblical tradition, in that literal castration involves simultaneously a threat to the life of the individual, the consequent impossibility of having intercourse (and thus of entering into that which Freud took to be paradigmatic of all intimate interpersonal—social—relations), and the impossibility of having children.

Sacrifice and Individual Survival

The fact that animals also constituted a major source of food supply serves to confound the meaning of sacrifice. The discussion thus far suggests that the ritual of sacrifice entailed two different psychological substitutions. First, the one for whose sake the sacrifice is made has been shifted from the father to God, essentially ascribing to God the infanticidal impulse of the father. Second, the victim of the sacrifice has been shifted from child to animal. We can deepen our understanding of the matter by observing the significance of the issue of the food supply.

Although the text indicates that Job is a wealthy man in terms of his possession of animals, giving their precise number and describing him as "the greatest of all the men of the east" by virtue of his "substance" (1:3), there is also a hint that the food supply is an issue when we compare the beginning and the end of the Book of Job. At the beginning of the book the text indicates that the brothers undertook the responsibility for feeding their sisters: "And his sons went and feasted in their houses, every one his day; and sent and called for their three sisters to eat and to drink with them" (1:4). At the end of the book, when Job's wealth is doubly restored to him, the text indicates that Job gave to the replaced daughters "inheritance among their brethren" (42:15), as though the authors wished to make sure that readers would understand that Job is finally providing for his daughters. The Septuagint version of the Book of Job is much more explicit about poverty having been an issue. It includes words from Job's wife in which she speaks of herself as "wandering about, or working for wages, from place to place and from house to house, wishing for the setting of the sun, that I may rest from the labours and sorrows I endure" (2:9).

We may presume that the biblical mind had learned one of the most primitive forms of "investment," to allow children to grow up as a provision against starvation in the future, analogous to allowing an animal to mature and to breed instead of eating it. Such an "investment policy" required, however, that the young be indoctrinated with a sense of responsibility for providing for those who had spared them in their childhood. Young persons rendering meat to the old is a ubiquitous theme in the Bible. It may be seen in the story of Cain and Abel, where the text indicates that "the Lord had respect unto Abel and to his offering" of meat (Gen. 4:4), "but unto Cain and his offering [of the fruit of the ground] he had not respect" (Gen. 4:5). There is the similar story of the demand by Isaac in his role as father for "savoury meat, such as I love" (Gen. 27:4) before giving the blessing. Indeed, obligation in the Bible is often exactly that of rendering meat offerings and other food to God. If the meat served is meat of animals, and it is in abundance, the conflict between the temptation of killing children and deference is hardly aroused. When there is shortage, however, the conflict between getting rid of children to conserve food and allowing them to grow up so that they can then supply food to their elders is aroused. The biblical references to child sacrifice are numerous, and one might suspect that, at times, when conditions were dire, a cannibalistic impulse was aroused in the biblical mind. That this is at least a possibility is indicated by the story told in 2 Kings, in which two women arranged that on one day they would eat the child of one and on another they would eat the child of the other. One of them bitterly complains over being betrayed: "So we boiled my son, and did eat him: and I said unto her on the next day, Give thy son, that we may eat him: and she hath hid her son" (6:29).

Thus, under conditions of shortage the biblical mind is brought to sin, brought to the killing of the children. If righteousness consists, in any part, in keeping the father supplied, and there is a shortage of food, and it is in some sense believed that the shortage is itself due to inadequate deference to the "father," the impulse to kill the child—

seemingly as an act of righteousness—is aroused. Thus, paradoxically, the major sin in the first place, killing the children, becomes what appears to be an act of righteousness, although, in the last analysis, killing the child is deference of the individual to his personal survival.

This deep paradox of the Judeo-Christian tradition, the convergence of the ultimate of righteousness and the ultimate of sin, is the basic theme of the Book of Job, even on the manifest level. Job's bitterness is the bitterness of confronting this paradox. The paradox is rooted in the fact that each generation is a transition between generations, and each would itself be immortal. Job comes to terms with this by allowing that there is a God, who is different from himself, and that the ways of this God are incomprehensible to man. The attribution of incomprehensibility to God, which is a major theological contribution of the Book of Job, allows the possibility that the paradox has a resolution, albeit unknown to man. We may interpret the Book of Job as indicating that sacrifice is ultimately unsatisfactory as a psychological mechanism. Job's sacrificing is the beginning and hardly the end of his difficulties. In seeming righteousness, the biblical mind in the Book of Job fulfills the wish to kill the children and comes to the realization that in the ultimate act of righteousness one is "cut off."

It has been recognized in the psychoanalytic literature that, although an unfulfilled wish may be involved in creating a neurotic condition, the resolution of the neurotic condition does not inhere in the satisfaction of the wish. We see this, for example, in the story of Oedipus and in Freud's treatment of the Oedipus complex. Freud identified what he took as one of the deepest wishes, that of having sexual relations with one's mother, in the story of Oedipus. Yet the fulfillment of the wish hardly brought happiness to Oedipus. Indeed, the fulfillment is the major condition of the tragedy. Similarly, the fantastic satisfaction of the wish does not result in happiness or fulfillment but is the nucleus of tragedy in the Book of Job. The sacrifice of animals failed either to appease the father or to satisfy the infanticidal wish in the biblical mind. In the Book of Job that mind has moved to the fantasy of engaging in the sacrifice of the children. But this fails; for then one is "cut off" and there is no possible comfort in the idea that one may be immortal through one's offspring. They are dead.

The Sacrifice of Self and Mortality

The biblical mind is thus brought to entertain the sacrifice of one's self. As the story has it, Satan is not satisfied that Job's children or his animals are dead. He must suffer disease. The tragedy of Job at once involved the loss of his children and disease.

The profoundest complaint that man can make to his creator is that, having made him, he made him mortal. An essential feature of man's condition is expressed metaphorically in the Genesis story, in which there are two trees: man ate only one of them and was cast forth from the Garden of Eden to prevent him from eating of the Tree of Life and living forever (Gen. 3:22). Having eaten of the first tree, he is capable of wisdom, understanding, and knowledge, the latter connoting and including generativity. But the fact of the matter is that individual man is mortal, and there is no way in which to stop the inexorable movement toward the death of the individual organism. Sacrifice might support an illusory hope of immortality, but it is only an illusion. Even the amputee whose life is saved by the sacrifice of his limb will eventually die. At some point the truth comes through that nothing one can do will make one's individual being immortal. For all of Job's sacrificing he must die. An immortal father-God who *might* spare man is a hollow fantasy, and to believe it costs man his maturity.

Contemplating the Book of Job helps us to appreciate one of the major defects of the Judeo-Christian tradition, the tendency to subsume death under punishment, to leave out the possibility of death which is not punishment. To conceive of death as resulting only from lack of virtue is essentially to adopt a view of death characteristic of the thought of a child, for whom neglect by or hostility from adults is the most likely cause of death. So conceiving of death perverts the fact that death is inevitable in time and will occur whether the life lived has been virtuous or not. Virtue might be associated with longevity, but it does not provide immortality.

In the Book of Job the cause of disease is attributed basically to God. But the fact remains that all human beings must eventually become diseased of something and die. Much of the discussion that Job has with his friends assumes that God causes death in each instance. But Job, at times, appears wiser than his three friends. For to Job the authors attribute the recognition that just to be born entails a sentence of death (14:1ff.). In the Book of Job there is a harbinger of the notion of "original sin," the sin in being born—that being born is the sin which is "punished" by the death to ensue in a finite number of days. "Man that is born of a woman is of few days" (14:1), for "Who can bring a clean thing out of an unclean? Not one" (14.4).

The Book of Job seeks to refute the thesis that virtue and reward, vice and punishment, are necessarily associated. The ultimate refutation of this thesis in the biblical sequence is the story of Jesus, in which one who is eminently virtuous, even to the point of having been born without original sin, still suffers. The Book of Job is a step in this refutation because in it the seemingly righteous man is made to suffer precisely as a test of his righteousness. Job's quarrel with his friends is about their assumption that suffering follows sin and that the amount of suffering is regulated by the amount of sin, which Job rejects. For Job knows full well that his righteousness, or any righteousness, does not give immortality. He asserts that the association is null, and he comes to recognize the deep sinfulness of believing that there is a separate God who rewards virtue and punishes vice. For if such were the case one could work toward one's immortality by wilfully being righteous, which in itself would be an attempt to disobey God's wish that man not eat of the Tree of Life. In short, Job knows that it is sinful to believe that God rewards the righteous with immortality; he knows it is not true; he knows that death is inexorable.

There are two major points in life which are beyond the scope of the individual will. One is conception; the other is death. Between these, but not including them, the will of the individual has its proper sphere. To fancy one's self one's own creator, or to place death within the power of the will, are the real sins of mankind. This Job understands. And this, I believe, Freud understood when he stressed the fantasy of presence and witness to the primal scene, on the one hand, and the death instinct, on the other.

At the end of the Book of Job, God is presented as manifesting anger against Job's three friends, commanding them "offer up for yourselves a burnt offering" (42:8). For them, who still believe in the relationship of virtue and vice to reward and punishment and who have not quite appreciated the fact that death is inexorable in spite of all, sacrifice is still an appropriate activity. But for Job the mechanism is no longer appropriate. He rather will have his children, will provide for them, and will sacrifice no more on behalf of them. After a long life he will die, comfortable in having eaten of the first tree, but no longer lusting after the second.

NOTES

1. The transposition of the two middle characters of the Hebrew of Job's name yields "enemy."

2. H. M. Kallen, *The Book of Job as a Greek Tragedy* (Moffat, Yard and Company, 1918).

3. I. J. Gerber, *The Psychology of the Suffering Mind* (Jonathan David Company, 1951), p. 35.

4. W. B. Stevenson, *The Poem of Job* (Oxford University Press, 1947), p. 22.

5. D. Bakan, *The Duality of Human Existence: An Essay on Psychology and Religion* (Rand McNally, 1966), pp. 205ff.

6. *The Talmud: Baba Bathra*, trans. M. Simon and I. W. Slotki (Soncino Press, 1935), pp. 76–77.

7. Ibid., p. 81.

8. Stevenson, pp. 23–24.

9. The Talmud: Baba Bathra, p. 81.

10. Bakan, *The Duality of Human Existence*, p. 59.

11. L. Ginzberg, *The Legends of the Jews*, trans. H. Szold (Jewish Publication Society, 1961), Vol. 1, p. 326.

12. D. Bakan, *The Duality of Human Existence*, pp. 222ff.

PART III

Erik H. Erikson

E rik H. Erikson was born in Frankfurt, Germany, in 1902 and died in Harwich, Cape Cod, Massachusetts, in 1994. During his lifetime, he was best known for the emphasis in his writings on the issue of identity, a term that was virtually synonymous with his name, and for his related theory of the life cycle as comprised of eight major psychosocial crises. In later life, he tried to bring attention to another issue of deep concern to him—what he called "pseudo-speciation"—but public and professional interest in this problem fell far short of that accorded identity.

As I mentioned in the general introduction, Erikson's first book was *Childhood and Society,* published in 1950 and revised in 1963. This was to remain his best-known work in spite of the fact that he wrote several more acclaimed books, including *Gandhi's Truth,* published in 1969, which received the Pulitzer Prize in general nonfiction and the National Book Award in philosophy and religion. Other books include *Young Man Luther* (1958), *Identity and the Life Cycle* (1959), *Insight and Responsibility* (1964), *Identity: Youth and Crisis* (1968), *Dimensions of a New Identity* (1974), *Life History and the Historical Moment* (1975), *Toys and Reasons* (1977), and *Life Cycle Completed* (1982). His wife, Joan, contributed to his work and wrote several books of her own, including *Wisdom and the Senses* (1988), which emphasizes the role of the sense perceptions at each phase of psychological development. Erikson is unique among the authors included here in having received his psychoanalytic training in Vienna (where Freud was still practicing), and under the special tutelage of Freud's daughter Anna, herself a major psychoanalytic figure specializing in work with children.

Erikson's interest in religion is evident throughout the corpus of his writings and is perhaps most explicit in his second major book, *Young Man Luther*, which focuses on Martin Luther's identity problems and their partial resolution—by displacement—through religious faith. His interest in religious subjects was related, to a considerable degree, to his own identity conflicts, which were rooted in the fact that the identity of his natural father remained a mystery to him throughout his life. He once confided to a young minister that his personal religious concerns were connected heavily to the mystery of his paternity.[1] As his natural father was a Gentile and his mother was Jewish (both were Danish), his identification with Judaism, the faith in which his mother and stepfather reared him, was significantly compromised from a relatively early age; his height and other physical features won him the nickname of "goy" among his Jewish peers in the orthodox synagogue in Karlsruhe, Germany, where his mother had settled shortly after his birth.[2]

As a young man he expressed interest in Protestantism, which itself had a somewhat marginal status in the largely Catholic city of Karlsruhe. Later, his marriage to Joan Serson, a Canadian-American daughter of an Episcopalian clergyman, contributed to what he came to call his "borderline" existence.[3] His subsequent name change— from Homburger, his stepfather's name, to Erikson—has been a matter of considerable controversy but seems to be a reflection of his concern to find his own identity. His early attraction to art, a career he abandoned in his mid-twenties in part because of his technical difficulties with paints, also had bearing on his religious struggles.

The selections from his writings included here are a very small sample of his writings on religion. The first selection focuses on the celebrated film *Wild Strawberries*, by Swedish director Ingmar Bergman. Erikson uses this vehicle's focus on a day in the life of its main character, Dr. Isak Borg, to bring his life cycle theory to life. It can be argued that this theory is itself inherently religious, an argument that Erikson himself invited when he acknowledged that it is more akin to religious world views, which attempt to create an image of the whole of life, than to fine-grained psychological constructs based on careful empirical measurement.[3] In *Toys and Reasons*, he likened his life cycle construct to ritual, confessing that one could easily view this construct as his attempt to give "ceremonial reassurances" not unlike the "greeting ritual" initiated by the mother in her relations with her infant, especially to those who may doubt whether life has any encompassing meaning.[4]

Supporting this view of his life-cycle conception is the fact that he expanded on Freud's stages of infancy and childhood (i.e., the oral, anal, genital, and latency stages), adding four additional (and much extended) stages to include adolescence and three adult periods. By referring to these stages in *Childhood and Society* as "the ages of man," he was also making explicit reference to Shakespeare's *As You Like It* (act 1, scene 7) where "the melancholy Jacques" compares life to a stage, having many players and scenes, and comprising "seven ages." First employing the seven-ages formula, Erikson subsequently realized, with his wife's assistance, that he had omitted their own developmental stage of "generativity and stagnation" (even as Shakespeare had failed to include the playwright, the generator of the play itself, in his conception of the seven ages of life). Thus, Erikson's very creation of the life-cycle theory was a manifestation of middle-adult generativity. (In later writings, the more expansive and allusive word "age" was frequently replaced by the developmental term "stage," a natural outgrowth of Erikson's tendency to represent his model in chart form.) Given its association with Shakespeare and with images from world religions (for example, the Hindu schema of three adulthood stages leading to a fourth stage of renunciation or disappearance),[5] Erikson clearly intended that his life- cycle theory be understood as more than a psychosexual (Freud's emphasis) or even psychosocial model (Erikson's own theoretical orientation), seeing it rather as a means to study life in all its complexities.

From a religious point of view, then, one of the most notable features of the essay on Bergman's Dr. Borg is Erikson's allusion to Borg's "revelatory sensation of grand simplicity," when he seems to gain a transcendent vision of the whole of his life during the celebration in the cathedral. This experience enables him to put national, ideological, professional, and religious claims and commitments into perspective and to see them as a reflection of the human propensity toward pseudo-speciation, that is, the division of the human species into arbitrarily constructed subspecies. (Freud addressed this tendency and its negative social effects in *Group Psychology and the Analysis of the Ego* and *Civilization and Its Discontents* with his allusion to "the narcissism of minor differences" that separate otherwise similar national groups, and Kristeva has more recently addressed it in her chapter on foreignness and universality in *Strangers to Ourselves.)* The final scene at the beach, where Dr. Borg witnesses his parents from a distance, makes Erikson's point that the life cycle is, indeed, cyclical, confirming (as T. S. Eliot expresses it in *Four Quartets*) that "in my end is my beginning." Because this essay was written relatively late in Erikson's career, we may view it as his most mature rendition of his life-cycle theory (and, not incidentally, as its most religious formulation).

The second selection is from *Young Man Luther*. It focuses on the central role of the mother-infant relationship in religion, especially as defining religion's primary concern with matters of trust and mistrust. While Freud's concern with the Father-God of the Judaeo-Christian tradition led him to emphasize the Oedipal conflict as the dynamic core of religion, and thus to view guilt as its central theme, Erikson emphasizes the priority of the maternal role and thus views mistrust (and resulting estrangements) as equally fundamental religious themes. To be sure, Freud's writings on religion (for example, *Totem and Taboo* and *Moses and Monotheism*) recognize that mother goddesses have always played an important role in religion, preceding the emergence of the theme of the primordial father, but Freud also emphasizes that goddess worship is a threat to the Judaeo-Christian tradition's monotheistic focus. Informed by Freud's argument, Erikson recognizes that Luther, himself resolutely monotheistic, rejected any idealization, much less deification, of the mother, as reflected in his vehement reaction against the elevation of Mary in the medieval church to which he was heir. On the other hand, Erikson also recognizes that Luther sought from the Father-God the recognition the son can only receive from the mother. Thus, he alludes to Luther's view that one may be reborn "out of the matrix of the scriptures," adding, " 'Matrix' is as close as such a man's man will come in saying 'mater.' . . . I think that in the Bible Luther at last found a mother whom he could acknowledge: he could attribute to the Bible a generosity to which he could open himself, and which he could pass on to others, at last a mother's son." [6]

This does not mean that Erikson minimizes the role of the father in religion, any more than he minimizes it in individual development. From his earliest to his latest writings, he emphasized the power (and cruelty) of the superego, which he associated with paternal authority, though he also recognized that a father who is able to "hold" his child emotionally enables the child to relinquish the need to remain encapsulated within the maternal matrix. Emphasizing the mother's place in the religious economy, however, permits Erikson to take account of and explore the complex set of parent-child dynamics and their relationships in religion. As he writes in *Young Man Luther:* "Father religions have mother churches."[7] Added to this is the individual's self-relationship and the corresponding image of God as preparental, an image which is so much a part of Christian and Eastern forms of mysticism. (Freud, who affirmed a "father of personal prehistory" prior to significant experience of one's actual father, did not, however, envision there being a *nonparental* image of God.) Later, Erikson's emphasis in *Young Man Luther* on this third religious nostalgia—the "pure self itself" preceding both maternal and paternal images—was expanded into the "sense of 'I' " which he accorded a prominent place in his essay on the Galilean sayings of Jesus.

This selection from *Young Man Luther* also illustrates Erikson's life-cycle theory, especially the first two stages ("Basic Trust vs. Basic Mistrust" and "Autonomy vs. Shame and Doubt"). It places the experience of the transition from the first to the second stage in a religious context, noting how religious melancholy develops in this transitional period, as the child engages in a desperate struggle for life, taking by force the life provisions that the provider withholds (often for the purpose of ensuring that her child will develop the capacity to fend for himself). In this transition, the child experiences the loss of innocence and the formation of conscience, and religion now takes the form of "secondary appeasement." Erikson thus views Luther's religious struggle as centering on how one may regain the original "basic" or "primal" trust once it has been shattered by the desperate will to live exemplified in the "autonomy vs. shame and doubt" conflict. His view that for the adult Luther the Bible *(sola scriptura)* became the "maternal matrix"—a truly generous mother—is directly relevant to this search for a new foundation for "basic trust," a "basic trust" that is viable this side of the "autonomy vs. shame and doubt" experience.

The third selection, "The Ritualization of Everyday Life," is from *Toys and Reasons,* published in 1977. In 1966, Erikson published an essay, "The Ontogeny of Ritualization in Man," in which he presented his understanding of how human development is supported by ritual behaviors involving an agreed-upon interplay between at least two persons who repeat it at meaningful intervals and in recurring contexts, an interplay that should have adaptive value for all participants. The middle section of *Toys and Reasons,* an expansion of this earlier essay, centers on the five childhood stages and one adolescent stage in his original formulation of the life cycle, and collapses the three adulthood stages into one. It assigns a central ritual element to each of the remaining six stages. These are Infancy and the Numinous, Childhood

and the Judicious, Play Age and the Dramatic, School Age and the
Formal, Adolescence and the Ideal, and Adulthood and Ritual Sanction. In the excerpt presented here, which centers on the first of these
ritual elements—"Infancy and the Numinous"—Erikson assigns religion to the first stage of the ritualization process. This selection invites
comparison with Freud's "Obsessive Actions and Religious Practices,"
as it recognizes that religion has its origins in an adaptive form of
human ritualization—the "greeting ritual" that occurs between
mother and infant on a recurrent, daily basis. Thus, for Erikson, religion is not inherently pathological, though it may be perverted into
the pathological "ritualism" of *idolism*. He also recognizes that religion, when viewed in light of the ritualization of everyday life, may assume perverted forms that are not only psychopathological (i.e.,
obsessions and compulsions) but also psychosocial (e.g., a leader's
manipulation and exploitation of his charismatic appeal). Lest
Erikson's emphasis on the origins of religion in the mother-infant relationship appear to be an endorsement of a more "benign" view of religion than Freud's, one should pay close attention to the emotional
ambivalences, especially from the mother's side, in his representation
of the greeting ritual.

The fourth selection, "Shared Visions," is from the third section of
Toys and Reasons. It reflects a convergence of Erikson's lifelong tendency to bring his earlier interest in a career in art to bear on his understanding and practice of psychoanalysis, and shows how religion is
the common link between them. His analysis of the *Annunciation*
painting undoubtedly had deep personal significance for him in light
of his illegitimate conception, as it depicts two rooms, the one Mary's
bedroom, the other leading "our eyes straight to . . . a window opening on the town." The first is a scene of despair, the second one of
hopeful expectation. His account of an exceedingly brief dream of an
agoraphobic patient, which immediately follows his reflections on the
Annunciation, leads to analysis of her associations with two paintings.
The first is the *Circumcision of Christ*, with whom she identifies in her
suffering at the hands of her father; the other is a painting of a goddess
with six breasts, who symbolizes not only maternal generosity but
also, and more importantly, the transgressive allure of the sensual life,
from which her agoraphobia provided a paralyzing restraint. Erikson
views his interpretation of these paintings as an instance of "the
Freudian version of enlightenment." By penetrating the meanings
these paintings had for her, he was able to help relieve her of her psychological immobility. The rationale behind this version of enlighten-

ment is that a patient's anxieties may become manageable through achievement of insight into their causes.

The final selection is a very brief excerpt from an expansive essay on the sayings of Jesus, published when Erikson was seventy-nine years old and originally intended as the first section of a book-length study of Jesus, one that he was unable to complete. He draws on the work of biblical scholars (most notably, Norman Perrin of the University of Chicago) who represented the "form-critical" approach to biblical interpretation. Their specific concern was to identify the "authentic core" of those sayings and deeds attributed to Jesus by developing and applying criteria designed to distinguish those features of the gospels and other early writings (for example, the extracanonical Gospel of Thomas) which reflected Jesus' local context from those which were related to the concerns of the early Christian church as it spread beyond the borders of Galilee. While not preserved verbatim, the "authentic sayings" are the ones that remain when those reflecting the early church's preoccupations, attributed to Jesus, are excluded.

The material included here focuses on Erikson's concept of "the sense of 'I,' " intimated in *Young Man Luther* but more fully developed in his "Theoretical Interlude," in *Identity: Youth and Crisis*, where he drew a distinction between the ego (which is largely preconscious) and the "I," or one's consciousness of being a self. In this earlier treatment, he proposed that the "counterplayers" to the ego are the environment, both as it exists outside oneself (in the real world) and as it has been internalized through identification, while the counterplayer of the "I" is "the deity who has lent this halo [that is, this sense of "I"] to a mortal and is Himself endowed with an eternal numinousness certified by all 'I's who acknowledge this gift."[8] For Erikson, evidence that this sense of "I" is absolutely critical to the formation of personal identity is the example of autistic children, who struggle desperately "to grasp the meaning of saying 'I' and 'You' and how impossible it is for them, for language presupposes the experience of a coherent 'I.' "[9] The aging adult who suffers from Alzheimer's disease or from senility engages in the same desperate struggle. In his essay on Jesus, Erikson seeks to recover this feature of Freud's psychology—Freud's own differentiation of "I" from "ego"—as the fundamental basis of his version of enlightenment, and to demonstrate that Jesus drew attention to this sense of "I" through his simple but pointed sayings, especially those that located the "I" in the human body.

The selections included here lean most heavily toward Erikson's later writings on religion. This is partly because his later writings did not receive the attention his earlier writings commanded, especially during the enormous popularity he enjoyed in the 1960s as a Harvard professor and sage commentator on the social and political troubles in America and abroad. A more intrinsic reason, however, is that his later writings reflect the maturation of his lifelong effort to articulate his own religious views in a manner convincing to himself.

NOTES

1. Lawrence J. Friedman, *Identity's Architect: A Biography of Erik H. Erikson* (New York: Scribners, 1999), 439.

2. See Erik H. Erikson, " 'Identity Crisis' in Autobiographic Perspective," in *Life History and the Historical Moment* (New York: W. W. Norton, 1975), 17–47.

3. He was greatly influenced by Paul Tillich's autobiography, *On the Boundary* (New York: Scribners, 1966).

4. Erik H. Erikson, *Toys and Reasons: Stages in the Ritualization of Experience* (New York: W. W. Norton, 1977), 116.

5. Erik H. Erikson, *Gandhi's Truth: On the Origins of Militant Nonviolence* (New York: W. W. Norton, 1969), 36–39.

6. Erik H. Erikson, *Young Man Luther: A Study in Psychoanalysis and History* (New York: W. W. Norton, 1958), 208.

7. Ibid., 263.

8. Erik H. Erikson, *Identity: Youth and Crisis* (New York: W. W. Norton, 1968), 220.

9. Ibid., 217.

CHAPTER 12

Reflections on Dr. Borg's Life Cycle

ERIK H. ERIKSON

Ingmar Bergman's motion picture *Wild Strawberries* records an old
Swedish doctor's journey by car from his place of retirement to
the city of Lund. There, in the ancient cathedral, Dr. Isak Borg is to
receive the highest honor of his profession, a Jubilee Doctorate marking fifty years of meritorious service. But this journey by car on
marked roads through familiar territory also becomes a symbolic pil-
grimage back into his childhood and deep into his unknown self. For
the doctor has been dreaming strangely of late. "It is as if I'm trying to
say something to myself which I don't want to hear when I'm
awake"—so he says during the course of the day to his companion on
the ride, his daughter-in-law Marianne, who (for reasons of her own)
does her best to confront him in their conversations with a number of
disturbing, but at the end liberating, truths both about himself and
about the Borgs generally. At the end of the day, the ceremonial honor
bestowed on him seems almost unreal or, at any rate, transcended by
a certain simple depth of wisdom that he has gained—and by a decision through which he and his immediate family find themselves
firmly and subtly united.

I shall use Bergman's screenplay in order to present a conception
of the life cycle and of the generational cycle which I find admirably illuminated in it and illuminated, for once, in a memoir which begins
with the end—that is, it demonstrates how a significant moment in old
age reaches back through a man's unresolved adulthood to the dim beginnings of his awareness as a child. To use the screenplay, however,
means to retell it in my own words, which is already a first step in
interpretation. But it also allows me to select quotations from

Bergman's text and to describe his imagery, both of which are apt to get lost in the somewhat cumbersome experience of most non-Swedish audiences who must read the captions and ignore the foreign dialogue, as they attempt to view the picture in all its detail.

The prologue of the screenplay begins with a scene depicting the old doctor noting down the events and the reflections of that memorable day. Sitting at his massive desk, on which we see family pictures and writing utensils in faultless array, the white-haired, slightly stooped but solid old man with a square, handsomely aged face introduces himself as Dr. Isak Borg, age seventy-six, a Swede, and, of course, a Lutheran (for "a mighty fortress," in Swedish, is *an vaeldig borg*). He has outlived nine brothers and sisters and has been widowed for many years. He is the father of one married but childless son, also a doctor, who, in fact, lives and teaches at Lund. Borg says of himself in a voice both pedantic and somewhat querulous, as if somebody had accused him of something:

> At the age of seventy-six, I feel that I'm much too old to lie to myself. But of course I can't be too sure. My complacent attitude toward my own truthfulness could be dishonesty in disguise, although I don't quite know what I might want to hide. Nevertheless, if for some reason I would have to evaluate myself, I am sure that I would do so without shame or concern for my reputation. But if I should be asked to express an opinion about someone else, I would be considerably more cautious. There is the greatest danger in passing such judgment. In all probability one is guilty of errors, exaggeration, even tremendous lies. Rather than commit such follies, I remain silent.
>
> . . . As a result, I have of my own free will withdrawn almost completely from society, because one's relationship with other people consists mainly of discussing and evaluating one's neighbor's conduct. Therefore I have found myself rather alone in my old age. This is not a regret but a statement of fact. All I ask of life is to be left alone and to have the opportunity to devote myself to the few things which continue to interest me, however superficial they may be.[1]

Incidentally, at the doctor's feet, as he writes at his desk, is a Great Dane bitch, to all generous appearances a recent mother. Knowing Bergman, we realize this must be symbolic of a major theme to come. In the meantime, we note in Borg's opening statement a strange half-awareness that he can maintain a certain strained integrity only by withdrawing ("of my own free will") from sociability and attending to his own restricted sphere of interests. It is fascinating how, from the beginning, Bergman the director reveals in small visual and auditory hints a "classical" case of compulsive character: here, it is the old man's defensive voice and his punctilious manners that indicate with how much self-restriction he has paid for that seeming autonomy of proud withdrawal. It is, indeed, as if in the journey to come we were to be led from the compulsive "rituals" of a lonely old man, through some everyday ritualizations of his culture, to a grand ritual which both seals and permits a transcendence of his over-defined professional existence.

As for psychoanalytic symbolism, the imagery does not, in fact, use the symbols indicative of the repressed unconscious (or does so only in well defined moments), but rather those denoting a tacit knowledge of the dimensions of existence that dwell in our preconscious and that we can become aware of in all its simplicity and depth in special moments, whether brought about by the "natural" crises of life, or by a meaningful confrontation with a significant person, or, indeed, by fitting ceremonies. As we shall see, all three conditions come together in Dr. Borg's journey: old age, confrontation, ceremonial. The result is that of a transcendent simplicity rather than a mystical rapture or an intellectual reconstruction. I am reminded here of what a minister friend recently said to a man who had felt induced to participate in the Eucharist, but could not explain to his skeptical wife what had "happened." What, he asked of my friend, should he tell her? "Tell her," he said, "that you ate bread and drank wine."

Only the rarest rituals convey this kind of truth, but works of art are bridges to them. I found in this screenplay an incomparable representation of the wholeness of the human life cycle—stage by stage and generation by generation—which again and again was also conveyed to my students, and which I now feel I should spell out for this new generation of adults who (after all we have learned about childhood and youth) feel impelled to comprehend, not without some reluctance and distaste, what adulthood and old age are really all about.

Now, my choice of this movie, year after year, in my undergraduate course on "The Human Life Cycle" at Harvard, has of course also earned me some more or less friendly suspicions from my students. Some said I looked like Dr. Borg, for which my thanks, although who *could* look like Victor Sjoestroem? Or did I, with my background, wish I had become just such a doctor? Now, there is a "connection" between the movie and my childhood, for Lund lies on the Ore Sund, on the Danish side of which (only twenty miles away) I spent the sunniest summers of my early years visiting my uncles' country houses and being taken for boat rides. But when it comes to some students' further queries whether such affinities might not be the reason for my seeing such a detailed resemblance between this movie and my views of the human life cycle, I can only register such suspicion as an essential aspect of any conception of the whole of life: for can our concepts and can our terms ever transcend the observations and values that are part of our own limited existence—and of the illustrations we choose? Nevertheless, it so happens that this screenplay is a good one, as well as the only one of its kind and, furthermore, that it would well lend itself to a social critique demarcating what is universal in it and what hopelessly culture- and class-bound.

I will, then, proceed, after a summary of each major scene, to offer my terms for the psychosocial stages and crises encountered, and I will even capitalize them in order to point up the scheme to be accounted for systematically in the second part of this paper.

The Dream

This screenplay opens with a view, as it were, from tomb to womb, or more exactly, from the coffin to the cradle. It begins with a dream in which the doctor comes face to face with his own corpse. This dream is the psychic background for the day's events; we shall learn only later what—besides the dreamer's age—was the dream's own "cause."

In the dream memoir we see Borg briskly, if on not too firm legs, pursuing his "usual morning stroll" through some familiar but now, indeed, very empty streets, their facades shining in the northern summer's morning light. The "silence was absolute," and his footsteps echoed rhythmically. Over a store, apparently shared by a watchmaker and an optometrist, there hung a large clock by which he usually set his own watch for the exact time. But now it had no hands, and two large eyes-with-eyeglasses that hang beneath it appear to have been bloodied. The doctor pulled out his own watch: it, too, was without hands, and when he held it to his ear, he heard, instead, his own heart beat wildly. But, ah, there *was* somebody standing there in all the emptiness: a man with a felt hat, his back to Borg. On being eagerly touched, the man turned. He had "no face," and promptly collapsed. On the sidewalk lay only a heap of clothes with some liquid oozing out of them: the person was gone.

Up the empty street now came the sound of trotting hoofs as church bells began to toll. An ornate hearse appeared. As it passed, one of the wheels got stuck on a lamp post, broke off, and struck a church wall right behind the doctor. The hearse began to sway, somewhat like a cradle, with an eery creaking sound strangely reminiscent of a tortured birth cry. A coffin, splintered, lay on the ground, and from it a corpse reached out for the doctor. It had, in fact, the doctor's face "smiling scornfully." The dreamer awakened.

Let us see: Footsteps that echo; bells that toll; a clock that ticks but does not tell time; a heart that thumps and pounds. It may be that, thus enumerated, the symbolism might seem almost trite. But there is the overall imagery and, of course, a sequence of utterly convincing close-ups of the old man's facial expression, ranging from outright fear to the daily dread known to all old people: when will it all suddenly stop. And then there is an inkling of a personal, a neurotic, anxiety revealed only in the imagery. The text says that the other man's, the double's, face was "empty." Yet, his appearance shows thin lips tightly drawn down and eyelids pressed hard together: tight-sphinctered, then, and caricaturing a retentive personality—holding and keeping out. That other person, that double, collapses and spills his lifeblood in the gutter—a theme to be repeated that day in a number of wasteful and destructive "spillings."

Awakened, the dreamer, as if to ban a curse with a formula, pronounces: "My name is Isak Borg. I am still alive. I am seventy-six years old. I really did feel quite well." The viewer's first impression is that the dream tries to tell the dreamer—is it "merely because of his advancing age or in view of the approaching "crowning" event in his life, or for some other reason?—that he must not permit his official and so isolated self to beckon him into the grave. Perhaps he must as yet learn to die?

Let me, at this point, briefly and didactically introduce some capitalized terms for the last crisis of the Life Cycle. In my publications on the subject, I have postulated a dialectic struggle in old age between a search for Integrity and a sense of Despair and Disgust (or Disdain). These contraries, in dynamic balance, are essential to a final human strength: Wisdom. While, at this point, I will not try to explain or defend these terms, they should denote to the reader some of the qualities of Borg's inner, as well as social, discord and suggest that these qualities can be present, in some simple form, in any old person. If I also assume that these qualities have precursors in earlier crises throughout the life cycle, "crisis" at any age does not necessarily connote a threat of catastrophe but rather a turning point, a crucial period of increased vulnerability and heightened potential. "Cycle," in turn, is meant to convey the double tendency of individual life to "round itself out" as a coherent experience and to form a link in the

chain of generations from which it receives and to which it contributes both strength and fateful discord.

It will take Dr. Borg's whole journey (and this whole paper) to
come to a closer formulation of the old-age crisis in the light of the
whole course of life.

The Decision

It is three o'clock in the morning, a Swedish summer dawn, and Borg
suddenly knows what he must do: he must go to Lund by car rather
than, as planned, by airplane. We learn only gradually that this is, indeed, a fateful decision, for the fourteen hours required for the trip
also allow for a number of half-planned, half-improvised events. But
we know immediately that such autonomy itself is utterly surprising;
for in a scene both humorous and pathetic, it becomes clear that the
widower lives in some antagonistic interdependence with a very bo-
somy and very possessive housekeeper named Agda. She has been
with the family for forty years, many of them with him alone. She is
his age, but (typically?) he refers to her as "an old woman." Awakened
by Borg (his nightclothes in disarray), she can only ask, "Are you sick,
Professor?" Hearing his decision, she is upset and hurt: he is destroying, she says, the most solemn day of her life. Whereupon he mumbles
that they are not married, and she praises God for it. But she gets up,
dramatically packs his clothes, and sulkily serves breakfast, anticipat-
ing with some disgust that she must fly ahead alone to get things ready
in Lund.

But then a houseguest appears, awakened by the old couple's bick-
ering. She is a beautiful, clear-eyed, strong-faced woman in a dressing
gown: Marianne, son Evald's wife. She has been visiting and now asks
whether she can accompany the doctor to Lund. Thus, truly, the scene
is set for the most significant of a number of masterly encounters. For
as they leave the big city and drive into the countryside, Bergman
makes the most of the alternative possibilities of the perspectives provided by the automobile. We first see the car from the air, moving with
other tiny vehicles on a central urban traffic circle, choosing their destined exit. Then, focusing on the car's interior, we see the rest of the
world move by. Both driver and passenger can look ahead at near and
distant goals or inward into the sequence of their thoughts; they can
throw sideward glances away from each other, or look at each other
with rare, sudden, and necessarily fleeting visual engagements. Whoever is driving can glance at the rear-view mirror and see what is ap-

proaching or perceive the faces of whoever happens to be in the back
seat. This moving stage also permits dozing off—and dreaming! Thus,
Bergman civilizes the mechanical range of a car's interior for his own
story-telling purposes. Let me list the scenes that follow and then
characterize some in my terms.

First, as Borg drives along dreamily (maybe thinking of his
dream), he is obviously made uncomfortable by the young woman's
presence. Marianne, with a determination born of some circumstance
that for a while remains a secret, decides to confront him with his discomfort: one cannot help thinking of Cordelia, driving Lear's despair
to the surface. It all begins—as it will later end—with small, even
petty, items which yet betray basic attitudes. She, nervous, wants to
smoke, he stops her, nastily. She says the weather is nice, he predicts a
storm. Suddenly, she asks him his "real" age—for no "real" reason. But
under the impact of his dream, he knows that she, too, wonders when
he will die. Pettily, still, he thinks of the money her husband owes him,
pleads principle: "a bargain is a bargain." Evald, he is sure, understands this, for they are "alike," as she, indeed, admits they are. Then
the bombshell: "But he also hates you." An indescribable horror appears on his face, but he keeps calm. Asked why she doesn't like him,
she elaborates on the fact that she has now stayed with him a month
with the "idiotic idea" that he may help Evald and her, but that he had
refused adamantly to hear about their marital trouble, suggesting that
maybe she needs a quack or a minister. He is half amused, half
shocked to hear some of the uglier things he has said. She concludes
that she does not dislike him, but "I feel sorry for you." Second look of
terror, startled to the core. But they both maintain amenities—even
some amusement.

The issue is joined. And the interplay (one could speak of the interlocking) between his dreams and her behavior leads to surprising
acts on his part. First, he, of all people, wants to tell her his dream. She
claims no interest. But there soon comes a chance to involve her in his
life: arriving at a side road, he swings the car into it, to lead her down
to a house by the sea where he had spent much of his childhood and
youth.

But before we attend to that sunny scenery and to the wealth of
reveries which are about to emerge, I must confess one of those "clinical" impressions which seemed to explain why the old man and the
young woman, at that time, experience one another as living in an increasingly tense polarity. If it is true (the text does not confirm it) that
in Borg's dream the noise made by the broken-down hearse, as it

sways like a cradle, eerily reflects the crying of a newborn, then the old doctor's medical intuition may well have told him that the reason for proud Marianne's seeking help from him is that she is pregnant, and that his reaction to pregnancy is, to say the least, deeply ambivalent (recall the Great Dane bitch). But if this is so, the issue that is joined is Marianne's concern over harboring a new Borg and the old man's sudden awareness that he who is close to death must yet learn to affirm life. This assumption is necessary to recognize Marianne's (and, as we shall see, her husband's) aggravated life crisis as being what I have called the psychosocial crisis of *Generativity versus Stagnation or Self-Absorption*. Generativity includes, in its wider sense, the mature drive to generate and regenerate products and ideas; but the birth cry emanating from the hearse begs us on this day of professional triumph to consider generativity in its procreative essence. For each such crisis I have postulated an emergent "virtue," in the sense of a vital strength necessary for the life cycle as well as for the cycle of generations. *Wisdom* is the virtue of the last crisis; *Care*, for the mature stage of adulthood. In that mature stage, fate, as well as the life lived so far, decides whom and what one is committed to take care of so as to assure the next generation's life and strength. But where *Disdain* is the destructive counterpart to Wisdom, I would nominate *Rejectivity* as the counterpart to Care. And I suggest that it is this rejective trend which Marianne recognizes as an all-too-well-rationalized developmental defect in Dr. Borg—and a generational one in the Borgs. In her, a strong ethical determination seems to have been awakened that the future must not be forfeited to what is dead in the Borgs' past, even as Borg's old-age struggle against despair makes him comprehend that what he has become must not be all that he is and must not be all that he leaves behind. To paraphrase William James, he must find behind his relatively peaceful and yet disdainful isolation not only his "murdered self" but also his murderous one, so he may find his living and life-giving self.

The Strawberry Patch

They are driving down the side road to a point where they can see the old summer house. The facade of the house first looks like that tightly closed face of the dream's alter ego: it "slept behind closed doors and drawn blinds." Marianne, in fact, calls it "a ridiculous old house," and she decides to take a quick dip in the sea, leaving Borg to his reveries. In a dreamlike fashion, he knows where to go: to the strawberry patch.

He sits down in the grass and slowly eats some strawberries "one by one," almost ritually, as if they had a consciousness-expanding power. And, indeed, he now hears somebody play a piano, and suddenly the house appears transformed. The facade comes alive, "sun glittered on the open windows," and the place seems to be "bursting with life," although no one is in sight as yet.

Then, he sees her: his "first love," his cousin Sara, as she had been (now nearly sixty years ago), a blond, "light-hearted young woman" kneeling in the patch in a "sunyellow cotton dress." She is gathering strawberries into a small basket. He calls, she does not hear. Then his elder brother Sigfrid appears in a college student's white cap, self-assured to the point of sassiness. He wants to make love to her, and, over her weakening protests that she is engaged to Isak and that he, Sigfrid, is of all the Borg brothers the most "awful . . . unbearable . . . stupid . . . idiotic . . . ridiculous . . . cocky," he embraces her with a passionate kiss which she reciprocates. Then she falls weeping to the ground, the strawberries are spilled, and a red spot appears on her dress: he has, she cries, turned her into a "bad woman, at least nearly." She is a fallen woman, then, and one senses that this whole earthy scene, beyond its precious gaiety and its symbolic reference to defloration, points to something primeval, some garden, long forfeited by Isak.

Borg continues to "dream": a breakfast gong sounds, a flag is raised (the flag of Swedish-Norwegian unity, to be exact), and a crowd of brothers, sisters, and cousins converge on the house. The festivity is presided over by a dictatorial aunt. The center of attention is nearly deaf Uncle Aron, whose birthday it is. "The only ones missing were Father, Mother, and I," says Borg significantly. Somebody announces that Isak is out fishing with his father—"a message," Borg later notes, at which he felt "a secret and completely inexplicable happiness," wondering at the same time what he should do in this "new old world which I was suddenly given the opportunity to visit." It is impossible to describe the noisy and gay, intimate and yet also somewhat grating, birthday scene that follows. As old man Borg appears to watch his childhood milieu, it becomes clear that he had always felt like an isolated onlooker in all that gaiety and activity which, to a withdrawn and sensitive boy, must have seemed marked by some overpopulation. A series of skirmishes are fought between the authoritarian aunt and a succession of healthy, boisterous children who protest their right to be. At the end, it is Sara who takes the brunt of all the impertinent vitality, for two unspeakable twin sisters in braids who always chant in unison announce that they saw Sara and Sigfrid kiss in the patch. Sara runs out of the room onto the veranda. There, she tearfully confesses to her older cousin Charlotta how much she loves Isak, but that he (who will kiss her only in the dark) is simply too mysterious a man for her: so "enormously refined" and sensitive, so "extremely intellectual," and so moralistically aloof.

And now I should, because I said I would, relate the brief but obviously central scene of the spilled wild strawberries to one of the stages of life. It is that of young adulthood, with its manifold playful intimacies which must mature into a quality of Intimacy—in friendship, in erotic life, and in work. The related danger is some form of Isolation—and it becomes immediately probable that it was when he lost Sara to Sigfrid that something in Isak turned away from women and that he remained not only wanting in Love—the strength of this stage—but, again, possessed of a pervasive Exclusivity. There is, in fact, a symbolic hint pointing way back in Isak's life, for, in the Bible, Sara was Isak's mother; and we realize that Isak had known his mother as a very young woman. Is Sara's name an allusion to the fact that she had been old when young, or that he had lost his young mother, too, to another man? The breakfast scene seems to affirm this in the noisiest way possible, for six brothers and sisters were born during Isak's childhood; it seems also to illustrate the ruthless politics of a large and, in summer, extended family. As the aunt calls for order, respect, and propriety, each youngster in his or her way fights for survival. And it becomes all the more painfully clear that Isak's way of autonomy had been gifted isolation—and so, perhaps, had his father's been. At any rate, they went fishing together—sharing, maybe, a certain exclusiveness from the family.

Didactically speaking, this childhood scene would permit us, step by step, to sketch the way in which, in comparison to the others, Isak resolved his childhood crises by acquiring some specialized strengths that would later serve him well in a professional career in his cultural setting, but for which he would have to pay with a certain compulsive self-restriction that began to possess him early. If it is his central life-long endeavor which is to be crowned that day, so are all the unresolved early and later crises to be faced along the way.

We almost forgot Uncle Aron: he is a man in his second childhood, prepared for his special day by some secret libation—also witnessed and announced by the twins. He is sung to lustily, as Isak will be later in the day, although Aron is nearly deaf: these familial ritualizations prepare us for the more ironic aspects of the coming ceremony.

Maybe being like Uncle Aron could save one much existential trouble—and some bad dreams? In the meantime, the silly twins seem to have prepared us for another and more weighty double appearance—a second Sara.

Passengers

As Isak Borg, overwhelmed by his reveries, sits by the patch and only slowly comes to with a strong feeling of emptiness and sadness, a most real, blond and tanned young girl, as if jumping down from a tree, awakens him fully. Obviously a member of Sweden's contemporary *jeunesse d'oree*, she is dressed in shorts and is sucking on an unlit pipe. "Is this your shack?," she inquires, and presently asks whether the "jalopy" by the house is his. Instead of being shocked, however, he is amused, for the girl looks like a reborn Sara (and is played by the same actress, now with a pageboy haircut). And her name is Sara. She is on her way to Italy, and she would like a ride to the other coast. He agrees, and in his benign mood tells returning Marianne that he has offered the young girl a ride. As they approach the car, it turns out that two strapping young men are part of the bargain: they are going to Italy with Sara. But Borg seems ready to accommodate them all. In fact, a strange bond exists between him and little Sara, who, now an apparition in his rear-view mirror, adds a dimension of rejuvenation to the day. What is their stage? The three young represent contemporary youth in search of something worthy of their awakening *Fidelity;* they are working hard at defining their *Identity:* one of the two boys wants to become a doctor and plays the atheistic rationalist; the other intends to be a minister and defends God's existence. Both, however, when driven to defense or offense, display a certain naive *Cynicism,* which is the natural contrary to adolescent Fidelity. They both love Sara—or so says Sara, who, appropriately sitting between them, announces to Borg with a charming mixture of cynicism and sincerity that she is playing them out against each other, while remaining a virgin. So now they are hitchhiking to Italy, where young Northerners of that day expected the southern sun to melt away their *Identity Confusion.*

Before we describe the other surprising appearances, let me point out an implicit scheme in this sequence—a scheme by which Borg meets up, as he now seems almost driven to do, with his past selves and counterplayers. We have "located" his acute crisis in the conflicts natural to old age and Marianne's in those of the center of adulthood; we have also suggested that in his opening dream he had reached back to that somehow unfulfilled center stage in himself. We will find that in each subsequent encounter he faces individuals who personify earlier stages of life (as the young portray the identity crisis) and help him to return to the corresponding stage of his own life through some reverie or dream.

Borg, in watching Sara in the rear-view mirror, seems eminently relaxed, almost meditative. But suddenly, utter fear forces his whole attention forward: he sees a little black car approaching on the wrong side of the road. He swerves his car safely off the road, while the other car overturns into a ditch (one is reminded of the broken-down hearse). What, after a moment of stunned paralysis, they see emerge is a—mysteriously unharmed—middle-aged couple who, it turns out, have been quarreling and immediately continue to do so. The man, the doctor notes, is limping, but he explains that he has been "crippled for years," and (as he says his wife says) not only physically. As they, too, become passengers in the Borgs' car (occupying the folding seats) they continue on with their habitual reciprocal harangue seemingly aggravated by the "death scare" lived through, and yet obviously not the cause of it. The man, who introduces himself as Alman, grants that his wife's scorn may be good psychotherapy for her, while she announces that he is a Catholic who probably perceives the accident to be God's punishment. Thus, the two ministering professions continue as an ideological double theme, full of sarcasm and obscure dread. The husband even accuses his wife, apparently an unsuccessful actress, of playing at having cancer: "She has her hysterics and I have my Catholicism." Suddenly, the wife hits the husband in the face. Marianne, who is now driving, stops the car and quietly orders the couple to get out "for the children's sake" (born and unborn, one senses). And so, Borg records, they "quickly drove away from this strange marriage."

It will have occurred to the viewer that the full car contained a complete representation of the precariousness of adulthood, from the young people in the back seat who are on the way to the land where they hope as yet to find their adult identities as well as each other, to the couple who have just about lost each other and themselves, to the old man and the young woman who are just beginning to find each other in the attempt to prevent a forfeiture of an all too overdefined adulthood. Here Marianne is the heroine; in her now dominant determination to care, she does not hesitate to break up the antics of the two self-absorbed and hopelessly antagonistic adults as being destructively unethical. For if the simplest moral rule is not to do to another what you would not wish to have done to you, the ethical rule of adulthood is to do to others what will help them, even as it helps you, to grow.

As the car is now relieved of the spectacle of the "strange marriage"—which one suspects seemed so foreign to Borg only because he had not as yet faced the strangeness of that part of his own adult past— he and all the others seem emptied and exhausted, as if they, as well as the car, need refueling. So, first a gas station, then the midday meal.

Midday

What grace had saved Borg for those transformations symbolized by that one day's journey? Sara, we now know, had been and still is with him. And in all his self-absorption he apparently had been a good doctor. The gas station happens to be in the very center of southern Sweden where Borg had practiced for fifteen years before he became a researcher and professor in the city. The big, blond gas-station owner immediately recognizes him. After all, the doctor had delivered him and all his brothers. He called his wife ("she beamed like a big strawberry in her red dress") and suggested that they name their coming baby (a boy, of course) Isak. (Will Isak, them, be a godfather to his clientele, yet not a grandfather in his own family?) Payment for the gasoline is refused: "There are some things that can never be paid back." And Isak, with a tragic glance, suddenly thinks aloud: "Perhaps I should have remained here." He should have stayed in touch, then, at least with those to whom he could offer competent and truly needed service—as a member of one of those mediating professions who thereby earn a kind of social and existential exemption. And yet, a pitiless awareness may be telling him then and there how much love one can receive—from patients and students—for what one also does for honor and for money. How many old people, maybe without knowing it, mourn for just that period of their lives?

There follows, again, an idyllic scene: a midday meal on a terrace overlooking Lake Vaettern. Over the table, they now face each other, and with the help of some consciousness-expanding wine, Isak and Marianne become part of a midsummer celebration. Anders, the future pastor, suddenly recites a religious poem. Victor, the scientific rationalist, protests: they had sworn to each other that they would not discuss God. He advocates looking biological death "straight in the eye." Finally, Victor asks the doctor's opinion. But Borg has been musing; and as Marianne lights his cigar for him (he, who had refused to let her smoke her cigarette), Isak, instead of offering an opinion, recites a poem: "Where is the friend I seek everywhere? / Dawn is the time of loneliness and care . . . / When twilight comes. . . ." He asks Anders for help, but it is Marianne who continues: "When twilight comes, I am still yearning." And as Sara, moved to tears ("for no reason at all"), says: "You're religious, aren't you, Professor," Isak continues: "I see His trace of glory and power, / In an ear of grain and the fragrance of a flower," and Marianne concludes, "In every sign and breath of air. / His love is there."

The poem, the setting, the tone seem to confirm the sense in which every human being's *Integrity* may be said to be religious (whether explicitly or not), namely, in an inner search for, and a wish to communicate with, that mysterious, that Ultimate Other: for there can be no "I" without an "Other," no "We" without a shared "Other." That, in fact, is the first revelation of the life cycle, when the maternal person's eyes shiningly recognize us even as we begin to recognize her. And it is the hope of old age, according to St. Paul's promise.

This poem, no doubt, will accompany Borg to the end of this day. But first, he must encounter life's earliest Other who, so human fate dictates, makes the very origins of *Hope* a variably discordant matter. After a long silence, Isak arises abruptly and announces that he will visit his old mother, who lives nearby. Marianne wants to come along. She takes his arm, he pats her hand.

From the sunny lakeside, they walk to a house surrounded by a wall "as tall as a man." Inside, his mother, in a black dress with lace cap, looks up sharply from an "incongruous desk." Her estranged living becomes apparent as she, having accepted his embrace, asks with a suspicious glance whether Marianne is his wife and, if so, would she leave the room, for "she has hurt us too much." Introduced, she learns that Marianne has no children and announces that *she* has had ten; all are dead now, except Isak. None of the twenty grandchildren ever visit her, except Evald. And she has fifteen great-grandchildren whom she has never seen. "I am tiresome, of course . . . and I have another fault. I don't die." They are waiting for her money. . . . She asks to have a large box full of toys brought to her, saying she has "tried to think which of you owned that." She lifts out toys, one after the other, names the owners, chats about them. And then, painfully echoing Isak's opening monologue at his desk, she concludes: "It doesn't pay much to talk. Isn't it cold in here?," and, looking at the darkening sky in the window, "I've always felt chilly . . . mostly in the stomach." She lifts a last item from the box: her father's old gold watch. Drumbeats in the background: the dial is handless! Isak recalls his dream, the hearse, and "my dead self." But his mother concludes with one warming memory: how little Sara always cradled her cousin Sigbritt's infant boy. Now he is going to be fifty years old! She wants to give the watch to him: "It can probably be repaired?" (Again, was the mother once motherly like this Sara?)

When kissing her goodbye, Isak notes that his mother's face is "very cold but unbelievably soft and full of sharp little lines." Marianne, who has watched all this with silent horror, curtsies, and once outside again takes Isak's arm. Isak is now "filled with gratitude toward this quiet, independent girl with her naked, observant eyes." Perhaps he feels that Evald, although his son and his mother's grandson, in marrying Marianne may have reversed the fate that was symbolized by his mother's father's watch, which had mysteriously entered the dream that had started him on this journey. It may have been this hope that gave Isak the courage to confront himself in yet another, more deeply "humiliating" dream.

In the meantime we have learned that old-age *Despair* and *Disgust* may be handed on from generation to generation, where conditions (and even quite "comfortable" conditions) have become an inexorable hindrance to renewal.

The Last Examination

As Marianne takes the wheel (is she in charge now?) all are resting, the boys in angry sullenness over yet another disputation, little Sara bored with them both. Isak sleeps and dreams profusely. Astonished at his productivity when he writes it all down later, he wonderingly includes a defensive note about his lack of enthusiasm for the psychoanalytic theory of dreams "as the fulfillment of desires in a negative or positive direction." He also wonders whether this new twilight experience of memories and dreams is a sign of senility, or even a "harbinger of approaching death." In abstracting the extraordinary dream sequence here, I can only continue to point to that motivation in old age so miraculously understood by the middle-aged playwright, namely, to experience and, in fact, also to affirm total *Despair* in order to gain some integrated sense of one's life: for is the life cycle, seen as a whole, perhaps a revelation? (And are dreams not merely "self-revealing?")

Back at the strawberry patch, in a continuation of the morning's reverie, Isak again encounters the original Sara of his youth who, with pitying tears, holds a mirror to his face, forcing him to see himself "old and ugly in the sinking twilight." Is Sara also another Other—his own female Self? For she says that she has been unintentionally cruel by not exposing him to himself. She now announces that she will marry his brother: "It's all a game." He smiles, an unforgettable smile that seems to hurt his whole face. And she says sharply that he, a professor emeritus, ought to know why it hurts, but she is sure he doesn't. She throws the mirror away.

Sigbritt's little boy is crying. She must hurry to him. "Don't leave me," begs Isak. She says she does not understand him, for he stammers. But it doesn't "really matter" anyway.

The day becomes utterly fateful and threatening in a darkening twilight. Blackbirds are screeching like furies. With tears streaming down her face, Sara, up in the arbor, cradles the little boy with lullaby words: "Soon it will be another day." The child calms down, but Isak wants to scream "till my lungs (are) bloody."

The wind dies, the house again looks festive. Sara plays the piano, Sigfrid listens. They sit down to a candlelit dinner, celebrating "some kind of event." Isak watches through the glass door, pressing his hand against the frame, where there is a nail. It pierces his hand, producing a wound like one of the stigmata. As if this identification with Christ the Crucified seemed too self-indulgent a gesture, the scene and the moonlight now turn utterly cold and cruel. Mr. Alman, of all people, appears, stiffly polite, and insists that the professor come into the house, which has turned into some kind of laboratory. Taken into the very lecture room where he used to give his polyclinical examinations, he now must himself take an examination before a silently hostile audience, which includes the young passengers. Asked to inspect a specimen, he can only see his own eye mirrored in the microscope. Asked to read a mysterious formula on the blackboard which tells of a doctor's first duty, he cannot make it out. Alman intones calmly, politely: "*A doctor's first duty is to ask forgiveness.*" Yes, of course, he knew that, laughs Isak, reduced to wincing despair. Alman persists: "*You are guilty of guilt.*" (Is that sin?) Now the old man, typically, claims infirmity: after all, he has a bad heart! Another judgment: "*There is nothing concerning your heart in my papers.*" Finally, Isak is to diagnose a woman patient. She looks like Mrs. Alman (and one is reminded of the implied parallel between the Almans' marriage and his own). His diagnosis: "She is dead." The patient laughs wildly. A third judgment: *He does not know when a woman is alive.* The inquisitor summarizes his guilt as "indifference, selfishness, lack of consideration." He stands so accused by his wife, Borg now learns, and he must confront her. But she has been dead for years? Come, demands the inquisitor.

He leads him out into a primeval forest. The moon is shining "like a dead eye." The ground, covered with decaying leaves, is swampy and porous underfoot, filled with snakes. They now stand by a charred ladder leaning against a burned-out hut. In a clearing, Isak sees Karin, his wife, a strong, sensual woman, being seduced by a disgusting but virile man, and she "received the man between her open knees." The inquisitor states the exact date: "Tuesday, May 1, 1917." May Day. Isak now has seen, but has not heard, the worst. For as the lovers then sit and talk, the woman sadly yet scathingly predicts what Isak will say when she confesses. He will feel sorry for her, like "God himself," and say with a sickening nobility, "You shouldn't ask forgiveness from me. I have nothing to forgive." (But he will not think of asking for forgiveness.)

The inquisitor has the last word, mocking any attempt to gain some superiority from mere self-revelation. "Everything has been dissected. A surgical masterpiece." The Penalty? "Of course, loneliness." "Is there no grace?," asks the dreamer. But the other claims not to know.

Fleetingly, Isak once again tries to appeal to Sara, who once more materializes. "If only you had stayed with me. . . . Wait for me." He wants to cry like a child, but he can't. That escape is also gone.

The message of the dream seems clear: Isak, who has learned how to study, to heal, and to preserve life, has not been alive to a woman's (nor to his own) feelings, and so he has had to watch the women in his life, although they loved him, turn to other men. He has learned, to paraphrase Freud's formula for adulthood, to work but not to love. Here, in fact, a psychoanalytic interpretation seems inescapable. For why does he once more turn to Sara, who, again, personifies the young mother: "If you had only stayed with me"? We must assert an infantile trauma behind these scenes of seduction with which, it is clear, he has unconsciously colluded in his adult life. It is what Freud has called the primal scene, the child's observation or imagination of parental lovemaking that makes an Oedipus out of the boy and alienates him from his own Id—the snaky swamp—as well as from betraying parents. What does the charred ladder mean? Is it an existential or a sexual symbol? Could it not represent the stages of life, rung after rung, here marred by what was burnt out on each?

New Life

As Borg wakes up, he finds that the car is standing still and that he is alone with Marianne. The "children" are in the woods. And he tells her what he thinks his dreams are trying to reveal to him: that he is dead, although he is alive. Her gaze darkens and she, once more perceiving a generational threat, says that Evald had used exactly the same words. "About me," says Isak, "Yes, I can believe that." But she counters, "No, about himself." A man of thirty-eight! Isak now begs to be told "everything."

So Marianne describes a haunting talk with Evald— the very talk that made her come to see whether Isak might be of help. She had taken Evald for a ride to the sea. Parked there, she had told him that she was pregnant. From her words it is clear that neither Evald nor she had tried much to prevent this. She intended to have the child. Evald had reacted as if trapped. He walked out into the rain, and as she followed him he refused to agree to any development that would force him "to exist another day longer than I want to"—not to speak of being responsible for a new human being. He referred to himself as an unwanted child, conceived in a marriage that was hell—and could he even be sure he was Borg's son? At the end, he cursed her "damned need to live, to exist and create life." Listening silently, Isak can only ask Marianne whether she does not wish to smoke.

She now sums up what we have learned of Isak's mother, of himself, and of his son as "more frightening than death itself." Not even the person she "loves more than anyone else" can take this child from her. Isak suddenly feels "shaken as never before." Perhaps he realizes what his first dream had tried to tell him. "Can I help you?," he asks.

Thus, in seemingly small matters and in small but significant gestures, some measure of *Care* is restored. But so has the power of *Rejectivity* been revealed, indeed from generation to generation. For if our generative concerns are held together by a world image which dictates what we consider relevant for the generational succession of our own "kind," it is clear that we are also (more or less consciously) possessed and obsessed by prejudices and convictions which exclude vigorously and even viciously some "other kinds" as weak or bad, foreign or inimical. In fact, such enmity often exists in relation to our closest neighbors—geographic, ideological, conceptual—who may share many of our generative concerns but differ in some minutiae which can suddenly loom devastatingly large; and, of course, it can exist within one's family, or be turned against one's own children, and this especially where conflicting generative concerns make them suddenly appear as outsiders or worse. And while there can be no generativity without rejectivity, human survival demands that rejectivity be counteracted by faith or by insight; for what Freud has called the narcissism of small difference, often expressed in hidden or displaced rejections, can also be projected on an overdefined otherness adhering to the very largest issues and collective antagonisms of mankind, whether these antagonisms are territorial and invite periodical warfare, or credal and deny salvation to the infidels. So we are prepared to see the stage expand from the private and the inner lives of a few individual Swedes to an ancient cathedral rich with symbols and crowded with uniforms.

The Celebration

Now the great Jubilee must be lived through. The "children" come running, bringing him "with friendly, mocking eyes" large bouquets of wildflowers, bowing and chanting that he is so wise and venerable and has, no doubt, learned all prescriptions by heart. A few more hours and they arrive at Evald's house in Lund, greeted by Agda who is breathless from all the preparations while they, she is sure, had a "relaxing and convenient" drive. Evald, very handsome in tails, asks whether Marianne wants to go to a hotel, but she says gaily that she will stay "for another night," and she intends to go to the state dinner with him. Borg, with Agda's help, dresses in his best.

The festivities? In his notes, Borg describes them thus:

> Trumpet fanfares, bells ringing, field-cannon salutes, masses of people, the giant procession from the university to the cathedral, the white-dressed garland girls, royalty, old age, wisdom, beautiful music, stately Latin sentences which echoed off the huge vaults. The students and their girls, women in bright, magnificent dresses. . . .

Truly a crowing ritual for all he was: a doctor, a teacher, a Swede, a Lutheran, a patriot, a venerable old man. But this strange, symbolic rite now seems as "meaningless as a passing dream." Nevertheless, he marches along, upright and obedient, waving to little Sara. The preliminary ceremony in the cathedral (with its Gothic niches, its saints, its crucifix) is endless, and Borg and his two old co-jubilants suffer the specific discomforts of old men in sitting it out. Finally, he stands high up to be topped by the famous Lund doctor's hat. The archetypal comparison with a crown of jewels or of thorns may seem inescapable. But Borg, as he stands there, looks above and beyond the scene and begins "to see a remarkable causality in this chain of unexpected, entangled events." The English caption says something about "an extraordinary logic. . . ." Whatever the words, they seem to bespeak a revelatory sensation of grand simplicity.

In view of the trumpets, the bells, and the cannons in this populous final event, we must pause and change our theoretical tune as well. For Borg is no longer one of a small circle of mutually significant persons containable in an automobile, but one in a row of black-robed men solemnly marching to honor the "immortals" of their own kind. We must recognize in such ceremonies a heritage of both triumph and of deadly danger for human adulthood—the very triumph and the very danger which wisdom here transcends. No doubt, this rather noisy and playful Swedish version of a crowning ceremony is one of the most benign in human history, and one can well see Dag Hammarskjöld in that place—in fact, he is buried in that cathedral. Yet, in its combination of religious, military, national, and academic symbols, it is no doubt meant to remind us that mankind, so far, has been divided into what I have come to call pseudo-species: national, ideological, or religious bodies that consider their own kind the model image of mankind as fully intended in their version of creation and history, for the survival of which they are ready to kill as well as to die. Such shared identity, narrower or broader, in combination with superior accomplishments seems to be necessary for that joint sense of the reality which permits adults in their middle years to be defended against the absolute fact of death—and thus permits the full application, between adolescence and senescence, of matured energies and gifts to what the Hindus call "the maintenance of the world." But this means that adulthood is always also imprisoned in the pseudo-species (we see this, of course, more clearly in foreigners than in ourselves) and thus has remained, to some extent, a pseudo-adulthood, falling short of the potential of an all-human maturity. At the same time, we must acknowledge a universal goal in mankind which has, over the millennia, led to larger and larger units of an ever more inclusive identity. Marx, it seems, believed in a historical trend toward such a maturation by expanding unification. He spoke of history as an *Entstebungsakt*—a word that implies an evolving all-human adulthood. He could not foresee, perhaps, that mankind, when faced with this ultimate possibility, would also invent ultimate weapons for the defense of nations and ideologies and their empires and markets.

Here I should repeat, however, that by "pseudo" I do not mean to emphasize conscious deception but the all-human tendency to create symbols, artifacts and appearances, ideologies and world images in a grandiose effort to make one's own kind a spectacular and unique sight in the universe and in history. It is a prime human dilemma that pseudo-speciation can bring out the truest and the best in loyalty and cooperation, heroism and inventiveness, while committing different human "kinds" to a history of reciprocal enmity and destruction on an increasingly species-wide scale. Therefore, we have every reason to study what this moving picture so strongly reveals, namely, how large-scale adult commitments are prepared in the "politics" of small differences in everyday life and in each successive life stage. And we must learn to differentiate between the way in which such tendencies as *Exclusivity* and *Rejectivity* aggravate the *moralistic destructiveness* of public and private morals; and how virtues such as *Love* and *Care*, in turn, contribute to a more insightful and universal *ethics*.

As we thus recognize the contraries which arise in every individual as the necessary correlates of human strength, we may well pause to consider the special function which the more inclusive visions of the great religions and ideologies have had in daily life, namely, to counteract the divisive potential arising in every stage of human growth. Such "sinful" tendencies as exclusivity or rejectivity thus were counteracted, say, in the Christian world view by the universal concepts of Agape and Caritas. The subtle sarcasm, however, which pervades the ceremonial scenes of our moving picture serves to point to the ritualisms which in an idolistic and formalistic fashion soon take hold of any innovative world image—ritualisms which for a while may serve some conservational purpose but are apt sooner or later to neglect the vital interplay of historical change and individual life cycles.

In the meantime, we may grant even a certain character type of Swedish doctor and professor, and so obviously an affluent member of the middle class, a moment of integrity which expresses the destiny of the old anywhere, where personal and social conditions favor an integrative revelation offered in the very structure of existence. Where such conditions are wanting, whether for poverty or for affluence, for laissez-faire or autocracy, our critique and our protest must gain purpose and direction from the study of the resulting misery. It is the merit of *Wild Strawberries*, as of any other great drama, that implicit in it is also a social critique: one may consider only the suggestions of possessiveness and feudalism (recall the high walls around Mother Borg's lonely house) in Isak's and his son's isolation.

The Evening

Dr. Borg's moment of revelation is followed by restrained and therefore all the more universal signs that the "remarkable causality" which the old doctor had envisioned at the height of the ceremony is already working in those most closely related to his fate. Borg does not attend the banquet: for him, the day is over. He takes a cab home and finds Agda (who in the cathedral had watched him with possessive pride) making his bed and arranging his things just the way he likes them. In this quiet after the storm he tries to make peace with her. He even apologizes for his behavior that morning, which now seems long ago. She asks him once more whether he is perhaps not quite well. He answers dreamily, in words that must, indeed, alarm her, whether it is really so unusual for him "to ask forgiveness." He even offers her the mutual use of the more familiar *du* (equivalent to addressing one by his first name in English), but she "begs to be excused from all intimacies" and departs, pointedly leaving her door slightly ajar. She is, perhaps, still hoping for her ceremony. But all this impresses one as being their normal relationship, with an added touch of friendship.

Then he hears an utterly youthful duet, accompanied by a guitar, in the garden. Lifting the blinds, he sees "the children" serenading him. Sara announces that they have secured a ride all the way to Hamburg (with a deaconess). Finally, little Sara, supported by the garden wall, lifts up her eyes to his inclined face and says with playful feminine intuition: "Goodby, Father Isak. Do you know that it is really you I love, today, tomorrow, and forever?" Then they are gone.

He hears whispering voices in the foyer: Evald and Marianne. Evald comes to say goodnight. Marianne, it appears, has lost a heel, so she had to come home before the dance. Isak asks him to sit down. What is going to happen with them?

> EVALD: I have asked her to remain with me.
> ISAK: And how will it . . . I mean . . .
> EVALD: I can't be without her.
> ISAK: You mean you can't live alone?
> EVALD: I can't be without her. That's what I mean.
> ISAK: I understand.
> EVALD: It will be as she wants.

Then Isak finds himself mentioning the loan. Evald protests that he will pay it back. Isak: "I did not mean that." Evald insists. But at least, the "debt" is now a question of money only.

Marianne appears, dressed in rustling white. She asks whether he likes the shoes she is wearing. In some of the longest such shots, they fully face each other, exchanging thanks and saying, "I like you."

The couple leaves. Isak hears his heart bump and his old watch tick. The tower clock strikes eleven. It begins to rain. Preparing for sleep, he wanders back once more to the strawberry patch. It is summer. Everybody is there. Sara runs toward him, calling him "darling" and telling him that there are no strawberries left. The aunt wants him to find her father. Isak says: "I have already searched for him, but I cannot find either Father or Mother." But she takes him by the hand. Down by the beach "on the other side of the dark water," he sees "a gentleman" fishing, and further up the bank, his mother, in bright summer dress, reading. Isak can not make himself heard. But his father waves and his mother nods, both smiling in recognition. A truly primal scene. He tries to shout, but his cries "did not reach their destination." Yet, he felt "rather light-hearted."

Borg has arrived at the beginning: his first childhood. We could now, as usual in our work, reconstruct the stages of life from the first *Hope* up the whole intact ladder of developmental strengths which old Borg, as any old person, has lived by—or has now learned to mourn. How childlike or how childish his second childhood will be is left open.

Notes on a Conception of the Human Life Cycle

I must now amplify and make more systematic the brief formulation of the stages of life that I have so far used only as annotations to Bergman's scenes. I will use these scenes, in turn, as a way of illustrating a conception of the human life cycle to be presented in the form of a checkered chart. For if I set down once more the principles that guided me in formulating a succession of life stages, it is in order to reflect on the nature of a total conception.

Formulated world views contain, within larger and even eternal temporal perspectives, images of the course of life, or, at any rate, of ideal and evil adulthood, with varying perspectives on the preceding period of growing up toward this middle estate and the final period of decline and dying. The rare emphasis that the gospels place on the relation of a lasting childlikeness to the coming Kingdom must be seen as a prophetic countervoice to the ancient attitude toward the child as one who, if it survives at all, must be fashioned in the adult mold. For all world views must come to terms with the irreversible ambiguities and contradictions arising from the fact that the human species (besides other extreme specializations) must undergo a protracted period in which to grow up and to grow into the specifications of a given group in a given place on earth in a given period of history. Other species "know" where they belong, and their instinctual energies are tuned to their instinctive patterns of living. Human instinctuality employs a drive equipment of loves and hates that must be ready for a great variety of social settings in which to learn the intricacies of technology and the style of customs; wherefore it is characterized by a conflict-ridden dialectic of excessive drive energy and stringent inhibition, of anarchic license and fateful repression and self-restriction. It is, again, the world religions which have striven to provide an all-inclusive world view for the containment of such human extremes as self-seeking vanity and self-abnegating humility, ruthless power-seeking and loving surrender, a search for beliefs worth dying and killing for, and a wish to empathize and understand. As I have put it in my Jefferson Lectures, there seem to be two poles to human endeavor, namely, the felt necessity to "survive and kill" where both the territorial survival and the cultural identity of a human subspecies seem to depend on the defensive or offensive exclusion of (all) others; and the precept "die and become" where, on the contrary, ascetic self-denial to the point of self-sacrifice appears to be the only means to becoming more inclusively human. We know the long and violent history of the attempt on the part of empires and creeds alternately to counterpoint and reconcile or refute and exclude the belief systems that emerge from the truly "dread"-ful human dilemma of having to reconcile a heightened need for generational renewal in a "real" Here and Now with the certainty of individual death.

One must begin with such fundamentals if one wishes to understand the necessity for adults to arrive at some formula of adulthood and to gain some objective perspective on its precursors. Thus, one of the few grand divisions of life into stages, namely, the Hindu *asramas*, clearly acknowledges a broad middle range of "householding" in the service of the "maintenance of the world," preceded by a well defined age of apprenticeship and followed by a transcendence of the individual life cycle and an entry into a cycle of rebirths. This scheme, however, has little to say about the stages of childhood. And in Shakespeare's seven ages there is, between the mewling infant and the sighing lover, only the whining schoolboy. But then we must consider how long it took enlightened humanistic and scientific mankind to acknowledge and to chart the existence of developmental stages—physical and emotional, cognitive and social—in childhood and youth, not to speak of the highly diverse history of the treatment of children through the ages as creatures existing and developing at the whim of fate—and of the adults. No doubt, there has been a deep-seated adult

resistance (first discovered and explained by Freud) not only to the remembrance of one's own childhood, but also to the recognition in
children of developmental potentials which may upset the adult conviction of occupying in the universe a safe and sanctioned place with a
well defined point of view. Only the century of the child has made us
study childhood and, indeed, youth, not only as the causal precursors
of adulthood as it was and is, but also as a potential promise for what
adulthood may yet become. We still face powerful problems arising
from the relativity adhering to the adult's task of defining his position
as a person and as an observer in ongoing life.

As we pursue our specialized conceptions of the cycle of life, matters of overall orientation of mood remain with us, either in the ambiguities and contradictions inherent in the material under observation
or in controversies over our choice of formulations. When I, as a psychoanalyst, for example, describe a psychosocial scheme in which I
postulate for each stage of life an interplay between certain qualities
from which emerges, under favorable conditions, a new "virtue" or
vital strength, a number of recurrent questions arise. Do I do this on
the basis of clinical interpretation, thus succumbing either to the fatal-
ism of the psychopathologist or to the optimism of the therapeutic
utopian? Or am I pursuing a humanistic ideal with unavowed moralistic or esthetic demands impossible to live up to in daily life? Is my view
period- and classbound and does it suggest either conformity to the requirements of a given social milieu or, on the contrary, indulgence in
self-actualization? Do the overprivileged abide by such a scheme, and
can the underprivileged afford it, should they want it? And, closer to
home, are the assumed strivings conscious or unconscious?

Such questions are, of course, legitimate, and we have every reason to pose them to ourselves, whatever our method, for they may
open up unduly neglected aspects of the matter. But we must also recognize in them the (often cyclic) recurrence of attempts to resolve in
some dogmatic manner the ambiguities and contradictions adhering
to adulthood itself. For even quite methodical and well trained persons when faced with the question of adult values are apt to revive the
totalistic tendencies of their youth, whether they reassert or disavow
the stance once held. For what is at stake here are matters of professional identity and of belief systems couched in theory. Then there are
the pervasive trends of the times. For example, in critical and uncriti-
cal references to my scheme, the list of "negatives" *(Isolation, Stagnation, Despair)* are often blithely omitted, wherefore I appear—to some
for better and to others for worse— to postulate a series of ideal ac-

complishments *(Love, Care, Wisdom)* as desirable "achievements" for which the proper prescriptions should and must be found.

Here, I can do no more than to restate briefly the origin of my formulations in the history of my field. Many of us who have worked not only clinically but also in child guidance and in the development of children have recognized it to be our generation's task to demonstrate the complementarity between the so-called genetic point of view in psychoanalysis and a *developmental* one. The genetic approach reconstructs the way major emotional disturbances are rooted in early traumatic events which tend to exert a regressive pull on the present, and it opens the "pre-historic" part of the human life cycle, and thus the unconscious dynamics of human conflict, to systematic inspection. The developmental approach, in turn, is based on the direct observation of children: following the genetic leads, it opens our awareness to the full developmental potentials of all stages of life—that is, both the later stages, when disturbances often become fully manifest, and the earlier ones, to which they are clearly related. Furthermore, in developing or contributing to an inclusive human psychology, psychoanalysis can not shirk the task of accounting not only for the way the individual ego holds the life cycle together, but also for the laws which connect generational cycles with individual ones—and the social process with both. My terms reflect this original task, even as the first formulation of psychosocial stages is grounded in Freud's original discovery of the psychosexual stages in childhood and their fateful relationship to the major psychopathological syndromes at all ages. In my extension of the principle of stages to adulthood and old age, the dystonic aspect of each stage remains related to the potential for a major class of disorders. Although I have abstained from viewing Dr. Borg as a case, Bergman's remarkable clinical intuition would make it quite feasible to describe in his hero some core disturbances that might have made him (given some adverse psychogenic factors) somebody's client—a status which the professor so grimly abhors. If—to speak in diagnostic terms for a moment—his compulsive character in old age borders on the depressive and paranoid, it obviously goes back to some "classical" origins in the anal-urethral stage of libido development with its retentive-eliminative mode emphases and the resulting over-fastidiousness and strict adherence to mutually exclusive categories in matters of value. Yet, if we let our observations tell us not only what could go wrong in each stage but also what is all set to go right, we can well see what kept such a man together all those years for his crowning day.

But what, some will ask, justifies the introduction into a developmental scheme of such old-fashioned terms as *Wisdom* or *Hope?* And what could be their relationship to the unconscious conflicts that Freud has demonstrated to be central to human development? Can hope, for example, be unconscious? The answer is that hope is a prime adaptive ego quality, pervading consciousness and yet immerging in and remerging from the dynamic interplay of conscious and unconscious forces. Whether somebody judges himself, or is judged by others, to be full of hope and whether or not he is motivated to make the most of it by occasional or persistent display are matters of personality and of social role. Another is the pervasive, though not necessarily always visible, and most contagious rudimentary quality of hopefulness which (as its loss in the deepest regressions indicates) emerges from the earliest experiences of abandonment as well as of closeness and which, throughout life, must rely on the power of unconscious processes as well as on some confirmation by fate—and by faith.

If we say that Dr. Borg's initial statement of his old-age conditions seem to describe admirably a state of mind governed by a struggle for *Integrity* versus a sense of *Despair* and *Disgust,* and that out of this conflict a certain *Wisdom* may emerge under favorable personal and cultural conditions, then we certainly do not postulate the achievement of a total victory of *Integrity* over *Despair* and *Disgust,* but simply a dynamic balance in *Integrity*'s favor. "Versus" is an interesting little word, because it can mean a reciprocal antagonism carried further in "vice versa." Developmentally, it suggests a dialectic dynamics, in that the final strength postulated could not emerge without either of the contending qualities; yet, to assure growth, the syntonic, the one more intent on adaptation, must absorb the dystonic. If *Hope* is the first and fundamental human strength, emerging from *Primal Trust* versus *Primal Mistrust,* it is clear that the human infant must experience a goodly measure of mistrust in order to learn to trust discerningly, and that there would be neither conviction nor efficacy in an overall hopefulness without a (conscious and unconscious) struggle with a persistent temptation to succumb to hopelessness. Dr. Borg's initial condition illustrates how unconvincing a sense of integrity can be if it does not remain answerable to some existential despair and some disgust with the repetitiveness of human pretenses—including, of course, one's own. In speaking here of various "senses of," however, we refer only to their more conscious aspects, while *Integrity,* like all the other strengths, obviously must have foundations deep in the pre-

Chart 1. The Interplay of Successive Life Stages

	1	2	3	4	5	6	7	8
H. OLD AGE								Integrity vs. Despair, Disgust: WISDOM
G. MATURITY							Generativity vs. Self-Absorption: CARE	
F. YOUNG ADULTHOOD						Intimacy vs. Isolation: LOVE		
E. ADOLESCENCE					Identity vs. Identity Confusion: FIDELITY			
D. SCHOOL AGE				Industry vs. Inferiority: COMPETENCE				
C. PLAY AGE			Initiative vs. Guilt: PURPOSE					
B. EARLY CHILDHOOD		Autonomy vs. Shame, Doubt: WILL						
A. INFANCY	Trust vs. Mistrust: HOPE							

Chart 2

Maladaptive Tendency		Adaptive Strength		Malignant Tendency	
I. (Sensory Maladjustment)	Trust	HOPE		Mistrust	(Withdrawal)
II. (Shameless Willfulness)	Autonomy	WILL		Shame/ Doubt	(Compulsion)
III. (Ruthlessness)	Initiative	PURPOSE		Guilt	(Inhibition)
IV. (Narrow Virtuosity)	Industriousness	COMPETENCE		Inferiority	(Inertia)
V. (Fanaticism)	Identity Cohesion	FIDELITY		Role Confusion	(Repudiation)
VI. (Promiscuity)	Intimacy	LOVE		Isolation	(Exclusivity)
VII. (Overextension)	Generativity	CARE		Stagnation	(Rejectivity)
VIII. (Presumption)	Integrity	WISDOM		Despair	(Disdain)

conscious and the unconscious as the reservoir of what was distilled in the whole previous course of life, even as *Despair* and *Disgust* emerge only as the latest expression of fear, anxiety, and dread that have pervaded previous stages. *Despair* tells us that time is too short if not altogether too late for alternate roads to *Integrity;* this is why the elderly try to "doctor" their memories. Rationalized bitterness and disgust can mask that despair, which in severe psychopathology aggravates a senile syndrome of depression, hypochondria, and paranoic hate. For whatever chance man has to transcend the limitations of his self seems to depend on his full (if often tragic) engagement in the one and only life cycle permitted to him. By the same token, a civilization and its belief systems can be measured by the meaning they give to the full cycle of life, for such meaning (or the lack of it) cannot fail to reach into the beginnings of future generations.

All this was assumed when I came to the formulation that *Wisdom,* in whatever systematic or implicit, eloquent or quiet way it may be expressed, *is the detached and yet active concern with life itself in the face of death itself, and that it maintains and conveys the integrity of experience in spite of the Disdain over human failings and the Dread of ultimate non-being.* It will prove easiest, with the help of our movie, to illustrate the diagrammatic scheme for the cycle of life if we immediately counterpoint this last stage to the very first one. I have postulated that the first and most basic human strength of *Hope* emerges from the earliest conflict between *Primal Trust* and *Primal Mistrust.* Here, the formulation goes: *Hope is the enduring belief in the attainability of primal wishes, in spite of the dark urges and rages which mark the beginnings of existence and leave a lasting residue of threatening Estrangement.* Hope, then, is the ontogenetic basis of what in adulthood becomes faith; it is nourished in childhood by the parental faith which pervades patterns of care. It is almost unnecessary to reiterate that the movie's last scenes, in the face-to-face emphasis on mutual recognition and trust, can be related both to the primal meeting of the eyes of the newborn with those of the maternal person and to St. Paul's dictum about what is beyond the glass darkly.

If I now distribute the stages of life and the life crisis in a diagram, *Hope* "belongs" in the lower left corner and *Wisdom* in the upper right, while the horizontal and the vertical meet in the upper left. All the earlier conflicts can thus be seen to reach into, and to be renewed on, the level of the last, as they are on each level in between—but always renewed in terms of the conflict which dominates that level. In A8, then, *Primal Trust* and *Wisdom* meet, and so do *Primal Mistrust* and *Despair.*

But here another problem of theory enters that easily becomes one of ideology: are we saying that the need for a faith is "nothing but" a life-long fixation on primal trust, childlike in the beginning and illusional at the end? Or that primal trust is "simply" the ontogenetic foundation of a capacity for some faith necessary both for terminal peace and for the renewal of life from generation to generation?

The movie, as we saw, links the contemporary cast of individuals who appear in the course of Borg's journey with the important figures of his early years, and it thus gives us a chance to populate the empty boxes on the top line of the chart.

At this point, however, I must spell out the *epigenetic* principle which alone excuses the use of such a chart:

(a) Each combination of primal qualities had its stage of ascendance when physical, cognitive, emotional, and social developments permit its coming to a crisis. These stages of ascendance constitute the diagonal.

(b) Each such stage has its precursors (below the diagonal) which must now be brought up (vertically) to "their" maturational crisis.

(c) Each such crisis (as already stated) must at the advent of succeeding crises (above the diagonal) be brought up to the new level of the then dominant conflict.

In Borg's case it is clear how his own terminal conflicts open up all his earlier ones, as personified by the younger persons who confront him (in fact or in fantasy) on his journey. To enter what we already know on the top line from right to left, his own ruefully unresolved crisis of *Generativity versus Stagnation* (H8) is renewed by his confrontation with Marianne, who herself is undergoing this same crisis in its age-specific form (H7) and is forcing her husband Evald to face it on his level. Borg's unresolved *Intimacy Crisis* (H6) we also reencountered, personified in the "accidental" couple, the Almans, and relived in his reveries and dreams.

These are the adult stages proper. They first emerge when a person is ready to commit the strengths, which have matured earlier, to the "maintenance of the world" in historical space and time. They now must combine in the qualities of *Love* and *Care, Love* matures through the crisis of *Intimacy versus Isolation;* it establishes a mutuality with new individuals in wider affiliations, thus transcending the exclusivity of earlier dependencies. *Care,* in turn, is the concrete concern for what has been generated by love, necessity, or accident, thus counteracting the *Rejectivity,* which resists the commitment to such obligation.

Nobody in this cast, however, nor, indeed, in life is neatly "located" in one stage; rather, all persons can be seen to oscillate between at least two stages and move more definitely into a higher one only when an even higher one begins to determine the interplay: thus, if Borg, in the last stage that can be formulated as developmental, is in a renewed struggle with the two earlier ones, he is so in the face of death or, at any rate, senility; and if Marianne's struggle for generativity is still weighed down by that for intimacy, she is also alarmed at her—and especially her husband's—increasing age and threatening ossification.

Moving further left on the chart and thus to the contemporary representatives of ever earlier stages of life, we encounter the triad of young people. The young men, as we saw, are still in the midst of the struggle for *Identity* and certainly in the grips of some *Identity Confusion* which they are trying to resolve by pointing up (and underscoring with blows) each other's inconsistencies. Little Sara, however, will not let them forget the approaching stage when being "in love" must mature into *Love* and when "intimacies" must amount to a pervasive sense of, and capacity for, *Intimacy*. What is still awake of Borg's *Identity Crisis* (H5) comes to the fore in the declamations of the midday meal and in a playful, even impulsive, yielding to feelings and notions which might well have become a more important part of his identity had they not been finally subdued by the loss of Sara, who is, as first loves are apt to be, both the female Other and the feminine Self—that is, the Self which such a man considers too feminine to acknowledge. To continue our formulations: *Fidelity is the ability to sustain loyalties freely pledged in spite of the inevitable contradictions and confusions of value systems.* It is the cornerstone of identity, and it receives inspiration from confirming ideologies and affirming companions.

The consideration of the twelve squares in the chart's upper right corner reminds us of another pervasive misunderstanding. For theoretical, as well as clinical, historical, and autobiographic reasons,[2] Identity terms have been emphasized in my writings and have subsequently been widely accepted or rejected on the assumption that in my scheme *Identity* was the teleological aim and end of growing up. The *Identity Crisis* is, to say the least, pivotal; but Dr. Borg's case illustrates poignantly what happens when *Identity*, because of some earlier partial arrests and especially because of a retreat from *Intimacy*, is overdefined in terms of occupation and civic role and whatever character restriction they may foster. The "achievement" of an overformulated identity, then, may sacrifice too early a measure of *Identity Confusion* salutary for some playful variability in later choices.

In this connection, it must be emphasized that all the psychosocial strengths associated with our scheme postulate an active adaptation rather than a passive adjustment—that is, they change the environment even as they make selective use of its opportunities. Thus, the "maintenance of the world" could by no means be effected by mere servitude and compliance; it means rather a continuous reciprocal facilitation of social and psychological development and of larger and smaller institutions and—where such facilitation has become impossible—radical changes in social mores and institutions. It is for this reason that the study of the life cycle leads to that of biography and history and of social and economic conditions. The implication here is that, if individuals do not find in daily ritualizations as well as in the rituals of a society that affirmation and confirmation suggested here, both individual and generational cycles will show symptoms of pathology that point to specific needs for social change. We can, at any rate, recognize in Victor, Anders, and little Sara some readiness for ideological controversies that could, in principle, involve them in a turbulent moratorium or in some ideological movement of varying revolutionary or reactionary potentials. The actual social involvements of our young ideologists seem as yet open, even as they watch with some mixture of awe and mockery how the older generation goes about honoring itself. As for Marianne, I can well see her taking an active hand in communal life, after her encounter with the mixture of professional service and generational isolation presented by her two doctors.

To conclude, in speaking of the human life cycle and of the place of adulthood and of old age in it, no conception would be sufficient without reference to the *relativity* of the three cycles:

(a) All the emergent strengths are necessary to complete the individual cycle, although, as we saw, no such cycle can escape variable emphases on the inhibiting and isolating qualities of human development which foster fear and anxiety.

(b) Any fulfillment of the individual life cycle, far from being simply a matter of finding terminal clarity, can only fulfill what is given in the order of things by remaining responsible and by contributing continuous solutions to the ongoing cycle of generations.

The generational cycle in all its intricacies, in turn, is vital to the maintenance of evolving *social structures* which must facilitate the emergence of the life stages or else suffer social and political pathology.

According to the retrospective logic of this presentation, we conclude with a few formulations concerning the stages of childhood. As

Dr. Borg, on his journey, crosses the Swedish countryside (and moves further left on our chart), he encounters his erstwhile patients who obviously represent his most satisfying personal involvement in the "maintenance of the world" at a time when his sexual and familial intimacy was slowly going bankrupt. His patients had provided the renewal in his adult life of the strengths he had developed throughout his childhood and youth: the strength of *Purposefulness* and of *Competence* which also came to occupy the center of his *Fidelity.*

Let me add here the corresponding formulations: Rudimentary *Purposefulness is the courage playfully to imagine and energetically to pursue valued goals, uninhibited by the defeat of infantile fantasies, by the guilt they aroused, and by the punishment they elicited.* It invests ideals of action, and it is derived from the example of the childhood milieu. *Competence,* in turn, *is the free exercise of dexterity and intelligence in the completion of tasks, unimpaired by infantile inferiority.* It is the basis for cooperative participation in technologies, and it relies, in turn, on the logic of tools and skills. But if the first one, namely, *Competence,* emerges from the infantile struggle of *Industry versus Inferiority,* and *Purpose* from that of *Initiative versus Guilt,* these original conflicts are faced in the doctor's reveries and dreams. His examination dream, as we saw, confronts him with the fact that his very competence in professional life has permitted him to become insensitive to a deep feeling of inadequacy (here expressed in his failure to recognize when a woman and, by implication, when he himself is "dead" or "alive") and to bypass his deepseated sense of being "guilty of guilt."

The vivid reverie of his early childhood milieu leads back to an even earlier stage in childhood (B2) in which the rudiments of a person's *Will* receive some lasting characteristics as it emerges from the conflict between a sense of *Autonomy* and the sense of *Shame*—which, like *Guilt,* is deeply ingrained in the human make-up and is used by all cultures to impose special choices and restrictions on a child's development. *Will is the unbroken determination to exercise free choice as well as self-control, in spite of early experiences of shame and self-doubt caused by uncontrolled willfulness and of rage over being controlled.* As we saw, the great childhood scene illustrates with vital humor how all the children and young people learn to stand up to the demanding and scolding aunt who represents, no doubt, in a reverie all too benign, the potentially cruel, moralistic side of such a milieu. The implication seems to be, quite in accord with psychopathology and characterology, that Isak, more than any of the other children, submitted to his milieu's moralism to an extent that restricted his spontaneity and playfulness, and that this made him, in fact, the compulsive character that he became.

But as Sara, who had by then assumed the role of the young maternal person, leads Isak to the shore where he and his parents exchange smiles of recognition—if now at the safe distance of terminal resignation—she seems to restore the trust of the first stage, without which Isak could not have become what he is and could not have dreamed as he did.

I hope to have indicated in the first part of this paper that a good story does not need a chart to come alive and, in the second, that a chart, and especially one with so many empty boxes, can use a good story.

NOTES

1. I. Bergman, *Four Screenplays of Ingmar Bergman,* trans. Lars Malmstrom and David Kushner (New York: Simon and Schuster, 1960).

2. Erik H. Erikson, " 'Identity Crisis' in Autobiographic Perspective," in *Life History and the Historical Moment* (New York: W. W. Norton, 1975), pp. 17–47.

CHAPTER 13

From *Young Man Luther*

ERIK H. ERIKSON

1

Nietzsche's fitting diagnosis that Luther wanted to speak to God directly and without a trace of embarrassment describes Martin's more personal and more impatient version of St. Paul's "For now we see through a glass, darkly, but then face to face: now I know in part, but then shall I know even as also I am known." But Martin's search was also younger and sadder: "He who sees God as angry does not see Him rightly but looks upon a curtain, as if a dark cloud had been drawn across His face."

The search for mutual recognition, the *meeting face to face*, is an aspect in his and in all religion which we must consider if we are to understand the deepest nostalgia of lonely youth. True lovers know this, and they often postpone the self-loss feared in the sexual fusion in order that each may gain more identity in the other's glance. What it means *not* to be able to behold a face in mutual affirmation can be learned from young patients, who, unable to love, see, in their more regressed states, the face of the therapist disintegrate before their horrified eyes, and feel themselves fall apart into fragments of oblivion. One young man patient drew and painted dozens of women's faces, cracked like broken vases, faded like worn flowers, with hard and ungiving eyes, or with eyes like stars, steely and blinking, far away; only when he had painted a whole and healthy face did he know that he could be cured, and that he was a painter. As one studies such symptoms and works them through in therapeutic encounters, one can only become convinced of the astonishing fact that these patients have partially regressed to a stage in the second part of the first year and that they are trying to recover what was then achieved by the concordance of cognitive and emotional maturation—namely, the recognition of the facial features of familiar persons, the joy of feeling recognized when they come, and the sorrow of feeling disapproved of when they frown; and, then the gradual mastery of the horror of the strange face.

It is remarkable to behold how in the infant's development into a human-being with the capacity for a firm "object-relationship"—the ability to love in an individualized sense—growing cognitive ability and maturing emotional response early converge on the face. An infant of two to three months will smile even at half a face; he will even smile at half a painted dummy face, if that half is the upper half of the face, is fully represented, and has at least two clearly defined points or circles for eyes; more the infant does not need, but he will not smile for less. Gradually, however, other conditions are added, such as the outline of a (not necessarily smiling) mouth; and only toward the eighth month does the child energetically indicate that certainly no dummy and not even a smiling face as such can make him respond with maximum recognition; from then on he will only respond to familiar people who act as he has learned to expect—and act friendly. But with this recognition of familiarity and friendliness also comes the awareness of strangeness and anger; not because the child, as many parents feel, has suddenly become fearful, but because he now "knows," he has an investment in those who are committed to his care, and he fears the loss of that investment and the forfeiture of that commitment. The activity which begins with something akin to a small animal's inborn response to minimum cues develops, through the gradual recognition of the human face and its expression, to that degree of social discrimination and sensitivity which marks the human being. And once he has made the investment in humanity and its learning processes, the human child knows fears and anxieties quite unthinkable in the small animal which, if it survives at all, has its environment cut out for it as a field of relatively simple and repetitive signs and techniques.

Mothers, of course, and people with motherly responses, like to think that when even a small baby smiles, he is recognizing them individually as the only possible maternal person, as the mother. This, up to a point, is good. For the timespan of man's dependence on the personal and cultural style of the person or persons who first take care of him is very long: and the firmness of his early ego-development depends on the inner consistency of the style of that person. Therefore, the establishment of a mutual "fixation"—of a binding need for mutual recognition between mother and child—is essential. In fact, the infant's instinctive smile seems to have exactly that purpose which is its crowning effect, namely, that the adult feels recognized, and in return expresses recognition in the form of loving and providing. In the beginning are the generous breast and the eyes that care. Could this be one of the countenances which religion promises us we shall see again, at the end and in another world? Is there an ethology of religion?

Those who fail in their once-bornness want to have another chance at being born. It often seems as though they want to be made over by the same mothers who give physical birth to them; but this, as we can now see, would be too literal an assumption. For that "first birth," to which all of their symptoms are related, is the emergence of their consciousness as individuals, a consciousness born from the interplay of recognitions. Whoever is the maternal attendant to that early phase is man's first "environment," and whatever environment is then first experienced as such remains associated with "mother." On the security of that first polarisation of a self and a maternal matrix are built all subsequent securities. "Mother" is the person (or the persons) who knows how to convincingly offer provision and screening: the provisions of food, warmth, stimulation in answer to the infant's searching mouth, skin, and senses; and the screening of the quality and quantity of his intake so as to avoid both over- and understimulation. The new human being, therefore, experiences his appetites and aversions together with the personal care (and care means provision and caution) he gets. They form his first world; but so do those moments when he feels uncared for, alone with his discomfort and his rage. For these, however, he has at his disposal signals with an immediate appeal to the mother, which sooner or later bring more or less response from her: the regularity and predictability of her responses are the infant's first world order, the original paradise of provision. During the first year of life, the reality of the provider thus gradually emerges from the original matrix as a coherent experience, a verified fact, a sound investment of love and trust—and the infant has matured enough to experience coherently, verify reasonably, and invest courageously.

This bipolarity of recognition is the basis of all social experience. Let nobody say that it is only the beginning, it passes, and it is, after all, childish. Man is not organized like an archaeological mound, in layers; as he grows he makes the past part of all future, and every environment, as he once experienced it, part of the present environment.

Dreams and dreamlike moments, when analysed, always reveal the myriad past experiences which are waiting outside the gates of consciousness to mingle with present impressions. Man at all times wants to be sure that the original bipolarity is intact, especially when he feels tired, doubtful, unsure, alone—a fact which has been utilized by both theology and psychoanalysis.

In that first relationship man learns something which most individuals who survive and remain sane can take for granted most of the time. Only psychiatrists, priests, and born philosophers know how sorely that something can be missed. I have called this early treasure "basic trust"; it is the first psychosocial trait and the fundament of all others. Basic trust in mutuality is that original "optimism," that assumption that "somebody is there," without which we cannot live. In situations in which such basic trust cannot develop in early infancy because of a defect in the child or in the maternal environment, children die mentally. They do not respond nor learn; they do not assimilate their food and fail to defend themselves against infection, and often they die physically as well as mentally.

One may well claim for that earliest meeting of a perceiving subject with a perceived object (which, in turn seems to "recognize" the subject) the beginning of all sense of identity; this meeting thus becomes the anchor-point for all the developments which culminate, at the end of adolescence, in the establishment of psychosocial identity. At that point, an ideological formula, intelligible both in terms of individual development and of significant tradition, must do for the young person what the mother did for the infant: provide nutriment for the soul as well as for the stomach, and screen the environment so that vigorous growth may meet what it can manage.

Of all the ideological systems, however, only religion restores the earliest sense of appeal to a Provider, a Providence. In the Judaeo-Christian tradition, no prayer indicates this more clearly than "The Lord make His Face to shine upon you and be gracious unto you. The Lord lift up His countenance upon you and give you peace"; and no prayerful attitude better than the uplifted face, hopeful of being recognized. The Lord's countenance is apt to loom too sternly, and His son's on the cross to show the enigmatic quality of total abandonment in sacrifice; but painters and sculptors fashion a faintly smiling face for the Madonna, graciously inclined toward the infant, who responds with peace and gaiety until, in the Renaissance, he stands up and, fully confident, motions away from her. We can see the search for the same smile of peace in the work of Eastern painters and sculptors, although their Buddhas seem closer to being the over-all parent *and* the child, all in one. It is art, the work of the visually gifted and the visually driven, in conjunction with religion, which puts such emphasis on the face; thought expresses the original symbiotic unity as a state of being firmly and yet flexibly held, imbedded in a *Way*.

One must work with children who cannot learn to say *I*, although they are otherwise healthy, and beautiful, and even soulful, to know what a triumph that common gift of "I" is, and how much it depends on the capacity to feel affirmed by maternal recognition. One basic task of all religions is to reaffirm that first relationship, for we have in us deep down a lifelong mistrustful remembrance of that truly *meta*-physical anxiety; *meta*—"behind," "beyond"—here means "before," "way back," "at the beginning." One basic form of heroic asceticism, therefore, one way of liberating man from his existential delimitations, is to retrace the steps of the development of the I, to forgo even object relations in the most primitive sense, to step down and back to the borderline where the I emerged from its matrix. Much of Western monasticism concentrates on prayer and atonement, but the Eastern form cultivates the art of deliberate self-loss: Zen-Buddhism is probably its most systematic form.

2

"I did not know the Christchild any more," Luther said later, in characterizing the sadness of his youth: he had lost his childhood. In a moment of terror he appealed, not to the Madonna, but to his father's occupational saint, St. Anne. But he always objected to the Madonna's mediation in the then popular scheme of religion. He wanted God's recognition. A long way stretched ahead of him before he was able to experience, through Christ rather than through Mary, the relevance of the theme of mother and child in addition to that of father and son. Then he could say that Christ was defined by two images: one of an infant lying in a manger, "hanging on a virgin's tits," *and* one of a man sitting at his Father's right hand.

But what destroyed in our infantile past, and what destroys in the depth of our adult present, that original unity which provides the imagery of our supreme hopes? All religions and most philosophers agree that it is will—the mere will to live, thoughtless and cruel self-will. In one of the few passionate passages of his *Varieties of Religious Experience*, William James describes specifically one of the manifestations of the will to live:

The normal process of life contains moments as bad as any of those which insane melancholy is filled with, moments in which radical evil gets its innings and takes its solid turn. The lunatic's visions of horror are all drawn from the material of daily fact. Our civilization is founded on the shambles, and every individual existence goes out in a lonely spasm of helpless agony. If you protest, my friend, wait till you arrive there yourself! To believe in the carnivorous reptiles of geologic times is hard for our imagination—they seem too much like mere museum specimens. Yet there is no tooth in any one of those museum-skulls that did not daily through long years of the foretime hold fast to the body struggling in despair of some fated living victim. Forms of horror just as dreadful to their victims, if on a smaller spatial scale, fill the world about us today. Here on our very hearths and in our gardens the infernal cat plays with the panting mouse, or holds the hot bird fluttering in her jaws. Crocodiles and rattlesnakes and pythons are at this moment vessels of life as real as we are; their loathsome existence fills every minute of every day that drags its length along; and whenever they or other wild beasts clutch their living prey, the deadly horror which an agitated melancholiac feels is the literally right reaction on the situation.

It may indeed be that no religious reconciliation with the absolute totality of things is possible. Some evils, indeed, are ministerial to higher forms of good; but it may be that there are forms of evil so extreme as to enter into no good system whatsoever, and that, in respect of such evil, dumb submission or neglect to notice is the only practical recource.[1]

The tenor of this mood is immediately convincing. It is the mood of severe melancholy, intensified tristitia, one would almost say tristitia with teeth in it. James, at this point, takes recourse to the "geologic times" far behind us, and to the reptiles way below us—creatures who devour one another without sin and are not condemned for it by any religion. He also cites the playfully cruel domestic cat, who shares with man an ecology of intermediary human institutions. The cat does not feed itself in direct interdependence with a sector of nature, but receives food, as man does, as a result of a social division of tool-labor. The cat's relation to the mouse has thus lost the innocence of ecological interdependence, and the cat's needs are refined, like ours.

James is clinically and genetically correct, when he connects the horror of the *devouring* will to live with the content and the disposition of melancholia. For in melancholia, it is the human being's horror of his own avaricious and sadistic orality which he tires of, withdraws from, wishes often to end even by putting an end to himself. This is not the orality of the first, the toothless and dependent, stage; it is the orality of the tooth-stage and all that develops within it, especially the prestages of what later becomes "biting" human conscience. There is, it would seem, no intrinsic reason for man's feeling more guilty or more evil because he employs, enjoys, and learns to adapt his gradually maturing organs, were it not for the basic division of good and bad which, in some dark way, establishes itself very early. The image of a paradise of innocence is part of the individual's past as much as the race's. Paradise was lost when man, not satisfied with an arrangement in which he could pluck from the trees all he needed for upkeep, wanted more, wanted to have and to know the forbidden—and bit into it. Thus he came to know good and evil. It is said that after that he worked in the sweat of his brow. But it must be added that he also began to invent tools in order to wrest from nature what it would not just give. He "knew" at the price of losing innocence; he became autonomous at the price of shame and gained independent initiative at the price of guilt. Next to primary peace, then, secondary appeasement is a great infantile source of religious affect and imagery.

In a strange counterpart to the quotation from James, Luther later pictured God himself as a devourer, as if the wilful sinner could expect to find in God's demeanor a mirror of his own avarice, just as the uplifted face of the believer finds a countenance inclined and full of grace: "He gorges us, with great eagerness and wrath . . . he is an avaricious, a gluttonous fire." Thus, in the set of god-images in which the countenance of the godhood mirrors the human face, God's face takes on the toothy and fiery expression of the devil, or the expressions of countless ceremonial masks. All these wrathful countenances mirror man's own rapacious orality which destroys the innocent trust of that first symbiotic orality when mouth and breast, glance and face, are one.

The Luder family, while traditional in structure, offered an extreme degree of moralistic paternalism, and, quite probably, a minimum degree of that compensatory free-for-all of small and highly satisfying delinquencies which barnyard, street, or park can provide for lucky children. The father's prohibitory presence, and the anticipation of his punishment seem to have pervaded the family milieu, which thus became an ideal breeding ground for the most pervasive form of the Oedipus complex—the ambivalent interplay of rivalry with the father, admiration for him, and fear of him which puts such a heavy burden of guilt and inferiority on all spontaneous initiative and on all phantasy. Where rebellion and deviousness are thus successfully undercut, and where, on the other hand, the father's alcoholic, sexual, and cruel self-indulgence obviously break through his moralistic mask, a child can only develop a precocious conscience, a precocious self-steering, and eventually an obsessive mixture of obedience and rebelliousness. Hans Luder was a "jealous God," one who probably interfered early with the mother's attempt to teach her children how to be before he taught them how to strive.

At first, of course, fathers are non-mothers, the other kind of person. They may be part of the maternal environment, but their specificity is experienced only later—when, exactly, I cannot say. Freud's oedipal father has clarified much, but, as sudden clarifications do, he has also obscured much. True, fathers are impressive as the mothers' powerful counterplayers in contexts not quite knowable, and yet deeply desirable and awe-provoking. But they are also importantly involved in the awakening of the child's identity. Fathers, it appears, were there before we were, they were strong when we were weak, they saw us before we saw them; not being mothers—that is, beings who make the care of babies their business—they love us differently, more dangerously. Here, I think, is the origin of an idea attested to by myths, dreams, and symptoms, namely, that the fathers (as some animal fathers do) could have annihilated us before we became strong enough to appear as their rivals. Much of the thanks we bring to potentially wrathful gods (who, we think, know our thoughts) is really thanks for their generosity in suffering us to live at all. Thus, we owe our fathers two lives; one by way of conception (which even the most enlightened children can visualize only very late in childhood); the other by way of voluntary sponsorship, of a paternal love.

In anxiety and confusion, children often seem to take refuge from their fathers by turning back to their mothers. But this occurs only if the fathers are not there enough, or not there in the right way. For children become aware of the attributes of maleness, and learn to love men's physical touch and guiding voice, at about the time when they have the first courage for an autonomous existence—autonomous from the maternal matrix in which they only seem to want to remain forever. Fathers, if they know how to hold and guide a child, function somewhat like guardians of the child's autonomous existence. Something passes from the man's bodily presence into the child's budding self—and I believe that the idea of communion, that is, of partaking of a man's body, would not be such a simple and reassuring matter for so many were it not for that early experience. Who never felt thus generated, "grown," as an individual by his father or fathers, always feels half annihilated, and may perhaps be forced to seek a father in the mother—a role for which the mother, if she assumes it, is blamed afterwards. For there is something which only a father can do, which is, I think, to balance the threatening and forbidding aspects of his appearance and impression with the guardianship of the guiding voice. Next to the recognition bestowed by the gracious face, the affirmation of the guiding voice is a prime element of man's sense of identity. Here the question is not so much whether in the judgment of others the father is a good model or a bad one, but whether or not he is tangible and affirmative. Intangibly good fathers are the worst.

3

It takes a particular view of man's place on this earth, and of the place of childhood within a man's total scheme, to invent devices for terrifying children into submission, either by magic, or by mental and corporeal terror. When these terrors are associated with collective and ritual observances, they can be assumed to contain some inner corrective which keeps the individual child from facing life all by himself; they may even offer some compensation of belongingness and identification. Special concepts of property (including the idea that a man can ruin his own property if he wishes) underlie the idea that it is entirely up to the discretion of an individual father when he should raise the morality of his children by beating their bodies. It is clear that the concept of children as property opens the door to those misalliances of impulsivity and compulsivity, of arbitrariness and moral logic, of brutality and haughtiness, which make men crueler and more licentious than creatures not fired with the divine spark. The device of beating children down—by superior force, by contrived logic, or by vicious sweetness—makes it unnecessary for the adult to become adult. He need not develop that true inner superiority which is naturally persuasive. Instead, he is authorized to remain significantly inconsistent and arbitrary, or in other words, childish, while beating into the child the desirability of growing up. The child, forced out of fear to pretend that he is better when seen than when unseen, is left to anticipate the day when he will have the brute power to make others more moral than he ever intends to be himself.

Historically, the increasing relevance of the Roman concepts of law in [Hans] Luder's time helped to extend the concept of property so that fatherhood took on the connotation of an ownership of wife and children. The double role of the mother as one of the powerless victims of the father's brutality and also as one of his dutiful assistants in meting out punishment to the children may well account for a peculiar split in the mother image. The mother was perhaps cruel only because she had to be, but the father because he wanted to be. From the ideology inherent in such an arrangement there is—as we will see in Luther's punitive turn against the peasant rebels—only one psychological and a few political steps to those large-scale misalliances among righteousness, logic, and brutality that we find in inquisitions, concentration camps, and punitive wars.

The question, then, whether Martin's fears of the judgment day and his doubts in the justice then to be administered were caused by his father's greater viciousness, or by his own greater sensitivity, or both, pales before the general problem of man's exploitability in childhood, which makes him the victim not only of overt cruelty, but also of all kinds of covert emotional relief, of devious vengefulness, or sensual self-indulgence, and of sly righteousness—all on the part of those on whom he is physically and morally dependent. Some day, maybe, there will exist a well-informed, well-considered, and yet fervent public conviction that the most deadly of all possible sins is the mutilation of a child's spirit; for such mutilation undercuts the life principle of trust, without which every human act, may it feel ever so good and seem ever so right, is prone to perversion by destructive forms of conscientiousness.

Of Luther's mother we know little. Didn't she stand between the father and the son whom she had suckled? Whose agent was she when she beat him "for one nut"? Did she disavow him on her own when he became a monk—a disavowal responsible for her one rather sandwiched mention in the *Documents of Luther's Development*: "I became a monk," Luther is quoted as saying, "against the wishes of my father, of my mother, of God, and of the Devil." And what did she feel when she bore and lost so many children that their number and their names are forgotten? Luther does mention that some of her children "cried themselves to death," which may have been one of his after-dinner exaggerations; and at any rate, what he was talking about then was only that his mother had considered these children to have been bewitched by a neighbor woman. And yet, a friend of Luther's who visited her in her old age reported that Luther was her "spit and image."

The father seems to have been standoffish and suspicious toward the universe; the mother, it is said, was more interested in the imaginative aspects of superstition. It may well be, then, that from his mother Luther received a more pleasurable and more sensual attitude toward nature, and a more simply integrated kind of mysticism, such as he later found described by certain mystics. It has been surmised that the mother suffered under the father's personality, and gradually became embittered; and there is also a suggestion that a certain sad isolation which characterized young Luther was to be found also in his mother, who is said to have sung to him a ditty: "For me and you nobody cares. That is our common fault."

A big gap exists here, which only conjecture could fill. But instead of conjecturing half-heartedly, I will state, as a clinician's judgment, that nobody could speak and sing as Luther later did if his mother's voice had not sung to him of some heaven; that nobody could be as torn between his masculine and his feminine sides, nor have such a range of both, who did not at one time feel that he was like his mother; but also, that nobody would discuss women and marriage in the way he often did who had not been deeply disappointed by his mother— and had become loath to succumb the way she did to the father, to fate. And if the soul is man's most bisexual part, then we will be prepared to find in Luther both some horror of mystic succumbing and some spiritual search for it, and to recognize in this alternative some emotional and spiritual derivatives of little Martin's "pre-historic" relation to his mother.

Paradoxically, many a young man (and son of a stubborn one) becomes a great man in his own sphere only by learning that deep passivity which permits him to let the date of his competency speak to him. As Freud said in a letter to Fliess, "I must wait until it moves in me so that I can perceive it." This may sound feminine, and, indeed, Luther bluntly spoke of an attitude of womanly conception—*sicut mulier in conceptu*. Yet it is clear that men call such attitudes and modes feminine only because the strain of paternalism has alienated us from them; for these modes are any organism's birthright, and all our partial as well as our total functioning is based on a metabolism of passivity and activity.

The theology as well as the psychology of Luther's passivity is that of man in the *state of prayer,* a state in which he fully means what he can say only to God: *Tibi soli peccavi,* I have sinned, not in relation to any person or institution, but in relation only to God, to *my* God.

In two ways, then, rebirth by prayer is passive: it means surrender to God the Father; but it also means to be reborn *ex matrice scripturae nati,* out of the matrix of the scriptures. "Matrix" is as close as such a man's man will come to saying "mater." But he cannot remember and will not acknowledge that long before he had developed those wilful

modes which were specifically suppressed and paradoxically aggravated by a challenging father, a mother had taught him to touch the
world with his searching mouth and his probing senses. What to a
man's man, in the course of his development, seems like a passivity
hard to acquire, is only a regained ability to be active with his oldest
and most neglected modes. Is it coincidence that Luther, now that he
was explicitly teaching passivity, should come to the conclusion that a
lecturer should feed his audience as a mother suckles her child? Intrinsic to the kind of passivity we speak of is not only the memory of
having been given, but also the identification with the maternal giver:
"the glory of a good thing is that it flows out to others." I think that in
the Bible Luther at last found a mother whom he could acknowledge:
he could attribute to the Bible a generosity to which he could open
himself, and which he could pass on to others, at last a mother's son.

4

Luther inspired a religious movement which grew out of and subsequently perpetuated an extreme emphasis on the interplay of initiative and guilt, and an exclusive emphasis on the divine Father-Son.
Even in this scheme, the mother remains a counterplayer however
shadowy. Father religions have mother churches.

One may say that man, when looking through a glass darkly, finds
himself in an inner cosmos in which the outlines of three objects
awaken dim nostalgia. One of these is the simple and fervent wish for
a hallucinatory sense of unity with a maternal matrix, and a supply of
benevolently powerful substances; it is symbolized by the affirmative
face of charity, graciously inclined, reassuring the faithful of the unconditional acceptance of those who will return to the bosom. In this
symbol the split of autonomy is forever repaired: shame is healed by
unconditional approval, doubt by the eternal presence of generous
provision.

In the center of the second nostalgia is the paternal voice of guiding conscience, which puts an end to the simple paradise of childhood
and provides a sanction for energetic action. It also warns of the inevitability of guilty entanglement, and threatens with the lightning of
wrath. To change the threatening sound of this voice, if need be by
means of partial surrender and manifold self-castration, is the second
imperative demand which enters religious endeavor. At all cost, the
Godhead must be forced to indicate that He Himself mercifully
planned crime and punishment in order to assure salvation.

Finally, the glass shows the pure self itself, the unborn core of creation, the—as it were, preparental—center where God is pure nothing: *ein lauter Nichts,* in the words of Angelus Silesius. God is so designated in many ways in Eastern mysticism. This pure self is the self no longer sick with a conflict between right and wrong, not dependent on providers, and not dependent on guides to reason and reality.

These three images are the main religious objects. Naturally, they often fuse in a variety of ways and are joined by hosts of secondary deities. But must we call it regression if man thus seeks again the earliest encounters of his trustful past in his efforts to reach a hoped-for and eternal future? Or do religions partake of man's ability, even as he regresses, to recover creatively? At their creative best, religions retrace our earliest inner experiences, giving tangible form to vague evils, and reaching back to the earliest individual sources of trust; at the same time, they keep alive the common symbols of integrity distilled by the generations. If this is partial regression, it is a regression which, in retracing firmly established pathways, returns to the present amplified and clarified.[2] Here, of course, much depends on whether or not the son of a given era approaches the glass in good faith: whether he seeks to find again on a higher level a treasure of basic trust safely possessed from the beginning, or tries to find a birthright denied him in the first place, in his childhood. It is clear that each generation (whatever its ideological heaven) owes to the next a safe treasure of basic trust; Luther was psychologically and ideologically right when he said in theological terms that the infant *has* faith if his community *means* his baptism. Creative moments, however, and creative periods are rare. The process here described may remain abortive or outlive itself in stagnant institutions—in which case it can and must be associated with neurosis and psychosis, with self-restriction and self-delusion, with hypocrisy and stupid moralism.

Freud has convincingly demonstrated the affinity of some religious ways of thought with those of neurosis.[3] But we regress in our dreams, too, and the inner structures of many dreams correspond to neurotic symptoms. Yet dreaming itself is a healthy activity, and a necessary one. And here, too, the success of a dream depends on the faith one has, not on that which one seeks: a good conscience provides that proverbially good sleep which knits up the raveled sleeve of care. All the things that made man feel guilty, ashamed, doubtful, and mistrustful during the daytime are woven into a mysterious yet meaningful set of dream images, so arranged as to direct the recuperative powers of sleep toward a constructive waking state. The dreamwork fails and the dream turns into a nightmare when there is an intrusion of a sense of foreign reality into the dreamer's make-believe, and a subsequent disturbance in returning from that superimposed sense of reality into real reality.

Religions try to use mechanisms analogous to dreamlife, reinforced at times by a collective genius of poetry and artistry, to offer ceremonial dreams of great recuperative value. It is possible, however, that the medieval Church, the past master of ceremonial hallucination, by promoting the reality of hell too efficiently, and by tampering too successfully with man's sense of reality in this world, eventually created, instead of a belief in the greater reality of a more desirable world, only a sense of nightmare in this one.

I have implied that the original faith which Luther tried to restore goes back to the basic trust of early infancy. In doing so I have not, I believe, diminished the wonder of what Luther calls God's disguise. If I assume that it is the smiling face and the guiding voice of infantile parent images which religion projects onto the benevolent sky, I have no apologies to render to an age which thinks of painting the moon red. Peace comes from the inner space.

NOTES

1. W. James, *The Varieties of Religious Experience*, (Longmans, Green and Company, 1935), p. 40.

2. See E. Kris, *Psychoanalytic Explorations in Art* (International Universities Press, 1952), p. 177.

3. S. Freud, *The Future of an Illusion*, trans. W. D. Robson-Scott (Liveright Publishing Corporation, 1949).

CHAPTER 14

Ritualization in Everyday Life

ERIK H. ERIKSON

W hen in psychopathy we speak of an individual's "handwashing ritual," we mean that he scrubs his hands, in tortured solitude, until they become raw, and yet he never feels clean. But this blatantly contradicts the anthropological meaning of the word, which assigns to "ritual" a deepened communality, a proven ceremonial form, and a timeless quality from which all participants emerge with a sense of awe and purification. Ritualization in our sense is anything but neurotic symptomatology where it supports the formation of a set of behavior patterns combining human propensities in a cultural system within a circumscribed section of nature and technology. Thus daily ritualization can serve as adaptive interplay deemed central to both the natural and the social universe.

This said, it must be clear that we would expect ritualization to be a major link between the ego's propensity for orientation in space and time and the world views dominating (or competing in) a society. In psychopathology, however, we can (and should) study the way ritualized schemes of behavior have fallen apart, isolating persons and their lonely conflicts. We may then offer therapeutic ritualizations which provide new insights into human adaptation. But only in the study of "live" ritualization in everyday life can we learn how persons and conflicts find a mutual fit in generational patterns, or how, indeed, the lack of true ritualization or its decline into false ritualism can lead to social pathology.

Such insights, it seems, might be particularly important in periods of rapid change, where ritualization (of a more punitive, say, or a more permissive kind, or of a different assignment of sex roles) disintegrates under the impact of changing ideology and technology. New ritualizations, however, emerge only where some dominant ethos emerges in consonance with new material facts, a new sense of reality, and new incentives for interplay in actuality.

Infancy and the Numinous: The Light, the Face, and the Name

Let us begin, then, with the way the maternal person and the infant greet each other in the morning. The awakening infant awakens in the maternal person a whole repertoire of emotive, verbal, and manipulative behavior. She approaches him with smiling or worried concern, brightly or anxiously voicing some appellation, and goes into action: looking, feeling, sniffing, she discovers possible sources of discomfort and initiates services to be rendered by rearranging the infant's position, by picking him up, and so on. This daily event is highly ritualized, in that the mother seems to feel obliged, and not a little pleased, to repeat a performance arousing in the infant predictable responses, which, in turn, encourage her to proceed. Such ritualization is at the same time highly individual ("typical" for the particular mother and also tuned to the particular infant) and yet also stereotyped along some traditional lines subject to anthropological description. It is more or less freely given and responded to, and more or less coerced by duty. The whole procedure is superimposed on the periodicity of physical needs close to the requirements of survival; it is also an emotional necessity in the generational process; and it counts on the child's growing cognitive capacity and eagerness.

This bit of playful routine can be properly evaluated only as a small but tough link in the whole formidable sequence of generations. As mother and infant meet in the first ritualization described so far, the infant brings to the constellation his vital needs (among "instinctual" drives subsumed as oral, sensory, and tactile in libido theory) and the necessity to have disparate experiences made coherent by mothering. The mother in her postpartum state is also needful in a complex manner: for whatever instinctive sense of mothering she may be endowed with, and whatever instinctual gratification she may seek in being a mother, she also needs to become a mother of a special kind and in a special way. This she becomes by no means without an anxious avoidance (sometimes phobic, often superstitious) as well as some more or less subdued anger over the coerciveness of routine and role. Along with the positive image of a mothering received by and watched in people of her own kind, there are elements of a negative identity, namely, what she must not do or be lest she resemble "other" kinds and ways typical for persons or groups whom she (more or less consciously) dislikes or despises, hates, or fears as godless or evil, unhygienic or immoral—or guided by images of womanhood protested by her. Luckily, the mother is affirmed in her new role by identification with those who mothered her well; while her own motherhood is reaffirmed as benevolent by the increasing responsiveness of the infant. The infant, in turn, develops a benevolent self-image (a certified narcissism, we may say) grounded in the recognition of an all-powerful and mostly benevolent (if sometimes strangely malevolent) Other. While the mother's postpartum condition enhances this interplay, it is clear that sooner or later any truly maternal person can replace the "birth mother."

Let us take the fact that the mother calls the infant by a name. This may have been carefully selected and perhaps certified in some name-giving ritual, held to be indispensable by the parents and the community. Yet, whatever procedures have given meaning to the name, that meaning now exerts a certain effect on the way in which the name is repeated during the greeting procedure—together with other emphases of caring attention which have a very special meaning for the maternal person(s) and eventually for the child. Thus, the mother also refers to herself with a special designation. This mutual assignment of a very special meaning is, I think, the ontogenetic source of one pervasive element in human ritualization, which is based on a *mutuality of recognition*, by face and by name.

There is much to suggest that man is born with the need for such regular and mutual affirmation and certification: we know at any rate that its absence can harm an infant radically, by diminishing or extinguishing his search for impressions which will verify his senses. This need will reassert itself in every stage of life as a demand for ever new, ever more formalized and more widely shared ritualizations (and, eventually, rituals) which repeat the face-to-face "recognition" and the name-to-name correspondence of the hoped for. Such ritualizations range from the regular exchange of greetings affirming a strong emotional bond, to traditional greetings affirming a reciprocity of roles, to singular encounters in love or inspiration, and, eventually, in a leader's "charisma" as confirmed by (more or less) exquisite statues and paintings, or by mere multiplied banners and televised appearances. All such meetings at their best embody seeming paradoxes: they are *playful* and yet *formalized;* quite *familiar* through repetition, they yet renew the *surprise* of recognition. And while the ethologists will tell us that ritualizations in the animal world must, above all, be *unambiguous* sets of signals which avoid the arousal of conflicting instinctive patterns, we suspect that in man the overcoming of *ambivalence* (as well as of ambiguity) is one of the prime functions of ritualization. For as we love our children, and children in general, they can also arouse hate and murderous disdain, even at best they will find us arbitrary in rejection and possessive in acceptance, if not potentially dangerous and witchlike. What we love or admire is always also threatening; awe becomes awfulness, and benevolence harbors the danger of being consumed by wrath. Therefore, ritualized affirmation, reaching from daily life to religious rites, becomes indispensable, as a periodical experience and must in changing times find new and meaningful forms.

This is a heavy burden to place on an infant's daily awakening, and, indeed, only the whole sequence of stages of ritualization can make this list of essentials plausible. Yet psychopathology confirms this early burdening. Of all psychological disturbances which we have learned to connect ontogenetically with the early stages of life, the deepest and most devastating (as Spitz and Bowlby have shown) are those in which the light of mutual recognition and of hope is early forfeited in autistic and psychotic withdrawal. For the earliest affirmation soon becomes much needed reaffirmation in the face of the fact that the very experiences which through ritualization give a measure of security also expose the growing being to a *series of estrangements:* these, too, we must try to specify as we deal with each developmental stage. In the first stage, I submit, it is a sense of *separation* and *abandonment* which is never quite overcome by periodical reassurance of familiarity and mutuality; while this first and dimmest affirmation, this sense of a hallowed presence, contributes to humankind's ritual-making a pervasive element which is best called the *numinous*. This designation betrays my intention to follow the earliest into the last: and, indeed, we recognize the numinous as an indispensable aspect of the devotional element in all periodical observances. However, it must be clear that of all institutions that of organized religion has the strongest claim to being in charge of the numinous: the believer, by appropriate gestures, confesses his dependence and childlike faith and seeks, by appropriate offerings, to secure the privilege of being lifted up to the very bosom of the divine which, indeed, may be seen to graciously respond, with the faint smile of an inclined face. The numinous assures us of *separateness transcended* and yet also a *distinctiveness confirmed*, and thus of the very basis of a sense of "I," renewed (as it feels) by the mutual recognition of all "I"s joined in a shared faith in one all-embracing "I Am."

As we proceed through ontogeny, however, let us be aware also of those deceptive and self-deceptive trends which are the shadow of all make-believe and of playful ritualization. I will attempt to name for each stage one element of that pervasive social pathology by which ritualization in its "measured" relation to over-all reality is perverted into what could be called pseudo-ritualization, or more simply, *ritualism*. This takes many forms, from mere compulsive compliance with daily rules to the obsessive-repetitive expression of fanatic and delusional visions. The first of these ritualisms may be called *idolism*, which distorts the reverence for the truly numinous. Such an "ism," of course, often fits in with prevailing character types and with important social trends and yet is apt to lose its playful relation to both fact and principal and become habitual and obsessive. The numinous thus can be lost in adulation—an attitude falling short (and this is the main point) of the psychosocial and generational integration inherent in a true sense of veneration or even adoration. The illusory image of perfection—including that of the self-image—implied in the relation of idolizer and idol is, of course, distorted by an excess in that libidinal attachment to the self which we call narcissism, after the mythical young man who perished rather than abandon his (and with his, a dead twin sister's) face reflected in a mountain pool: a double mirroring, then, instead of a commitment to a living love.

If, again, I have dwelt unduly long on the first stage, I have also declared my principles of presentation. But there remains one question which we must ask about each element of ritualization: as it survives in and grows with the growing person, what does it contribute to and what does it demand of the community's vision? Here we must underline once more the changing fields of vision successively experienced in the process of growing up from a supine newborn to the kind of upright creature we are.

Man's inner structure, we said, has evolved together with his institutions. The human being which at the beginning wants, in addition to the fulfillment of oral and sensory needs, to be gazed upon by the primal parent and to respond to the gaze, to look up to the parental countenance and to be responded to, continues to look up, and to look for somebody to look up to, and that is somebody who will, in the very act of returning his glance, lift him up. It is clear that the religious element in any collective vision responds to this first stage. In the Visconti Hours, where Barbello depicts Maria's death, God in heaven is shown holding in his arms her spirit in the form of a swaddled baby, and "returning the gaze of Mary's soul." This closes the cycle of the first stage as projected on the whole of existence. In religion, vision becomes Revelation, and revelatory spectacles, all confirming the immortality of the "I," if also under strict rules and often awful threats of total abandonment. Now, each religion has its own political structure; and politics proper always competes with religion (joining it, tolerating it when it must, and absorbing it when it can) in order to promise, if not a life beyond, then a new deal on this earth, and a Leader smiling charismatically from the placards. Yet, in any true ritual as well as in any working combination of all ritualizations, this one element tends to be integrated with all others.

Table 1. Ontogeny of Ritualization

infancy	mutuality of recognition					
early childhood	↓	discrimination of good and bad				
play age	↓	↓	dramatic elaboration			
school age	↓	↓	↓	rules of performance		
adolescence	↓	↓	↓	↓	solidarity of conviction	
elements in adult rituals	NUMINOUS	JUDICIAL	DRAMATIC	FORMAL	IDEOLOGICAL	GENERATIONAL SANCTION

CHAPTER 15

Shared Visions

ERIK H. ERIKSON

Visions on the Wall

I began this book [*Toys and Reasons*] with one child's play construction, reviewed some play theories, and came to the conclusion that I have no reason to revise the suggestion made in my first book [*Childhood and Society*], namely, that play on a toy stage is only one model of the human proclivity to project onto a circumscribed "microsphere" an arrangement of figures which dramatizes a moment of fate. In child's play we saw the model for the creative vision which later uses a circumscribed field, a "plane" (and to *explain* means to spread something out for clearer comprehension), a stage, or a blueprint to gain mastery over what he is in the process of becoming by means of evolutionary and historical, technical and personal developments. But I also had to point to the fear, the anxiety, and the dread which overwhelm man, small or big, when he finds his hoped-for leeway checkmated by inner inhibitions or by blind circumstances, a fate imposed on him by visible or invisible enemies: in fact, I indicated that where man does not have enemies he often must invent them in order to create boundaries against which he can assert the leeway of the new man he must become.

The ontogenetic cultivation of a viewpoint, I then explained in the second part, is accomplished by a minute *ritualization* of daily life, which leads from the smallest items of personal interplay to the ceremonial get-togethers of cultural events—all saying, "This is the way *we* see, and say, and do things, and it is the *human* way." Visions are grounded in facts verifiable in some detail and yet arranged to fit within a cosmology and an ideology that unite groups of human beings in mutual actualizations.

I will now describe the manifestation of such visions in a number of fields, beginning with those closest to me by avocation and vocation, namely art and psychoanalysis. This, at any rate, permits me to begin again by sharing a visual experience. Recently, Hellmut Wohl gave a paper in San Francisco, "On Point of View."[1] In this, he related the formal perspective of Renaissance painting to the Christian faith it was to propagate, and both perspective and faith to the need for a vision of hope. He wrote: "Aesthetic vision offers a model for the formulation of ideas in terms of a coherent point of view. [It thus] signifies the reaffirmation of basic trust—perhaps the deepest criterion for the measure of coherence that a point of view represents. Finally, aesthetic vision provides both an ideal and a standard of that wholeness which a point of view imparts to reality."

In the De Young Museum, we saw the Van Borsig *Annunciation* ascribed to a Flemish master of the early sixteenth century. In all its anonymity and simplicity it immediately seemed to us to unite many of the basic elements of man's playful vision, from its ontogenetic origins in what can be seen to its most existential visionary meaning. An *Annunciation*, of course, is a visitation announcing the Eternal Prospect, the expectation that the child to be born will be the Child who will forever save in man some portion of what childhood promises: The "Kingdom." There is Mary, then, the to-be-elect. Becoming aware of the angel's presence and glance, she lowers an open book, and we can see that the page she had studied (and a page, too, is a framed visual field) is "illuminated": it shows the biblical theme of a kneeling figure before an apparition of light—is it Moses, the prophet of the old law, as Christ will be of the new? But Mary is almost overshadowed by the presence of the angelic messenger with the commanding glance, who brings the word that within her will be the Child, the guarantor of a New Man. And, indeed, the Holy Spirit, the agent, can be seen floating down on a golden and piercing ray of light.

The stage, in the foreground of which all this takes place, has two doorframes opening up on two rooms in the background. The one behind Mary reveals her bed; the other leads our eyes straight to two further frames: a window opening on the town; and, beside it, an open triptych with rounded panels: in its brightness, it could easily be mistaken for another window (a "wind-eye"). It, too, shows a kneeling figure before an apparition of light, and we are reminded that to face the east means to be "oriented" in a world in which the darkness of night always opens up on the dawn.

If I pointed out that the play constructions of children as well as corresponding visions seem to reveal a need of human consciousness to be central to the world rather than shunted to the periphery and to be chosen in one's newness rather than negligible, then we must certainly recognize Mary's womb as being, at that moment, in the center of the universe—as is, indeed, that of any woman pregnant with child, and every child newly born: new eyes to be set on the world, a new face to be recognized, a new name becoming the mark of a new "I," and (who knows) a new person full of a grace not yet betrayed by the "human condition."

Yet, to encompass the total world view of which this small picture portrays only the promising beginning, and to envisage all the dimensions we recognized in our "ordinary" play construction, we would have to include such other paintings as those that might surround an *Annunciation* on the walls of any studio, any church, or any museum. One picture may depict that child as the grown Son of Man, his hand raised, in the persuasive gesture of blessing; another crying his last cry, his hands nailed to a cross, in the dreadful night of Golgotha. One may know the Son of God benevolently saluting the saved and elect in Heaven, another majestically discarding those to be damned in Hell, another depict one of the crowned heads who with ceremonial splendor have represented the crucified carpenter's son through history; in another, we may see spread before us a battlefield, hallowed *"in hoc signo,"* with the felled infidels piled up in wounded and dying agony.

Thus, only a whole ensemble of themes, linking a special creation in the past with the certainty of a prophesied future, provides the Eternal Prospect with a perspective that gives meaning to all births and deaths and the enigmas in between. And once established, a new world view acquires not only a renewed identity symbolical of eternal renewal, but also techniques and rituals, hierarchies and battle lines, which vastly elaborate the original vision of the believing "I" bound with other mortal "I"s through one divine "I"—the one that assuredly Is. Only thus does man feel protected against the doom of some primal curse—is it that of non-existence?—and able to face the verdict of a last judgment where only the elect few will be saved, while all others—those excluded from choices—will perish. Thus we make a political deal with mortality and infinity; and let us not overlook the fact that the most transcendent of visions will become rooted in establishments (such as churches) that politicize existential needs and come to live off human aloneness and death; for whether or not we can truly perceive ourselves as physically dead, our soul fears above all to be alone and to be inactivated in eternity. (For the dread of a forfeited identity, I found a supreme formula on the tombstone of one who was beheaded in the very century when this *Annunciation* was painted: "My youth is gone, and yet I am but young; I saw the world, and yet I was not seen.")

That quiet *Annunciation,* then, in which the light and spirit, the face and the word come together, derives its persuasiveness from the recurrent cataclysmic dread of total darkness and spiritual death, of facelessness and meaninglessness. But let us not forget that to be magically convincing, the painter must be in technical command of an art providing a living style for the play with forms. Only then will his work appeal to the deepest needs of the viewer and confirm faith with demonstrated truth.

To keep this in mind is of the essence, as we mention other "frames" or spheres—some seemingly totally foreign to each other. That a framed picture may share some configurations with a dream or with the proscenium of a theater is not difficult to claim; but that theater and theory may have common roots in experience as well as in language may be more so. And yet, these two words have in common "visible or visualized spheres arousing fascination and belief." In the same way, many words which we use every day have emerged from word roots related to seeing: that a fact is evident because any willing person can see it—that is evident. Yet, there are very central words which contain a linguistic root marking them as visible: an idea as a model in the inner eye; history as a visualized continuum of events; and wisdom as a final overview—with some wit to spare. Thus does all true perspective affirm the original organ of comprehension in an imaginative creature born with stereoscopic vision—and a need for a perspective and an outlook.

Perspective at its best gives a transcendent order to what is visible from a given position in space, and leads from what is closest to a point revealed in the far distance. It thus opens and limits us to our point of view, foreshortening all that is distant and hiding all that happens to be behind the objects seen. Far from deserving to be taken for granted, however, an elaborate emphasis on perspective is itself an expression of a particular world view. By the same token, in gloriously affirming a visible world order as well as the orderliness of vision, art can give an aesthetic glow even to subjects of damnation and despair. It can illuminate the grandest illusions and outshine with realism itself the very lowness of daily life. We treasure Rembrandt for illuminating so grandly and so simply the transcendence of everyday hereness.

The Dream Screen

As I now turn to my own field of observation, psychoanalysis, it seems only one step (and it was so in my own life) from the pictures on the wall to the images dreamed at night.

The late Bertram Lewin has provided us with a term which can help us to find in psychoanalytic introspection a counterpart to those toy tables and playing boards and game fields which we have been discussing. He called the background on which we see our dreams the dream screen. In his book, *The Image and the Past*, he is fully aware of the role of vision in the dreams and the memories which patients report and which psychoanalysts hear, meditate upon, and interpret. In discussing the question of what goes on in the psychoanalyst's head as he listens to his patient, Lewin suspects (with others) that the psychoanalyst's remarkable ability to listen to many people for hours must to some extent rely on a "sublimated scopophilia," that is, a higher kind of voyeurism which permits him to endure long working days visualizing what he hears.[2] But so must the patient translate into words what often "comes to mind" as images on an inner screen—and Freud said, long ago: "Even in those whose memory is not normally of a visual type, the earliest recollections of childhood retain far into life the quality of sensory vividness."

But if vision is, as we saw, the basic organizer of the sensory universe and if the beholding of one person's face by another is the foundation of a sense of mutuality, then the classical psychoanalytic treatment situation itself is an exquisite deprivation experiment. Freud created the arrangement, it is said, because he did not like to be stared at, which can only mean that a patient's avid wish to see the therapist's facial response interfered with the theory builder's wish to think before he responded. But it is also the genius of this clinical invention that it systematically provokes the patient's "free" verbal associations by creating a visual void, which invites the rushing in of old images seeking a healing mutuality. Above all, this setting serves to intensify what we call transference, that is, a transfer to the unseen listener of important personages of the past, and especially the primal parent—and this often with all the dread of being abandoned and the rage over being ignored. All this, of course, is eminently instructive in regard to what "down there" is left over from "way back" and can be deeply and uniquely therapeutic. But we also know that classical psychoanalysis is a cure for which a patient must be relatively healthy in the first place and gifted for this specific ascetic combination of introspection and verbalization. And as, sooner or later, every field must become aware of the way in which its principal procedure influences the nature of the observed, we will, in our context, pursue some of the fate of the visual in the classical procedure.

Let me tell, then, of the shortest dream ever reported to me. I have come back to it over the years because it demonstrates how a clinical datum of utmost brevity can prove to be like the hub of a wheel in which a great number of meanings are conjoined. It was the first dream reported by a young woman patient. German-speaking, but versed in Romance languages, the young woman reported, in a tone half shy and half daring me to see what I could make of *that,* a dream consisting only of the word S[E]INE—lit up against a dark background. The first letter E was in brackets. The whole word obviously referred to the river that flows through Paris: and, indeed, it had been in Paris and on leaving the Louvre that the patient as a young girl had first been overcome by the symptom of agoraphobia that now brought her to analysis. But if she had seen a disturbing picture there, she did not remember it. And, indeed, the form of her dream suggested that what she saw so overly clearly in neon-light letters corresponded to some dark spot in her mind: maybe some amnesia. But what did those letters say? There seemed to be a linguistic puzzle hidden in this one word. "To see," in German, is *sehen,* a word that is often pronounced like the French "Seine." So, we have "seen by the Seine." But *seine* is also a German word, meaning "his"; and if we cross out the letter in brackets, we have the Latin word *sine,* meaning "without." Taken together, the word puzzle seems to say that the patient, by the Seine, had seen (somebody) without his (something). In the course of her free associations, and along some detours, the patient eventually remembered a picture that had shocked her deeply: it was a *Circumcision of Christ.* Being Catholic, she had, as a curious small girl, guiltily wondered what was behind the Savior's loincloth: here the Christ child was without it and defenselessly exposed to ritual surgery.

Her shock, however, had been, as we say, overdetermined: for the picture, it soon became plausible, had reminded her of a most traumatic experience in childhood when she had been catheterized by her father, a pediatrician, because of a bladder condition that was reducing the flow of urine. This memory caused in the patient a deep panic, and increased a certain squirming on the couch which now appeared to represent the apprehension that something like that medical procedure was going to be repeated in the psychoanalytic situation. She was, however, able to describe the early experience in emotional detail:

besides the pain endured, the shame and a certain rage over having to expose herself to her father had been intense, for while she herself could not see what he saw and did, the procedure did make her void. Those versed in these matters will note that in psychoanalytic libido theory we include the age of five, when all this happened, in the phallic (or, as I prefer to call it, the infantile genital and locomotor) stage, and it will be obvious how traumatic at that stage an event was that both immobilized and exposed the little girl—in an "oedipal" context.

This dream eventually proved strategic in helping to clarify the patient's early neurosis and personality development. But if we now ask in what way this first dream also dwelt on the "psychoanalytic situation," we must turn to the "initiation" of the procedure. When she had come for her first hour, I had informed her that she was to lie on the couch, facing away from me; and she was to let her thoughts come freely and to verbalize them candidly, no matter how painful or shameful they might seem to her. Now, in presenting me with the dream, she seemed to challenge me even as she declared herself ready to play my game. The basic theme of the dream obviously compared the Christ child's and her own predicament to the clinical ritual commanding her to assume a supine position in which she could not see me but was to permit what in my trade we, indeed, refer to as the "free flow" of verbal associations so that I might detect unconscious ideas that might prove embarrassing to her. The idea of flow, at any rate, connects the image of the river with the urinary focus of her memories and the basic requirement of her treatment.

The special combination of rage and shame aroused by this all too suggestive situation finally leads us to the meaning of the bracketed letter E. This being my initial, it suggested some trick of "transference," that is, a transfer on the psychoanalyst of highly conflicted feelings originally attached to a significant figure in childhood. In this sense, it can be seen to reveal the further thought that she might wish to "turn the tables" and to expose *me:* a mocking projection of both the Savior's and her own predicament. Here, then, the patient's passively suffered self-exhibition, according to a well-known reversal, is actively turned against me with an aggressive voyeurism which, in fact, is also natural for the very stage of childhood when she was traumatized. This interpretation could only confound the patient's embarrassment, but also led to some (luckily not infrequent) shared laughter over the tricks of the unconscious which can condense—and give away—all these meanings in one word.

But here I have followed only one main trend of thought suggested in the patient's multilingual dream puzzle. The French-speaking reader will have missed, at least by association, some reference to the word *sein*—breast. And, indeed, the patient eventually remembered another painting that had shocked her. Ascribing it to Rubens, she recalled a goddess with six breasts—an obvious counter-vision to the *Circumcision*, for it added a theme of utmost plentitude where the other theme so sharply subtracted. Yet, this was too fleshly an affirmation of femininity for the young girl, who at the time had felt attracted to—as well as disquieted by—the sensual emphasis in women's dress (décolleté) and the seductive masculine mores of Parisian life. While the first picture, then, pointed to an infantile trauma suffered during a specific infantile stage, the second symbolized the cultural atmosphere which in the adolescent girl had aroused voyeuristic and exhibitionistic wishes and thus set the libidinal tone for the whole traumatic and, as it were, re-repressive experience, now relived in the psychoanalytic situation.

We can, then, see in this first dream of an admittedly rather "classical" case an infantile and an adolescent trauma in interplay with the psychoanalytic situation. A parallelism of such clarity that is revealed so promptly is, of course, rare. It must usually be reconstructed from many obscure details over a long period of treatment. But the example may make it plausible that in thus enforcing the patient's concentration on the sequence of emerging images, the treatment intensified a "natural" self-healing process, which Bertram Lewin formulated thus: "All recapturing of the pictorial past, whether as dream picture, screen memory, new memory of repressed traces, etc., could include, besides the more obvious wish fulfillments and defensive formations, an equivalent of an attempt at explanation and cure."[3] Freud had gone further in claiming that even "The delusions of patients appear to me to be the equivalent of the constructions which we build up in the course of an analytic treatment—attempts at explanation and cure."[4]

Finally, it must interest us that this dream leads to two "visions on the wall" and especially to one that belongs in the same religious context as does our *Annunciation:* somewhere they could very well hang in the same hall. And in both of them we can see at work the particular proclivity of the ego which interests us here, namely a private space-time orientation in interplay with a world view which gives structure and meaning to the multiplicity of experience. It must be clear that the patient's traumatic reaction to the extreme imagery of the *Circumcision* was codetermined by her ready identification with the Christ child in his infantile predicament and, in fact, in the whole vision of suffering suggested by Christ's life and death. Her neurosis was codetermined by the fact that this identification had been elaborated into a deeply masochistic vision, with many irrational aspects. In her late adolescence, this vision was in intense conflict with another one which came into full bloom in the Parisian atmosphere: the exhibitionistic and voyeuristic indulgence in erotic temptation. These coexisting visions aggravated her confusion by alternately suggesting two totally different identities: her agoraphobia resolved this conflict by making her a patient. But the promise of a psychoanalytic cure opened up a third vision, namely, the promise of enlightenment, as a mediator between sexuality and spirituality. Finally, the humor and the artistry of this play on the dream screen certified not only to the tricky powers of the unconscious but also to the dreamer's specific linguistic giftedness and expressed the hope that the new woman, liberated by psychoanalysis from her infantile bondage, would see the light, would be able to move and look around freely and use her talents. Thus, to the ancient Christian and the modern French visions was added the Freudian version of Enlightenment.

NOTES

1. H. Wohl, "On Point of View," *Boston University Journal*, Vol. 20 (Autumn, 1972, pp. 16–21.)

2. B. Lewin, *The Image and the Past* (International Universities Press, 1968).

3. Ibid., pp. 21–22.

4. S. Freud, "Constructions in Analysis," in *The Standard Edition of the Complete Psychological Works of Sigmund Freud*, vol. 23, James Strachey (ed.). (London: Hogarth Press, 1964), p. 268.

CHAPTER 16

The Galilean Sayings and the Sense of "I"

ERIK H. ERIKSON

The episodic art form of gospels such as St. Matthew's, one-sided as each may be, conveys the combination in Jesus' ministry of an extensive capacity to address the wide variety of groups found in Galilee, and yet to be, potentially, in contact with each individual encountered. In this connection, a scene stands out which I, as a psychoanalyst, felt I had good reason to quote in my Jefferson lectures,[1] and this especially because Jefferson had omitted it from his authentic data. It is the story of a woman who had lost not only her blood for twelve years but also all her money on physicians, none of whom had helped her at all. Finding herself in a big crowd surrounding Jesus, she did not dare to, or could not, approach him directly, but she pressed in behind him and touched his garment.

> And straightway the fountain of her blood was dried up; and she felt in her body that she was healed of that plague. And Jesus, immediately knowing in himself that virtue had gone out of him, turned him about in the press and said, "Who touched my clothes?" And his disciples said unto him, "Thou seest the multitude thronging thee, and sayest thou, 'Who touched me?'" And he looked round about to see her that had done this thing. But the woman fearing and trembling, knowing what was done in her, came and fell down before him, and told him all the truth. [Mark 5:29–34]

This illustrates Jesus' selective responsiveness to one person reaching out for him in a big crowd. What he then said to her—that will open up a whole new subject to us.

I have suggested that the sense of *I* is one of the most obvious facts of existence—indeed, maybe *the* most obvious—and that it is, at the same time, one of the most elusive: wherefore psychologists are apt to consider it a philosophical rather than a psychological concern. I will discuss later how my teacher, Sigmund Freud, managed (almost) to ignore it. But it is true, of course, that this subjective sense dwells on the very border of our conscious existence, though no doubt its health is dependent on such qualities of our psychosocial life as our sense of identity. In the Bible, the most direct reference to the human *I* is in the form of an inner light, that is, of a luminosity of awareness. The original Galilean saying is reported in Matthew's account: "Nor do men light a lamp and put it under a bushel, but on a stand, and it gives light to all in the house" (5:15). "The eye is the lamp of the body. So, if your eye is sound, your whole body will be full of light, but if your eye is not sound, your whole body will be full of darkness. If, then, the light in you is darkness, how great is the darkness!" (6:22). And, indeed, our sense of *I* gives to our sensory awareness a numinous center.

It is no wonder, then, that our most eloquent recent witness for the inner light is a blind man, Jacques Lusseyran, who lost his eyesight through an accident at the age of seven and a half. He later wrote (in "The Blind in Society"):

> Barely ten days after the accident that blinded me, I made the basic discovery . . . I could not see the light of the world any more. Yet the light was still there. . . . I found it in *myself* and what a miracle!—it was intact. This "in myself," however, where was that? In my head, in my heart, in my imagination? . . . I felt how it wanted to spread out over the world. . . . The source of light is not in the outer world. We believe that it is only because of a common delusion. The light dwells where life also dwells: within ourselves. . . . The second great discovery came almost immediately afterwards. There was only one way to see the inner light, and that was to love.

This numinosity, however, seems lost when it is too eagerly concentrated on for its own sake, as if one light were asked to illuminate another. No wonder that dictionaries avoid the matter! I have before me a psychological dictionary which does not even mention *I*. My thesaurus, in turn, refers first to a "self-designating pronoun" and then to "the spiritual personality"—and nothing in between.

Actually, writers who take the sense of *I* seriously will first of all ask what is the *I*'s counterplayer. They may indeed begin with the second pronoun, you, and end with the soul's sense of a divine Thou. To my developmental orientation the most telling "map" depicting the development of the sense of *I* would be the whole list of personal pronouns, from *I* to *They*, as each one first gets to be pronounced and understood correctly in childhood, and then as it is meaningfully experienced and reexperienced throughout life. The beginnings of the sense of *I* itself, one should think, can only emerge in a newborn out of the counterplay with a sensed *You* in the maternal caretaker—whom we shall call the Primal Other; and it seems of vital importance that this Other, and, indeed, related Others, in turn experience the new being as a *presence* that heightens *their* sense of *I*. It is this interplay, I think, that helps the original sense of *I* gradually face another fundamental counterplayer, namely, *my Self*—almost an Inner Other. But the original interplay of *You* and *I* remains the model for a mutual recognition throughout life, up to a finite expectation to which St. Paul gave the explicitly religious form of an ultimate meeting now only vaguely sensed beyond "a glass, darkly" (the Ultimate Other, then).

Now, one glance at the list of all personal pronouns reveals a whole developmental program in their sequence: for while *I* and *you* form the original dyad, this dyad soon turns into a number of triads as a series of *hes* or *shes* (and, indeed, a world of *its*) become additional counterplayers within varied connotations: paternal, fraternal, sororal, and so on. And as this happens, the plural concepts *we, you* and *they* become both verbal necessities and the bearers of important emotional involvements. Thus, the system of pronouns, beginning with *I* and *you*, is built into a ground plan ready to unfold in stages; and one can well see how each of them, once learned, serves a widening experience as it includes, on every stage, new counterplayers. Take, for example, the necessity—especially in any patriarchal and monotheistic system—to transfer some of the earliest forms of a sense of *I* from their maternal origin to strongly paternal and eventually theistic relationships. Or consider the crisis of adolescence as a transfer of the identity elements formed in childhood and youth to the productive milieu in which one expects to find one's psychosocial identity. Or, again, how the sense of *we* acquired in one's family of origin ("my kind") must be extended to the family and the community one marries into—and, indeed, to one's own new family in which one must help to generate new beings with their own sense of *I*.

Throughout this establishment of new boundaries of *We, Ourselves*, dictated as it is by the realities and the ideology of work and production, there also emerges a gradual demarcation of the decisive borderlines beyond which live those definitely other Others—those *theys* and *thems* whom one has learned to repudiate or to exclude as foreign, if not nonhuman altogether. These habitual rejections, in turn, have helped to give a clearer outline to one's own "true Self" or to those variant "selves" which are either proudly or fatalistically accepted as a self-description within the contemporary world of roles. And yet, throughout all these critical stages with all their involvements, there remains for the *I* a certain existential solitariness which, in these pages, we depict as seeking love, liberation, salvation.

Some Authentic Sayings of Jesus

The "Authentic Sayings": According to the form critics, this means the "earliest form" known of such a saying that can plausibly be traced to Mark (the first gospel, later independently used by Matthew and Luke) and/or to the even earlier collection of sayings called Q (for the German "Quelle," meaning "source")—if, furthermore, the occurrence of such a form can be shown to be "neither possible nor probable" in ancient Judaism or in the early Church. As we will see (our first example will consist of exactly five words), sayings which survive such a scrutiny are of immense simplicity, especially if seen against the background of the spatial and temporal sweep of the world imagery of much of the preceding Judaic religiosity *and* of the gospels to follow. But such simplicity, we will claim, is of their essence. At the same time, however, the gospels' specific art form permits us, as we have already seen, at least to imagine these simple sayings as spoken within the context of a most vivid encounter. Here let me go back to the story of the woman who was cured of a persistent flow of blood. This example, in its healing aspects, can be seen immediately to be as close to our day and work as it seems to have surprised the Galilee of that day. For, to permit myself a professional and even theoretical response, it makes good sense in modern terms that Jesus, in the midst of a thick throng, should have felt the touch of the desperate woman, and felt it as an acute loss of a powerful quantity of something vital. For this is comparable to and, indeed, is a parabolic representation of a certain interplay or mutual "transfer" of energy (Freud called it libido, that is, love-energy) which is assumed to take place and must be understood—as "transference"—in any therapeutic situation.

But now, what *did* Jesus say, having been "touched" in this manner? *"Your faith has healed you."* The King James version is "My daughter, thy faith hath made thee whole"—which underlines the loving as well as the holistic character of all healing. At any rate, he acknowledges the woman's aptitude for trust and her determination to reach him as an essential counterpart to his capacity to help her. Nor is this the only time that Jesus specifies this "interpersonal" and active condition. There was a blind beggar (Mark 10:46–52) seated at the roadside, shouting for the "son of David." Jesus first "activated" him by having somebody call to him, thus inducing him to throw off his cloak, spring up, and come to *him*. Then Jesus said, "Your faith has made you well." And there were the four friends (Mark 2:1–5), who were trying to bring a paralyzed man on a stretcher through the door of the house in which Jesus was teaching. Unable to get through, they broke open the roof "over the place where Jesus was" and lowered the stretcher through. This time, Mark says, when Jesus saw their faith, he said to the sick man, "My son, yours sins are forgiven"—a rabbi's claim to the right of absolution which resulted in a bit of theological argument from some lawyers: "Why does the fellow talk like that?"

It will be clear that Jesus' therapeutic formula is only one of many sayings, all cohering in a basic orientation (to be illustrated further) which emphasizes the individual's vital core in the immediate present rather than in dependence on traditional promises and threats of a cosmic nature. If I relate this to the sense of *I*, it will appear to be simplistic, and certainly too "superficial" for a psychoanalyst. Yet, as we have said, to be active (as well as central, continuous and whole), or at any rate not to feel inactivated (or peripheral and fragmented), is one of the most essential dimensions of a sense of *I*. I would consider Jesus' emphasis on the patient's propensity for an active faith, then, not only a therapeutic "technique" applied to incapacitated individuals but an ethical message for the bystanders as part of a population which at that time must have been weakened in its sense of being the master—or unsure of a faith that could promise to become master—of its collective fate. And as for the enduring meaning of this saying let me here note only that this orientation reasserted itself in the history of psychotherapy with Freud's decision to make the hysterical patient *work* for recovery by letting his or her own inner voice direct "free associations" in search of the underlying conflicts instead of merely submitting to hypnosis.

And—to pursue our second concern—what did Freud say about the human sense of *I*? Certainly, in his search for a scientific psychology he did not wish to be sidetracked into man's age-old claim to a soul—which all too often has seemed to become a "narcissistic" center of human self-illusion. He concentrated on the means by which man's consciousness may be made useful in the process of calling to mind what to mankind's vast detriment had become denied and repressed in ontogeny and phylogeny. And so he emphasized what he called the human *Ich*—the right word for *I* in German, but always (and sometimes questionably) translated into English as "ego." And it is true that the *Ich* as ego to him became a primarily unconscious inner organization of experience on which human adaptation and sanity depend: the "ego gives mental processes an order in time and submits them to reality testing." Therefore, if it is disturbed its control must be restored by insight; but where is insight located? Freud cautiously claims that "On this ego [*an diesem Ich*] hangs consciousness"—a phenomenon, then, "on the periphery of the ego."

But here we face an issue of vast importance in the understanding of Freud's original concepts. If Freud himself in the early days of theory-formation uses the term *Ich* alternately for a conscious surface phenomenon and for a largely unconscious ordering of experience, one cannot blame his translators for refusing to make themselves responsible for a decision as to when the context might suggest *I* rather than ego. Freud himself, however, wonders aloud what right he has to narrow down the importance of a conscious sense of *I*. "At first we are inclined greatly to reduce the value of the criterion of being conscious since it has shown itself so untrustworthy," he claims; and then he must admit, "But we should be doing it an injustice. As may be said of our life, it is not worth much, but it is all we have. Without the illumination thrown by the quality of consciousness, we should be lost in the obscurity of depth-psychology: but we must attempt to find our bearings afresh." Here again, the translator has given in to Freud's usual tendency *not* to overdo the significance of a numinous sense of aliveness. For the word translated as "illumination" is "die Leuchte," a word denoting, indeed, luminosity, and this in the two senses of the Galilean saying, that is, a "Leuchter"—a lamp—and a "Leuchte," i.e., a luminous quality, a shining light. This whole "skeptical" remark, then, in which our consciousness, whatever its worth, is compared with life itself, is in all its caution not too far from the psalmist's acknowledgment of a light given by the creator to the apple of the eye.

And while Freud remains, as it were, religiously scientific because he is determined to pursue his mission, which is to find a truly analytical method to study human obsession (whether "evil" or "sick"), he comes, in the statement quoted, as close as he may wish to the saying, "but when thine eye is evil, thy body also is full of darkness" (Luke 11:34, King James version); except that he continues to pursue the darkness behind consciousness, attempting to reveal some structural divisions in man's psyche—that is, besides the ego, the superego, and, finally, the id, an inner caldron of drives and passions.

Here, as far away from the *I* as we can get, another Galilean saying seems to have expressed a "new disposition" most decisive for a self-aware human attitude. When challenged by some Pharisees who saw his disciples sit down to a meal without washing their hands properly and without seeming concerned about "the washing of pots and cups and vessels of bronze," Jesus says tough things, as Mark reports it, about their "teaching as doctrines the precepts of men," thus "making void the word of God through your tradition." Mark continues: "And he called the people to him again, and said to them, 'Hear me, all of you, and understand: there is nothing outside a man which by going into him can defile him; but the things which come out of a man are what defile him' " (Mark 7:14–16). And later, Jesus added for the sake of his questioning disciples: " 'Do you not see that whatever goes into a man from outside cannot defile him, since it enters, not his heart but his stomach, and so passes on?' (Thus he declared all foods clean.) And he said, 'What comes out of a man is what defiles a man. For from within, out of the heart of man, come evil thoughts, fornication, theft, murder, adultery, coveting, wickedness, deceit, licentiousness, envy, slander, pride, foolishness' " (Mark 7:18–22).

Our form critics, I presume, would not underwrite as authentic the exact list of evils emanating from within, although every believer in the id must acknowledge them. But as to Jesus' simple insistence on the fate of what comes in ("es geht den natuerlichen Gang," Luther puts it: it takes the natural course), it seems to do away with many deeply ingrained distinctions between clean and unclean which serve the phobic avoidances and the compulsive purifications by daily and weekly ritualisms—at the time probably reinforced in Pharisaic circles by their disdain for the intrusion into Jewish life of Hellenic mores. By then, of course, Jesus had publicly demonstrated not only his unorthodox daily habits but also the liberality of his choice of table fellows. In calling the inner caldron the "heart" of man, however, he certainly points to an *inner* seat of passionate conflict from which emerge the multiple temptations by which the sense of *I* is ruefully inactivated and which it therefore can experience as an inner chaos—an id. And yet, the *I* can possibly manage some of them only by that radical awareness which Jesus here demands.

I have now come dangerously close to claiming that the authentic Jesus does, indeed, make sensible sense in terms of our present-day pursuits. So it is time to present a saying which puts exorcism more explicitly into the (literally) widest actuality in which the Galilean Jesus felt he was operating—that is, the Kingdom: "But if it is by the finger of God that I cast out demons, then the kingdom of God has come upon you" (Luke 11:20). Luther renders this "den Teufel austreiben," that is, "to cast out the devil," and continues: "so kommt je das Reich Gottes zu Euch," that is, "and so, every time, the reign of God comes upon you." The saying itself is said to have "high claims on authenticity," even if Matthew speaks of God's "spirit" rather than "finger"—but then the gospel writers often modify what in the original version seems to them to be a bit extreme. I like the finger, however, because it continues the theme of touch which was so prominent in the episode with the woman; except that here, of course, it is the finger of God which is operative through Jesus' action and makes the Kingdom—well, how shall we put it— come? have come? forever coming? For here we seem to have some play with time appearing in special contrast to those grand prophetic predictions of the kingdom as some final act in history such as decisive redemption. And if the Kingdom is so vague in its temporal boundaries, *where* is it? This question Jesus answers in another context: "Behold, the kingdom of God is in the midst of you" (Luke 17:21). The Greek original, *entos hymōn*, presumably can mean "between you" as well as "within you," for Luther's translation, "inwendig in Euch," claims just that.

In all these forms, the saying is considered "absolutely characteristic of oral tradition." Thomas, in fact, in his Gnostic way, presents an apparently independent parallel: "The kingdom is within you and it is without you. If you will know yourselves, then you will be known and you will know that you are the sons of the Living Father" (Thomas 3). And again, being asked by the Pharisees (to trick him, no doubt) when the kingdom was coming, Jesus answered: "The kingdom of God is not coming with signs to be observed" (Luke 17:20). This could be seen to contradict the first saying we quoted where Jesus, in fact, refers to his own observable act of healing; but Luther, again, seems to be on the right track, for he translates "not coming with signs to be observed" as "kommt nicht mit ausserlichen Gebaerden"; it does not "come with extraneous gestures."

If I may say in my own words what I understand all this to mean: these quotations make it clear that Jesus speaks of the Kingdom as an experience of inner as well as interpersonal actualization open to every individual who accepts his mediation. Since Jehovah, as we saw, is a god whose very being is action, such initiative, it seems, is now certified as a property of human existence—if through Jesus' mediation. For to be the voice announcing such an actuality as a potential in the here and now of every individual—that, it seems, is the essence of

Jesus' ministry: "if it is by the finger of God that I . . ." We have seen that one of the conditions for the realization of such a potential is faith, which, of course, includes repentance. But, again, it is an individual decision to become aware of universal sin in one's own personal form which, of course, also means to acknowledge these universal potentials in one's neighbor. All of which implies that the "kingdom" is no longer (if it ever was) a static territory or a predictable time span: it is a dominion *(malkuth shamayim)* in motion, a Coming, a Way—a fulfillment in the present which contains an anticipation of a future.

Why do I repeat here what has been said often and better? I wish, of course, to relate it to the concept of an *I*-time, for which I have postulated, among others, the qualities of activity and wholeness, and to which I must now add that of *centrality*, a being present in the center of events. Thus, repentance as an active choice (and the Greek word for it is *metanoia*, translated by Luther as "Umkehr"—"turnabout") makes one central to one's life-space. With all the pain of penitence inherent in the word, one need not be inactivated by bad conscience, nor banned by divine judgment; and this seems to be a step toward the alertness of the sense of *I*, which is also implied in that repeated encouragement: "Be aware! Be wakeful! Watch!"

Having related some sayings concerned with the boundaries of adult existence, we turn to one which focuses on the beginnings of human life: childhood. Mark 10 refers to an episode when the disciples rebuked some people who brought their children ("even infants," according to Luke) to Jesus so that they might be touched by him. Indignantly, he said: " 'Let the children come to me, do not hinder them; for to such belongs the kingdom of God. Truly, I say to you, whoever does not receive the kingdom of God like a child shall not enter it.' And he took them in his arms and blessed them, laying his hands upon them" (Mark 10:14–16). This is a total affirmation of the radiant potentials of childhood. This is the more astonishing as today we consider ourselves the discoverers of childhood, its defenders against all those history-wide negative attitudes which permitted proud and righteous as well as thoughtless adults to treat children as essentially weak or bad and in dire need of being corrected by stringent methods, or as expendable even to the point of being killed.

A detrimental counterpart of these attitudes is, of course, a more modern sentimentalization of childhood as an utterly innocent condition to be left pampered and unguided. In view of these and other trends, and especially of the Judaic concentration on bookish learning for spiritual improvement, Jesus' saying seems simply revolutionary. But it must be seen that he refers to an adult condition in which child-likeness has not been destroyed, and in which a potential return to childlike trust has not been forestalled. What is suggested, then, is a preservation and reenactment of the wonder of childhood: the "inno-cent eye" and ear. Consider in this connection the series of sayings commending the "seeing eyes" and "hearing ears" which can compre-hend the parables tacitly.

Keeping in mind the patriarchal days in which this was said, one cannot help noticing, on Jesus' part, an unobtrusive integration of ma-ternal and paternal tenderness. And, indeed, if we ask what reassur-ance for the individual *I* may be hidden in this and the following intergenerational sayings, it is, I think, the confirmation of *continuity* of the stages of development. The adult must not feel that the step of faith expected of him demands his leaving the child or, indeed, his youth behind him: on the contrary, only the continuation into matu-rity of true childlikeness guarantees his faith. Perrin, in this context, speaks of the child's ready trust and instinctive obedience; and I have held in my own writings that the strength of infancy is basic trust, de-veloped in the interaction of the budding *I* with the "primal Other," namely, the maternal person (or persons). This continues into adult-hood as a mutuality between growing perceptiveness and a dis-cernible order in the universe. As to an "instinctive obedience," this, too, calls for a correspondence with the pedagogic instinct in adults. But this is the point, and probably was the point in Jesus' time: the im-position of a merely compelling obedience, with disregard of the child's natural tendency to conform, can almost guarantee inner am-bivalence leading either to rebellious negation or to that widespread compulsiveness of adjustment which then is apt to find an expression in personal scrupulosity and shared ritualisms—which Jesus preached against as dangerous to faith.

I have now counterposed a few examples of the style and the logic of Jesus of Nazareth's original sayings with some of the dimensions of the human sense of *I*. I did so because I share the belief that the ele-mental sayings that emerged in the millennium "before Christ," and in Jesus' own short life, all deal with dimensions of human conscious-ness in a new manner nowadays expressed in the terms of *individual-ity* and *universality,* that is, a more aware *I* related to a more universal *We,* approaching the idea of one mankind. In my chosen context, how-ever, I could not attempt to look back on the roots of these sayings in the Judaic world; nor could I review some of Freud's dramatic conjectures concerning the archaic and infantile origins of the Mosaic religion—and its gradual self-transcendence through spirituality and intellectuality. As to Jesus' ministry, I had to stop short of the Judaean Passion that followed the Galilean period after Jesus' decision to confront militantly but nonviolently the violence latent in the political and spiritual deals between the Roman and the priestly establishments by which mortally endangered Israel had learned to live. Here, the son of man took chances not just with the lost ones but also with those who act out so strenuously the roles they find appropriate for their superior identity.

What followed was the crucifixion and the reported resurrection of him who thus became Christ and whose course of life was then creatively mythologized—from the nativity to the ascension. What was then recorded in writing for the Hellenistic world in the services of the mother churches of Christianity developed another kind of authenticity best illustrated by the then emerging victorious symbolisms—such as that of the cross, which, in its utter simplicity, seems to combine the form of homo erectus with his arms all-inclusively extended and that of the son of man dying a deliberately human death under the most vulnerable conditions, only to be resurrected as the savior. Or think of the maternal Madonna who gradually occupied such a shining ceremonial center. The ensuing history of ritualization, however, with all its wealth of new social, cultural, and artistic forms, eventually could not escape manufacturing its own kind of compulsive ritualism, including a new pseudo-speciation which permitted the saved species to use even the Christian faith as a rationale for crusades—and murderous hate.

All this must make us even more attentive to the study of the origins and eventual evolution of those simplest revelatory formulations. For their very brevity and simplicity of manifest meaning could never be contrived, and could emerge only when their time had come. They must count as an event central to our Judaeo-Christian heritage—a step in human comprehension and self-awareness which is by no means fully expressed in, or restricted to, its ecclesiastic fate.

NOTE

1. Erik H. Erikson, *Dimensions of a New Identity* (New York: W. W. Norton and Company, 1974).

PART IV

D. W. Winnicott

Donald Woods Winnicott was born in 1896 in Plymouth, England, and died in London in 1971. He attended Jesus College, Cambridge, where he took a degree in biology and then medicine. As a young medical resident at St. Bartholomew's Hospital in London, he intended to become a general medical practitioner in the countryside, but these plans were jettisoned when a friend lent him a copy of Freud's *Interpretation of Dreams*, which made such a powerful impression on him that he immediately decided to remain in London to undergo a personal analysis. He was also influenced at the time by a book on Freud by Oskar Pfister, the Swiss clergyman and supporter of psychoanalysis, who was later to write a major book in the psychoanalysis of religion, *Christianity and Fear*. Winnicott's decision to enter psychoanalysis was also accompanied by a desire to become a children's doctor, and throughout his life as a psychoanalyst he drew on his experience as a pediatrician, specializing in work with children and adolescents.[1]

Among his publications, the most widely circulated are *The Maturational Process and the Facilitating Environment* (1965), *Playing and Reality* (1971), and a posthumously published collection of essays and talks, *Home Is Where We Start From* (1986). Throughout his career, he wrote brief essays in a simple, almost conversational style, eschewing complex psychoanalytic terms in favor of language deriving from his interactions with children and their mothers.

His acute powers of observation (a capacity he shared with Erikson, whose ability to relate to children was a hallmark of his own career) led to the proposal of several original concepts, usually put forward as hypotheses, the best known of which is presented in the lead essay in *Playing and Reality*, "Transitional Objects and Transitional Phenomena."[2] An excerpt from this paper is the first selection from Winnicott's writings included here. While he made only a passing reference to religion in this essay, the basic idea expressed there has been adopted by several scholars for the psychoanalytic study of religion, including Paul W. Pruyser, W. W. Meissner, and Ana-Maria Rizzuto, resulting in Winnicott's being viewed as a major contributor to the psychoanalytic study of religion in spite of the fact that he did not address the subject of religion in any sustained or systematic way. He often gave talks to religious groups but left them to devise their own applications of his ideas to religious phenomena.

His thesis in the essay is that in addition to the "inner reality" of the individual and the "external reality" or environment, there is an intermediate area of experiencing to which inner reality and external life both contribute. He thinks of this intermediate area as a kind of "resting place" for the individual engaged in the perpetual human task of keeping inner and outer reality separate yet interrelated. He perceived this third reality in the infant's tendency to use her fists, fingers, and thumbs for instinctual satisfaction, and then after a few months to play with dolls or some other special objects, becoming, as it were, "addicted" to them. These objects stand at the nexus of the inner world and outer reality, having a foot in both, and thus are not clearly differentiated as either "me" or "not-me." He emphasizes the infant's use of a transitional object as a defense against anxiety, especially of the depressive type, and notes that the object may become vitally important to the infant at the time of going to sleep. He also indicates that the object is the recipient of ambivalent feelings, of both instinctual loving and hating, and is thus subject to being caressed one moment and mutilated the next. To accomplish its purpose, the object must survive both forms of contact, but mere survival is not enough, as it must also be perceived to respond or react to the infant's affections or blandishments, "to give warmth, or to move, or to have texture, or to do something that seems to show it has vitality or reality of its own."[3]

Eventually, these objects lose their emotional significance for the child; in effect, the child grows out of them. The reason why this normally occurs without their being mourned (or repressed) is that the infant has replaced the objects with a whole transitional field or sphere, which exists independently of any specific object, having taken on a reality of its own. While the fetishistic quality of the original transitional objects of infancy has implications for religion, the transitional sphere, with its variety of objects, has played a more important role in the psychoanalysis of religion, largely because Winnicott suggested that this intermediate state is the very "substance of *illusion,* that which is allowed the infant, and which in adult life is inherent in art and religion, and yet becomes the hallmark of madness when an adult puts too powerful a claim on the credulity of others, forcing them to acknowledge a sharing of illusion that is not their own."[4]

In effect, Winnicott here adopts Freud's view of illusion in a way that Freud did not, even suggesting it has status equal to the objective world (that is, those aspects of the external world toward which one takes a purely analytical attitude). Thus, he makes the case that, epistemologically, the convictions that form with regard to the transitional sphere are not inferior to those that involve the more stringent criteria of reality-testing. This is because the transitional sphere is a neutral area of experience which is not to be challenged: "Of the transitional object it can be said that it is a matter of agreement between us and the baby that we will never ask the question: 'Did you conceive of this or was it presented to you from without?' The important point is that no decision on this point is expected. The question is not to be formulated."[5] On the other hand, Winnicott notes that the transitional sphere is the locus not only of illusion but of disillusionment as well, the latter occurring when the objects within the sphere prove unreliable. Among adults, the equivalent to the object's failure to survive the infant's caresses and mutilations is the failure of the belief or practice to remain credible, or effective, especially perhaps in the alleviation of anxiety.

That his concepts of the transitional object and sphere have been employed in the psychoanalytic study of religion is a result that Winnicott seems to have anticipated—though surely not in its scope and influence—in his view that the transitional object has symbolic value. He notes in this regard that the wafer as used in Christian Eucharistic ceremonies may be thought of as a kind of transitional object.[6] Illustrative of such employment is Paul W. Pruyser's application, in *Between Belief and Unbelief,* of Winnicott's concept to the roles of magic and mystery in religion, to the trust in God exhibited by Job, and to the appeal and affront of ritual.[7] In *The Play of the Imagination,*

Pruyser added the theme of transcendence and addressed Freud's view of religion as illusion from a Winnicottian perspective, urging the development of skill in "illusion-processing" lest the religious use of the "illusionistic sphere" become perverted by lack of vigilance and false premises, succumbing to "dumb superstition." [8] In *Psychoanalysis and Religious Experience,* W. W. Meissner applied Winnicott's concept to the dimension of faith, the God-representation, the use of symbols, and the experience of prayer, noting their transitional aspects and their impact on psychic adjustment.[9] The second selection involving Winnicott's work is an excerpt from Meissner's chapter, "Religion as Transitional." While this selection departs from this volume's focus on the primary writings of the six authors included here, this was deemed appropriate in Winnicott's case because of his influence on the psychoanalysis of religion despite the fact that he did not develop this application himself. Meissner is a psychoanalyst and a Jesuit priest.

The third essay in this section, on the use of an object, gives particular attention to Winnicott's insistence that the transitional object is not only related to but also put to some use. In his essay on transitional objects and phenomena, he had noted that object use follows sequentially from object-relating and reflects the fact that the object is not merely a creation of the self but exists quite independently of the self, as not-self. His essay on object use develops this point further, emphasizing that in order for its independent existence to be secured, thereby enabling the infant to experience herself as an independent existent as well, the object must survive her attempt to destroy it. When it does so, achieving "object-constancy," it can be "used" by the self, not in the sense of exploitation but in the sense of being a resource in times of difficulty or need, expectancy and longing, joy and exaltation. In effect, the reality of the self is secured by the object's capacity not to be "undone" by the infant, either by succumbing to the infant's destructive behavior or by retaliating against the infant. That the mother *is* capable of such retaliation is suggested in Winnicott's essay, "Hate in the Countertransference," where he lists eighteen reasons why a mother may resent—even have hateful feelings, however transient these may be—toward her infant child.[10]

This selection sets the stage for the fourth, which is explicitly concerned with religion, and written by a professor of English literature. The author, Brooke Hopkins, has devoted much of his attention to applying Winnicott's concept of the transitional sphere to the interpretation of literary texts, itself a popular use of Winnicott's work.[11] In the essay included here, and in a subsequent essay on the capacity to believe, he addresses specifically religious themes.[12] More specifically, he applies Winnicott's theme of object-use to the Christian belief in the resurrection of Jesus. Hopkins contends that, as a transitional object in light of his ability to attract both devotion and animosity, Jesus' "object-constancy" is demonstrated in his survival of the crucifixion. Viewed thus, the Christian belief in original sin is also illumined, in that this belief emphasizes the permanence of the believer's destructive impulses and, therefore, of the necessity for Jesus to survive over and again, thus being a symbol of acceptance, of reassurance of divine favor, and of a nondespairing attitude toward the future. In addition to his employment of Winnicott's essay on object-use, Hopkins draws on Winnicott's own appropriation of Melanie Klein's concern with reparation in her well-known essay, "Love, Guilt, and Reparation." Thus, he relates Winnicott's concept of object-use to the theme of sin, repentance, and reparation for damages which Christianity adopted from Judaism. Following Winnicott's own allusion to the Christian Eucharist, he also notes that this rite reenacts the destruction and survival of the object, thus integrating the mythic (the resurrection theme) and ritual dimensions (the sacrament) of the Christian religion.

While Winnicott's concept of transitional objects and transitional sphere does not directly challenge Freud's view that religion may have historical truth without having material truth, applications of the concept (by Hopkins, Pruyser, Meissner, and others) to religion help to explain why religion itself has managed to survive throughout human history. As Pruyser indicates in *The Play of the Imagination*, the intermediate region of experiencing is the locus of both transcendence and mystery, two related forms of human experience to which religion is especially sensitive. These applications of Winnicott's ideas to religion have not, however, given sufficient attention to his emphasis on the fact that the object has her own ambivalent feelings toward the infant. As he writes in his aforementioned essay, "Hate in the Countertransference," "The mother, however, hates her infant from the word go. I believe Freud thought it possible that a mother may in certain circumstances have only love for her boy baby; but we may doubt this. . . . A mother has to be able to tolerate hating her baby without doing anything about it. She cannot express it to him."[13] When this view is applied to religion, it shows Winnicott's further relevance to the themes that Freud addresses in "The Moses of Michelangelo' (i.e., Moses' seething hatred for the people, which he nonetheless controls) and Bakan raises in his interpretation of Job. To some extent, Pruyser recognizes this darker side of God, noting that the "deity is not nice" to Job, yet Job continues to believe in Him because of his "trust that there is more to God than he has thus far experienced."[14] What Bakan emphasizes, though, is not so much that God may not always be "nice" but that God—as the Book of Job portrays him—has an infanticidal impulse toward his "children" that must be appeased by means of animal sacrifices or (as in the case of Job himself, a prefigurement of Jesus) a representative victim.

NOTES

1. For a fuller account of his life, see Dodi Goldman, *In Search of the Real: The Origins and Originality of D. W. Winnicott* (Northvale, N.J.: Jason Aronson, 1993).

2. "Transitional Objects and Transitional Phenomena," in D. W. Winnicott, *Playing and Reality* (London and New York: Tavistock/Routledge, 1982), 1–25.

3. Ibid., 5.

4. Ibid., 3.

5. Ibid., 12.

6. Ibid., 6.

7. Paul W. Pruyser, *Between Belief and Unbelief* (New York: Harper & Row, 1974).

8. Paul W. Pruyer, *The Play of the Imagination: Toward a Psychoanalysis of Culture* (New York: International Universities Press, 1983).

9. W. W. Meissner, *Psychoanalysis and Religious Experience* (New Haven: Yale University Press, 1984).

10. D. W. Winnicott, "Hate in the Countertransference," in *In One's Bones: The Clinical Genius of Winnicott*, ed. Dodi Goldman (Northvale, N.J.: Jason Aronson, 1993), 15–24.

11. See Peter L. Rudnytsky, ed., *Transitional Objects and Potential Spaces: Literary Uses of D. W. Winnicott* (New York: Columbia University Press, 1993).

12. Brooke Hopkins, "Winnicott and the Capacity to Believe," *International Journal of Psycho- Analysis* 78 (1997): 485–97.

13. Winnicott, "Hate in the Countertransference," 22–23.

14. Pruyser, *Between Belief and Unbelief*, 202.

CHAPTER 17

Transitional Objects and
Transitional Phenomena

D. W. WINNICOTT

It is well known that infants as soon as they are born tend to use
fist, fingers, thumbs in stimulation of the oral erotogenic zone, in
satisfaction of the instincts at that zone, and also in quiet union. It
is also well known that after a few months infants of either sex become
fond of playing with dolls, and that most mothers allow their infants
some special object and expect them to become, as it were, addicted to
such objects. There is a relationship between these two sets of phenomena that are separated by a time interval, and a study of the development from the earlier into the latter can be profitable, and can make
use of important clinical material that has been somewhat neglected.

The First Possession

Those who happen to be in close touch with mothers' interests and
problems will be already aware of the very rich patterns ordinarily displayed by babies in their use of the first "not-me" possession. These
patterns, being displayed, can be subjected to direct observation.
There is a wide variation to be found in a sequence of events that starts
with the newborn infant's fist-in-mouth activities, and leads eventually on to an attachment to a teddy, a doll or soft toy, or to a hard toy. It
is clear that something is important here other than oral excitement
and satisfactions, although this may be the basis of everything else.
Many other important things can be studied, and they include:

1. The nature of the object.
2. The infant's capacity to recognize the object as "not-me."
3. The place of the object—outside, inside, at the border.

4. The infant's capacity to create, think up, devise, originate, produce an object.

5. The initiation of an affectional type of object-relationship.

I have introduced the terms "transitional objects" and "transitional phenomena" for designation of the intermediate area of experience, between the thumb and the teddy bear, between the oral erotism and the true object-relationship, between primary creative activity and projection of what has already been introjected, between primary unawareness of indebtedness and the acknowledgement of indebtedness ("Say: 'ta' "). By this definition an infant's babbling and the way in which an older child goes over a repertory of songs and tunes while preparing for sleep come within the intermediate area as transitional phenomena, along with the use made of objects that are not part of the infant's body yet are not fully recognized as belonging to external reality.

Inadequacy of Usual Statement of Human Nature

It is generally acknowledged that a statement of human nature in terms of interpersonal relationships is not good enough even when the imaginative elaboration of function and the whole fantasy both conscious and unconscious, including the repressed unconscious, are allowed for. There is another way of describing persons that comes out of the researches of the past two decades. Of every individual who has reached to the stage of being a unit with a limiting membrane and an outside and an inside, it can be said that there is an *inner reality* to that individual, an inner world that can be rich or poor and can be at peace or in a state of war. This helps, but is it enough?

My claim is that if there is a need for this double statement, there is also need for a triple one: the third part of the life of a human-being, a part that we cannot ignore, is an intermediate area of *experiencing*, to which inner reality and external life both contribute. It is an area that is not challenged, because no claim is made on its behalf except that it shall exist as a resting-place for the individual engaged in the perpetual human task of keeping inner and outer reality separate yet interrelated.

It is usual to refer to "reality-testing," and to make a clear distinction between apperception and perception. I am here staking a claim for an intermediate state between a baby's inability and his growing ability to recognize and accept reality. I am therefore studying the substance of illusion, that which is allowed to the infant, and which in adult life is inherent in art and religion, and yet becomes the hallmark of madness when an adult puts too powerful a claim on the credulity of others, forcing them to acknowledge a sharing of illusion that is not their own. We can share a respect for *illusory experience,* and if we wish we may collect together and form a group on the basis of the similarity of our illusory experiences. This is a natural root of grouping among human beings.

I hope it will be understood that I am not referring exactly to the little child's teddy bear or to the infant's first use of the fist (thumb, fingers). I am not specifically studying the first object of object-relationships. I am concerned with the first possession, and with the intermediate area between the subjective and that which is objectively perceived.

Development of a Personal Pattern

There is plenty of reference in psychoanalytic literature to the progress from "hand to mouth" to "hand to genital" but perhaps less to further progress to the handling of truly "not-me" objects. Sooner or later in an infant's development there comes a tendency on the part of the infant to weave other-than-me objects into the personal pattern. To some extent these objects stand for the breast, but it is not especially this point that is under discussion.

In the case of some infants the thumb is placed in the mouth while fingers are made to caress the face by pronation and supination movements of the forearm. The mouth is then active in relation to the thumb, but not in relation to the fingers. The fingers caressing the upper lip, or some other part, may be or may become more important than the thumb engaging the mouth. Moreover, this caressing activity may be found alone, without the more direct thumb-mouth union.

In common experience one of the following occurs, complicating an auto-erotic experience such as thumb-sucking:

   (i) with the other hand the baby takes an external object, say a part of a sheet or blanket, into the mouth along with the fingers; or

  (ii) somehow or other the bit of cloth is held and sucked, or not actually sucked; the objects used naturally include napkins and (later) handkerchiefs, and this depends on what is readily and reliably available; or

 (iii) the baby starts from early months to pluck wool and to collect it and to use it for the caressing part of the activity; less commonly, the wool is swallowed, even causing trouble; or

 (iv) mouthing occurs, accompanied by sounds of "mum-mum," babbling, anal noises, the first musical notes, and so on.

One may suppose that thinking, or fantasying, gets linked up with these functional experiences.

All these things I am calling *transitional phenomena*. Also, out of all this (if we study any one infant) there may emerge some thing or some phenomenon—perhaps a bundle of wool or the corner of a blanket or eiderdown, or a word or tune, or a mannerism—that becomes vitally important to the infant for use at the time of going to sleep, and is a defense against anxiety, especially anxiety of depressive type. Perhaps some soft object or other type of object has been found and used by the infant, and this then becomes what I am calling a *transitional object*. This object goes on being important. The parents get to know its value and carry it round when traveling. The mother lets it get dirty and even smelly, knowing that by washing it she introduces a break in continuity in the infant's experience, a break that may destroy the meaning and value of the object to the infant.

I suggest that the pattern of transitional phenomena begins to show at about four to six to eight to twelve months. Purposely I leave room for wide variations. Patterns set in infancy may persist into childhood, so that the original soft object continues to be absolutely necessary at bed-time or at times of loneliness or when a depressed mood threatens. In health, however, there is a gradual extension of range of interest, and eventually the extended range is maintained, even when depressive anxiety is near. A need for a specific object or a behavior pattern that started at a very early date may reappear at a later age when deprivation threatens.

This first possession is used in conjunction with special techniques derived from very early infancy, which can include or exist apart from the more direct autoerotic activities. Gradually in the life of an infant teddies and dolls and hard toys are acquired. Boys to some extent tend to go over to use hard objects, whereas girls tend to proceed right ahead to the acquisition of a family. It is important to note, however, that *there is no noticeable difference between boy and girl in their use of the original "not-me" possession*, which I am calling the transitional object.

As the infant starts to use organized sounds ("mum," "ta," "da") there may appear a "word" for the transitional object. The name given by the infant to these earliest objects is often significant, and it usually has a word used by the adults partly incorporated in it. For instance, "baa" may be the name, and the "b" may have come from the adult's use of the word "baby" or "bear."

I should mention that sometimes there is no transitional object except the mother herself. Or an infant may be so disturbed in emotional development that the transition state cannot be enjoyed, or the sequence of objects used is broken. The sequence may nevertheless be maintained in a hidden way.

Summary of Special Qualities in the Relationship

1. The infant assumes rights over the object, and we agree to this assumption. Nevertheless, some abrogation of omnipotence is a feature from the start.
2. The object is affectionately cuddled as well as excitedly loved and mutilated.
3. It must never change, unless changed by the infant.
4. It must survive instinctual loving, and also hating and, if it be a feature, pure aggression.
5. Yet it must seem to the infant to give warmth, or to move, or to have texture, or to do something that seems to show it has vitality or reality of its own.
6. It comes from without from our point of view, but not so from the point of view of the baby. Neither does it come from within; it is not a hallucination.
7. Its fate is to be gradually allowed to be decathected, so that in the course of years it becomes not so much forgotten as relegated to limbo. By this I mean that in health the transitional object does not "go inside" nor does the feeling about it necessarily undergo repression. It is not forgotten and it is not mourned. It loses meaning, and this is because the transitional phenomena have become diffused, have become spread out over the whole intermediate territory between "inner psychic reality" and "the external world as perceived by two persons in common," that is to say, over the whole cultural field.

At this point my subject widens out into that of play, and of artistic creativity and appreciation, and of religious feeling, and of dreaming, and also of fetishism, lying and stealing, the origin and loss of affectionate feeling, drug addiction, the talisman of obsessional rituals, etc.

Illusion and the Value of Illusion

The mother, at the beginning, by an almost 100 per cent adaptation affords the infant the opportunity for the *illusion* that her breast is part of the infant. It is, as it were, under the baby's magical control. The same can be said in terms of infant care in general, in the quiet times between excitements. Omnipotence is nearly a fact of experience. The mother's eventual task is gradually to disillusion the infant, but she has no hope of success unless at first she has been able to give sufficient opportunity for illusion.

In another language, the breast is created by the infant over and over again out of the infant's capacity to love or (one can say) out of need. A subjective phenomenon develops in the baby, which we call the mother's breast.[1] The mother places the actual breast just there where the infant is ready to create, and at the right moment.

From birth, therefore, the human being is concerned with the problem of the relationship between what is objectively perceived and what is subjectively conceived of, and in the solution of this problem there is no health for the human being who has not been started off well enough by the mother. *The intermediate area to which I am referring is the area that is allowed to the infant between primary creativity and objective perception based on reality-testing.* The transitional phenomena represent the early stages of the use of illusion, without which there is no meaning for the human being in the idea of a relationship with an object that is perceived by others as external to that being.

The idea illustrated in *Figure 1* is this: that at some theoretical point early in the development of every human individual as infant in a certain setting provided by the mother is capable of conceiving of the idea of something that would meet the growing need that arises out of instinctual tension. The infant cannot be said to know at first what is to be created. At this point in time the mother presents herself. In the ordinary way she gives her breast and her potential feeding urge. The mother's adaptation to the infant's needs, when good enough, gives the infant the *illusion* that there is an external reality that corresponds to the infant's own capacity to create. In other words, there is an overlap between what the mother supplies and what the child might conceive of. To the observer, the child perceives what the mother actually presents, but this is not the whole truth. The infant perceives the breast only in so far as a breast could be created just there and then. There is no interchange between the mother and the infant. Psychologically the infant takes from a breast that is part of the infant, and the mother gives milk to an infant that is part of herself. In psychology, the idea of interchange is based on an illusion in the psychologist.

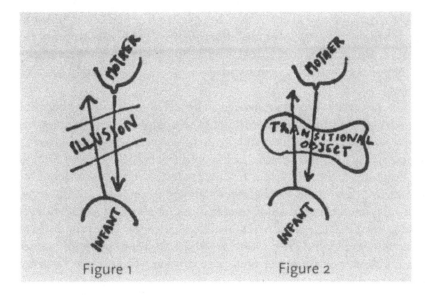

Figure 1   Figure 2

In *Figure 2* a shape is given to the area of illusion to illustrate what I consider to be the main function of the transitional object and of transitional phenomena. The transitional object and the transitional phenomena start each human being off with what will always be important for them, i.e. a neutral area of experience which will not be challenged. *Of the transitional object it can be said that it is a matter of agreement between us and the baby that we will never ask the question: "Did you conceive of this or was it presented to you from without?" The important point is that no decision on this point is expected. The question is not to be formulated.* This problem, which undoubtedly concerns the human infant in a hidden way at the beginning, gradually becomes an obvious problem on account of the fact that the mother's main task (next to providing opportunity for illusion) is disillusionment.

Development of the Theory of Illusion-Disillusion

It is assumed here that the task of reality-acceptance is never completed, that no human being is free from the strain of relating inner and outer reality, and that relief from this strain is provided by an intermediate area of experience which is not challenged (arts, religion, etc.). This intermediate area is in direct continuity with the play area of the small child who is "lost" in play. In infancy this intermediate area is necessary for the initiation of a relationship between the child and the world, and is made possible by good-enough mothering at the early critical phase. Essential to all this is continuity (in time) of the external emotional environment and of particular elements in the physical environment such as the transitional object or objects.

The transitional phenomena are allowable to the infant because of the parents' intuitive recognition of the strain inherent in objective perception and we do not challenge the infant in regard to subjectivity or objectivity just here where there is the transitional object. Should an adult make claims on us for our acceptance of the objectivity of his subjective phenomena we discern or diagnose madness. If, however, the adult can manage to enjoy the personal intermediate area without making claims, then we can acknowledge our own corresponding intermediate areas, and are pleased to find a degree of overlapping, that is to say common experience between members of a group in art or religion or philosophy.

Summary

Attention is drawn to the rich field for observation provided by the earliest experiences of the healthy infant as expressed principally in the relationship to the first possession. This first possession is related backwards in time to auto-erotic phenomena and fist- and thumb-sucking, and also forwards to the first soft animal or doll and to hard toys. It is related to the external object (mother's breast) and to internal objects (magically introjected breast), but is distinct from each.

Transitional objects and transitional phenomena belong to the realm of illusion which is at the basis of initiation of experience. This early stage in development is made possible by the mother's special capacity for making adaptation to the needs of her infant, thus allowing the infant the illusion that what the infant creates really exists. This intermediate area of experience, unchallenged in respect of its belonging to inner or external (shared) reality, constitutes the greater part of the infant's experience, and throughout life is retained in the intense experiencing that belongs to the arts and to religion and to imaginative living, and to creative scientific work. An infant's transitional object ordinarily becomes gradually decathected, especially as cultural interests develop.

What emerges from these considerations is the further idea that paradox accepted can have positive value. The resolution of paradox leads to a defense organization which in the adult one can encounter as true and false self organization (Winnicott, 1960a).

NOTE

1. I include the whole technique of mothering. When it is said that the first object is the breast, the word "breast" is used, I believe, to stand for the technique of mothering as well as for the actual flesh. It is not impossible for a mother to be a good-enough mother (in my way of putting it) with a bottle for the actual feeling.

CHAPTER 18

Transitional Phenomena in Religion

W. W. MEISSNER

T he thesis we wish to pursue here, following the suggestion of Winnicott, is that religion partakes of the character of transitional phenomena or the transitional process and as such achieves its psychological reality and its psychic vitality in the potential space of illusory experience. It shares this participation in the illusory with other aspects of human culture but is unique among them because of the extent to which it impinges on what is most immediate and personal in man's psychic life, namely, man's sense of himself— his meaning, purpose, and destiny.

While many aspects of religious experience might lend themselves readily to an analysis of transitional and illusory aspects, I will select for the present discussion the dimension of faith, the God-representation, the use of symbols, and the experience of prayer. My purpose in treating these areas is simply to demonstrate their transitional aspects and some of their impact as such on psychic adjustment. In so doing, I must regrettably ignore many other components of these complex psychic experiences.

1

The faith experience has a number of attributes that characterize it as a form of transitional experience. The believer does not regard his faith as a matter of wishful hallucination or of purely subjective implications. Rather, his faith speaks to him of the nature of the world in which he lives, of the meaning and purpose of his existence there, and, in most religious traditions, of the relationship of that world and himself to a divine being who creates, loves, guides, and judges. At the same time that faith asserts, however, it cannot demonstrate the independent reality of the spiritual world and to which it lays claim. Consequently, the experience of faith is not totally subjective, nor is it totally objective. Rather, it represents a realm in which the subjective and the objective interpenetrate.

The question we are addressing here is not that of the truth value of the believer's faith. The point, rather, is that to envision his faith solely in subjective terms, as essentially did Freud, is to do a disservice to the believer and actually to distort the substance of his belief. The experience of faith, however, is neither exclusively subjective nor wholly objective by reason of its own intentionality; rather, it is a realm in which both the subjective and objective poles of experience contribute to the substance of belief.

There are also parallels to the infant's experience with the mother in the experience of faith. The believer's faith does not spring from a vacuum but comes to life within a context of belief. The capacity for faith is vitalized in a family environment in which faith plays a more or less significant role, and in the context of a community of believers that presents the individual with a more or less systematically elaborated and coherent set of doctrines to be believed. In this sense, the emergence of faith is much like the infant's creation of the mother. The what and how of belief in any given religious tradition are presented to the child in such a manner that he can respond to them and conjoin them to his own inner need to believe. In this sense, then, the young believer comes to create beliefs in conjunction with the objective reality of a set of beliefs that he finds in his environment.

Obviously, the vicissitudes of this process are complex and extremely variable. The extent to which individuals accept the belief system of an established religious community varies considerably. Ultimately at issue are the establishment and maintenance of the individual's sense of identity in relation to and in the context of a community that he comes to accept as part of his view of himself, his life, and his world, in reciprocation of its acceptance of his individuality as part of the community of believers.

The need and capacity to integrate oneself with such a community must be balanced against the need to rebel and to find and express one's individuality. In some basic sense, the individual, personal faith of the believer is always somewhat removed from, and in tension and dialectical interaction with, the belief or dogma of his religious community. Rarely, if ever, is the sense of faith and commitment complete.

At the extremes of differentiation and disparity, one finds expressions of religious rejection, alienation, and rebellion, on the one hand, and complete submission and religious compliance, on the other. Between them lie infinite degrees of variation within which most human beings live out their religious convictions.

The faith of any human being, then, is both received from the religious community of his affiliation and created as a matter of internal and subjective expression. In this sense faith can be regarded as taking shape within the realm of illusory experience, and the faith of religious communities as being realized through the sharing of illusory experience within a given group of believers. Within any religious group, such sharing of illusion is a matter of degree that allows for both individual variation and a community of sharing.

2

An essential aspect of the faith experience is the individual's representation of the figure of God. Like other transitional objects, the experience of God or the God-representation is neither a hallucination nor is it totally beyond the reach of subjectivity; rather, it is located, in Winnicott's terms, "outside, inside, at the border." Unlike the teddy bear or the blanket, God is created out of representational derivatives that stem particularly from the child's experience of primary objects.

As a transitional object, God is also of a special order in that he does not follow the usual course of such objects—that is, he is not gradually decathected, ultimately to be forgotten or relegated to psychic limbo. Rather, the God-representation is cathected with increasing intensity during the pregenital years and reaches a peak during the high point of oedipal excitement. The representation that endures depends on the manner of the child's oedipal resolution and the resulting psychic compromises. Rather than lose force, the meaning of the God-representation is intensified by the oedipal experience. Even when the outcome is loss of meaning or rejection, God as a transitional object remains available for further processing, for further acceptance or rejection. Even in a state of relative abandonment or repression, the God-representation maintains the potentiality for revivification and further integration. The psychic process of creating and finding God— that is, this personalized representation acting as transitional object— continues through the course of the human life cycle.

While God shares the transitional space with other cultural representations, the God-representation has a special place in that it is uniquely connected to man's sense of himself, of the meaning and purpose of his existence and his ultimate destiny. Perhaps more important than anything else is the fact that once this transitional object representation is created, whether it is dormant or active, it remains available for continuing psychic integration. The God-representation reflects the ongoing process of exchange that develops in relation to the individual's evolving self-representation. This process is an authentic dialectic insofar as the God-representation transcends the subjective realm. As Rizzuto notes, "The transitional object representation of God can be used for religious purposes precisely insofar as he is beyond magic."[1] And as Winnicott notes, "The transitional object is never under magical control like the internal object, nor is it outside control as the real mother is."[2]

3

One of the striking aspects of religious culture is its use of material objects to signify various aspects of belief. This objective or material aspect of cultural expression has been referred to by anthropologists as "material culture." We are addressing here the concretization of signs and symbols of religious belief systems. In this category we can include the crucifix, the cross, the symbolic actions and gestures of the Roman Catholic Mass, bread and wine as symbols of the Body and Blood of Christ, the Star of David, the menorah, and the prayers and rituals of liturgical practice, whether in the Catholic church, the Protestant meeting house, or the Jewish synagogue. Each religion provides a rich lore of symbolic gestures and materials that embody and convey the content of its belief system. This applies not only to liturgical practice but to scriptural tradition as well. In this sense, Scripture acquires by reason of its privileged place in the body of religious belief a symbolic value beyond the mere content of the texts.

Such symbols, as they take their place within the religious system, are not to be envisioned merely in terms of their physical attributes. The crucifix is not just a piece of carved wood, nor is the Torah simply a roll of parchment with ancient writing on it. Rather, they are religious symbols and as such become the vehicles for the expression of meanings and values that transcend their physical characteristics. This symbolic dimension is not a product of the objects themselves, however; it can come about only by some attribution to them by the believer. Consequently, the objects as religious symbols are neither exclusively perceived in real and objective terms, nor simply produced by subjective creation. Rather, they evolve from the amalgamation of what is real, material, and objective as it is experienced, penetrated, and creatively reshaped by the subjective belief and patterns of meaning attributed to the object by the believer.

As is the case with other forms of transitional experience, this process can be misdirected into infantile or pathological channels. Just as the transitional object of the child can degenerate into a fetish object, transitional religious experience can be distorted in less authentic, relatively fetishistic directions that tend to contaminate and distort the more profoundly meaningful aspects of the religious experience. When this fetishistic course is followed, religious objects or practices begin to take on a magical quality that perverts their authentic religious impulse and meaning. Religious objects, prayers, and rites become magical talismans in the service of magical expectations and infantile needs.

4

A final place in which the transitional experience comes to fruition in the religious realm is in prayer. In this activity, the believer immerses himself in the religious experience in a more direct, immediate, and personal way than in any other aspect of his religious involvement— whether in common, as a liturgical function, or in private, as a more or less intrapsychic function.

It is here that the qualities of the God-representation and their relationship to the believer's self-representation become immediate. The God he prays to is not ultimately the God of the theologians or of the philosophers, nor is this God likely to be in any sense directly reconcilable with the God of Scripture. Rather, the individual believer prays to a God who is represented by the highly personalized transitional object representation in his inner, private, personally idiosyncratic belief system. Thus, all the unconscious and preconscious as well as conscious and reflective elements of the individual's relationship to God and the characteristics of his God-representation come into play. These may include elements that are more consciously mature and self-reflective but also elements that stem from earlier developmental levels and have a more infantile, dependent, and even narcissistic quality.

One might say that in prayer the individual figuratively enters the transitional space where he meets his God-representation. Prayer thus can become a channel for expressing what is most unique, profound, and personal in individual psychology. All the elements of transference that have become familiar to psychoanalysts can enter into the prayer experience and come to shape the individual's experience both of God and of himself in its context. Indeed, a great deal more can and should be said about the psychology of prayer, but our purpose here is only to indicate the extent to which it shares in the quality of transitional experience and expresses another aspect of the illusory dimension of religious experience.

NOTES

1. Ana-Maria Rizzuto, *The Birth of the Living God* (Chicago: University of Chicago Press, 1979), p. 180.

2. D. W. Winnicott, "Transitional Objects and Transitional Phenomena," in *Playing and Reality* (New York: Basic Books, 1971), p. 10.

CHAPTER 19

The Use of an Object and
Relating through Identifications

D. W. WINNICOTT

I propose to put forward for discussion the idea of the use of an object. The allied subject of relating to objects seems to me to have had our full attention. The idea of the use of an object has not, however, been so much examined, and it may not even have been specifically studied. When I speak of the use of an object, however, I take object-relating for granted, and add new features that involve the nature and the behavior of the object. For instance, the object, if it is to be used, must necessarily be real in the sense of being part of shared reality, not a bundle of projections. It is this, I think, that makes for the world of difference that there is between relating and usage.

If I am right in this, then it follows that discussion of the subject of relating is a much easier exercise for analysts than is the discussion of usage, since relating may be examined as a phenomenon of the subject, and psychoanalysis always likes to be able to eliminate all factors that are environmental, except in so far as the environment can be thought of in terms of projective mechanisms. But in examining usage there is no escape: the analyst must take into account the nature of the object, not as a projection, but as a thing in itself.

For the time being may I leave it at that, that relating can be described in terms of the individual subject, and that usage cannot be described except in terms of acceptance of the object's independent existence, its property of having been there all the time. You will see that it is just these problems that concern us when we look at the area that I have tried to draw attention to in my work on what I have called transitional phenomena. But this change does not come about automatically, by maturational process alone. It is this detail that I am concerned with.

In clinical terms: two babies are feeding at the breast. One is feeding on the self, since the breast and the baby have not yet become (for the baby) separate phenomena. The other is feeding from an other-than-me source, or an object that can be given cavalier treatment without effect on the baby unless it retaliates. Mothers, like analysts, can be good or not good enough; some can and some cannot carry the baby over from relating to usage.

I should like to put in a reminder here that the essential feature in the concept of transitional objects and phenomena (according to my presentation of the subject) is *the paradox, and the acceptance of the paradox:* the baby creates the object, but the object was there waiting to be created and to become a cathected object. I tried to draw attention to this aspect of transitional phenomena by claiming that in the rules of the game we all know that we will never challenge the baby to elicit an answer to the question: did you create that or did you find it?

I am now ready to go straight to the statement of my thesis. It seems I am afraid to get there, as if I fear that once the thesis is stated the purpose of my communication is at an end, because it is so very simple. To use an object the subject must have developed a *capacity* to use objects. This is part of the change to the reality principle.

This capacity cannot be said to be inborn, nor can its development in an individual be taken for granted. The development of a capacity to use an object is another example of the maturational process as something that depends on a facilitating environment. In the sequence one can say that first there is object-relating, then in the end there is object-use; in between, however, is the most difficult thing, perhaps, in human development; or the most irksome of all the early failures that come for mending. This thing that there is in between relating and use is the subject's placing of the object outside the area of the subject's omnipotent control; that is, the subject's perception of the object as an external phenomenon, not as a projective entity, in fact recognition of it as an entity in its own right.

This change (from relating to usage) means that the subject destroys the object. From here it could be argued by an armchair philosopher that there is therefore no such thing in practice as the use of an object: if the object is external, then the object is destroyed by the subject. Should the philosopher come out of his chair and sit on the floor with his patient, however, he will find that there is an immediate position. In other words, he will find that after "subject relates to object" comes "subject destroys object" (as it becomes external); and then may come *"object survives destruction by the subject."* But there may or may not be survival. A new feature thus arrives in the theory of object-relating. The subject says to the object: "I destroyed you," and the object is there to receive the communication. From now on the subject says: "Hullo object!" "I destroyed you." "I love you." "You have value for me because of your survival of my destruction of you." "While I am loving you I am all the time destroying you in (unconscious) *fantasy*." Here fantasy begins for the individual. The subject can now use the object that has survived. It is important to note that it is not only that the subject destroys the object because the object is placed outside the area of omnipotent control. It is equally significant to state this the other way round and to say that it is the destruction of the object that places the object outside the area of the subject's omnipotent control. In these ways the object develops its own autonomy and life, and (if it survives) contributes-in to the subject, according to its own properties. In other words, because of the survival of the object, the subject may now have started to live a life in the world of objects, and so the subject stands to gain immeasurably; but the price has to be paid in acceptance of the ongoing destruction in unconscious fantasy relative to object-relating.

Let me repeat. This is a position that can be arrived at by the individual in early stages of emotional growth only through the actual survival of cathected objects that are at the time in process of becoming destroyed because real, becoming real because destroyed (being destructible and expendable). From now on, this stage having been reached, projective mechanisms assist in the act of *noticing what is there*, but they are not *the reason why the object is there*. In my opinion this is a departure from theory which tends to a conception of external reality only in terms of the individual's projective mechanisms.

The central postulate in this thesis is that, whereas the subject does not destroy the subjective object (projection material), destruction turns up and becomes a central feature so far as the object is objectively perceived, has autonomy, and belongs to "shared" reality. This is the difficult part of my thesis, at least for me. It is generally understood that the reality principle involves the individual in anger and reactive destruction, but my thesis is that the destruction plays its part in making the reality, placing the object outside the self. For this to happen, favorable conditions are necessary. This is simply a matter of examining the reality principle under high power. As I see it, we are familiar with the change whereby projection mechanisms enable the subject to take cognizance of the object. This is not the same as claiming that the object exists for the subject because of the operation of the subject's projection mechanisms. At first the observer uses words that seem to apply to both ideas at one and the same time, but under scrutiny we see that the two ideas are by no means identical. It is exactly here that we direct our study.

At the point of development that is under survey the subject is creating the object in the sense of finding externality itself, and it has to be added that this experience depends on the object's capacity to survive. (It is important that "survive," in this context, means "not retaliate.") It appears to me that the idea of a developmental phase involving survival of object does affect the theory of the roots of aggression. It is no good saying that a baby of a few days old envies the breast. It is legitimate, however, to say that at whatever age a baby begins to allow the breast an external position (outside the area of projection), then this means that destruction of the breast has become a feature. I mean the actual impulse to destroy. It is an important part of what a mother does, to be the first person to take the baby through this first version of the many that will be encountered, of attack that is survived. This is the right moment in the child's development, because of the child's relative feebleness, so that destruction can fairly easily be survived. However, even so it is a tricky matter; it is only too easy for a mother to react moralistically when her baby bites and hurts. But this language involving "the breast" is jargon. The whole area of development and management is involved, in which adaptation is related to dependence.

It will be seen that, although destruction is the word I am using, this actual destruction belongs to the object's failure to survive. Without this failure, destruction remains potential. The word "destruction" is needed, not because of the baby's impulse to destroy, but because of the object's liability not to survive, which also means to suffer change in quality, in attitude.

CHAPTER 20

Jesus and Object Use: A Winnicottian Account of the Resurrection Myth

BROOKE HOPKINS

N o one will deny the centrality of the myth of the resurrection to Christian theology. To be sure, accounts of Christianity are as various as the spectrum, but if Christians can be said to be united in anything, it is in the belief that Jesus of Nazareth was crucified, died, buried, and rose again in the flesh, both to forgive men for the sins they had committed and to proclaim his eternal love.[1] This is the central event in Christian history, an event that is commemorated and reenacted in an endless variety of communal and private contexts by Christians throughout the world. Regardless of the objective truth of this account, it would be hard to deny its deep emotional and psychological appeal for millions of believers. That appeal, however, has never been adequately explained in emotional and psychological terms, and this is what I would like to try to do.

The purpose of this essay, then, will be to offer an account of the resurrection myth. The terms of the account will be psychoanalytic, largely Winnicottian, in character. This is not only because Winnicott's work tends to be far more sympathetic to the role played by cultural and religious phenomena in human development than Freud's does.[2] It is also because Winnicott's writing, particularly his writing on the paradoxical role of aggressive and destructive impulses in human development, sheds direct light on the process dramatized by the myth itself— specifically, the destructiveness embodied by the act of crucifixion and the central fact of Jesus' reappearance, his acceptance of the world that tried to destroy him. These seem to reflect developmental processes Winnicott describes as leading to the capacity to "use" objects, that is, the capacity to experience them as separate from oneself, as reliable and constant despite their separateness.[3] Of course, Winnicott's own work does not stand wholly outside the circle of cultural influence. And, while he tends to disapprove of many aspects of conventional Christian morality, particularly that which "continues to create and re-create God as a place to put that which is good in [man] himself, and which he might spoil if he kept it in himself along with all the hate and destructiveness which is also to be found there,"[4] it might be the case that his underlying conception of infant and adult relationships is formed and influenced by, perhaps even drawn out of, a tradition in which destructiveness, rejection, aggression, and yet survival and forgiveness are the central themes. If so, this is simply another version of the hermeneutic circle. But we will leave such ultimately unanswerable questions aside for the time being in order to pursue our goal; let us first look briefly at the central features of the myth itself.

Two things stand out in the account: the destructiveness of Jesus' death on the cross and the miracle of his survival, the fact that he continues to love despite the terrible offence committed against his body in the act of crucifixion. The former, of course, serves to represent the Christian concept of sin in its starkest and most uncompromising form, the murder of the Messiah, the God/man who came to bring peace into the world. One has only to think of the vivid depictions of Jesus' crucifixion to recall the physical violence of the act—the scourged flesh, the agony of the last moments, and the callousness of those who inflicted the pain. Suffering is almost an understatement. The latter aspects of the account, Jesus' miraculous survival of the murderous acts committed against his person, serve to represent the Christian concept of redemption, redemption through love; they offer the promise of salvation for the individual and for mankind as a whole. Jesus' resurrection serves as definitive proof for believers of his godhood and the promise of eternal life, while his forgiveness of those who caused his suffering likewise serves as proof of the permanent and complete nature of his divine love. These, then, are the two central features of Jesus' story: the subjection to destructive attacks and the survival of those attacks, the ability to accept remorse, to continue to love those who inflicted them. Destructiveness and continuing love are the salient features of the central event of Christian history, the event that lies at the heart of Christian doctrine.

Like all "cultural objects,"[5] objects that inhabit that "potential space"[6] in which individuals and groups do their most creative living, the story of Jesus' death and resurrection mirrors fundamental developmental processes. In this case, I want to argue, the processes are those whereby the infant and, later, the adult, comes to acknowledge his or her own destructive impulses and, as a consequence of that acknowledgment, comes to discover the otherness, the reality of the object whose destruction was desired. In the case of the myth, and the historical events upon which it is based, of course, those desires are actually acted out. Jesus *is* crucified. But that is precisely what renders the myth such a powerful reflection of the processes it embodies, the processes whereby the survival of the object and its lack of retaliation for the destructive impulses directed against it are what transforms it into a *genuine* object of love.

According to Winnicott, the original object in human experience is the mother or, more precisely, the mother's breast. This is the original object of the infant's love. Paradoxically, however, this is also the original object of its aggression and destructiveness as well, the fantasized "attack and destruction" that inevitably accompanies "full blooded id-drives," particularly in the act of feeding.[7] From the infant's perspective, to take nourishment from the mother, to swallow the contents of her body, is inseparable in fantasy from destroying her. Furthermore, since "the instinct-driven episodes . . . have acquired the full force of fantasies of oral sadism and other results of fusion," the infant's acts in feeding are genuinely aggressive in nature. But this aggression is transformed in its very occurrence and is in the end productive. The key to the successful outcome of this process, according to Winnicott, is the mother's capacity to survive the attacks directed against her, "to continue to be herself, to be empathic towards her infant, to be there to receive the spontaneous gesture, and to be pleased." This is what "makes the infant able to hold the anxiety" it inevitably feels, and "the anxiety held in this way becomes altered in quality and becomes a sense of guilt."[8] The process here is a transitional one. In the course of it the infant comes to feel guilt or, even more favorably, to transform latent guilt feelings for destructive fantasies into constructive, reparative behavior. Thus the infant achieves a new sense of the other—the mother—and of the reliability of her love. This results in what Winnicott calls "the development of the capacity for concern," a capacity that can only develop in the infant with the mother's survival of its attacks. Winnicott calls this a "benign cycle," a cycle that somehow makes constructive, positive use of destructiveness in the infant's discovery of the world.[9]

The process described above occurs at the earliest stages of development. According to Winnicott, however, it also repeats itself in later relationships involving various forms of transference: projection, idealization, and destructive fantasies. In his seminal paper, "The Use of an Object and Relating through Identification," Winnicott describes the process whereby what he calls the "subject" comes to relate to the "object" (in the sense in which that term is used in object relations theory) as something external, as fundamentally different from itself and as something that can be loved; this is to be able to *use* it. (By "use," it should be stressed, Winnicott does not mean manipulate or exploit; he means simply experience as something external, *different* from oneself.) These adult relationships also involve destructiveness, the subject's fantasized destruction of the object and, if the object survives, a new appreciation for its otherness, for what its survival has meant in terms of the subject's growth.

The first stage in this adult process of coming to use objects Winnicott calls "object-relating." That is when the subject relates to the object as "a bundle of projections," as part of, an extension of, itself, just as the infant did at the earliest stages of its relationship with the mother, the mother's breast, before its destructive fantasies and attending changes in perception made her real.[10] The transition between "object-relating" and "object-use" Winnicott describes as "the most difficult thing, perhaps, in human development." What it involves is "the subject's placing of the object outside the area [of its] omnipotent control . . . the subject's perception of the object as an external phenomenon, not as a projective entity . . . recognition of it as an entity in its own right."[11] This comes about through the subject's fantasized destruction of the object. The process here is an essentially dialectical one. Destruction of the object in fantasy leads to the discovery of the object's reality, its otherness, and vice versa: "the subject is being destroyed in fantasy as fantasy and is felt as real because of this, at the same time its realness makes *fantasy* destructiveness possible."[12] This results eventually in the creation of a new space, no longer a "potential space," but what Michael Eigen calls an "area of faith," an area in which the subject can relate to the object as "in some basic way outside [its] boundaries, [as] 'wholly other.' " This, Eigen goes on,

> opens the way for a new kind of freedom, one *because* there is radical otherness, a new realness of self-feeling exactly because the other is now felt as real as well. The core sense of creativeness that permeates transitional experiencing is reborn on a new level, in so far as genuine not-me nutriment becomes available for personal use. The subject can *use* otherness for true growth purposes and, through the risk of difference as such, gains access to the genuinely new.[13]

By this process, according to Winnicott, the subject comes "to live a life in a world of objects," always keeping in mind that "the price has to be paid in acceptance of the on-going destruction in unconscious fantasy relative to object-relating." The key word here is "acceptance"; this is the measure of the subject's growth.

In both the infant and adult developmental processes, the crucial factor in the scenario is the object's survival, its lack of retaliation against the subject for the subject's destructive fantasies. This provides the context for *both* the subject's rediscovery of the object as separate from, as external to, itself *and* its recognition of the destructive nature of its fantasies, its recognition of fantasy generally. Winnicott captures this moment in the following passage:

> After "subject relates to object" comes "subject destroys object" (as it becomes external); and then may come "*object survives* destruction by the subject." But there may or may not be survival. A new feature thus arrives in the theory of object relating. The subject says to the object: "I destroyed you," and the object is there to receive the communication. From now on the subject says: "Hullo object," "I destroyed you." "I love you." "You have value for me because of your survival of my destruction of you." "While I am loving you I am all the time destroying you in (unconscious) *fantasy.*" [14]

The importance of this moment in the Winnicottian scheme of things cannot be overestimated. It represents a kind of rebirth for the subject in the recognition of the object's reality. The object's survival of destructiveness, its lack of retaliation, its being "there to receive the communication" are everything here. For these characteristics of the object are what enable the subject to experience love in the genuine sense of that word, love for another as other and not the product of one's "projective mental mechanisms." This is what enables the object to "contribute-in to the subject, according to its own properties." It is what enables the object to be *used.*

There is, as is not uncommon in Winnicott, a genuine paradox here. Fantasized destruction, "the quality of 'always being destroyed,'" is what contributes (from the subject's point of view) to the reality of the object, its "object-constancy" and its ability to "feed back other-than-me substance into the subject." At the same time, this nurturing in turn contributes to "the subject's sense [of its own] aliveness," [15] to its ability to see itself as an object, as (presumably) something that could be of use as well. "In this way," Winnicott writes, "a world of shared reality is created," a "world of objects" each of which is separate and unique. Again, survival is everything. It is the object's survival of, its lack of retaliation for, the subject's destructive fantasies that alone enables the subject to grow, and to be able to regard both the object and itself as independent entities.

How, then, does the myth of the resurrection mirror this process? Let us step back for a moment and view the Gospels from a distance. They were written, of course, in a variety of different contexts and for a variety of different audiences. At the core of each of them, however, lies the passion and death of Jesus and, with the probable exception of Mark, his return, his reappearance. Like all narratives, these invite participation in the story. They invite identification on the part of their readers with the main figures and situations, both with those who betrayed and murdered Jesus and with Jesus himself—that is, both with those who acted out their destructive fantasies and with the object they destroyed. Thus, the narrative gives its audience the opportunity to reenact one of the most basic developmental patterns, the destruction/survival/rebirth pattern we have been examining. It does this by inviting the reader to experience the destructive drives that contribute to human development both from the point of view of those who act them out and from the point of view of their object, from both points of view at once.

The object, of course, is depicted in the Gospels as a figure who attracted both devotion and animosity, a highly cathected figure and therefore one vulnerable to "radical decathexis."[16] The Gospels stress, among other things, Jesus' patience, his mildness, his remarkable capacity to heal. Above all, Jesus is depicted as good, as loving, as kind, especially to those considered socially unacceptable and to children, and his teachings are depicted as capable, if followed, of bringing about the reign of universal love. As they are represented, his betrayal and crucifixion constitute destructive acts of the most basic and primitive sort, the acting out in reality of unconscious destructive fantasies that serve to threaten this love.

But the Gospels also depict Jesus' resurrection, his survival of those destructive attacks. History, the "facts," are of little relevance here. What matters is what Jesus' resurrection meant to those who believed it and what it symbolizes for those who continue to do so. And, as it is depicted, that survival of, that lack of retaliation for, destructive impulses represents Jesus' capacity to love, even more importantly, to "be there to receive" love when it comes, even from those who attempted to destroy him or those who acquiesced in that attempt. Thus the resurrection story provides a clear analogue to Winnicott's account of the destruction/survival paradigm. Like the mother whom the infant believes it has destroyed but who is always there, continuing to love, like the object of the subject's destructive fantasies which remains constant despite them, Jesus is depicted as harboring no urge to retaliate, no urge to pay back those who betrayed or even murdered him. His attitude is one of infinite forgiveness, just the sort of forgiveness that makes possible "the explosion of the introjection-projection circle"[17] dramatized above: " 'Hullo object!' 'I destroyed you.' 'I love you.' 'You have value for me *because* of your survival of my destruction of you' " (italics added). It is Jesus' "quality of 'always being destroyed' " that makes him an object, in Winnicott's terms, that can be *used*, that is, experienced as something external, something independent, "wholly other." Because Jesus is not only always being destroyed (in fantasy) but also always surviving that destruction, he stands, so to speak "outside the area of omnipotent control," outside "the area of objects set up by . . . projective mental mechanisms."[18] He is, in fact, completely autonomous. What is crucial about this quality of externality in the account, however, is the way it frees those who believe in Jesus' survival of the (their unconscious) attacks upon him to "live in a world of objects . . . a world of shared reality." This is because, being external, being experienced against "a backcloth of unconscious destruction," Jesus has now achieved "object-constancy," has become an object of trust and, having become an object of trust, can "feed back other-than-me substance," especially love, into those who trust in him. But there is a price. The experience of Jesus' independent reality and continuing love is possible only with the "acceptance of the ongoing destruction in unconscious fantasy relative to object relating," that is, only if the believer is able to acknowledge the permanence of his destructive impulses, or what Christianity calls sin.

The theologian Rowan Williams has argued that the essence of the resurrection doctrine is "the invitation to *recognize one's victim as one's hope*,"[19] and that "to recognize my victim as my hope involves the recognition of the fact that I victimize, and of the identity of my victim."[20] This involves, Williams says, both self-discovery and discovery of the other, in this case, Jesus, "the symbolic figure who transcends the order of human violence, a figure first to be identified with my victim and then with myself, in a continuing process of meditation and reinterpretation."[21] What Williams does not recognize is that part of that "continuing process" involves the continuing reenactment of processes outlined by Winnicott, not only the acknowledgment of one's own destructive impulses but "the development of the capacity for concern" for the other and for what the other has come to represent, and the eventual transition from object-relating to object-use that produces "a world of shared reality." Jesus' symbolic, transcendent status is a measure of the "object-constancy" believers grant him in this process. He has become, quite literally, the symbol of trust.

From this Winnicottian reading of the resurrection story I think it is possible to see why the account would have such (relatively) lasting appeal, as a "symbol," as "a vehicle of human self-interpretation and a challenge to human self-interpretation."[22] The figure of Jesus is, on some level, a maternal imago, or at least one who, in our culture at least, represents certain strikingly (albeit stereotypically) feminized qualities: patience, nurturance, the ability to love. (He represents other qualities, of course, but they are not so relevant here.) And Jesus' murder embodies, on some level, the infant's fantasized destruction of the mother, as well as the adult subject's fantasized destruction of the loved object, its radical decathexis. The violence of the act, the assault on Jesus' body, his hands, his feet, his side, is fundamental here. The crucifixion (as it is represented) is an essentially corporeal act. As a representation of destructive drives, it could not be more brutally honest. Jesus *is* the body in pain, the pain human beings inflict, in fantasy or in reality, upon one another from infancy on. This is Jesus' "quality of 'always being destroyed,' " the correlate of the Christian sense of sin. Yet if Jesus, as an analogue of the mother or of the loved object, is "always being destroyed," he is also *always surviving,* always *not retaliating* against those who, in their "sinfulness," destroy him; rather, he is always waiting for and accepting their love. He is, in fact, in his survival of destructive impulses and in his refusal to retaliate, the embodiment of "object-constancy," of trust and love.

These elements are at least part of what accounts for the tremendous potency of the myth of the resurrection for those who believe in it, the way it *simultaneously* reenacts the destruction of the loved object and its survival, the possibility of continued love. Two essential things are acknowledged by the account—destructiveness, which, according to Winnicott, "creates the quality of externality" in things, and the survival of that destructiveness, which makes it possible for the object "to feed back other-than-me substance into the subject" (1971:93). A doctrine, a "symbol" that acknowledged less to its believers, would tell only part of the story. This one manages, for those who are able to accept its full consequences, a good deal more, feeds "back other-than-me substance into" them as well.

It might now be possible to see why a sacrament like that of the

eucharist has such appeal. Winnicott had already made a few observations on the symbolic function of the sacrament for Catholics and
Protestants in his paper on transitional objects. "For the Roman
Catholic community," he observes, the wafer "is the body [of Christ],
and for the Protestant community it is a *substitute*, a reminder, and is
essentially not, in fact, actually the body itself." [23] This points to differences in the ways the two communities experience potential space,
how much illusion, how much play is tolerated. But in both traditions
the body, or the wafer that symbolizes the body, is *eaten;* it is incorporated, in a way that reenacts the infant's incorporation of the mother,
her breast, the nourishment from her body. In both the infant's interaction with the mother and in the religious rite, something disappears, is destroyed.

In both cases, the mouth is the vehicle of that disappearance, that
destruction. Yet in both cases, something survives. In the case of the
infant, what survives is the mother, who remains as she was despite
the "id-drives" directed against her body and who can begin to become, on account of her survival and lack of retaliation, a symbol of
object-constancy (the way other transferential objects will in later life,
under analogous circumstances). In the case of the sacrament, it is
Jesus himself who survives, even though the wafer, his body, is eaten;
he survives both bodily *and* symbolically—that is, both in his physical
(or spiritual) body, represented by the bread and wine, and in the spiritual body represented in Christian doctrine by the community, in the
spirit of love between its members. Every time the believer takes the
sacrament, he must acknowledge his own destructiveness (in eating
the wafer, the symbol of the body, or the actual body itself) and his
own faith that the love-object survives and continues to love. Thus, the
sacrament, like the account of the resurrection, involves destructiveness, yet involves it as something that can become, under the right circumstances, ultimately creative of a world of shared reality which can
be used by those who share it.

We have been talking about symbols, and the developmental origins of their potency and appeal. There should be, I hope, nothing reductive in this. In fact, our account should only render those aspects
of the Christian myth and practice of which we have been exploring
the psychological roots all the more noteworthy. After all, this account
gives us a way of seeing them in a new, and perhaps more deeply
human, light, as arising "out of human nature" and not imposed
"from outside." [24] Read, as we have been reading them, in a Winnicottian context, they are representations of some of the most basic

human drives and impulses—destructiveness and the painfully achieved capacity for "object-constancy" and trust. For, and this is where Winnicott differs so profoundly from Freud, symbolic and therefore cultural representations of the sort we have been examining here are not necessarily expressions of the human impulse to *escape* or *avoid* painful "reality." They can be powerful ways of *facing*, indeed of creating, reality, of continuing a process begun nearly at birth, a process of making things, including both transitional and cultural objects, that render experience a bit more comprehensible. This is called "reality-testing." It takes place in the "intermediate area of *experiencing,*"[25] where we have just been.

NOTES

1. I am treating the resurrection story as myth here not in its pejorative sense but to describe a story that appeals on a "primordial" level to some of the most basic human impulses and needs and that "provides the structure of identity and cohesion of particular human groups and ways of life." A. Wilder, *Theopoetic: Theology and the Religious Imagination* (Fortress Press, 1976), pp. 73–74.

2. W. W. Meissner, *Psychoanalysis and Religious Experience* (Yale University Press, 1984).

3. D. W. Winnicott, "The Use of an Object and Relating Through Identifications," *Playing and Reality* (Tavistock-Routledge, 1982), p. 86.

4. D. W. Winnicott, "Morals and Education," in *The Maturational Processes and the Facilitating Environment: Studies in the Theory of Emotional Development* (International Universities Press, 1963), p. 94.

5. R. Kuhns, *Psychoanalytic Theory of Art: A Philosophy of Art on Developmental Principles* (Columbia University Press, 1983), p. 21.

6. D. W. Winnicott, "The Location of Cultural Experience," in *Playing and Reality*, p. 103.

7. D. W. Winnicott, "The Development of the Capacity for Concern," in *The Maturational Processes and the Facilitating Environment*, p. 76.

8. Ibid., p. 77.

9. See Melanie Klein: "Here is a benign circle, for in the first place we gain trust and love in relation to our parents, next we take them, with this love and trust, as it were, into ourselves; and then we can give from this wealth of loving feelings to the outer world again." From "Love, Guilt, and Reparation," in M. Klein and J. Riviere, *Love, Hate, and Reparation* (New York: W. W. Norton and Company, 1964), p. 115.

10. Winnicott, "The Use of an Object," p. 88.

11. Ibid., p. 89.

12. M. Eigen, "The Area of Faith in Winnicott, Lacan and Bion," *The International Journal of Psycho-Analysis*, Vol. 62 (1981), p. 417.

13. Ibid., p. 415.

14. Winnicott, "The Use of an Object," p. 90.

15. Eigen, p. 415.

16. A. Green, "The Object in the Setting," in S. A. Grolnick and L. Barkin (Eds.), *Between Reality and Fantasy: Transitional Objects and Phenomena* (Jason Aronson, 1978), p. 184.

17. Eigen, p. 415.

18. Winnicott, "The Use of an Object," p. 94.

19. R. Williams, *Resurrection: An Easter Meditation* (Darton, Longman, and Todd, 1982), pp. 11, 19.

20. Ibid., p. 25.

21. Ibid., p. 26.

22. Ibid., p. 26.

23. D. W. Winnicott, "Transitional Objects and Transitional Phenomena," in *Playing and Reality*, p. 6.

24. D. W. Winnicott, "Children Learning," in *Home is Where We Start From* (New York: W. W. Norton and Company, 1986), p. 143.

25. Winnicott, "Transitional Objects and Transitional Phenomena," p. 2.

PART V

Heinz Kohut

Heinz Kohut was born in Vienna in 1913 and emigrated to the United States in 1938 to escape the Nazis. He received his medical degree from the University of Vienna and was trained in neurology and psychiatry at the University of Chicago. He received psychoanalytic training at the Chicago Institute for Psychoanalysis, where he served as teacher, training analyst, and member of the staff until his death in 1981. In addition to scores of professional papers and published lectures, he wrote three books: *The Analysis of the Self* (1971), *The Restoration of the Self* (1977), and *How Does Analysis Cure?* (published posthumously in 1984).

Although Kohut was Jewish, he regularly attended the Unitarian Church in Hyde Park on Chicago's South Side, and, according to Charles B. Strozier, he appeared to be deeply ambivalent about his own Jewishness. Strozier notes that "many of his close friends at the University of Vienna during the 1930s had no idea he was Jewish. He never told Jewish jokes or used Yiddish expressions or made any reference to Jewish cultural traditions (and he looked baffled whenever anyone did any of these things in his presence)."[1] The explanation may simply lie in the fact that his family was "a cultured, well-off, and highly assimilated Viennese family" or that Kohut was seeking to avoid the fate that eventually befell him (being forced to leave Austria), but Strozier suspects that it had deeper psychological roots, and he points to some statements Kohut made toward the end of his life involving his assessment of Nazi concentration camps as notable less for their overt cruelty and more for their absence of empathy. An empathyless environment, in his view, is far worse than cruelty, as it is even more dehumanizing.[2]

Empathy, then, was key to Kohut's therapeutic method, and the primary basis for his belief, contradicting Freud, that narcissistic personalities are in fact treatable. Other disagreements with Freud centered on their conceptions of the human condition—Kohut portrayed the difference as one between Freud's "guilty self" and his own "tragic self"—which were ultimately traceable to Freud's Oedipus-complex theory and Kohut's acceptance of it only within the larger picture of self-development. In his view, the self develops well before Oedipal conflicts occur, and the very presence of a firm self is a precondition for the experience of these conflicts. Like Bakan, he notes that Freud neglected Oedipus's abandonment as an infant as the fateful precursor to the tragic events that followed, but he also claims that merely pointing out Freud's neglect is insufficient to counter the "magical" grip that Freud's version of the Oedipus complex exerts on psychoanalysis. More importantly, one needs a "countermagic," and for this Kohut nominates the story of Odysseus, who in the very prime of his life, with a young wife and infant son, refused to join the war of the Greeks against the Trojans. When a delegation sent by the Greeks came to see him, he feigned insanity by plowing his land with an ox and ass yoked together, flinging salt over his shoulder into the furrows, and wearing a silly, cone-shaped hat on his head. But one of his visitors suspected foul play and picked up Odysseus's infant son, Telemachus, and threw him in front of the plow. Without the slightest hesitation, Odysseus made a semicircle around the child with his plow to avoid hurting him. The delegation immediately concluded that Odysseus was sane. Kohut notes that this myth portrays a healthy father-son relationship, while Laius's and Oedipus's story portrays one that is already disturbed.[3] Thus, the Odysseus story counters the Oedipus story by depicting the father's empathy toward his son.

In time, Kohut felt that his differences with Freud were so fundamental that he began to refer to his work as "self psychology" and suggested that there may well be unbridgeable obstacles between his own views and those who continued to work within the parameters of classical psychoanalysis. While his orientation was broadly cultural and not focused on religion per se, he did from time to time note his disagreements with Freud on religion as well. In an interview reported by Strozier, Kohut took exception to *The Future of an Illusion*, criticizing

Freud for applying the yardstick of scientific values to religion. He suggested that there are three great cultural enterprises: "Science deals with cognitive issues, with explanations. Art deals with beauty, creating beautiful things, pleasing things. And religion is neither one nor the other." Its unique function is to "shore up, to hold together, sustain, and make harmonious, to strengthen, man's self."[4] Kohut made much the same point in the concluding pages of *The Restoration of the Self* when he observed that playwright Eugene O'Neill dealt with "man's leading psychological problem—the problem of how to cure his crumbling self," and especially cited his play *The Great God Brown*, in which Brown declares near "the end of his long day's journey into night, after a life torn by uncertainty about the substance of his self: 'Man is born broken. He lives by mending. The grace of God is glue.' " Kohut asks: "Could the essence of the pathology of modern man's self be stated more impressively?"[5]

Except for such occasional references, however, Kohut did not write about religion in his major books, and he broached the subject only when it was integral to a patient's pathology. He left to others the task of applying his theories and concepts to religion. Most applications of this sort have involved his concept of the "selfobject," which lies at the heart of his theory. By selfobject, he means something very close to what Winnicott identifies as object-relating. It refers to the process by which the infant establishes and maintains her emerging self through a primary narcissistic relationship with her caregivers and later their symbolized substitutes. The selfobject is so called because, initially, the self does not experience it as separate. Thus, it is self-related and not, strictly speaking, an "other" having an independent existence. The infant takes the very being of the other into herself and experiences her soothing as indistinguishable from her own. This is narcissism—"my world is me"—but it is healthy narcissism, and an absolutely essential experience for the subsequent normal growth and development of the child. If the caregivers fail to support the infant's need for self-soothing and self-idealization, a weak or defective self-structure occurs, and this has negative implications throughout childhood and well into adulthood.

In an interview in which Strozier raised the issue of religion, Kohut commented that "as a supportive selfobject, religion is not poor by a long shot. Freud's concern was with religion as irrational dogma. But he ignored the supportive aspect of religion."[6] In another interview concerned with "cultural selfobjects," he commented on the need to be "accepted and mirrored— there has to be the gleam in some mother's eye which says it is good you are here and I acknowledge your being here and I am uplifted by your presence. There is also the other need: to have somebody strong and knowledgeable and calm around with whom I can temporarily merge, who will uplift me when I am upset. Originally, that is an actual uplifting of the baby by the mother; later that becomes an uplifting feeling of looking at a great man or woman and enjoying him or her, or following in his or her footsteps."[7] He went on to talk about the misguided idealization of Hitler by the German people, but he could have developed this point in a more positive direction, noting, for example, that religious personages—such as Mary and Jesus—may serve as selfobjects who transcend the limitations of their own cultural-historical contexts.

The first selection from Kohut's writings included here is an article coauthored with Ernest S. Wolf, his colleague at the Chicago Institute of Psychoanalysis. Concerned with self disorders and their treatment, it presents the major tenets of his self psychology. This essay has its basis—as does self psychology itself—in the treatment of patients afflicted with narcissistic personality disorder, the disorder that he considers most emblematic of our age and reflected in a poorly formed self. Situating this primary concern with narcissism within a broader framework of self-pathologies, he and Wolf identify four syndromes of self-pathology (the understimulated, fragmentary, overstimulated, and overburdened self), and then focus on the narcissistic personality types (including ideal-hungry, merger-hungry, and contact-shunning personalities). Given the pejorative connotations of the word "narcissism" in social discourse, and the tendency to take a moralistic view of it, we should note that Kohut and Wolf are using the term in its clinical sense.

In the second selection, "Forms and Transformations of Narcissism," Kohut laments the fact that even within the therapeutic community there is a tendency to view narcissism—"the libidinal investment of the self"—in a negative fashion: "Where such a prejudice exists it is undoubtedly based on a comparison between narcissism and object love, and is justified by the assertion that it [narcissism] is the more primitive and the less adaptive of the two forms of libido distribution." He contends, however, that these views do not stem primarily "from an objective assessment either of the developmental position or of the adaptive value of narcissism" but are instead "due to the improper intrusion of the altruistic value system of Western civilization." This leads the therapist to attempt "to replace the patient's narcissistic position with object love, while the often more appropriate goal of a transformed narcissism (i.e., of a redistribution of the patient's narcissistic libido, and of the integration of the primitive psychological structures into the mature personality) is neglected." Also overlooked is the contribution of narcissism to health, adaptation, and achievement.

Thus, this essay takes exception to the rather negative view of narcissism prevalent in psychoanalysis since Freud. Kohut viewed narcissism as a phase-appropriate expression of ambitions which, in early childhood, elicited unempathic responses from parental figures. When confronted by such deflating responses, the child embarked on a life-strategy of concealment of the resulting sense of shame, humiliation, and absence of self-respect through a variety of self-defensive and self-aggrandizing behaviors. Because religious worldviews extol object-love as an ethical ideal, however, Kohut's essay is a challenge not only to more traditional psychoanalytic views on narcissism, but also to religious worldviews that fail to take the narcissistic condition and its self-limiting effects into account. On the other hand, most if not all of the characteristics of transformed narcissism (creativity, empathy, wisdom, acceptance of personal transience, humor) have received support from other religious viewpoints. If these characteristics are central to Kohut's own religious viewpoint, as they would appear to be, they reveal a philosophical orientation not too dissimilar to Freud's own. We should bear in mind, however, that the essay was a relatively early one, written long before Kohut envisioned his "self psychology."

The third selection is from Kohut's most popular book, *The Restoration of the Self,* and focuses on the case of "Mr. X.," in whose self-pathology religion was a very significant factor. Kohut points to the role of religion in Mr. X.'s early relationship with his mother, the sexualization of his relation to religion in late adolescence, and his desire to enter the ministry. Central to his pathology was his unfulfilled desire to merge with an idealizable, admired father, glimpses of which he had experienced during childhood. Kohut views Mr. X. as a fragmented self, described in the Kohut and Wolf essay as a chronic or recurrent condition of the self "which arises in consequence of the lack of integrating responses to the nascent self in its totality from the side of the selfobjects in childhood." Kohut presents the analytic process as one in which the pole of the self that carries Mr. X.'s idealized goals is strengthened through a reactivation of his relation with his real father, the idealized selfobject of his infancy and childhood. The selection concludes with a more general discussion from the "Epilogue" of

The Restoration of the Self involving the contrast Kohut wishes to draw
between Freud's "mental-apparatus psychology" and his own "self-
psychology." Here, Kohut notes that his approach, also based in realism, is nonetheless more hopeful regarding the chances of individuals
like Mr. X. for a productive, even joyful existence.

From the perspective of religion, it is noteworthy that an important feature of the therapeutic process in Mr. X.'s case was that his reactivation of the relation with the selfobject of the real father of his
childhood entailed a simultaneous disengagement from the father-
surrogate (the Father of the Trinity), the assumption being that the
latter was too much identified with the mother and her unconscious
image of her own father (Mr. X.'s grandfather). Significantly, several of
Freud's early associates wrote papers on the role of grandparents, and
especially grandfathers, in the development of neuroses and explored
in considerable depth the "reversal of generations" phenomenon,
where the child replaces parents with earlier progenitors.[8] In an association drawing on Freud's argument in *Totem and Taboo*, the Harvard
psychologist Henry Murray made an explicit association between his
maternal grandfather, his own image of God as a child, and the primordial father: "Of all these progenitors I was acquainted only with
my daughter-venerated grandfather, aloof toward me, but a kindly
gent whose white bearded visage resembled God's as painted, say, by
Tintoretto. Remembering him I have been led to surmise that the
image and concept of Yahweh must have come not from the all-too-
familiar father figure, but from the more remote and lordly grandfather, the overruling patriarch of the clan."[9] Thus, Kohut's case of Mr.
X. prompts us to ask whether the grandfather, especially the maternal
one as mediated through the mother's idealization of him, is the primary source of the child's "Father of personal prehistory"?

The fourth Kohut selection, from *How Does Analysis Cure?*, centers on agoraphobia in women and uses this to illustrate differences
between classical Freudian approaches to psychopathology and
Kohut's self psychology approach. (It also relates to Erikson's essay,
"Shared Visions," also involving an agoraphobic patient). While his
discussion does not address religion per se, his analysis of agoraphobia has significance for religion in light of his comment that Freud ignored "the supportive aspect of religion" and of his view of cultural
selfobjects as providing what the infant looks for in her parents—that
is, not only acceptance and mirroring, but also "somebody strong and
knowledgeable and calm" with whom she can temporarily merge,
who will uplift her when she is upset. Kohut's analysis of agoraphobia

centers on the failure of the parental figure to provide such strength and calmness—especially to be the "calming structure" that the infant requires—because the parent has a self defect. (In this case, it is primarily but not exclusively the mother; in other forms of psychopathology, it may be the father.) The question this raises is whether religion can, albeit in a substitutionary way, provide the "calming structure" that parents, for whatever reasons, were unable to offer. Kohut's comments on the supportive aspect of religion, and his explicit reference to the Madonna and Child in an interview which focused on cultural selfobjects and the continuity of the self,[10] suggest that this is the very role that he envisions religion playing. Perhaps this provides an explanation for why religion, especially in its mythic and ritual aspects, has tended to remain so closely attached to the psychodynamics of parent-child relationships.

The fifth selection is an excerpt from a very long essay on courage which was published posthumously. This selection may be read as a further development of views set forth by Kohut in "Forms and Transformations of Narcissism," in that several of the indicators of the transformation of narcissism identified there are presented here in his discussion of persons of remarkable courage. These include the ability to be empathic, the capacity to contemplate one's own impermanence, a sense of humor, and wisdom. By the time he wrote "On Courage," however, Kohut had gone beyond the earlier essay by formulating his concept of the "nuclear self," which, as the essay he wrote with Wolf indicates, is a bipolar structure that develops in early childhood, with archaic nuclear ambitions forming the one pole and archaic nuclear ideals forming the other. Thus, in the essay on courage, he identifies this nuclear self with what Erikson calls "the sense of 'I' " and argues that the acts of courage by the anti-Nazis portrayed in the essay are a reflection of the individual's nuclear self, not an expression of psychopathology (for example, "martyr complex"). Nor are they to be viewed as superordinate acts of altruism. Rather, they are integral to the individual's sense of "I" and are primarily expressive of the idealized pole of the nuclear self. Thus, they grow out of the individual's self, as integral to it, and not, as some religionists would have it, as acts of self-denial.

This selection concludes with a discussion of tragedy, reflecting Kohut's view, presented in several of his writings, that whereas Freud's prototypical self was "guilty" (for having harbored ambitions against the father), the self central to Kohut's theorizing is characterized by tragedy (the "tragic self"). The tragedy lies in the fact that the fulfillment of the goals and idealized aspirations of one's nuclear self will necessarily remain elusive, owing to the limitations and finitude of human existence. Here Kohut also distinguishes his view of tragedy from Freud's by emphasizing the centrality of the nuclear self, rather than guilt, in the tragic life. He concludes with a qualified endorsement of Freud's idea of the "death-instinct," supporting the basic idea itself but recontextualizing it, that is, from the psychobiological locus to which Freud ascribed it to its locus in the nuclear self.[11] Religion receives explicit mention in the essay in his interpretation of the tragedy of the life and death of Jesus of Nazareth.

NOTES

1. Charles B. Strozier, "Heinz Kohut's Struggles with Religion, Ethnicity, and God," in *Religion, Society, and Psychoanalysis: Readings in Contemporary Theory*, ed. Janet Liebman Jacobs and Donald Capps (Boulder: Westview Press, 1997), 173.

2. Ibid., 173–77.

3. Heinz Kohut, "Introspection, Empathy, and the Semicircle of Mental Health," in *The Search for the Self*, vol. 4, ed. Paul H. Ornstein (Madison, Conn.: International Universities Press, 1991), 561–65.

4. Quoted in Strozier, "Heinz Kohut's Struggles," 167.

5. Heinz Kohut, *The Restoration of the Self* (New York: International Universities Press, 1977), 287.

6. Heinz Kohut, *Self Psychology and the Humanities: Reflections on a New Psychoanalytic Approach*, ed. Charles B. Strozier (New York: W. W. Norton, 1985), 261.

7. Ibid., 226–27.

8. These include Karl Abraham's "Some Remarks on the Role of Grandparents in the Psychology of Neuroses"; Sandor Ferenczi's "The Grandfather Complex"; Ernest Jones's "The Significance of the Grandfather for the Fate of the Individual"; and Freud's own "The Occurrence in Dreams of Material from Fairy-Tales," in which he considered the role of the grandfather as a "father surrogate." All of these essays were written in 1913. Also relevant is Erik H. Erikson's "The Nature of Clinical Evidence," in *Insight and Responsibility* (New York: W. W. Norton, 1964), 47–80. This essay involves the case of a young man, who had been engaged in studies for missionary work abroad, whose dream of his grandfather was crucial to his treatment and eventual resolution of identity problems.

9. Henry Murray, in *A History of Psychology in Autobiography*, vol. 5, ed. Edwin C. Boring and Gardner Lindzey (New York: Appleton-Century-Crofts, 1967), 296.

10. Kohut, *Self Psychology and the Humanities*, 242.

11. Sigmund Freud, *Beyond the Pleasure Principle*, vol. 18 of *The Standard Edition of the Complete Psychological Works of Sigmund Freud*, ed. James Strachey (London: Hogarth Press, 1955), 3–64.

CHAPTER 21

The Disorders of the Self and Their Treatment

HEINZ KOHUT AND ERNEST S. WOLF

D uring recent years the psychoanalytic investigation of certain frequently encountered patients led to the recognition of a definable syndrome which at first appeared to be related to the psychoneuroses and neurotic character disorders. It was clear from the outset that these patients are characterized by a specific vulnerability: their self-esteem is unusually labile and, in particular, they are extremely sensitive to failures, disappointments and slights. It was, however, not the scrutiny of the symptomatology but the process of treatment that illuminated the nature of the disturbance of these patients. The analysis of the psychic conflicts of these patients did not result in either the expected amelioration of suffering or the hoped-for cessation of undesirable behavior; the discovery, however, that these patients reactivated certain specific narcissistic needs in the psychoanalytic situation, i.e. that they established "narcissistic transferences," made effective psychoanalytic treatment possible.

The psychopathological syndrome from which these patients suffer was designated as *narcissistic personality disorder.* The narcissistic transferences which are pathognomonic for these syndromes were subdivided into two types: (1) the *mirror transference* in which an insufficiently or faultily responded to childhood need for a source of accepting-confirming "mirroring" is revived in the treatment situation, and (2) the *idealizing transference* in which a need for merger with a source of "idealized" strength and calmness is similarly revived. As the understanding of the symptomatology, core psychopathology, and treatment of the narcissistic personality disorders increased, in particular via the investigation of the narcissistic transferences, it be-

came clear that the essence of the disturbance from which these patients suffered could not be adequately explained within the framework of classical drive-and-defense psychology. In view of the fact that
it is a weakened or defective self that lies in the center of the disorder,
explanations that focused on conflicts concerning either the libidinal
or the aggressive impulses of these patients could illuminate neither
psychopathology nor treatment process. Some progress was made
by expanding the classical libido theory and by revising the classical
theory of aggression. Specifically, the weakness of the self was conceptualized in terms of its underlibidinizations—as a cathectic deficit, to speak in the terms of Freudian metapsychology—and the
intense aggressions encountered in the narcissistic personality disorders were recognized as the responses of the vulnerable self to a variety of injuries.

The decisive steps forward in the understanding of these disorders, however, were made through the introduction of the concept of
the selfobject and via the increasing understanding of the self in
depth-psychological terms. *Selfobjects* are objects which we experienced as part of our self; the expected control over them is, therefore,
closer to the concept of the control which a grown-up expects to have
over his own body and mind than to the concept of the control which
he expects to have over others. There are two kinds of selfobjects;
those who respond to and confirm the child's innate sense of vigor,
greatness and perfection; and those to whom the child can look up
and with whom he can merge as an image of calmness, infallibility
and omnipotence. The first type is referred to as the mirroring selfobject, the second as the idealized parent imago. The *self*, the core of our
personality, has various constituents which we acquire in the interplay with those persons in our earliest childhood environment whom
we experienced as selfobjects. A firm self, resulting from the optimal
interactions between the child and his selfobjects is made up of three
major constituents: (1) one pole from which emanate the basic strivings for power and success; (2) another pole that harbors the basic
idealized goals; and (3) an intermediate area of basic talents and skills
that are activated by the tension-arc that establishes itself between
ambitions and ideals.

Faulty interaction between the child and his selfobjects result in a
damaged self—either a diffusely damaged self or a self that is seriously damaged in one or the other of its constituents. If a patient
whose self has been damaged enters psychoanalytic treatment, he re-
activates the specific needs that had remained unresponded to by the

specific faulty interactions between the nascent self and the selfobjects of early life—a selfobject transference is established.

Depending on the quality of the interactions between the self and its selfobjects in childhood, the self will emerge either as a firm and healthy structure or as a more or less seriously damaged one. The adult self may thus exist in states of varying degrees of coherence, from cohesion to fragmentation; in states of varying degrees of vitality, from vigor to enfeeblement; in states of varying degrees of functional harmony, from order to chaos. Significant failure to achieve cohesion, vigor, or harmony, or a significant loss of these qualities after they had been tentatively established, may be said to constitute a state of self disorder. The psychoanalytic situation creates conditions in which the damaged self begins to strive to achieve or to re-establish a state of cohesion, vigor and inner harmony.

Once the self has crystallized in the interplay of inherited and environmental factors, it aims towards the realization of its own specific program of action—a program that is determined by the specific intrinsic pattern of its constituent ambitions, goals, skills and talents, and by the tensions that arise between these constituents. The patterns of ambitions, skills and goals; the tensions between them; the program of action that they create; and the activities that strive towards the realization of this program are all experienced as continuous in space and time—they are the self, an independent center of initiative, an independent recipient of impressions.

The Secondary and the Primary Disturbances of the Self

The experiential and behavioral manifestations of the *secondary disturbances of the self* are the reactions of a structurally undamaged self to the vicissitudes of life. A strong self allows us to tolerate even wide swings of self-esteem in response to victory or defeat, success or failure. And various emotions—triumph, joy, despair, rage—accompany these changes in the state of the self. If our self is firmly established, we shall neither be afraid of the dejection that may follow a failure nor of the expansive fantasies that may follow a success—reactions that would endanger those with a more precariously established self.

Among the secondary disturbances belong also the reactions of the self to physical illness or to the incapacities of a structural neurosis, e.g. the dejection or the anger experienced when incurable muscular paralysis or chronic neurotic anxiety inhibit a person from pursuing his central self-enhancing goals. And even certain reactions of relatively undamaged layers of the self to the consequences of its own primary disturbances—such as dejection over the fact that a damaged self's vulnerability has led to social isolation—should be counted among the secondary disturbances of the self.

The *primary disturbances of the self* can be divided into several subgroups, depending on the extent, severity, nature and distribution of the disturbance. If serious damage to the self is either permanent or protracted, and if no defensive structures cover the defect, the experiential and behavioral manifestations are those that are traditionally referred to as *the psychoses*. The nuclear self may have remained noncohesive (schizophrenia) either because of an inherent biological tendency, or because its totality and continuity were not responded to with even minimally effective mirroring in early life, or because of the interplay between or convergence of biological and environmental factors. It may have obtained a degree of cohesion but because of the interaction of inherent organic factors and a serious lack of joyful responses to its existence and assertiveness, it will be massively depleted of self-esteem and vitality ("empty" depression). It may have been almost totally deprived during the crucial periods of its formation of the repeated wholesome experience of participating in the calmness of an idealized adult (i.e. of a merger with an idealized selfobject), with the result, again decisively influenced by inherent biological factors, that an uncurbed tendency toward the spreading of unrealistically heightened self-acceptance (mania) or self-rejection and self-blame ("guilt"-depression) remains as a serious central weak spot in its organization.

A second subgroup of primary disorders of the self are the *borderline states*. Here the break-up, the enfeeblement, or the functional chaos of the nuclear self are also permanent or protracted, but, in contrast to the psychoses, the experiential and behavioral manifestations of the central defect are covered by complex defenses. Although it is in general not advisable for the therapist to tamper with these protective devices, it is sometimes possible to make the patient's use of them more flexible by reconstructing the genesis of both the central vulnerability and of the chronic characterological defense. It may, for example, be helpful to the patient to understand the sequence of events, repeated on innumerable occasions, when as a child his need to establish an autonomous self was thwarted by the intrusions of the parental selfobject. At the very point, in other words, when the nascent self of the child required the accepting mirroring of its independence, the selfobject, because of its own incompleteness and fragmentation fears, insisted on maintaining an archaic merger.

A significantly more resilient self is found in the next subgroup, the *narcissistic behavior disorders*, even though the symptoms which these individuals display—e.g. perverse, delinquent or addictive behavior—may expose them to grave physical and social dangers. But the underlying disorder, the break-up, enfeeblement or serious distortion of the self, is only temporary in these cases, and with the support of increasing insight into the genetic roots and the dynamic purpose of their symptomatic behavior, they may become able to relinquish it and to substitute for it more mature and realistic supports for their self-esteem.

Closely related to the narcissistic behavior disorders are the *narcissistic personality disorders* where break-up, enfeeblement or serious distortion of the self are also only temporary but where the symptoms—e.g. hypochondria, depression, hypersensitivity to slights, lack of zest—concern not primarily the actions and interactions of the individual but rather his psychological state.

Of the patients who suffer from disorders of the self, only those with narcissistic behavior and personality disorders are capable of tolerating the frustrations of the reactivated narcissistic needs of their vulnerable self to which the working-through process in analysis exposes them without a protracted fragmentation or depletion of the self. In other words, of all the primary disorders of the self only narcissistic behavior and personality disorders are analyzable.

The Aetiology of Self-Pathology

In view of the fact that the disorders of the self are, by and large, the results of miscarriages in the normal development of the self, we shall first present an outline of the normal development of the self. It is difficult to pinpoint the age at which the baby or small child may be said to have acquired a self. To begin with, it seems safe to assume that, strictly speaking, the neonate is still without a self. The new-born infant arrives physiologically pre-adapted for a specific physical environment—the presence of oxygen, of food, of a certain range of temperature—outside of which he cannot survive. Similarly, psychological survival requires a specific psychological environment—the presence of responsive-empathic selfobjects. It is in the matrix of a particular selfobject environment that, via a specific process of psychological structure formation called *transmuting internalization*, the *nuclear self* of the child will crystallize. Without going into the details of this structure-building process, we can say (1) that it cannot occur without a previous stage in which the child's mirroring and idealizing needs had been sufficiently responded to; (2) that it takes place in consequence of the minor, non-traumatic failures in the responses of the mirroring and the idealized selfobjects; and (3) that these failures lead to the gradual replacement of the selfobjects and their functions by a self and its functions. And it must be added that while gross identifications with the selfobjects and their functions may temporarily and transitionally occur, the ultimate wholesome result, the autonomous self, is not a replica of the selfobject.

If we keep in mind the processes by which the self is created, we realize that, however primitive by comparison with the self of the adult the nuclear self may be, it is already at its very inception a complex structure, arising at the end-point of a developmental process which may be said to have its virtual beginnings with the formation of specific hopes, dreams and expectations concerning the future child in the minds of the parents, especially the mother. When the baby is born, the encounter with the child's actual structural and functional biological equipment will, of course, influence the imagery about its future personality that had been formed by the parents. But the parental expectations will, from birth onward, exert a considerable influence on the baby's developing self. The self arises thus as the result of the interplay between the new-born's innate equipment and the selective responses of the selfobjects through which certain potentialities are encouraged in their development while others remain unencouraged or are even actively discouraged. Out of this selective process there emerges, probably during the second year of life, a nuclear self, which, as stated earlier, is currently conceptualized as a bipolar structure; archaic nuclear ambitions form one pole, archaic nuclear ideals the other. The tension arc between these two poles enhances the development of the child's nuclear skills and talents— rudimentary skills and talents that will gradually develop into those that the adult employs in the service of the productivity and creativity of his mature self.

The strength of these three major constituents of the self, the choice of their specific contents, the nature of their relationship—e.g. which one of them will ultimately predominate— and their progress towards maturity and potential fulfilment through creative actions, will be less influenced by those responses of the selfobjects that are shaped by their philosophy of child rearing than by those that express the state of their own nuclear self. In other words, it is not so much what the parents do that will influence the character of the child's self, but what the parents are. If the parents are at peace with their own needs to shine and to succeed insofar as these needs can be realistically gratified, if, in other words, the parents' self-confidence is secure, then the proud exhibitionism of the budding self of their child will be responded to acceptingly. However grave the blows may be to which the child's grandiosity is exposed by the realities of life, the proud smile of the parents will keep alive a bit of the original omnipotence, to be retained as the nucleus of the self-confidence and inner security about one's worth that sustain the healthy person throughout his life. And the same holds true with regard to our ideals. However great our disappointment as we discover the weaknesses and limitations of the idealized selfobjects of our early life, their self-confidence as they carried us when we were babies, their security when they allowed us to merge our anxious selves with their tranquility—via their calm voices or via our closeness with their relaxed bodies as they held us—will be retained by us as the nucleus of the strength of our leading ideals and of the calmness we experience as we live our lives under the guidance of our inner goals.

It is only in the light of our appreciation of the crucial influence exerted on the development of the self by the personality of the selfobjects of childhood, that we are able to trace the genetic roots of the disorders of the self. Psychoanalytic case histories tended to emphasize certain dramatic incidents, certain grossly traumatic events—from the child's witnessing the "primal scene" to the loss of a parent in childhood. But we have come to incline to the opinion that such traumatic events may be no more than clues that point to the truly pathogenic factors, the unwholesome atmosphere to which the child was exposed during the years when his self was established. Taken by themselves, in other words, these events leave fewer serious disturbances in their wake than the chronic ambience created by the deep-rooted attitudes of the selfobjects, since even the still vulnerable self, in the process of formation, can cope with serious traumata if it is embedded in a healthily supportive milieu. The essence of the healthy matrix for the growing self of the child is a mature, cohesive parental self that is in tune with the changing needs of the child. It can, with a glow of shared joy, mirror the child's grandiose display one minute, yet, perhaps a minute later, should the child become anxious and overstimulated by its exhibitionism, it will curb the display by adopting a realistic attitude vis-a-vis the child's limitations. Such optimal frustrations of the child's need to be mirrored and to merge into an idealized selfobject, hand in hand with optimal gratifications, generate the appropriate growth-facilitating matrix for the self.

Some parents, however, are not adequately sensitive to the needs of the child but will instead respond to the needs of their own insecurely established self. Here are two characteristic illustrations of pathogenic selfobject failures. They concern typical events that emerge frequently during the analysis of patients with narcissistic personality disorders during the transference repetitions of those childhood experiences that interfered with the normal development of the self. We must add here that the episodes depicted in the following vignettes are indicative of a pathogenic childhood environment only if they form part of the selfobjects' *chronic* attitude. Put differently, they would not emerge at crucial junctures of a selfobject transference if they had occurred as the consequences of a parent's unavoidable *occasional* failure.

First illustration: A little girl comes home from school, eager to tell her mother about some great successes. But the mother, instead of listening with pride, deflects the conversation from the child to herself, begins to talk about her own successes which overshadow those of her little daughter.

Second illustration: A little boy is eager to idealize his father, he wants his father to tell him about his life, the battles he engaged in and won. But instead of joyfully acting in accordance with his son's need, the father is embarrassed by the request. He feels tired and bored and, leaving the house, finds a temporary source of vitality for his enfeebled self in the tavern, through drink and mutually supportive talk with friends.

Psychopathology and Symptomatology

In the following we will present some syndromes of self-pathology, arising in consequence of the developmental failures described in the preceding section. It is clear that in many if not in most instances the various forms of self-disturbance which we separate from each other in the following classification will not be clearly identifiable in specific patients. Mixtures of the experiences characteristic of different types will often be present and, even more frequently, one and the same patient will experience the one or the other of the pathological states of the self at different times, often even in close proximity. The following descriptions should, however, be clinically helpful because they point out frequently occurring clusters of experience.

The *understimulated self.* This is a chronic or recurrent condition of the self, the propensity to which arises in consequence of prolonged lack of stimulating responsiveness from the side of the selfobjects in childhood. Such personalities are lacking in vitality. They experience themselves as boring and apathetic, and they are experienced by others in the same way. Individuals whose nascent selves have been insufficiently responded to will use any available stimuli to create a pseudo-excitement in order to ward off the painful feeling of deadness that tends to overtake them. Children employ the resources appropriate to their developmental phase—such as head-banging among toddlers, compulsive masturbation in later childhood, daredevil activities in adolescence. Adults have at their disposal an even wider armamentarium of self-stimulation—in particular, in the sexual sphere, addictive promiscuous activities and various perversions, and, in the non-sexual sphere, such activities as gambling, drug and alcohol-induced excitement, and a life style characterized by hypersociability. If the analyst is able to penetrate beneath the defensive façade presented by these activities, he will invariably find empty depression. Prototypical is the compulsive masturbation of lonely, "un-mirrored" children. It is not healthy drive-pressure that leads to the endlessly repeated masturbation, but the attempt to substitute pleasurable sensations in *parts* of the body (erogenous zones) when the joy provided by the inhibition of the *total* self is unavailable.

The *fragmenting self.* This is a chronic or recurrent condition of the self, the propensity to which arises in consequence of the lack of integrating responses to the nascent self in its totality from the side of the selfobjects in childhood. Occasionally occurring fragmentation states of minor degree and short duration are ubiquitous. They occur in all of us when our self-esteem has been taxed for prolonged periods and when no replenishing sustenance has presented itself. We all may walk home after a day in which we suffered a series in self-esteem-shaking failures, feeling at sixes and sevens within ourselves. Our gait and posture will be less than graceful at such times, our movements will tend to be clumsy, and even our mental functions will show signs of discoordination. Our patients with narcissistic personality disorders will not only be more inclined to react with such fragmentation symptoms to even minor disappointments, but their symptoms will tend to be more severe. If a normally tastefully dressed patient arrives in our office in a dishevelled attire, if his tie is grossly mismatched, and the color of his socks does not go with that of his shoes, we shall usually not go wrong if we begin to search our memory with the question whether we had been unempathic in the last session, whether we had failed to recognize a narcissistic need. Still more serious degrees of fragmentation will finally be encountered during the psychoanalytic treatment of the most severely disturbed patients with narcissistic personality disorders. Here a patient might respond to even minor rebuffs, whether from the side of the analyst or in his daily life, with a deep loss of the sense of the continuity of his self in time and of its cohesiveness in space—a psychic condition that produces profound anxiety. The feeling, in particular, that various body parts are beginning not to be held together anymore by a strong, healthy awareness of the totality of the body-self, leads to apprehensive brooding concerning the fragments of the body, often expressed by the patient in the form of hypochondriacal worry concerning his health. Unlike the chronic hypochondriacal preoccupations encountered in some psychoses, however, even the most severe and quasi-delusional analogous worries in the narcissistic personality disorders are the direct consequence of some specific, identifiable narcissistic injury, and they disappear, often with dramatic speed, as soon as a bridge of empathy with an understanding selfobject has been built.

The *overstimulated self*. The propensity towards recurrent states during which the self is overstimulated arises in consequence of unempathically excessive or phase-inappropriate responses from the side of the selfobjects of childhood, either vis-a-vis the activities of the grandiose-exhibitionistic pole of the child's nascent self or vis-a-vis the activities of the pole that harbors the guiding ideals, or both.

If it was the grandiose-exhibitionistic pole of a person's self that had been exposed to unempathic overstimulation in childhood, then no healthy glow of enjoyment can be obtained by him from external success. On the contrary, since these people are subject to being flooded by unrealistic, archaic greatness fantasies which produce painful tension and anxiety, they will try to avoid situations in which they could become the center of attention. In some such individuals creativity may be unimpaired so long as no exhibition of the *body*-self is involved, directly or indirectly. In most of them, however, the creative-productive potential will be diminished because their intense ambitions which had remained tied to unmodified grandiose fantasies will frighten them. In view of the fact, furthermore, that the selfobjects' responses had focused prematurely and unrealistically on the fantasied performance or the fantasied products of the self but had failed to respond appropriately to the exhibitionism of the nascent nuclear self of the child as the initiator of the performance and as the shaper of products, the self will, throughout life, be experienced as separate from its own actions and weak in comparison with them.

Such people will tend to shy away from giving themselves over to creative activities because their self is in danger of destruction by being siphoned into its own performance or into the product it is shaping.

If it is predominantly the pole that harbors the ideals that had been overstimulated—e.g. by the unempathically intense and prolonged display of a parental selfobject in need of admiration—then it will be the persisting, intense need for the merger with an external ideal that will threaten the equilibrium of the self. Since contact with the idealized selfobject is, therefore, experienced as a danger and must be avoided, the healthy capacity for enthusiasm will be lost—the enthusiasm for goals and ideals which people with a firm self can experience vis-a-vis the admired great who are their guide and example or with regard to the idealized goals that they pursue.

Closely related to the overstimulated self is the *overburdened self*. But while the overstimulated self is a self whose ambitions and ideals had been unempathically responded to in isolation, without sufficient regard for the life *in toto*, the overburdened self is a self that had not been provided with the opportunity to merge with the calmness of an omnipotent selfobject. The overburdened self, in other words, is a self that had suffered the trauma of unshared emotionality. The result of this specific empathic failure from the side of the selfobject is the absence of the self-soothing capacity that protects the normal individual from being traumatized by the spreading of his emotions, especially by the spreading of anxiety. A world that lacks such soothing selfobjects is an inimical, a dangerous world. No wonder, then, that a self that had been exposed in early life to states of "overburdenedness" because of the lack of soothing selfobjects, will under certain circumstances experience its environment as hostile. During states of "overburdenedness" in adult life—e.g. after the therapist had been unempathic, in particular by failing to give to his patient the right interpretation with regard to his emotional state, or by pouring too much insight into him all at once, oblivious to the fact that the absorption of the new understanding confronts the patient with an excessive task— a patient might dream that he lives in a poisoned atmosphere or that he is surrounded by swarms of dangerous hornets; and, in his wakeful awareness, he will tend to respond to otherwise hardly noticeable stimuli as if they were attacks on his sensibilities. He will, for example, complain of the noises in the therapist's office, of unpleasant odors, etc. These reactions of patients with narcissistic personality disorders, especially when they involve an overall attitude of irritability and suspiciousness, may at times strike us as alarmingly close to those we encounter in the psychoses, in particular of course in paranoia. Unlike the more or less systematized, chronic suspiciousness and counter-hostility of the paranoiac, however, these manifestations of the overburdened state of the self appear, like the analogous hypochondriacal preoccupations in states of self-fragmentation, always as the direct consequence of a specific narcissistic injury, as a consequence of the unempathic, overburdening response of a selfobject. They disappear speedily when an empathic bond with the selfobject has been re-established, i.e. in therapy, when a correct interpretation has been made.

Behavioral Patterns and the Injured Self

It is with a good deal of reluctance that the psychoanalyst undertakes to present a typology of behavior, even if he has been able to correlate his descriptions of frequently occurring clusters of specific surface manifestations with specific underlying dynamic constellations or with specific foci of genetic experience. The best efforts of the past are no exception to the rule that the simplified correlation of specific patterns of manifest behavior with universally present psychological conditions which of necessity forms part of any such typology will, in the long run, impede scientific progress. Why then, do we persist in the attempt to devise characterologies? The answer is that such classifications, even though we must be aware of the fact that they may eventually limit our thinking and stand in our way, can for a while be valuable guides in psychological territory in which we feel not yet at home. So we will throw caution to the winds and outline some frequently encountered narcissistic personality types.

Mirror-hungry personalities thirst for selfobjects whose confirming and admiring responses will nourish their famished self. They are impelled to display themselves and to evoke the attention of others, trying to counteract, however fleetingly, their inner sense of worthlessness and lack of self-esteem. Some of them are able to establish relationships with reliably mirroring others that will sustain them for long periods. But most of them will not be nourished for long, even by genuinely accepting responses. Thus, despite their discomfort about their need to display themselves and despite their sometimes severe stage fright and shame they must go on trying to find new selfobjects whose attention and recognition they seek to induce.

Ideal-hungry personalities are forever in search of others whom they can admire for their prestige, power, beauty, intelligence, or moral stature. They can experience themselves as worthwhile only so long as they can relate to selfobjects to whom they can look up. Again, in some instances, such relationships last a long time and are genuinely sustaining to both individuals involved. In most cases, however, the inner void cannot forever be filled by these means. The ideal-hungry feels the persistence of the structural defect and, as a consequence of this awareness, he begins to look for—and, of course, he inevitably finds—some realistic defects in his God. The search for new idealizable selfobjects is then continued, always with the hope that the next great figure to whom the ideal-hungry attaches himself will not disappoint him.

Alter-ego-personalities need a relationship with a selfobject that by conforming to the self's appearance, opinions, and values confirms the existence, the reality of the self. At times the alter-ego-hungry personalities, too, may be able to form lasting friendships—relationships in which each of the partners experiences the feelings of the other as if they had been experienced by himself. "If thou sorrow, he will weep; if thou wake, he cannot sleep; thus of every grief in heart he with thee doth bear a part" (Shakespeare, *The Passionate Pilgrim*). But again, in most instances, the inner void cannot be filled permanently by the twinship. The alter-ego-hungry discovers that the other is not himself and, as a consequence of this discovery, begins to feel estranged from him. It is thus characteristic for most of these relationships to be short-lived. Like the mirror-and ideal-hungry, the alter-ego-hungry is prone to look restlessly for one replacement after another.

The preceding three character types in the narcissistic realm are frequently encountered in everyday life and they should, in general, not be considered as forms of psychopathology but rather as variants of the normal human personality, with its assets and defects. Stated in more experience-distant terms, it is not primarily the intensity of the need that brings about the typical attitude and behavior of these individuals but the specific direction into which they are propelled in their attempt to make up for a circumscribed weakness in their self. It is the location of the self-defect that produces the characteristic stance of these individuals, not the extent of the defect in the self. By contrast, the following two types are characterized less by the location of the defect and more by its extent. They must, in general, be considered as lying within the spectrum of pathological narcissism.

Merger-hungry personalities will impress us by their need to control their selfobjects in an enactment of the need for structure. Here, in contrast to the types sketched out before, it is the need for merger that dominates the picture, the specific type of merger, however—whether with a mirroring or an idealized selfobject or with an alter-ego—is less important in determining the individual's behavior. Because the self of these individuals is seriously defective or enfeebled, they need selfobjects in lieu of self-structure. Their manifest personality features and their behavior are thus dominated by the fact that the fluidity of the boundaries between them and others interferes with their ability to discriminate their own thoughts, wishes and intentions from those of the selfobject. Because they experience the other as their own self, they feel tolerant of his independence: they are very sensitive to separations from him and they demand—indeed they expect without question—the selfobject's continuous presence.

Contact-shunning personalities are the reverse of the merger-hungry just described. Although for obvious reasons they attract the least notice, they may well be the most frequent of the narcissistic character types. These individuals avoid social contact and become isolated, not because they are disinterested in others, but, on the contrary, just because of their need for them is so intense. The intensity of their need not only leads to great sensitivity to rejection—a sensitivity of which they are painfully aware—but also, on deeper and unconscious levels, to the apprehension that the remnants of their nuclear self will be swallowed up and destroyed by the yearned-for all-encompassing union.

The Treatment of the Narcissistic Behavior and Personality Disorders

The essential therapeutic goal of depth-psychology is the extensive amelioration or cure of the central disturbance, not the suppression of symptoms by persuasion or education, however benevolently applied. Since the central pathology in the narcissistic behavior and personality disorders is the defective or weakened condition of the self, the goal of therapy is the rehabilitation of this structure. True, to external inspection, the clusters of symptoms and personality features that characterize the narcissistic behavior disorders on the one hand, and the narcissistic personality disorders, on the other hand, are completely different: the self-assertive claims of the first group appear to be too strong, those of the second not strong enough. But depth-psychological investigation demonstrates that the psychopathological basis of both disorders—the disease of the self—is, in essence, the same.

Since the psychopathology of both major types of analysable dis-

orders is identical, it follows that despite their divergent symptomatology—noisy demands and intense activity in the social field in the
narcissistic behavior disorders; shame and social isolation in the narcissistic personality disorders—the process of treatment also is identical in its essence. And the same, of course, holds for the nature of the
wholesome result that is achieved by the treatment: it is the firming of
the formerly enfeebled self, both in the pole that carries the patient's
self-confidently held ambitions and in the pole that carries his idealized goals. It only needs to be added now that the patient's revitalized
self-confidence and the revitalized enthusiasm for his goals will ultimately make it possible for him, whether he suffered from a narcissistic behavior disorder or a narcissistic personality disorder, to take up
again the pursuit of the action-poised program arched in the energic
field that established itself between his nuclear ambitions and ideals,
i.e., will make it possible for him to lead a fulfilling, creative-
productive life.

CHAPTER 22

Forms and Transformations of Narcissism

HEINZ KOHUT

A lthough in theoretical discussions it will usually not be disputed that narcissism, the libidinal investment of the self, is per se neither pathological nor obnoxious, there exists an understandable tendency to look at it with a negatively toned evaluation as soon as the field of theory is left. Where such a prejudice exists it is undoubtedly based on a comparison between narcissism and object love, and is justified by the assertion that it is the more primitive and the less adaptive of the two forms of libido distribution. I believe, however, that these views do not stem primarily from an objective assessment either of the developmental position or of the adaptive value of narcissism, but that they are due to the improper intrusion of the altruistic value system of Western civilization. Whatever the reasons for them, these value judgments exert a narrowing effect on clinical practice. They tend to lead to a wish from the side of the therapist to replace the patient's narcissistic position with object love, while the often more appropriate goal of a transformed narcissism (i.e., of a redistribution of the patient's narcissistic libido, and of the integration of the primitive psychological structures into the mature personality) is neglected.

There exist, however, a number of acquisitions of the ego which, although genetically and dynamically related to the narcissistic drives and energized by them, are far removed from the preformed narcissistic structures of the personality, and which therefore must be evaluated not only as transformations of narcissism but even more as attainments of the ego and as attitudes and achievements of the personality. Let me first enumerate those whose relationship to narcissism I shall discuss. They are: (i) man's creativity; (ii) his ability to be empathic; (iii) his capacity to contemplate his own impermanence; (iv) his sense of humor; and (v) his wisdom.

1

First we will briefly examine the relationship of narcissism to *creativity*. Like all complex human activities, artistic and scientific creativity serves many purposes, and it involves the whole personality, and thus a wide range of psychological structures and drives. It is therefore to be expected that the narcissism of the creative individual participates in his creative activity, for example, as a spur, driving him toward fame and acclaim. If there existed no further connection between narcissism and creativity, however, than the interplay between ambition and superior executive equipment, there would be no justification for discussing creativity specifically among the transformations of narcissism. It is my contention, however, that while artists and scientists may indeed be acclaim-hungry, narcissistically vulnerable individuals, and while their ambitions may be helpful in prompting them toward the appropriate communication of their work, the creative activity itself deserves to be considered among the transformations of narcissism.

The ambitions of a creative individual play an important role in his relationship to the public, i.e., to an audience of potential admirers; the transformation of narcissism, however, is a feature of the creator's relationship to his work. In creative work narcissistic energies are employed which have been changed into a form to which I refer to as idealizing libido, i.e., the elaboration of that specific point on the developmental road from narcissism toward object love at which an object (in the sense of social psychology) is cathected with narcissistic libido and thus included in the context of the self.

The analogy to the mother's love for the unborn fetus and for the newborn baby is inviting, and undoubtedly the single-minded devotion to the child who is taken into her expanded self, and her empathic responsiveness to him are similar to the creative person's involvement with his work. Nevertheless, I believe that the creative person's relationship to his work has less in common with the expanded narcissism of motherhood than with the still unrestricted narcissism of early childhood. Phenomenologically, too, the personality of many unusually creative individuals is more childlike than maternal. Even the experiments of some of the great in science impress the observer with their almost childlike freshness and simplicity.

The indistinctness of "internal" and "external" is familiar to all of us in our relationship to the surrounding air which, as we take it in and expel it, is experienced by us as part of our selves, while we hardly perceive it as long as it forms a part of our external surroundings. Similarly, the creative individual is keenly aware of those aspects of his surroundings which are of significance to his work and he invests them with narcissistic-idealizing libido. Like the air which we breathe, they are most clearly experienced at the moment of union with the self. The traditional metaphor which is expressed by the term "inspiration" (it refers both to the taking in of air and to the fertilizing influence of an external stimulation upon the internal creative powers) and the prototypical description of creativity ("and the Lord God formed man of the dust of the ground, and breathed into his nostrils the breath of life; and man became a living soul" [Genesis 2:7]) support the assertion that there exists a close psychological proximity, on the one hand, between respiratory and creative inspiration and, on the other hand, between the coming to life of dust and the creative transformation of a narcissistically experienced material into a work of art.

The well-established fact, furthermore, that creative people tend to alternate during periods of productivity between phases when they think extremely highly of their work and phases when they are convinced that it has no value, is a sure indication that the work is cathected with a form of narcissistic libido. The fact, too, that the artist's attitude to his work is similar to that of the fetishist toward the fetish, lends support to the idea that, for the creator, the work is a transitional object and that it is invested with transitional narcissistic libido. The fetishist's attachment to the fetish has the intensity of an addiction, a fact which is a manifestation not of object love but of a fixation on an early object that is experienced as part of the self. Creative artists, and scientists, may be attached to their work with the intensity of an addiction, and they try to control and shape it with forces and for purposes which belong to a narcissistically experienced world. They are attempting to re-create a perfection which formerly was directly an attribute of their own; during the act of creation, however, they do not relate to their work in the give and take mutuality which characterizes object love.

2

I am now turning to *empathy* as the second of the faculties of the ego which, though far removed from the drives and largely autonomous, are here considered in the context of the transformation of narcissism. Empathy is the mode by which one gathers psychological data about other people and, when they say what they think or feel, imagines their inner experience even though it is not open to direct observation. The groundwork for our ability to obtain access to another person's mind is laid by the fact that in our earliest mental organization the feelings, actions, and behavior of the mother had been included in our self. This primary empathy with the mother prepares us for the recognition that, to a large extent, the basic inner experiences of people remain similar to our own. Our first perception of the manifestations of another person's feelings, wishes, and thoughts occurred within the framework of a narcissistic conception of the world; the capacity for empathy belongs, therefore, to the innate equipment of the human psyche and remains to some extent associated with the primary process.

Nonempathic forms of cognition, however, which are attuned to objects which are essentially dissimilar to the self become increasingly superimposed over the original empathic mode of reality perception and tend to impede its free operation. The persistence of empathic forms of observation outside of psychology is, indeed, archaic and leads to a faulty, prerational, animistic conception of reality. Nonempathic modes of observation, on the other hand, are not attuned to the experiences of other people and, if they are employed in the psychological field, lead to a mechanistic and lifeless conception of psychological reality.

Nonempathic forms of cognition are dominant in the adult. Empathy must thus often be achieved speedily before nonempathic modes of observation are interposed. The approximate correctness of first impressions in the assessment of people, by contrast with subsequent evaluations, is well known and is exploited by skillful men of affairs. Empathy seems here to be able to evade interference and to complete a rapid scrutiny before other modes of observation can assert their ascendancy. The exhaustive empathic comprehension, however, which is the aim of the analyst requires the ability to use the empathic capacity for prolonged periods. His customary observational attitude ("evenly suspended attention"; avoidance of note taking; curtailment of realistic interactions; concentration on the purpose of achieving understanding rather than on the wish to cure and to help) aims at excluding psychological processes attuned to the nonpsychological perception of objects and to encourage empathic comprehension through the perception of experiential identities. The prototype of empathic understanding must be sought not only in the prehistory of the race but also in the early life of the individual. Under favorable circumstances, the faculty of perceiving the psychological manifestations of the mother, achieved through the extension of narcissistic cathexes, becomes the starting point for a series of developmental steps which lead ultimately to a state in which the ego can choose between the use of empathic and nonempathic modes of observation, depending on realistic requirements and on the nature of the surroundings that it scrutinizes.

3

Man's *capacity to acknowledge the finiteness of his existence*, and to act in accordance with this painful discovery, may well be his greatest psychological achievement, despite the fact that it can often be demonstrated that a manifest acceptance of transience may go hand in hand with covert denials. The acceptance of transience is accomplished by the ego, which performs the emotional work that precedes, accompanies, and follows separations. Without these efforts a valid conception of time, of limits, and of the impermanence of object cathexes could not be achieved. Freud discussed the emotional task which is imposed on the psyche by the impermanence of objects, be they beloved people or cherished values, and gave expression to the conviction that their impermanence did not detract from their worth. On the contrary, he said, their very impermanence makes us love and admire them even more: "Transience value is scarcity value in time."[1]

Freud's attitude is based on the relinquishment of emotional infantilism, an abandonment even of a trace of the narcissistic insistence on the omnipotence of the wish; it expresses the acceptance of realistic values. More difficult still, however, than the acknowledgment of the impermanence of object cathexes is the unqualified intellectual and emotional acceptance of the fact that we ourselves are impermanent, that the self which is cathected with narcissistic libido is finite in time. I believe that this rare feat rests not simply on a victory of autonomous reason and supreme objectivity over the claims of narcissism but on the creation of a higher form of narcissism.

Just as the child's *primary empathy* with the mother is the precursor of the adult's ability to be empathic, so his *primary identity* with her must be considered as the precursor of an expansion of the self, late in life, when the finiteness of individual existence is acknowledged. The original psychological universe, i.e., the primordial experience of the mother, is "remembered" by many people in the form of the occasionally occurring vague reverberations which are known by the term "oceanic feeling."[2] The achievement—as the certainty of eventual death is fully realized—of a shift of the narcissistic cathexes, from the self to a concept of participation in a supraindividual and timeless existence, must also be regarded as genetically predetermined by the child's primary identity with the mother. In contrast to the oceanic feeling, however, which is experienced passively (and usually fleetingly), the genuine shift of the cathexes toward a cosmic narcissism is the enduring, creative result of the steadfast activities of an autonomous ego, and only very few are able to attain it.

4

It seems a long way from the acceptance of transience and the quasi-religious solemnity of a cosmic narcissism to another uniquely human acquisition: *the capacity for humor.* And yet, the two phenomena have much in common. It is not by accident that Freud introduces his essay on humor with a man's ability to overcome the fear of his impending death by putting himself, through humor, upon a higher plane. "When . . . a criminal who was being led out to the gallows on a Monday remarked: 'Well, the week's beginning nicely,' " Freud says that "the humorous process . . . affords him . . . satisfaction." And Freud states that "humour has something liberating about it"; that it "has something of grandeur"; and that it is a "triumph of narcissism" and "the victorious assertion of . . . invulnerability." Metapsychologically, however, Freud explains that humor—this "triumph of narcissism"—is achieved by a person's withdrawing "the psychical accent from his ego" and "transposing it on to his super-ego."[3] Humor and cosmic narcissism are thus both transformations of narcissism which aid man in achieving ultimate mastery over the demands of the narcissistic self, i.e., to tolerate the recognition of his finiteness in principle and even of his impending end.

There is no doubt that the claim that the ego has mastered its fear of death is often not authentic. If a person is unable to be serious and employs humor excessively, or if he is unwilling to face the pains and labors of everyday living and moves along continuously with his head in the clouds, we will become suspicious of both the clown and the saint, and we will most likely be right in surmising that neither the humor nor the otherworldliness are genuine. Yet, if a man is capable of responding with humor to the recognition of those unalterable realities which oppose the assertions of the narcissistic self, and if he can truly attain that quiet, superior stance which enables him to contemplate his own end philosophically, we will assume that a transformation of his narcissism has indeed taken place (a withdrawal of the psychical accent from the "ego," as Freud puts it) and will respect the person who has achieved it.

A genuine decathexis of the self can only be achieved slowly by an intact, well-functioning ego; and it is accompanied by sadness as the cathexis is transferred from the cherished self upon the supraindividual ideals and upon the world with which one identifies. The profoundest forms of humor and cosmic narcissism therefore do not present a picture of grandiosity and elation but that of a quiet inner triumph with an admixture of undenied melancholy.

5

We have now reached our final subject matter, the human attitude which we call *wisdom*. In the progression from information through knowledge to wisdom, the first two can still be defined almost exclusively within the sphere of cognition itself. The term information refers to the gleaning of isolated data about the world; knowledge to the comprehension of a cohesive set of such data held together by a matrix of abstractions. Wisdom, however, goes beyond the cognitive sphere, although, of course, it includes it.

Wisdom is achieved largely through man's ability to overcome his unmodified narcissism and it rests on his acceptance of the limitations of his physical, intellectual, and emotional powers. It may be defined as an amalgamation of the higher processes of cognition with the psychological attitude which accompanies the renouncement of these narcissistic demands. Neither the possession of ideals, nor the capacity for humor, nor the acceptance of transience alone characterizes wisdom. All three have to be linked together to form a new psychological constellation which goes beyond the several emotional and cognitive attributes of which it is made up. Wisdom may thus be defined as a stable attitude of the personality toward life and the world, an attitude which is formed through the integration of the cognitive function with humor, acceptance of transience, and a firmly cathected system of values.

In the course of life the acquisition of knowledge clearly must be preceded by the gathering of information. Even from the point of view of its cognitive component, therefore, wisdom can hardly be an attribute of youth since experience and work must first have led to the acquisition of broadly based knowledge. Ideals are most strongly cathected in youth; humor is usually at its height during maturity; and an acceptance of transience may be achieved during the advanced years. Thus we can see again that the attainment of wisdom is usually reserved for the later phases of life.

The essence of this proud achievement is therefore a maximal relinquishment of narcissistic delusions, including the acceptance of the inevitability of death, without an abandonment of cognitive and emotional involvements. The ultimate act of cognition, i.e., the acknowledgment of the limits and of the finiteness of the self, is not the result of an isolated intellectual process but is the victorious outcome of the lifework of the total personality in acquiring broadly based knowledge and in transforming archaic modes of narcissism into ideals, humor, and a sense of supraindividual participation in the world. Wisdom is, in addition, characterized not only by the maintenance of the libidinal cathexes of the old ideals but by their creative expansion. And in contrast to an attitude of utter seriousness and unrelieved solemnity vis-a-vis the approaching end of life, the truly wise are able in the end to transform the humor of their years of maturity into a sense of proportion, a touch of irony toward the achievements of individual existence, including even their own wisdom. The ego's ultimate mastery over the narcissistic self, the final control of the rider over the horse, may after all have been decisively assisted by the fact that the horse, too, has grown old. And, lastly, we may recognize that what has been accomplished is not so much control but the acceptance of the ultimate insight that, as concerns the supreme powers of nature, we are all "Sunday riders."

In concluding this presentation let me now give a brief resume of the principal themes which I laid before you. I wanted to emphasize that there are various forms of narcissism which must be considered not only as forerunners of object love but also as independent psychological constellations, whose development and functions deserve separate examination and evaluation. In addition, I tried to demonstrate the ways by which a number of complex and autonomous achievements of the mature personality were derived from transformations of narcissism, i.e., created by the ego's capacity to tame narcissistic cathexes and to employ them for its highest aims.

I would finally like to say that I have become increasingly convinced of the value of these conceptualizations for psychoanalytic therapy. They are useful in the formulation of broad aspects of the psychopathology of the frequently encountered narcissistic personality types among our patients; they help us understand the psychological changes which tend to be induced in them; and, last but not least, they assist us in the evaluation of the therapeutic goal. In many instances, the reshaping of the narcissistic structures and their integration into the personality—the strengthening of ideals, and the achievement, even to a modest degree, of such wholesome transformations of narcissism as humor, creativity, empathy, and wisdom—must be rated as a more genuine and valid result of therapy than the patient's precarious compliance with demands for a change of his narcissism into object love.

NOTES

1. Sigmund Freud, "On Transience" (1916), in *The Standard Edition of the Complete Psychological Works of Sigmund Freud*, vol. 14, James Strachey (ed.). (London: Hogarth Press, 1957), p. 303.

2. Sigmund Freud, *Civilization and Its Discontents* (1930), in *The Standard Edition of the Complete Psychological Works of Sigmund Freud*, vol. 21, James Strachey (ed.). (London: Hogarth Press, 1961), pp. 64–73.

3. Sigmund Freud, "Humour" (1927), in *The Standard Edition of the Complete Psychological Works of Sigmund Freud*, vol. 21, James Strachey (ed.). (London: Hogarth Press, 1961), pp. 161–164.

CHAPTER 23

From *The Restoration of the Self*

HEINZ KOHUT

When he presented himself for analysis, Mr. X., twenty-two years old, had been rejected by the Peace Corps, which he had wanted to join in order to obtain the fulfillment of a lifelong wish-fantasy: to help underprivileged, suffering people. He admitted to the analyst that, although the rejection had been the immediate stimulus for his seeking treatment, he had contemplated undergoing psychotherapy even before applying to the Peace Corps, but then decided he would spend several years in the Peace Corps first. The real motive for his wish for treatment appeared to be shame about his sexual disturbance and, perhaps as a consequence of his shame, his social isolation and a pervasive sense of loneliness. His sex life, from early adolescence to the beginning of therapy, consisted of frequent masturbatory activities (several times a day, with addiction-like intensity) accompanied by homosexual fantasies. He had never had any actual sexual experiences—homosexual or heterosexual.

Mr. X.'s mother had idealized him and supported his open display of grandiosity—but only, as we will see, so long as he did not remove himself emotionally from her. Her attitude toward the boy's father had been strongly depreciative. Beginning in latency, the patient, a Lutheran, had felt a desire to enter the ministry, a desire that became even stronger during adolescence. Although I am not certain that his mother explicitly supported this vocational choice, it was undoubtedly related to the sphere of her influence over him. At any rate, it was the carrier of consciously entertained grandiose ideas (an identification with Christ), which, however, implicitly deprived him of independence and of masculine goals. The patient's mother had often read

the Bible to him when he was a child, laying stress on the relation between the boy Jesus and the Virgin. One of their favorite Bible stories—it later became a focus of many of the patient's daydreams—was
of the boy Jesus in the temple (Luke 2:41–52); and particular emphasis seems to have been given to the implication that ("sitting in the
temple surrounded by the teachers") Jesus was even as a child superior to the father figures ("and all who heard him were amazed at his
intelligence and the answers he gave").[1]

Although the patient's attempt to enter the Peace Corps was undoubtedly motivated by an offshoot of the original identification with
the figure of the Saviour, Mr. X. did not actually undertake steps that
would have led him to the ministry. Without investigating in detail the
endopsychic obstacles that stood in his way, I can give the following
psychodynamic summary: Mr. X. could not fit his earlier grandiose
preoccupations into the life pattern of a clergyman because his relation to religion had become sexualized. Beginning in late adolescence,
many of his masturbatory activities were accompanied by fantasies of
homosexual relations with the officiating pastor, particularly at the
moment of receiving Holy Communion. Although Mr. X.'s desire for
sexualized oral incorporation was thus quite close to the psychological surface, his deeply felt need for paternal psychological structure
was not expressed through *conscious* fellatio fantasies. The manifest
content of the relevant masturbatory fantasies—a fascinating synthesis of the sublimated symbolism of the Church and the patient's primary processes—concerned the crossing (!) of the powerful penis of
the pastor and his own at the moment of receiving the Host. Thus, at
the moment of climactic ejaculation, the patient's preoccupation with
a powerful man's penis, with oral incorporation, and with the acquisition of idealized strength found an almost artistically perfect expression in his sexualized imagery about the consummation of the most
profoundly significant symbolic act of the Christian ritual.

On the basis of Mr. X.'s conscious memories, the analyst had at
first surmised that he had hardly been in any meaningful emotional
contact with his father as a child and that the relationship to his father
had therefore become unimportant to him. It could be discerned in
retrospect, however, that in the initial diagnostic interviews Mr. X.
had alluded to a deep disappointment he had experienced concerning
his father. The analyst had not recognized the significance of these references to Mr. X.'s father, and the patient, too, was completely unaware at that point that he was alluding to an important emotional
need from his childhood. On the contrary, he presented the relevant

communication—the complaint that his mother had deprived him of his rightful share of the father's estate—entirely with reference to an issue of the more recent past (the disposition of the inheritance after his father's death) and expressed it with such bitterness and resentment that the analyst entertained the possibility of the presence of a hidden paranoia and was for a while in doubt whether the patient would be suitable for analysis. (In retrospect, it was possible to explain the meaning of this complaint: behind the manifest accusation that he had been short-changed with regard to his father's *financial* estate lay hidden the deeper reproach that his mother had deprived him of the opportunity of his rightful *psychological* inheritance by preventing him from relating admiringly to his father and from thus forming a self-structure guided by paternal ideals, values, and goals.)

The patient began to develop the theme of his attempt to turn from his mother to this father—to avail himself of a second developmental chance of acquiring a reliably cohesive self— comparatively late in the analysis. During the first two and a half years the analyst had focused her attention almost exclusively upon the patient's overt grandiosity (his arrogance, his isolation, his unrealistic goals); and she attempted to show Mr. X. that his grandiosity was, on the one hand, part of an "oedipal victory" and, on the other, that it was defensive—that it was buttressing the child's denial of the fact that, despite the mother's seeming preference for him, the father was still her real possessor, that he could punish (castrate) the little boy. Put briefly, she had tried to tell him that beneath his overt grandiosity lay the depression of an "oedipal defeat." In other words, the analyst's attention and interpretations had been focused on the overt grandiosity in which, as she and I came to recognize, the patient was no more than the agent of his mother's ambitions. What had remained disregarded was the patient's latent grandiosity, emanating from the boy's repressed grandiose-exhibitionistic self—an independent boyish self that had first yearned in vain for confirmation from the side of the mother and had then attempted to gain strength by merging with an idealizable, admired father.

But patients do not give up easily, and their unfulfilled childhood needs continue to assert themselves. Mr. X. was somehow able to indicate to the analyst that he had been misunderstood. One of the clues he provided was the following. Several weeks after the summer interruption marking the end of the second full year of analysis, he reported a touching sequence of events. He recalled that at the beginning of his vacation he had driven alone into a mountainous region, far from Chicago. While driving, he daydreamed a good deal of the time, as had been his wont throughout his life. The analyst assumed that Mr. X. was now beginning to tell her about how lonely he had felt when he was away from her. But his associations moved into a different direction. He recalled a very vivid daydream which apparently had almost the features of a real dream. The patient imagined that his car was not running smoothly, that the engine was beginning to work irregularly and finally stopped altogether. He looked at the fuel gauge and realized he had run out of gas. He then saw himself pulling the car over to the side of the road, coming to a stop on the shoulder of the expressway. In his fantasy he got out of the car and tried to signal to the passing cars that he needed help. But one after the other they kept rushing by, and his anxiety grew as he felt himself alone, helpless and powerless. But then a thought came to him. Had he not, long long ago, stashed away into the trunk of his car a can filled with gasoline? Could it be that it was still there and that he could find it and thus get moving again? He saw himself opening the trunk, looking at a heap of luggage and tools and a great variety of other, nondescript, discarded old objects. He dug into the heap and, by God!, here indeed was the old can—rusty, battered, dilapidated, yet still filled with gasoline—just what he had hoped to find, just what he needed. The daydream ended with his pouring the gasoline into the tank and driving off again.

He followed the recall of this daydream by an account of his wanderings through the wooded landscape of the beautiful region to which he had driven. Again he was alone, and again his mind was active during his walks. In particular, he kept reminiscing about an aspect of his childhood about which he had never before spoken in the analysis. He remembered that on very rare occasions he and his father had gone on walks through the woods, that during these walks there had been an intimacy, a closeness between father and son which otherwise had seemed to be totally absent from their relationship. And there was another feature that seemed immediately to be of potentially great significance: in contrast to the depreciated image of his father the patient had presented in the analysis up to that point, he now told the analyst that during these walks the father impressed him as a remarkable man, as an admirable teacher and guide. The father knew the names of the trees, he identified the tracks made by various animals, and he told his son about his having been a good hunter in his younger years who knew how to approach the game and how to kill it with a well-aimed shot. Needless to say, the boy had listened with delightful admiration to his father's stories and was an enthusiastic and attentive pupil when his father thus taught him the rudiments of the woodsman's craft. There was, however, another side to these experiences. Not only did they occur but rarely, they also remained isolated; they had not become integrated with the rest of Mr. X.'s personality, had existed only as enclaves in the boy's life (and in the father's relation to his son). Father and son never talked about these walks afterward, and, as if by a silent agreement, they never mentioned them in front of the mother.

Excursion into Theory

The structural basis of the patient's psychological disturbance was a vertical split in his personality (See Chart). One sector functioned by virtue of a still unbroken merger with his mother. The other sector harbored two not fully integrated constituents of his nuclear self—an unresponded-to grandiose-exhibitionistic fragment, and a fragment characterized by idealized-goal structures related to certain admiring attitudes toward his father. As we shall see shortly, the first of these two fragments of the nuclear self (the grandiose-exhibitionistic pole) was even more paralyzed than the second one (the pole that carried the masculine ideals). The nuclear self was, however, not only fragmented and weak, it was also out of touch with the functioning surface of the personality; it had gone into hiding. It had no communication with and no access to the conscious self-structures, but was separated from them by a horizontal split in the personality—it was repressed.

Thus, Mr. X.'s personality was divided into two sectors by a vertical split. In one sector, characterized by a sense of superiority, arrogant behavior, unworldly and religious aims, and identification with Christ, he maintained the old merger with his mother who permitted, and even encouraged, his expression of ideas of greatness—and his pursuit of life goals that were in harmony with them—so long as he did not break the merger-bond with her, so long as he remained the executor of her grandiosity. In the present context, however, we are not focusing on this sector, but on the second one where we encounter the condition to which I referred earlier as the "repression" of the structure that yearned for merger with the idealized parent imago and contained some rudimentary foci of already internalized nuclear ideals. The conditions present in this sector can, as I said, easily be depicted within the theoretical framework of the psychology of the self in the

The Case of Mr. X.—His Psychopathology and the Course of His Analysis

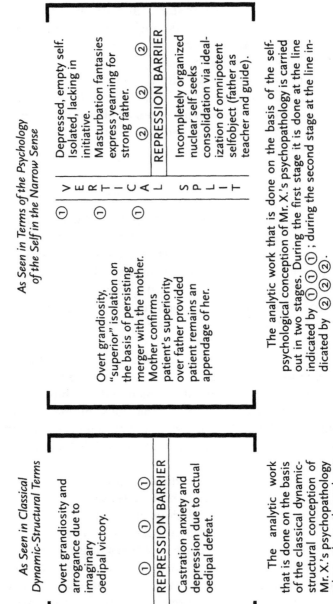

As Seen in Classical Dynamic-Structural Terms

Overt grandiosity and arrogance due to imaginary oedipal victory.

① ① ①

REPRESSION BARRIER

Castration anxiety and depression due to actual oedipal defeat.

The analytic work that is done on the basis of the classical dynamic-structural conception of Mr. X.'s psychopathology takes place throughout the analysis at the line indicated by ① ① ①.

As Seen in Terms of the Psychology of the Self in the Narrow Sense

Overt grandiosity, "superior" isolation on the basis of persisting merger with the mother. Mother confirms patient's superiority over father provided patient remains an appendage of her.

V E R T I C A L

① Depressed, empty self. Isolated, lacking in initiative.

① Masturbation fantasies express yearning for strong father.

① ② ② ②

REPRESSION BARRIER

S P L I T

Incompletely organized nuclear self seeks consolidation via idealization of omnipotent selfobject (father as teacher and guide). ② ② ②

The analytic work that is done on the basis of the self-psychological conception of Mr. X.'s psychopathology is carried out in two stages. During the first stage it is done at the line indicated by ① ① ①; during the second stage at the line indicated by ② ② ②.

narrower sense of the term: we will say that the nuclear self, especially that part of its nuclear greatness that is acquired through a merger with the idealized self-object, is walled off by repression (i.e., by a "horizontal split") from contact with the consciously perceived self. The course of Mr. X.'s analysis, in other words, can be described in schematic approximation as unrolling in two phases.

The first phase will focus on breaking down the barrier that maintained the vertical split in his personality. The removal of this barrier has the result that the patient will gradually realize that the self-experience in the horizontally-split sector of his personality—a self-experience of being empty and deprived which, although underemphasized, had always been present and conscious—constitutes his authentic self, and that the up to now predominant self-experience in the nondichotomized sector—the self-experience of overt grandiosity and arrogance—did not emanate from an independent self but from a self that was an appendage to the self of his mother.

The second phase of the analysis may be said to begin when, after the removal of the vertical barrier, the patient's attention has shifted from the nondichotomized to the dichotomized sector. Now the analytic work will focus on the horizontal barrier (the repression barrier) in the pursuit of the principal task of the analysis: to make conscious the *unconscious* structures that underlay the conscious self-experience. We can describe the goal of this second phase with the aid of the beautiful symbolic imagery Mr. X. employed in his daydream: the analysis should uncover the hidden supply of gasoline that can get him going again on the road of his life. Mr. X., in other words, is helped to discover the presence of a nuclear self that had been formed on the basis of his relation with the idealized self-object, his father.

The disturbing doubt, however, whether more than one valid solution to an analysis can exist is not allayed by the foregoing considerations. True, in a case such as that of Mr. X., a properly conducted analysis will unearth the patient's buried unconscious self which was derived from the idealized self-object, leading to this self's ascendancy and thus to the expression of hitherto unavailable ambitions and ideals. And indeed, as a result of the analytic work, the patient's personality underwent a gradual change, clearly in the direction of greater psychological health. Furthermore, with the greater inner freedom and resilience he thus attained, he was able to make certain decisions that led to the adoption of new goals. He gave up the thought of entering the ministry (or the Peace Corps) and turned towards goals more in tune with being a "teacher and guide"—a pattern that had molded his nuclear self in accordance with his merger with the idealized parent imago represented by his father on their walks through the woods.

Before the analytic process began to offer the patient truly effective means to fill in the structural defect, he could do no more than obtain fleeting relief through concretized erotized enactments. These found their most poignant expression in the patient's feeling suffused with male strength when he imagined the act of crossing his penis with the penis of the pastor at the moment of receiving the Host. It was the task of the analysis to move this need for a firm self— particularly for the pole of the self that was able to carry his idealized goals— from its addictive-erotic representation, which provided only a temporary sense of strength, back to the underlying need to reactivate the relation with the idealized self-object. Mr. X., in other words, had to reactivate the relation with the real father of his childhood; he had to shed the Christ-identification his mother had fostered in him, and simultaneously he had to disengage himself from the father-surrogate (the Father of the Trinity—the mother's unconscious imago of her own father) offered him by his mother. It was with the aid of the analytic work focused on the sector of his personality that harbored the need to complete the internalization of the idealized father imago to integrate the paternal ideal, after the analysis had shifted away from preoccupation with Mr. X.'s overt grandiosity, that structures began to be built, that a firming of the formerly isolated, unconscious self could take place through gradual transmuting internalizations.

I believe that I have adduced sufficient evidence in support of the claim that, in the case of Mr. X., a correctly responsive analysis would always, on the basis of intrinsic factors, become focused on the rehabilitation of the idealized parent imago and would in this way enable the patient to build up a properly functioning sectorial unit of his self.

Two Concepts of Psychological Cure

No satisfactory definition of the concept of a cure, and thus of the concept of a proper termination of an analysis, can be given if we fail to determine the patient's greatest terror— whether castration anxiety or disintegration anxiety—and his most compelling objective— whether conflict solution or the establishment of self-cohesion—or, stated in different terms, if we disregard the question whether the analysis had enabled him to perform those central psychological tasks through which he can establish the conditions that will guarantee his psychological survival. Because psychological health was formerly established through the solution of inner conflicts, cure, whether in a narrow or in a broad sense, was then seen exclusively in terms of conflict solution through the expansion of consciousness. But because psychological health is now achieved with ever-increasing frequency through the healing of a formerly fragmented self, cure, whether in a narrow or broad sense, must now also be evaluated in terms of achieving self-cohesion, particularly in terms of the restitution of the self with the aid of a re-established empathic closeness to responsive self-objects.

Our self—or should we say: the specific condition of our self?—influences our functioning, our well-being, the course of our life, both comprehensively and in depth. There are, on the one hand, many people with poorly constituted selves who, despite the absence of symptoms, inhibitions, and disabling conflicts, lead joyless and fruitless lives and curse their existence. And there are, on the other hand, those with firm, well-defined selves, who, despite serious neurotic disturbance—and yes, occasionally even despite their psychotic (or borderline) personalities—are leading worthwhile lives and are blessed with a sense of fulfillment and joy. It is the central position of the self within the personality that accounts for its broad influence on our life; and it is this central position that explains the vast increase in well-being provided for our patients by even a comparatively small improvement of self pathology. But in the absence of such improvement—however successful an analysis may have been in eradicating symptoms and inhibitions via a causal dynamic-genetic approach—the patient will remain unfulfilled and dissatisfied.

With regard to this second group of patients, analysts have, on the basis of their theoretical conviction that their patients' psychopathology was to be understood within the framework of conflict psychology and of the structural model of the mind, tended to shrug their shoulders in modest realism, consoling themselves with the thought that they have done all they possibly could. They have said, with Freud, that all they could do was to open new choices for their patients; or they have said, again with Freud, that they changed neurotic "misery into common suffering" over which they had no control.

I believe that some of these limitations can be seen in a different light—that a patient's continuing inability to make the right choices and his continuing inability to alter the suffering inflicted on him by unfortunate circumstances are in some cases at least (probably in many) not the result of unalterable internal or external factors, but of curable self pathology. Only increasing clinical experience, particularly the data of follow-up studies of analyses of narcissistic personality disorders, will give us reliable answers to the questions raised by the foregoing statement.

The two frames of reference—mental-apparatus psychology and self psychology—that permitted two different but complementary definitions of mental health, will also assist us now in our endeavor to formulate differentiating definitions of the concept of cure in the two classes of analyzable psychic disorders. In cases of structural conflict, the principal indicators that a cure has been established will be the disappearance or amelioration of the patient's neurotic symptoms and inhibitions, on the one hand, and his comparative freedom from neurotic anxiety and guilt, on the other. And, on the whole, the positive achievement of a good analysis in these cases will be confirmed by the fact that the patient is now able to experience the pleasures of life more keenly than before. In cases suffering from analyzable forms of self pathology, however, the principal indicators that a cure has been established will be the disappearance or the amelioration of the patient's hypochondria, lack of initiative, empty depression and lethargy, self-stimulation through sexualized activities, etc., on the one hand, and the patient's comparative freedom from excessive narcissistic vulnerability (the tendency, for example, to respond to narcissistic injuries with empty depression and lethargy, or with an increase of perverse self-soothing activities), on the other. And, on the whole, the positive achievement of a good analysis will here be confirmed by the fact that the patient is now able to experience the joy of existence more keenly, that, *even in the absence of pleasure,* he will consider his life worthwhile—creative, or at least productive.

NOTE

1. The atmosphere of family relationships indicated by the biblical passages quoted here is that of the constellation in which the mother belittles her husband, aggrandizes the son as long as he remains attached to her, but unconsciously harbors a deep awe of her own father. When his parents reproach him for his disappearance from home, Jesus replies, "Did you not know that I was bound to be in my Father's house?," referring to the temple as the house of the God-Father. (Translated into the language of depth psychology, he alludes here to the unconscious image of his maternal grandfather.)

CHAPTER 24

A Reexamination of Agoraphobia

HEINZ KOHUT

According to the traditional psychoanalytic view—a view that decisively influences the ambience of the analysis and the analyst's therapeutic strategy—the (female) patient's anxiety when unaccompanied in the street is the secondary, overt (conscious) manifestation of a specific underlying (unconscious) disturbance which is deemed primary. Namely, the patient's paralyzing fear arises in reaction to the mobilization of oedipal sexual wishes toward her father, as displaced upon the men whom she encounters in the street. The patient's panic—again in accordance with the traditional view—is no more than a symptom, and the relief the patient experiences when she is accompanied by a woman, in particular an older woman, is no more than a defensive maneuver. This maneuver is understandable as an enactment of the mother's presence which, by making the fulfillment of the oedipal desires impossible, short-circuits the fantasy and forestalls the outbreak of anxiety. Expressed most tersely in terms of Freud's earlier theories: the phobia is a symptom of an underlying anxiety hysteria in which libido is transformed into anxiety. Expressed most tersely in terms of the ego-psychological transformation of Freud's earlier theories: the ego reacts with panic and regressive infantilism to the mobilization of incestuous oedipal wishes.

Before proceeding to outline the self psychological evaluation of the syndrome of agoraphobia, I will first respond to a question that may well arise in many minds at this point. Why, it may be asked, do I choose agoraphobia as my sample of classical psychopathology, as the prototype of oedipal pathology of structural neurosis? Agoraphobia, after all, has for a long time been recognized as significantly interpenetrated by preoedipal pathology and thus should not be made to serve as a prototypical example of oedipal pathology.

I fully recognize the validity of the foregoing argument as far as agoraphobia per se is concerned, but I would be inclined to extend the same reasoning to all other forms of so-called oedipal pathology. Even in terms of ego psychology, in other words, pure oedipal neuroses are no longer encountered, or, to say the least, they must be considered a great rarity. But my present efforts should not be understood as an attempt to demonstrate that pure oedipal pathology is practically nonexistent; that could indeed be carrying coals to Newcastle. What I will try to illustrate, using the well-known syndrome of agoraphobia as an example, is the different viewpoint adopted by self psychology as it evaluates the significance of the clinical phenomena. I will add, furthermore, that I could easily have chosen any other of the classical syndromes, such as animal phobia, for my comparison. I have selected agoraphobia mainly for historical reasons, that is, in deference to the fact that agoraphobia came to play a prototypical role in Freud's writings and that it has served the same function for many generations of psychoanalytic instructors and students. But let us now return to the task we have set ourselves.

How does self psychology look at the phenomena presented by agoraphobia? The answer to this question is as simple as it is significant: What traditional analysis looked upon as secondary and peripheral self psychology sees as primary and central. This follows from the fact that self psychology considers the structural and functional deficiencies of the patient's self as the primary disorder and focuses its attention on them, whereas traditional analysis saw the content of conflicts as the primary disorder and focused on it. We believe, to return to our example, that the agoraphobic woman's essential illness is not defined by her unconscious wish for incestuous relations with her father and by her unconscious conflicts over them, but by the fact that she suffers from a structural deficiency of the self.

The causal role played by oedipal selfobjects in bringing about the pathogenic Oedipus complex has already been discussed at length and I will, therefore, only briefly repeat that when the little girl reached the oedipal stage, her phase-appropriate affection and assertive behavior did not elicit affectionate pride from her oedipal selfobjects. Instead, they were (preconsciously) stimulated and competitive, for they displayed guilt-inducing prohibitive attitudes, for example, via overt censure or emotional withdrawal. As a result, the child's unsupported oedipal self began to fragment, and isolated drive experiences and conflicts about them replaced the primary joyful experiences of the phase-appropriate affectionate and assertive whole self. These are the conditions which, I believe, prevail in all instances of subsequent pathology that arise on the basis of an Oedipus complex. The situation in the case of agoraphobia, however, has certain specific features to which I will now turn.

Although the breakup of the self accounts for both the disintegration of the agoraphobic woman's affectionate attitude toward the father in childhood (with pathogenic sexual fantasies replacing the former joyful warmth) and the tendency toward the spreading of anxiety and development of paralyzing panic, it is the faultily responsive *paternal* selfobject that accounts for the first aspect of the structural disease of the self (i.e., the ascendancy of an Oedipus complex) and the faultily responsive *maternal* selfobject that accounts for the second aspect (i.e., the patient's tendency to become overwhelmed by panic rather than being able to control her anxiety so that it can serve as a signal).[1] The mother, in other words, was apparently not able to provide a calming selfobject milieu for the little girl which, via optimal failures, would have been transmuted into self-soothing structures capable of preventing the spread of anxiety. It is this structural deficit, the deficiency in calming structures—a defect in the soothing functions of the idealized pole of the self—that necessitates the presence of a companion (a maternal woman who temporarily replaces the missing structure and its functions) to forestall the outbreak of anxiety. It was the nonempathic selfobject milieu of the oedipal phase, in other words, that both brought about the deleterious transformation of the little girl's originally affectionate attitudes into sexual drivenness and failed to provide the necessary conditions for the gradual internalization of those self structures that would have given self-confidence to the little girl and enabled her to remain calm despite conflict and tension.

To summarize: self psychology sees the failure of the oedipal selfobject milieu as the essential genetic factor in agoraphobia. It considers the pathological oedipal fantasies as a symptomatic consequence of the flawed selfobject response. Finally, it believes that in the adult symptomatology the addiction-like need for an accompanying woman is not to be viewed as a defensive maneuver but as a manifestation of the primary disorder: the structural defect of which both the unconscious oedipal fantasy and the conscious need for a female companion are symptoms. The fact that the sexual wish for the father can be kept outside of awareness ("repressed") while the re-

liance on the selfobject mother to curb the anxiety is conscious does
not mean that the first is the dynamic source (the cause) of the
patient's psychological illness and that the second arises in consequence of the first. The sexual wish for the father, in other words, despite being unconscious, is not "deeper" than the need for the
selfobject mother. The dynamic prime mover (the cause) of the disturbance and the "deepest" layer of the disease, as far as we can
determine at this time, is the flawed selfobject relationship that
transformed the positive experience of the oedipal stage, an upsurge
of affectionate and assertive feelings, into the potentially pathogenic
Oedipus complex. Vastly more important than the agoraphobic
woman's subsequent exposure to the unconscious incestuous desires
of the Oedipus complex, however, is the structural defect that followed from the failure of the idealized maternal selfobject to provide
the child with the idealized omnipotent calmness which, via transmuting internalization, should have become self-soothing, anxiety-
curbing psychic structure.

Is this lack of anxiety-curbing structure specific and circumscribed or general and diffuse? Did the selfobject milieu, in other
words, provide the child with sufficient opportunities of merging with
a calm idealized parent imago early in life and fail only vis-a-vis the
specific anxieties surrounding the new experiences of the oedipal
stage? Turning to the overt manifestations of the illness, is the agoraphobic's anxiety restricted to the pathological incestuous and compet-
itive-destructive drive fragments or is it more widespread, is there a
more general propensity to respond with panic vis-a-vis those various
inner and outer circumstances that would be responded to with limited fear, that is, by the appearance of an anxiety signal and secondarily with appropriate action, in those whose wholesome development
had provided them with adequate psychic structures?

Clinical experience, not speculation, must provide the answers to
these questions. We know clinically that there are various kinds of
phobias, that phobias occur in a spectrum that extends from those instances—now very rare but perhaps formerly much more frequent—
in which the panic is restricted to the mobilization of the Oedipus
complex to those instances—now clearly the vast majority—in which
the agoraphobic symptom is only one of many manifestations of a
widespread and nonspecific propensity to become anxious to the
point of panic states, disorganized action, or paralysis of all initiative.
In the former instances, the responses of the early selfobjects to the
"preoedipal" child's anxieties must have been adequate; in the latter

instances the responses of the selfobjects must have been faulty all along, beginning in early life. Still, for the sake of completeness, we must add that, even when the anxiety tendency is more diffuse, the uncovering of a concentration of unconscious oedipal strivings in the transference before the earlier selfobject failures begin to occupy center stage testifies to the fact that the deleterious responses of the selfobject intensified at the very point when the child reached the oedipal stage.

The most general statement that can be made about the pathogenic defect of the idealized selfobject in these phobias may be the following. Because the parental figure with whose power and calmness the child's self needs to merge has herself a self defect—I say "herself" because in the case of the agoraphobic woman it is the mother, whereas in other forms of psychopathology, whether oedipal or preoedipal, it is the father—she experiences the child's developmental progress (his emotionally moving away from her) as a threat to her cohesion. She therefore fails to respond with mirroring pride or with other appropriate reactions that the child needs in order to maintain her self-esteem and ensure her self-cohesion. Moreover, this parental failure comes at a moment when the child's self, in the midst of a pivotal forward move, is only precariously established and thus especially vulnerable.

Am I, it may be asked, despite all my excessive care to illuminate the problem of phobias from all possible sides, disregarding a factor which for Freud was potentially more important than childhood experience, namely, the biological factor, in Freud's early terms: the strength of the drive, in later terms: a congenital inherited possible weakness of the ego? Is the phobia not also, to a greater or lesser extent, due to the fact that the infantile sexual demands are, *ab initio*, especially great in some children and/or the defensive and sublimatory powers of the ego are, *ab initio*, especially weak? Should we not say, with Freud, that it is faulty biological equipment which we may ultimately have to hold responsible for both the oedipal phobias and the diffuse propensity to experience excessive anxiety?

This is not the place to explain my position vis-a-vis the so-called psychobiological attitude. As I have stated repeatedly since 1959 when I first clarified my operational position, I do not believe we are dealing with separate biological and psychological universes, but with two approaches to reality. When science approaches reality via extrospection (and vicarious extrospection), we call it physics or biology; when it approaches it via introspection (and empathy), we call it psychology.

Both instruments of observation have limits. Only a specific, strictly delimited part of reality can be approached via introspection and empathy: our own inner life and the inner life of others. Our inner lives, moreover, are not graspable via extrospection, even though the possibility (thought contents) may become decipherable via physical data such as electromagnetic tracings of the activity of our brains. At present, however, the psychological approach, with all its limitations, is the only useful one for investigating the inner life of man, including his psychopathology.

Still, even though at present we have, outside of the area of organic disturbances extensive enough to lead to "organic" psychopathology, no clear-cut proof that variations in biological equipment contribute to the fact that some individuals experience drive-wishes with greater intensity than others, or are less able to transform primitive urges into socially acceptable actions than others, and that some individuals cannot curb the spreading of their emotions and develop panic states or depression and/or elation, it stands to reason that our biological inheritance should influence these psychological functions. In practice, analysts do not need to be told that these considerations should in clinical work only be an explanation of last resort, that the search for psychological causes must remain paramount. But there is another set of factors that must not be neglected in this context. Granted that variations in congenital equipment exist, the response of the selfobject milieu to congenital shortcomings must by all means be taken into consideration, and any resulting psychopathology—for example, an excessive tendency to develop panic states or an inability to curb anxiety—must be explained not only in terms of the congenital defect, but also with regard to the failure of the selfobjects to respond adequately to an especially trying situation. Specifically, we must ask whether the parents were able to fill the specific or excessive needs of certain children, and, if not, why they were unable to do so and how specifically they failed. The capacity of a parent to respond empathically to the unusually great or highly specific selfobject need of a child is, in the last analysis, a function of the firmness of the cohesion of the parent's self. Certainly neither in such cases nor, indeed, in the case of any selfobject failure do we judge the selfobject's shortcomings from a moral point of view. Such an attitude would be foolish since the parental disability is an outgrowth of the deepest early experiences that influenced the development of the parent's responsibility and is thus beyond direct control; it would also be completely out of keeping with the approach of the scientist whose aim is neither to blame nor exculpate but to establish causal-motivation chains that explain the empathically gathered, psychological data.

NOTE

1. S. Freud, *Inhibitions, Symptoms and Anxiety, The Standard Edition of the Complete Psychological Works of Sigmund Freud*, Vol. 20, James Strachey (ed.). (Hogarth Press, 1959), pp. 75–114.

CHAPTER 25

On Courage

HEINZ KOHUT

Courage can be defined as the ability to brave death and to tolerate destruction rather than to betray the nucleus of one's psychological being, that is, one's ideals. There are genetic,
dynamic, and structural aspects of such fortitude, as well as certain
auxiliary devices which the psyche employs in order to maintain its
resolve.

One striking characteristic of unusually courageous individuals is
that at certain critical moments or stages of their lives they create imagery concerning an all-powerful figure on whom to lean for support.
This idealized figure may be a personified god or a prototypical historical figure or a charismatic person who is living in the present. The
spectrum of such falsification of reality, employed in the service of es-
tablishing a courage-supporting relationship to an idealized figure,
extends from (a) temporary delusions and hallucinations, via (b)
grossly aggrandizing distortions in the evaluation of people who in reality have only ordinary and moderate endowment, to (c) an illusional, concretizing, vivid idealization of truly inspiring personages
who are either temporally or spatially remote from the hero who,
however, in his fantasy, will feel that he is deriving concrete support
from leaning on them.

To the first group of falsifications or courage-supporting mechanisms belong experiences such as hearing the voice of God or seeing
visions in which God appears as the hero. Such messages that the
courageous individual receives are delivered from the supernatural
powers with the aid of supposedly meaningful but, in fact, accidental
occurrences. Some of these experiences are tradition-bound and stan-

dardized, like "the call" from a personified god heard at a specific time and place by those embarking on a career as missionaries.

A good example of the second type of falsification of reality engaged in by heroic people is the intense, unrealistic idealization of the physical, mental or moral powers of people who in reality possess only ordinary, moderate endowment. I call this phenomenon the "transference of creativity." A genius, frightened by the boldness of his pioneering discoveries and yearning to relieve his loneliness, creates for himself the figment of a vastly overestimated figure on whom he leans temporarily but whom he discards (i.e., from whom he withdraws his idealization) after his essential work has been achieved. During the transference of creativity itself, the genius projects his own mental powers onto someone else. He assigns his discoveries temporarily to that other person and feels humble toward and dependent upon this idealized protector, mentor and judge, who is in essence his own creation.

In some of these examples (especially in those involving the relationship to hallucinated god figures) it may, on superficial scrutiny, seem difficult to draw a clear-cut line of demarcation with the psychoses. But the third type of falsification of reality, in which courage is supported through a leaning on or a merger with inspiring prototypical figures, does not generally raise serious doubts about the sanity of those who cling to these bonds, even though with this group one may occasionally encounter experiences of hallucinatory vividness and temporary delusion-like distortions.

It is not difficult to recognize that all these falsifications of reality, which are so dramatic at certain critical times in the lives of courageous individuals, are variations on the single theme of regression in the developmental line of a specific narcissistic configuration, that of the idealized, omnipotent selfobject. It is my impression, however, that in many instances of great heroism it is not an intensely cathected value system alone which is the primary motivation for the courageous thought or deed. As I will try to show, this motivation arises from the entire *nuclear self* of the individual and not from his values alone. The re-concretization of the ego ideal, however—that is, its (regressive) transformation into an omnipotent selfobject—becomes temporarily necessary as an auxiliary means by which the fulfillment of the nuclear self can be attained despite the most severe anxieties of dissolution to which man will expose himself voluntarily. The pseudo-delusions and pseudo-hallucinations of the hero are, therefore, created in response to a temporary great need; they occur as the outgrowth of conditions which resemble those of early childhood when, because of the psychological incompleteness which prevails at that stage, the young child's self-esteem regulation depends almost exclusively on the presence of selfobjects who admire the child or who allow the child to merge into their idealized perfection. Under certain anxiety-provoking conditions, then, the archaic need for support becomes so great that the omnipotent object will, regressively, arise out of the ego ideal and be, again, as it was once in early life, experienced as an archaic, prestructural, *external* power. Thus it may happen that an individual at the very peak of psychological independence—when he lives in fact more actively and expresses the goals of his nuclear self more completely than the average human being can ever hope to do—believes that he has no initiative and feels himself "lived" by influences from outside himself.

It seems apparent that courage cannot be easily explained as the personification and concretization of the ego-ideal. Nor does the hero simply mobilize irrational imagery and beliefs to support his rational, nonpathological pursuits. So what then prompts him to move forward, despite intimidation from within and without? He is compelled to proceed on his lonely road, even if it means his individual destruction, because he must shape the pattern of his life—his thoughts, deeds and attitudes—in accordance with the design of his nuclear self.

But what is this nuclear self for which I claim such an important place in psychological health and disease? It is that continuum in time, that cohesive configuration in depth, which we experience as the "I" of our perceptions, thoughts and actions. There are those who would postulate that a self—*the* self—is the center of our being from which all initiative springs and where all experiences end. I, however, do not agree for the following two reasons: (1) To posit a single self as the central agency of the psyche leads toward an elegant, simple theory of the mind, but also toward an unwarranted de-emphasis of the importance of the unconscious. And (2) this definition of the self is not derived from psychoanalytic material but from conscious experience. The decision to assign to a single self the most central position in the psyche is not—at least not at the present stage of psychoanalysis— forced on us by the necessity to accommodate specific data obtained through psychoanalytic observation, but it is made by choice in order to fashion a rounded and cohesive theory of thought, perception and action. The concept of a unitary, central self is an axiom introduced into analysis from the outside.

There is, however, a second approach to the conceptualization of the self. Although it does not lead immediately to a theory of the mind which is as elegant and cohesive as the first, it has my vote. I prefer to define the self as an abstraction derived from psychoanalytic clinical experience, not excluding psychoanalytically sophisticated observation outside the clinical setting. I consider the self as a potentially observable content of the mind. If we choose this approach we will recognize the simultaneous existence of different and even contradictory selves in the same person, of selves with various degrees of stability and of various degrees of importance. There are conscious, preconscious, and unconscious selves; there are selves in the ego, the id, and the superego; and we may discover in some of our patients incompatible selves, side by side, in the same psychic agency.

Among these selves, however, there exists one which is most centrally located in the psyche, one which is experienced by the individual as the basic one, and which is most resistant to change. I like to call this the *nuclear self*. It is composed of derivatives of the grandiose self (i.e., of the central self-assertive goals, purposes and ambitions), and of derivatives of the idealized parent imago (i.e., of the central idealized values). The nuclear self is thus that unconscious, preconscious and conscious sector in id, ego and superego which contains not only the individual's most enduring values and ideals but also his most deeply anchored goals, purposes and ambitions.

The nuclear self, however, is not immutable. The task of modifying and even of transforming it is repeatedly imposed on us throughout life under the influence of new internal and external factors. The modifiability of the nuclear self—at certain developmental junctures like adolescence and old age or under the influence of crucial environmental changes—is not a sign of disease and must not, in and of itself, be evaluated as a psychological or moral defect. On the other hand, we may justifiably deplore some behavior as the manifestation of a psychological shortcoming and of moral infirmity—like the actions and attitudes of those who quickly and opportunistically adjust their convictions under the influence of external pressures. Such behavior does not involve an alteration of the nuclear self but represents merely an adaptation on the psychological surface. In such individuals the nuclear self ceases to participate in the overt attitudes and actions and becomes progressively isolated and is finally repressed or disavowed. The psychological outcome, which is unfortunately more or less characteristic of the psychological makeup of the majority of adults, is not an individual striving toward a creative solution of his conflicts concerning the redefinition of his basic ambitions and values but a person who, despite his smoothly adaptive surface behavior, experiences a sense of inner shallowness and who gives to others an impression of artificiality.

The heroic individual's nuclear self is, therefore, not necessarily characterized by its immutability. As a matter of fact the hero's willingness to die sometimes comes about as a result of a creative change in his nuclear self, a change by virtue of which he gets out of step with the goals, ambitions and values of his environment. The capacity of the nuclear self to undergo changes, whether they take place slowly or occur abruptly (as in mystical experiences of illumination) is fully compatible with that firmness of attitude so characteristic of courage.

Such heroic individuals are therefore not psychotic. Nor are the hallucinations and delusional commands which the hero experiences as the motivators of his courageous actions and attitudes the manifestations of a dissolution of the self. The true motivator which propels the hero toward the heroic deed is his nuclear self; the hallucinated commands are merely temporary auxiliary mechanisms, secondarily created to serve the purposes of the hero.

In support of this claim I will discuss three features of some heroic individuals which place them clearly outside the realm of psychosis. The three features are: the presence of a fine sense of humor; the ability to respond to others with subtle empathy; and, generally at the time when the ultimate heroic decision has been reached and the agonizing consequences have to be faced, the suffusion of the personality with a profound sense of inner peace and serenity—a mental state akin to wisdom. This is something which never fails to impress the observer, including even persecutors, torturers and executioners. Heroes, in other words, achieve a high order of development in the narcissistic sector of their personality, and this developmental achievement is maintained during the decisive heroic period of their lives.

My examples of heroism are anti-Nazis who were active during the Second World War. They include the Austrian farmer, Franz Jaegerstaetter, and Hans and Sophie Scholl, who were two of the heroes of the Student Conspiracy in Munich in 1943. Specifically, I will discuss the presence of a sense of humor in Jaegerstaetter, of a high degree of empathy in Hans Scholl, and of serenity as a ubiquitous phenomenon present in all of these heroes but most noticeably manifested (and self-interpreted through a decisive dream) in Sophie Scholl. Finally, I will attempt to show the difference between two classes of heroes: those which I am discussing at this point—I will call them for simplicity's sake the *martyr heroes*—and those (exemplified in Nazi Germany by individuals belonging to such groups as the so-called Kreisauer Kreis and to the Oster-Canaris-Stauffenberg Circle) to whom I will refer as the *national resisters*.

The presence of a genuine sense of humor constitutes one reliable indication that there is no severe impairment in the narcissistic sector of the personality. It speaks in particular against the existence of, or even against the propensity for, a psychosis. Genuine humor can be achieved only when primitive forms of grandiosity have been relinquished—whether the grandiosity had previously been bound to the subject's grandiose self or had been focused on an idealized (aggrandized) selfobject. A paranoiac's coldly arrogant superiority and the hostile certainty of his own conviction about the powerful persecutor's inimical intentions are the very antithesis of a healthy humorous attitude toward the realistic limitations of oneself and of those one admires. It bears repeating that to be humorous is not the same as to be self-belittling or to be lacking in enthusiasm. Humor is fully compatible with a secure sense of self-esteem or with a warm devotion to values and ideals. It is, of course, true that there are times, outside of mental illness, when the serious, nonhumorous pursuit of the purposes of the self and a serious, nonhumorous devotion to ideals may be demanded of us. But when an individual has earnestly resolved to live in accordance with the central purposes of the self and in harmony with the highest idealized value and still preserve a sense of modesty and proportion, then we will feel that he has achieved a high degree of healthy mastery in the narcissistic sector of his personality. We can be certain that the core of his personality is sane and that the inner forces which propelled him toward heroic activity were not based on delusions when his ability to respond with humor is preserved in the face of the utmost sacrifices that man can make as he remains faithful to his nuclear self.

This was indeed the psychological state which prevailed in Franz Jaegerstaetter when he faced execution. Jaegerstaetter's letters to his wife from the prisons in which he was kept from March 2, 1943, until he was executed five months later on August 9, are a moving testimony to his modesty, his sense of proportion and his humor. He was neither self-belittling nor sarcastic, and he never lost his heroic resolve to suffer death rather than to compromise with evil. Jaegerstaetter's total correspondence should be studied by those who want to experience the full human resonance of his communications. Here a few samples will have to suffice.

In a letter written on March 19, Jaegerstaetter empathically imagines the strain which his imprisonment and the villagers' reactions to his anti-Nazi and anti-war stand must have imposed on his wife. He sympathizes with her concerning the amount of work that she now has to do because he is away. But then he adds, tongue in cheek: "I think it would be good for us occasionally to trade places for a week; such a rest would be good for you." Or, on April 4 he comments, with a touch of wry humor, about the food in prison: "Of course, you can easily understand," he writes, "that we are not getting fat on this diet; but that is not essential either, for they have not locked us in here in order to fatten us up."

The Scholls provide further evidence that many martyr heroes give evidence of a high degree of sublimation in the narcissistic sector. These two young Munich students were both executed on February 2, 1943: Hans Scholl was 22 at the time of his death and his sister Sophie Scholl was 19.

As a student of medicine Hans Scholl was released from regular military duties, but from time to time he was subject to active service on the front. At the beginning of one of these periods of service, on the way to the Russian front, the train which transported his company stopped at a small station in Poland. There he saw a line of women and young girls bent over doing heavy labor at the railroad tracks. The women had the yellow star of David affixed to their garments. Hans jumped from the train and walked toward the women. The first in the row as he approached them was an emaciated young girl. He noticed her slender hands and her intelligent, beautiful face, which seemed to express unspeakable sorrow. He tried to think of something that he could give her. He remembered that he had his "K-ration" with him— a mixture of chocolates, raisins, and nuts—and he stuck it into her pocket. The girl threw it back at him, with a harried but proud gesture. Hans smiled at her warmly and said, "I would so much have liked to give you a little pleasure." He bent down, picked a daisy, laid it upon the food package, and put the gift at her feet. Then he ran for the train which had begun to move. From the train window he saw the girl once more, standing up straight, looking after him. The white daisy was in her hair.

The journey of the true martyr hero leads him increasingly toward clarity concerning the essence of his nuclear self. The beginning of this journey may be marked by a shock-like recognition, which is often experienced as a revelation, i.e., as coming from outside. The revelation may occur at a time when some change of the external or internal milieu (including a basic alteration of the nuclear self) brings about a psychological disequilibrium. Suddenly there exists now a gap between the kind of behavior which would be in harmony with the self and the kind of behavior that is dictated by the demands of the environment. Once the martyr hero has become aware of his nuclear self (and of the inner and outer conflict situations to which he is brought by its demands), he can find no rest. At first it may seem that he is primarily afraid of the social consequences which he would have to face if he lived in conformity with the basic patterns of the nuclear self. His uneasiness, however, is in the main not due to the fear of the external forces which might oppose him; rather, his tensions are a manifestation of the fact that he is in a severe narcissistic disequilibrium until he has achieved the complete unification of his personality under the leadership of the nuclear self. As soon as the ultimate step in this direction is made and the ultimate decision has been reached (whether it be Churchill's becoming prime minister or Jaegerstaetter's resolve not to accept any further compromises with the demands of the Nazi war machine), the hero experiences a sense of relief and of inner peacefulness and serenity. These feelings are manifestations of the narcissistic balance which has come through the establishment of a state of complete harmony between the nuclear self and the rest of the personality.

In many of the martyr heroes, it is the set of central values and ideals, the heir to the archaic idealized object, which decisively defines the nuclear self. Thus, the ultimate state of narcissistic balance in such people blends the personality with the central values of the self. When such an identification has been achieved, the martyr hero has a sense of profound inner peace (narcissistic equilibrium) and even the experience of conscious pleasure that his ideals and his total personality have now become one. The general psychological setting in which these emotions occur is one of calmness and clarity. We see neither the fuzzy mysticism which characterizes certain regressive swings in narcissistic personality disturbances nor, of course, the anxious and bizarre mental state surrounding the delusional contacts with a bizarre god and with other distorted omnipotent figures which we encounter in the psychotic.

The most beautiful illustration of the essence of the experience of inner peace and serenity which the martyr hero achieves in the end is poignantly contained in the last dream of Sophie Scholl. It occurred during the night which preceded her execution. Sophie Scholl's dream should be compared with the dream of Jaegerstaetter. Jaegerstaetter's dream portrays the state of the psyche at the beginning of the martyr hero's road: It shows the first response of the psyche to the demands of the nuclear self, the first stirrings of recognition regarding the difficult road which lies ahead. Sophie Scholl's dream portrays the state of the psyche at the end of the martyr hero's road: It shows how the total personality is being given over to the essential sectors of the nuclear self, to the hero's idealized values.

Here is the account of Sophie Scholl's last dream. After she had been aroused from her sleep to face the day of her execution, she told the following dream to her cellmate. In the dream, she said, it was a sunny day, "and I carried a child, dressed in a long white garment, to be baptized. The path to the church led up a steep mountain; but I held the child firmly and securely. Suddenly there was a crevasse gaping in front of me. I had barely enough time to deposit the child on the far side of it, which I managed to do safely—then I fell into the depths." After Sophie had told her dream she immediately explained its meaning to her companion. The child, she said, is our leading idea ("unsere Idee")—it will live on and make its way to fulfillment despite obstacles ("wird sich durchsetzen").

Her behavior during the rest of the day (she was executed in the afternoon) testifies to the total absorption of her personality by her idealized values. Everything that is reported about her is in harmony with a sense of total narcissistic balance. She was calm and peaceful throughout the day. Her skin was glowing and fresh, her face radiant, with an expression of "wonderous [sic] triumph." Her lips were of a deep glowing red. She went to her execution without a trace of fear.

The Nuclear Self

I hope that the examination of courageous individuals, of heroic figures in history, has taken us some distance along the way toward the clarification of the position of the nuclear self in the human personality and of its function in the life of the individual. But there is still a great deal that may seem to have remained unclear. One might argue, for example, that the definition of the nuclear self rests on a kind of circular reasoning. We postulate that the nuclear self occupies the most central position in the personality and that other selves occupy positions which are more peripheral or more superficial in relation to the central one and, by implication at least, are less genuine. On the other hand, we conclude that the self which ultimately determines the admirable actions of the martyr-heroes is the nuclear self, because only the genuine, structurally most centrally located self could have such a powerful positive influence on the personality. There is a logical fallacy here in first hypothesizing courage to be a central characteristic of the nuclear self and then proving the hypothesis by demonstrating the unswerving courage and persistence of some exceptional, saint-like persons whose attitudes and deeds we see as the manifestations of their nuclear selves.

These are compelling arguments which cannot be disproved within the confines of a system of pure logic. But I do believe that the validity of the processes of fact-finding of empirical psychology can be gauged by these standards. First I would like to specify that, although my illustrative examples concerned certain individuals whose action I personally happen to admire and whose values and goals are similar to my own, my explanatory attempt concerns at this point only the ability of the heroic individuals to perform their actions, not the moral or social validity of their standards and goals. Secondly, steadfastness in the face of maximal threats and intimidations is not the only distinguishing and characteristic quality of the nuclear self. While I have no doubt that it is in general only the central self which is likely to prove itself indomitable in the face of torture and death, there might be instances when a defensive stance, resting on an image of the self which is located in a peripheral or superficial area of the psyche, is kept up for a long time and may in very exceptional cases be maintained even in the face of ultimate sacrifice. The gripping novel *Jud Süss* (1925) by Lion Feuchtwanger can perhaps be considered as a fictitious illustration of such an occurrence. Thus—to put the previous statements in a milder form—while it may appear to be very likely that the solitary martyr-hero is living out the pattern of his most deeply anchored and most central self, we must search for criteria which apply not only in these extreme cases but also in less dramatic ones.

Indeed, as I have indicated earlier, there is at our disposal another set of data which lends strong support to our hypothesis. This supportive evidence is obtained through the psychological investigation of a person's path toward the full dominance of his nuclear self, through the scrutiny of the depth-psychological significance of the steps which lead to the final equilibrium at the point when the central narcissistic structure achieves its total victory and a tranquil joy pervades the total personality. The careful empathic scrutiny of this last stage of quiet triumph in the face of death will protect us in particular against resorting to a routine, nonspecific judgment, i.e., dispensing with the evidence obtained from the actual psychological manifestations of the martyr-hero's experiences and explaining the progressive course of his development directly in the terms of a biologizing drive-psychology. The consummate peace achieved by the hero is, at least in certain instances, not the result of the instinctual gratification of a masochistic wish—the fulfillment of an expiatory death-wish (the victory of self-destructive aggressive strivings in the service of the superego, for example)—but the ultimate ascendancy of a firm and life-affirming self.

Courage and Tragedy

Analysts, beginning with Freud, have felt strongly attracted by the mystery of tragedy, which they have explained largely in terms of a psychology of passions (drives), inner conflicts concerning these passions (structural conflicts), and punishment for transgressions motivated by passions (the victory of the self-punitive forces in the superego and the ascendancy of the death instinct). In this view of tragedy, which sees man as striving for happiness through love and work, man comes to grief because he cannot master his unruly passions and must ultimately bow to the inevitable victory of the life-destructive forces as embodied in his aggressions, in his guilt, and in the inevitable end of his biological existence.

A psychoanalytic psychology of the self is able to provide us with a fresh chance to comprehend tragedy. I will step directly in *medias res* and make my central assertion: The art of the tragic—whether sung, told, or written as in the great epics; whether through music, on canvas, in stone, or on the stage—is concerned with man's attempt to live out the pattern of his nuclear self. And the tragic hero who is the protagonist of the great tragedies, which must be counted as among the most precious cultural possessions of mankind, is a man who, despite the breakdown of his physical and mental powers (e.g., Oedipus) and even despite his biological death (e.g., Hamlet), is triumphant because his nuclear self achieved an ascendancy which never will, indeed which never can, be undone.

Surrounded by the incessant flux of the human condition, confronted by the necessity of admitting the impermanence of all things dear to him, compelled finally to acknowledge the finiteness of individual existence not only in the abstract but also as it concerns his own beloved self, man comes closest to narcissistic fulfillment when he is able to realize the pattern of his most central self. The effacement or the death of the tragic hero is thus not an incidental occurrence. Its essential meaning is not to be seen as punishment for a code-transgressing deed, which sets in motion the pattern of guilt and retribution. It is instead a necessary component of the hero's achievement, for it is only in death that the hero's narcissistic fulfillment attains permanence. The survivors weep about the hero's fate, but the raised body of the hero as it is carried to the funeral pyre is not lamented as the remains of defeat would be. It is admired as the symbol of the hero's narcissistic triumph which, through his death, has now become absolute.

Every individual has two courses open to him and every individual, in one way or another, follows both of them. In his ordinary day every man lives by the pleasure and reality principles: He is the man of work and love. But no man is excluded from participating in the tragic dimensions of life. No man, however apparently insignificant his self-fulfilling goals and the idealized aspirations of his nuclear self, is at all times fully absorbed by the toils of work and by the pursuit of time-limited pleasures. There will be periods, or at least moments, in the life of every man when he becomes aware, even if only dimly, of a yearning that does not relate to the attainment of the pleasurable discharge of drive-wishes but to the compelling urge to realize the deep-rooted design of his nuclear self. Man is propelled by both of these forces, and human life lacking either of them is incomplete.

Society, too, needs tragic man. The tragic man senses the destiny of a people and of his potential role as it relates to this destiny. Ordinarily, leaders will be of the "work and love" type. In extraordinary times, however, in times of deep crisis, it will be a tragic man who will rise to lead and inspire a group whose deepest group-self—the confluence of the nuclear selves, i.e., of the basic ambitions, goals and ideals of the individuals who make up the group—has been threatened and needs to assert itself.

All art, including tragedy, is wish fulfillment. But our enjoyment of tragedy does not come from the pleasurable participation in the victory of a drive (the death instinct). That would be analogous to our enjoyment of the pleasurable participation in the wish-fulfilling world conjured up by the art of the happy ending. Simple comedies please us through the vicarious enjoyment of fulfilled libidinal wishes. Other branches of the art of the happy ending present us with artistically disguised denials of the reality of our limitations and frustrations. There is a great variety of ways by which the art of the happy ending, through more or less sophisticated means, is able to entertain the man of work and love. Our enjoyment of these art forms is derived from our temporary acceptance of the artistic assertion that a drive-wish has been fulfilled or from the functional analogue of this process, the artistic denial of the pains and frustrations of life. Tragedy, however, has another function: It gives the spectator, reader, listener or beholder the opportunity to experience, in temporary identification with the tragic hero, the unfolding, expansion and triumph of his own nuclear self.

It is a significant (and largely unexplored) fact that civilized man feels timid vis-a-vis the profound strivings of his nuclear self and that his ego seems fragile when it is faced by its demands. Civilized man has learned to work, he tries to obey the restrictions necessitated by communal life and yet, despite work and restrictions, he manages, directly and indirectly, to obtain a modicum of fulfillment of his drive-wishes. But the fetters of communal living have curtailed his freedom to express his deepest self even more than they have interfered with the opportunity to discharge his drives. Indeed, I believe that there are forces at work in this realm which are even more restrictive than the inhibiting precepts of civilized society. From the beginning of our awareness these forces have made us fearful of developing our self-expressive initiative and our creativeness. Perhaps from infancy onward the unfolding of our central selves has evoked frightening envious anger, which is a manifestation of the wounded narcissism of those around us. The full assertion of our nuclear selves is thus for most of us beyond the scope of our courage. We withdraw from our innermost goals and ideals, and we falsify and dilute them. It is in this sphere then that the buffering of art allows us a tolerable experience of self-affirmation in the form of our participation in the self-expression of the tragic hero on the stage. Great tragedy, as exemplified most tangibly in the tragic drama, is a repeatable, and thus a dosed, experience. It allows us, therefore, to participate in the emotional development of the tragic hero from doubt to decision and from dejection to triumph as his nuclear self attains realization and is made permanent through death. Paradoxically, the spectator, participating in the ultimate self-realization of the tragic hero, experiences his own self as more vigorous and cohesive than he ever can in his real life.

It is illuminating to compare *Hamlet*, the greatest tragic drama of Christian civilization, with the tragedy of the life and death of Jesus of Nazareth, the Christ and Savior of western religious belief. Despite some striking overt differences in the two life spans, there is much similarity. Both heroes are idealistic and beloved adolescents, both face the evils of the world, both turn away from their mothers although their mothers never cease to admire them, both appear to age rapidly as they are confronting the world of evil, both have their periods of doubt and despair, and both die in early manhood. In both cases their death coincides with the fulfillment of the deepest pattern of their nuclear selves, that is, in both instances seeming defeat is actually a narcissistic triumph. The hero's funeral which is ordered for Hamlet is, however, hardly more than a symbolic allusion to his triumph. The resurrection and ascension, symbolizing the full merger with the father ideal, is the glorified narcissistic triumph which permanently transforms the humiliated, suffering seeker into the God.

Stripped of dogmatic belief and sentimentalizing additions, the story of the gospels may, therefore, be regarded as a prototype of modern tragedy, as a link in that chain of the portrayals of western tragic man which leads from Sophocles to Shakespeare to O'Neill, and from the *Dying Persian* in the Thermae Museum to Grünewald's *Christ on the Cross* to Picasso's *Guernica*. The Marys faint and cry; the Pharisees, the men of work and love and everyday morality, sneer at the hero; Pilate, the wielder of worldly power, will not interfere with the unrolling of the predestined life, despite his wife's dreams. The hero's friends detach themselves one by one in order to survive as death approaches. And then, after one last weakness and doubt, as in all great tragedy, there comes the final fulfillment and the ultimate consummation of the nuclear self of the hero. The rest—the mythological details of the moment of death, the empty tomb, the reappearances—is symbolism. These are secondary additions, yet they remain in meaningful symbolic contact with the essence of the story, for they tell in various ways of the hero's narcissistic triumph, of his immortal divinity.

I know that one must not simplify the complexities of a powerful religious creation by separating one strand from the intricate web of the overall pattern. But it is indeed my conviction that the tragedy of man forms the very center of the stories told by the evangelists. The older tradition of the epic of the warrior hero has remained alive to serve as a paradigm for the prototypical hero of western civilization. But the story of Jesus—the Judaic tale of a hero's loyalty, even unto death, to the deepest pattern of his self—has influenced, in various ways, every western hero, whether on the field of battle, in artistic and scientific faithfulness, or, as described earlier, in the historically modest deeds of the, mostly unsung, Jaegerstaetters and Scholls.

Conclusion

Certain qualities and functions of the nuclear self, once this structure has been fully formed, cannot be comprehended unless the self is conceptualized as an independent, autonomous unit. There are other, broad areas of the personality outside the nuclear self. But once it has been laid down, the nuclear self strives to fulfill itself. It moves, from the time of its consolidation, toward the realization of its ambitions and ideals, which are the ultimate descendants of the child's grandiosity and exhibitionism and of his strivings to emerge with an idealized selfobject. And if an individual succeeds in realizing the aims of his nuclear self, he can die without regret. He has achieved the fulfillment of the tragic hero—not the painful death of guilty man who strives for pleasure—but a death which is "beyond the pleasure principle."

Guilty man wants to achieve redemption and reform himself and society. But an individual's deepest ambitions and ideals, once congealed to form the nucleus of his self, will drive and lead him with a force which, though hidden in most of us by conflict, fear and guilt, in its essence is independent of fear and guilt, of expiation and reform. Tragic man's death is not caused by guilt. It is not suicide, nor is it self-destructive. It is more closely related to a "death-instinct" than is the striving toward death experienced by guilty man. The death attained by tragic man must not be conceived, in analogy to Freud's conception of a psychobiological antagonism between Eros and Thanatos, as being in opposition to life. It is an integral part of the life curve of the self.

Julia Kristeva

J ulia Kristeva was born in Bulgaria in 1941 and went to France in 1965 as the recipient of a scholarship for Eastern European students. She studied with several major French intellectuals, including Lucien Goldman, Roland Barthes, and Claude Lévi-Strauss, and her psychoanalytic perspective owes a major debt to Jacque Lacan, whose primary appeal to her was his ability to link psychoanalysis with linguistics, intellectual history, and philosophy. While she attended his celebrated seminars, she came to know him personally when she asked him to contribute an article to a journal she edited called *Semiotica*. Subsequently, they worked together to plan a trip to China which was the basis for her book *About Chinese Women*.

Kristeva's initial reasons for entering personal psychoanalysis concerned her interest in the limits of language, language acquisition in children, the experience of poetry (which she refers to in an interview as "psychotic discourse"), and her sense that she needed to engage in such discourses on a personal level, "which meant participating in the experience of transference." In the course of her analysis, she became intensely aware of "that extraordinary thing we call motherhood," noting, "Mothers are the one who pass along the native tongue, but they also perform an important psychological role that we are still discovering. They perform a sort of miracle by separating themselves from their children while loving them and teaching them to speak. This gives them a corporeal and sensory pleasure as well as an intellectual one." [1]

Relatedly, important themes in her work have been an emphasis on the pre-Oedipal stage of development, and her interest in religious discourse: "It is often said that psychoanalysis can replace religion: first people confess and then you give them hope. That may be right, but it really isn't, for this hope is concomitant with the dissolution of the analytic contract [that is, the successful termination of the analysis]."[2] We live in a society and we will continue to live with illusions; religion offers both connections and illusions. What, then, does psychoanalysis offer? Not so much a substitute for religion (a new faith), since it represents the dissolution of illusions and connections, but the "analytical attitude" that Philip Rieff ascribes to Freud. As Kristeva puts it: "I am not fooled by them [these connections and illusions]. I am going to analyze them. Why? Because I want to create new connections, not to isolate myself but to explore with other people. This requires another relationship to social bonds, another morality that is different from religious morality."[3]

The selections included here represent a very small sampling of Kristeva's writings on religion, which easily rival Freud's in size and scope. Significantly, they also reflect her tendency to write intertextually (a term she herself employs) with Freud's writings on religion.[4] Thus, while she was trained in Lacanian-style psychoanalysis, her writings reflect a deep concern to engage Freud's own texts, and to do so less in the sense of developing an alternative position as to bring to light implications of Freud's writings, especially regarding the mother.

Certain unfamiliar terms that are central to Kristeva's thought recur throughout the selections presented here. The first is her distinction between the symbolic and the semiotic. This distinction, having roots in her study of linguistics prior to her involvement in psychoanalysis, identifies two distinguishable discourses which nonetheless need to be understood in relation to one another, as they are dialectically linked, and refer to the fundamental properties of language and its limits. The *symbolic* is the signifying property of language, or the effects of meaning that appear when linguistic signs are articulated into grammar and assume a syntactic structure. She identifies the symbolic with the paternal Law and Word. The *semiotic* are the effects of meaning that are not reducible to language or that may operate outside language, even if language is necessary as an immediate context or as a final referent. Examples of the latter are a child's repetition of words spoken by adults (echolalia), the play of colors in an abstract painting, or a piece of music that lacks signification but has meaning.[5] As the semiotic is prior to the symbolic in the development of the infant, it is identified with the mother. Poetry may be viewed as an especially exemplary form of the dialectic between the symbolic and the semiotic, as it tends to undermine the lawfulness of symbolic discourse, while using it, in order to give voice to the semiotic.

The second term is the French word *jouissance*, which is left untranslated in her writings, in part because it has figured prominently in theoretical discussions among French psychoanalysts, but also because its meanings are rich and varied, exemplifying the semiotic itself. In ordinary use, it may mean pleasure, enjoyment, delight, sensual pleasure, use, possession, but may also have connotations of suffering and agony. Kristevan scholars have linked it to Freud's libido (or drive-discharge) but have at the same time emphasized its superfluity, the fact that it cannot be contained within the structures or confines of the symbolic order. M. J. Reineke writes: "By *jouissance*, Kristeva refers to an excess and surplus of being . . . that establishes in humans the possibility of creation, communion, newness, pleasure, and transgression."[6]

The first selection, "Credo in Unum Deum," is from *In the Beginning Was Love*, which grew out of a series of lectures given by Kristeva to students of L'Ecole Sainte-Geneviève, a Catholic school in Versailles. This book may be read with Freud's *Future of an Illusion* in mind,[7] as it addresses the "imaginary" quality of religious, specifically Christian, formulas. The chapter reproduced here is preceded by a chapter in which Kristeva takes up Freud's "religion is illusion" thesis by recounting her work with a male analysand, and explores the meanings evoked by the word "credo" ("I believe"). The selection itself centers on the Nicene Creed and explores the "basic fantasies" (that is, desires and traumas) that underlie its various affirmations, including the desire for an "Almighty Father" and "Virgin Mother," and the trauma of abandonment in the figure of Christ dying on the cross and descending into hell. Thus, religion is an "illusion," but it is not the *credo quia absurdum* that Freud challenges in *The Future of an Illusion*, as it makes perfect sense as a reflection of fundamental human dreams and traumas. Thus, if not on the dogmatic level, it has a certain claim to truth (being psycho-logical).

The second selection, from *Black Sun: Depression and Melancholy*, centers on Hans Holbein's haunting painting of the dead Christ, in which the corpse is left strangely alone, endowing the painting with "a major melancholy burden." Kristeva does not disagree with Freud's association of melancholy with loss in "Mourning and Melancholy," but she emphasizes that it is essentially a mood, one that is traceable to the transition from the semiotic to the symbolic order in childhood (a transition that manifests itself in signs of childhood depression). The issue she addresses here is not the psychobiographical one of whether or to what extent Holbein himself suffered from melancholia. Rather, her concern is that the painting reflects the centrality of melancholia in the Christian religion, for it portrays Christ experiencing the separation which is the true anguish behind melancholia. Of course, Christianity also affirms the Resurrection and the Son's glorious return to the Father in Heaven. In Holbein's painting, though, Jesus is completely, abjectly alone, cut off from others, and from the Father himself. Then: "Who sees him? There are no saints. There is of course the painter. And ourselves." What, then, does the painting itself effect in us, the lone observers of this disturbing portrayal of the abandoned one? Kristeva turns to other paintings of Holbein for a provisional answer, noting that there is no exalted loftiness toward the beyond in the demeanor of the persons who populate these paintings, only the sense of the sober difficulty of standing here below, struggling with their own melancholy burdens. They are, however, standing, providing the horizontal dimension of the cross that is missing from (but implied by) the painting's verticality.

The next selection, from Kristeva's *Strangers to Ourselves*, uses Freud's essay " 'The Uncanny' " to explore our reactions to "foreigners," noting that many analysts have emphasized the frequency of the "uncanny" affect in phobias. This is not, however, an essay about foreigners as such, nor is it a utopian vision (as in the case of Erikson) of a humanity having matured beyond pseudospeciation. Instead, it proposes that Freud's analytic attitude teaches us "how to detect foreignness in ourselves," to recognize that there is a dimension of ourselves which is "uncanny" and strange to us. We do not, however, recognize it as our own until it comes to conscious awareness with the return of the repressed. The "foreigner" is not outside of us, but in us, and therefore we are all foreigners (which also means that there is no foreigner). What binds us together, ironically, is the death instinct, the most "uncanny" stranger of all, who, as Freud points out in *Beyond the Pleasure Principle*, resents the efforts of outside forces to usurp its own agencies, its own "right" to arrange for our death in its own way.

Two selections from Kristeva's *New Maladies of the Soul* follow. In "Reading the Bible," Kristeva takes note of the "human sciences" approach to the Bible. This necessarily sets limits, as it requires, at least initially, a disregard of the sacred powers to which the Bible attests, and a focus instead on its textual logics and rhetorics. From an exposition of several examples of this approach originally presented in her use of Leviticus to explore the theme of maternal abjection in *Powers of Horror*,[8] she concludes that they fail to address the issue of the linguistic subject of the biblical utterance: Who is speaking in the Bible? And for whom? From this, a psychoanalytic reading of the text becomes possible. What especially interests her in this regard is that the mother is noticeably absent and that one becomes a member of the discursive community in which the Bible is situated by separating from the mother. The maternal represents the limits of the biblical text, and, therefore, is the promised land, the utopia, to which the Bible points but does not itself embody. This essay, then, elaborates Kristeva's distinction between the symbolic order (in which the Bible itself is located) and the semiotic, which registers the limits of symbolic discourse, its inability to do more than identify (name) the desires that the semiotic represents.

The final selection, "The Wheel of Smiles," returns to Freud's monograph on Leonardo da Vinci. It, too, may be read in light of Kristeva's distinction between the semiotic and the symbolic order. Reflecting the circumstances of his own infancy, da Vinci's painting of the *Virgin and Child with St. Anne* has no place for the father. Thus, it portrays an unalloyed semiotic scene, one in which there are smiles all around: between mother and daughter, and mother and son. This painting has traditionally been interpreted as prefiguring Jesus' subsequent entry into the symbolic order (culminating in his death). Kristeva's essay does not reject this interpretation, but by directing attention to the compositional problems that Leonardo faced and overcame, her viewing focuses on the mutual gazes that give the painting an aura of eternal bliss. Thus, like Holbein's *Dead Christ*, da Vinci's *Virgin and Child with St. Anne*, when viewed psychoanalytically, reveals the desire that lies behind faith and is obscured by faith's symbolic order. These selections from Kristeva's work are all, therefore, concerned with the semiotic and the ways in which it struggles for representation in the predominantly symbolic order of Judaeo-Christian religion.

NOTES

1. Julia Kristeva, *Interviews*, ed. Ross Mitchell Guberman (New York: Columbia University Press, 1996), 10.

2. Ibid., 11.

3. Ibid.

4. Diane Jonte-Pace makes this point specifically in relation to Freud's texts

on religion in "Julia Kristeva and the Psychoanalytic Study of Religion: Rethinking Freud's Cultural Texts," in *Religion, Society, and Psychoanalysis: Readings in Contemporary Theory*, ed. Janet Liebman Jacobs and Donald Capps (Boulder, Colorado: Westview Press, 1997), 240–68.

5. Kristeva, *Interviews*, 21–22.

6. Martha J. Reineke, *Sacrificed Lives: Kristeva on Women and Violence* (Bloomington and Indianapolis: Indiana University Press, 1997), 24.

7. Jonte-Pace, 256.

8. Julia Kristeva, *Powers of Horror: An Essay on Abjection*, trans. Leon S. Roudiez (New York: Columbia University Press, 1982), ch. 4.

CHAPTER 26

Credo in Unum Deum

JULIA KRISTEVA

A n early Credo, known as the "Symbol of the Apostles," was in use throughout western Christendom by the tenth century. The Credo, based on the Nicene Creed of 325, was worked out by the Council of Constantinople in 381 and has remained in use to the present day.

Whoever is speaking in this text does not define his faith except in terms of its object. The God to whom he entrusts his vital speech—his heart—is a trinity. He is first of all the "Father Almighty," the "creator" not only of the person praying but of "all things visible and invisible." As if to bring himself closer to the person invoking his name, however, this God is also "Lord Jesus Christ, the only begotten Son of God." Begotten by God, he shares his essence, he is "one substance" with the Father; this is amplified by the statement that he is "begotten not made," since no creature can be identical with the Creator. This Son, with whom the person praying is supposed to find it easier to identify, is thus also a "son" (with a small s), a "minor" in some sense, yet still a "very God of very God," "Light of Light." Next we have various Christological assertions setting forth the history of the Son's time on earth. We are told that he came down from heaven for our salvation, that he made himself a man, becoming flesh by way of virgin birth from the body of a woman, the Virgin Mary. Like the person who invokes his name, this man suffered; he was crucified at a specific moment in history (under Pontius Pilate), he was buried, and on the third day (according to the sacred texts) he was restored to life and ascended to heaven and a place of glory at his Father's side. Ultimately he will return on Judgment Day to judge the living and the dead.

Following this christological excursus we return to the exposition of the trinity. The Holy Spirit is worshiped and glorified jointly with the Son and the Father in whom it "originates." (The Eastern and Western Churches differed on this question, the former denying that the Holy Spirit originates with both the Father and the Son.) Like the other two persons of the trinity, the Holy Ghost was mentioned by the prophets. It gives life and serves as mediator: it is "through the Holy Spirit" that the Son was incarnated in the Virgin Mary.

The Credo ends by mentioning the institution that sustains the faith and to which we must also give our hearts. The "catholic and apostolic" Church is the locus of ritual and faith: baptism, confession, remission of sins. Thus from the trinitarian nexus to its "political apparatus" the believer is provided with a structure of support with the help of which he will be able to obtain a reward that no human gift can possibly equal: resurrection and eternal life in the centuries to come.

Does anyone in the West *believe* in all the elements of this admirably logical and unified system? If believers do exist, aren't they many-faceted characters, prepared to accept the Credo in one of their parts or "personalities" while allowing others—the professional personality, the social personality, the erotic personality—to ignore it? Essential as this feature of contemporary religious belief is, it is not the question I wish to discuss here.

As an analyst, I find that the Credo embodies basic fantasies that I encounter every day in the psychic lives of my patients. The almighty Father? Patients miss one, want one, or suffer from one. Consubstantiality with the father and symbolic identification with his name? Patients aspire to nothing else, and the process is at once essential to psychic maturation and a source of pleasure (through assumption of the father's power and elevation to the summit of authority). More than any other religion, Christianity has unraveled the symbolic *and* physical importance of the paternal function in human life. Identification with this third party separates the child from its jubilant but destructive physical relationship with its mother and subjects it to another dimension, that of symbolization, where, beyond frustration and absence, language unfolds. Because of its insistence on the paternal function, Christianity shapes the preconscious formulation of the basic characteristic of male desire.

Thus the substantial, physical, incestuous fusion of men with their fathers both reveals and sublimates homosexuality. The crucifixion of God-made-man reveals to the analyst, always attentive to murderous desires with regard to the father, that the representation of

Christ's Passion signifies a guilt that is visited upon the son, who is himself put to death.

Freud interprets this expiation as an avowal of the oedipal murder that every human being unconsciously desires. But Christ's Passion brings into play even more primitive layers of the psyche; it thus reveals a fundamental depression (a narcissistic wound or reversed hatred) that conditions access to human language. The sadness of young children just prior to their acquisition of language has often been observed; this is when they must renounce forever the maternal paradise in which every demand is immediately gratified. The child must abandon its mother and be abandoned by her in order to be accepted by the father and begin talking. If it is true that language begins in mourning inherent in the evolution of subjectivity, the abandonment by the father—the symbolic "other"—triggers a melancholy anguish that can grow to suicidal proportions. "I detest him, but I am he, therefore I must die." Beyond the torment of suicide there is joy, ineffable happiness at finally rejoining the abandoned object.

The "scandal of the cross," the *logos tou stavron* or language of the cross, which some, according to Saint Paul, would call "foolishness" (I Cor. 1:18 and 1:23; Gal. 5:11) and which is indeed inconceivable for a god as the ancients understood the term, is embodied, I think, not only in the psychic and physical suffering that irrigates our lives *(qui irrigue notre existence)* but even more profoundly in the essential alienation that conditions our access to language, in the mourning that accompanies the dawn of psychic life. By the quirks of biology and family life we are all of us melancholy mourners, witnesses to the death that marks our psychic inception.

Christ abandoned, Christ in hell, is of course the sign that God shares the condition of the sinner. But He also tells the story of that necessary melancholy beyond which we humans may just possibly discover the other, now in the form of symbolic interlocutor rather than nutritive breast. In this respect, too, Christianity wins the adhesion of the masses; it supplies images for even the fissures in our secret and fundamental logic. How can we not believe?

A virgin mother? We want our mothers to be virgins, so that we can love them better or allow ourselves to be loved by them without fear of a rival. The unprecedented affirmation of symbolic paternity (carried to the point of insisting on the consubstantiality of father and son) could not have been made without reducing the weight of certain images, which would have made the burden of the father's symbolic authority too heavy to bear; those images have to do with procreative sexuality. By eliminating the mother as well as the father from the primal scene, the believer's imagination protects itself against a fantasy that is too much for any child to bear: that of being supernumerary, excluded from the act of pleasure that is the origin of its existence. Christianity, it must be said, avoids the whole question of procreation and is thus profoundly influenced by the idea of the virgin mother, which Catholicism, particularly in its more exuberant baroque forms, carried to an extreme.

More than one mother has been sustained in narcissistic equilibrium by the fantasy of having a child without the aid of a father; such women are not necessarily paranoid. Yet female hysterics, frequently touched by paranoia as well, relish the not-so-humble role of the virgin mother who is the "daughter of her son," mother of God, queen of the Church, and to top it all off the only human being who does not have to die (even her son must endure the cross). For her life ends according to Orthodox dogma in "dormition" and according to Catholic dogma in "assumption." Such a view of maternity has a strong appeal to man's imagination, as we have seen; it is particularly stimulating to artistic sublimation, as the example of Leonardo proves.[1]

Unfortunately, the proscription of female sexuality helped to infantilize half the human race by hampering its sexual and intellectual expression. Only advances in contraceptive technique have finally made it possible to lift that proscription. Previously, however, women received generous compensation in the form of praise of motherhood and its narcissistic rewards. Hence today, now that so-called artificial pregnancies have given concrete reality to the distinction between sexuality and procreation, femininity and maternity, the image of the virgin mother resonates with the daydreams of modern women with no particular religious vocation simply because there is no secular discourse on the psychology of motherhood.

The Trinity itself, that crown jewel of theological sophistication, evokes, beyond its specific content and by virtue of the very logic of its articulation, the intricate intertwining of the three aspects of psychic life: the symbolic, the imaginary, and the real. To the analyst, however, the representations on which the Credo is based are fantasies which reveal fundamental desires or traumas but not dogmas. Analysis subjects these fantasies to X-ray examination. It begins by individualizing: What about your father? Was he "almighty" or not? What kind of son were you? What about your desire for virginity or resurrection? By shifting attention from the "macrofantasy" to "microfantasy" analysis reveals the underlying sexuality, which prayer circumvents but does not really proscribe; for though the object of desire be transformed, desire itself remains the object of desire to be transformed, desire itself remains a feature of Christian discourse.

NOTE

1. Sigmund Freud, *Leonardo da Vinci and a Memory of His Childhood*, trans. Alan Tyson (New York: Norton, 1964).

CHAPTER 27

Holbein's Dead Christ

JULIA KRISTEVA

n 1522 Hans Holbein the Younger (1497–1543) painted a disturbing picture: *The Body of the Dead Christ in the Tomb*. The painting
represents a corpse stretched out by itself on a slab covered with a
cloth that is scarcely draped. Life size, the painted corpse is seen from
the side, its head slightly turned toward the viewer, the hair spread out
on the sheet. The right arm is in full view, resting alongside the emaciated, tortured body, and the hand protrudes slightly from the slab. The
rounded chest suggests a triangle within the very low, elongated rec-
tangle of the recess that constitutes the painting's frame. The chest
bears the bloody mark of a spear, and the hand shows the stigmata of
the crucifixion, which stiffen the outstretched middle finger. Imprints
of nails mark Christ's feet. The martyr's face bears the expression of a
hopeless grief; the empty stare, the sharp-lined profile, the dull blue-
green complexion are those of a man who is truly dead, of Christ forsaken by the Father ("My God, my God, why have you deserted me?")
and without the promise of Resurrection.

The unadorned representation of human death, the well-nigh
anatomical stripping of the corpse convey to viewers an unbearable
anguish before the death of God, here blended with our own, since
there is not the slightest suggestion of transcendency. What is more,
Hans Holbein has given up all architectural or compositional fancy.
The tombstone weighs down on the upper portion of the painting,
which is merely twelve inches high, and intensifies the feeling of permanent death: this corpse shall never rise again. The very pall, limited
to a minimum of folds, emphasizes, through that economy of motion,
the feeling of stiffness and stone-felt cold. The viewer's gaze penetrates

this closed-in coffin from below and, following the painting from left to right, stops at the stone set against the corpse's feet, sloping at a wide angle toward the spectators.

Italian iconography embellishes, or at least ennobles, Christ's face during the Passion but especially surrounds it with figures that are immersed in grief as well as in the certainty of the Resurrection, as if to suggest the attitude we should ourselves adopt facing the Passion. Holbein, on the contrary, leaves the corpse strangely alone. It is perhaps that isolation--*an act of composition*--that endows the painting with its major melancholy burden, more so than delineation and coloring. To be sure, Christ's suffering is expressed through three components inherent in lines and colors: the head bent backwards, the contortion of the right hand bearing the stigmata, the position of the feet—the whole being bonded by means of a dark palette of grays, greens, and browns. Nevertheless, such realism, harrowing on account of its very parsimony, is emphasized to the utmost through the painting's composition and location: a body stretched out alone, situated above the viewers, and separated from them.

Cut off from us by its base but without any prospect toward heaven, for the ceiling in the recess comes down low, Holbein's *Dead Christ* is inaccessible, distant, but without a beyond. It is a way of looking at mankind from afar, even in death—just as Erasmus saw folly from a distance. It is a vision that opens out not on glory but on endurance. Another, a new morality resides in this painting.

Christ's dereliction is here at its worst: forsaken by the Father, he is apart from all of us. Unless Holbein, whose mind, pungent as it was, does not appear to have led him across the threshold of atheism, wanted to include us, humans, foreigners, spectators that we are, forthrightly in this crucial moment of Christ's life. With no intermediary, suggestion, or indoctrination, whether pictorial or theological, other than our ability to imagine death, we are led to collapse in the horror of the caesura constituted by death or to dream of an invisible beyond. Does Holbein forsake us, as Christ, for an instant, had imagined himself forsaken? Or does he, on the contrary, invite us to change the Christly tomb into a living tomb, to participate in the painted death and thus include it in our own life, in order to live with it and make it live? For if the living body, in opposition to the rigid corpse, is a dancing body, doesn't our life, through identification with death, become a "danse macabre," in keeping with Holbein's other well-known depiction?

This enclosed recess, this well-isolated coffin simultaneously re-

Hans Holbein the Younger, *The Body of the Dead Christ in the Tomb*, 1521
(accession #318), distemper on limewood panel, 30.5 x 200 cm (Oeffentliche
Kunstammlung Basel, Kunstmuseum; photo: Oeffentliche Kunstammlung
Basel, Martin Bühler)

jects us and invites us. Indeed, the corpse fills the entire field of the
painting, without any labored reference to the Passion. Our gaze follows the slightest physical detail, it is, as it were, nailed, crucified, and
is riveted to the hand placed at the center of the composition. Should
it attempt to flee it quickly stops, locked in at the distressed face or the
feet propped against the black stone. And yet such walling in allows
two prospects.

On the one hand, there is the insertion of date and signature,
MDXXII H. H., at Christ's feet. Placing the painter's name, to which
was often added that of the donor, in that position was common at the
time. It is nevertheless possible that in abiding by that code Holbein
inserted himself into the drama of the Dead body. A sign of humility:
the artist throwing himself at God's feet? or a sign of equality? The
painter's name is not lower than Christ's body—they are both at the
same level, jammed into the recess, united in man's death as the essential sign of humanity, of which the only surviving evidence is the
ephemeral creation of a picture drawn here and now.

We have, on the other hand, this hair and this hand that extend beyond the base as if they might slide over toward us, as if the frame
could not hold back the corpse. The frame, precisely, dates from the
end of the sixteenth century and includes a narrow edging bearing the
inscription *Jesus Nazarenus Rex Judaeorum*, which encroaches upon
the painting. The edging, which seems nonetheless always to have
been part of Holbein's painting, includes, between the words of the inscription, five angels bearing the instruments of the martyrdom: the
shaft, the crown of thorns, the scourge, the flogging column, the cross.
Integrated afterwards in that symbolic framework, Holbein's painting
recovers the evangelical meaning that it did not insistently contain in
itself, and which probably legitimized it in the eyes of its purchasers.

Even if Holbein's painting had originally been conceived as a pre-
della for an altarpiece, it remained alone; no other panel was added to

it. Such isolation, as splendid as it is gloomy, avoided Christian symbolism as much as the surfeit of German Gothic style, which would
combine painting and sculpture but also add wings to altarpieces,
aiming for syncretism and the imparting of motion to figures. In the
face of that tradition, which directly preceded him, Holbein isolated,
pruned, condensed, reduced.

Holbein's originality lies then in a vision of Christly death devoid
of pathos and Intimist on account of its very banality. Humanization
thus reached its highest point: the point at which glory is obliterated
by means of graphics. When the dismal brushes against the nondescript, the most disturbing sign is the most ordinary one. Contrasting
with Gothic enthusiasm, humanism and parsimony were the inverted
products of melancholia.

We easily imagine Renaissance man as Rabelais depicted him: im-
posing, perhaps somewhat funny like Panurge, but boldly launched
on the pursuit of happiness and the wisdom of the divine bottle. Holbein, on the other hand, proposes another vision—that of man subject
to death, man embracing Death, absorbing it into his very being, integrating it not as a condition for glory or a consequence of a sinful nature but as the ultimate essence of his decentralized reality, which is
the foundation of a new dignity. For that very reason the picture of
Christly and human death with Holbein is in intimate partnership
with *In Praise of Folly* (1511) by Desiderius Erasmus, whose friend, il-
lustrator, and portrayer he became in 1523. Because he acknowledges
his folly and looks death in the face—but perhaps also because he
faces his mental risks, the risks of psychic death—man achieves a new
dimension. Not necessarily that of atheism but definitely that of a dis-
illusioned, serene, and dignified seance. Like a picture of Holbein.

At the heart of a disrupted Europe the quest for moral truth was
accompanied by excesses on both sides, while the realistic taste of a
class of merchants, artisans, and navigators promoted the rule of
strict discipline, but one already corruptible by gold. At such a world
of simple and fragile truths, the artist refused to cast an embellishing
gaze. If he embellished the setting or the clothing, he banished the illusion of having grasped the personality. A new idea was born in Europe, a paradoxical painterly idea—the idea that truth is severe,
sometimes sad, often melancholy. Can such a truth also constitute
beauty? Holbein's wager, beyond melancholia, is to answer, yes it can.

It is not my point to maintain that Holbein was afflicted with
melancholia or that he painted melancholy people. More profoundly,
it would seem, on the basis of his oeuvre (including his themes and

painterly technique), that a *melancholy moment* (an actual or imaginary loss of meaning, an actual or imaginary despair, an actual or imaginary razing of symbolic values, including the value of life) summoned up his aesthetic activity, which overcame the melancholy latency while keeping its trace. One has imagined for the young Holbein a secret and intense erotic activity, on the grounds of Magdalena Offenburg's having been the model for his Basel *Venus* (done earlier than 1526) and his *Laïs of Corinth*, and of the two illegitimate children he left in London. Charles Patin was the first to emphasize Holbein's dissipated life in his edition of Erasmus' *In Praise of Folly* (Basel, 1676). Rudolf and Margot Wittkower endorsed that interpretation and made a spendthrift of him: he would have squandered the considerable sums he was assumed to have received at the court of Henry VIII buying wild, opulent clothing, so much that he left only a paltry legacy to his heirs . . . [1] There is no serious evidence either to prove or to disprove such biographical assumptions, except for the legend of Magdalena Offenburg's own dissipated life. The Wittkowers, moreover, insist on ignoring the painter's work and consider as unimportant that his pictures do not in any way reflect the erotic and financial extravagance they ascribe to him.

From my point of view, that personality trait—assuming it is confirmed—in no way invalidates the depressive center the work reflects and overcomes. The economy of depression is supported by an omnipotent object, a monopolizing Thing rather than the focus of metonymical desire, which "might account for" the tendency to protect oneself from it through, *among other means*, a splurge of sensations, satisfactions, passions, one as elated as it is aggressive, as intoxicating as it is indifferent. It will be noted, nevertheless, that the common feature of those outlays is a *detachment*—getting rid of it, going elsewhere, abroad, toward others . . . The possibility of unfolding primary processes, spontaneously and under control, artfully, appears, however, as the most efficacious way of overcoming the latent loss. In other words, the controlled and mastered "expenditure" of colors, sounds, and words is imperative for the artist-subject, as an essential recourse, similar to "Bohemian life," "criminality," or "dissoluteness" alternating with "miserliness," which one observes in the behavior of such skylarking artists. Hence, very much like personal behavior, artistic *style* imposes itself as a means of countervailing the loss of other and of meaning: a means more powerful than any other because more autonomous (no matter who his patron is, isn't the artist master of his work?) but, in fact and fundamentally, analogous with or complementary to behavior, for it fills the same psychic need to confront separation, emptiness, death. Isn't the artist's life considered, by himself to start with, to be a work of art?

The Death of Christ

A depressive moment: everything is dying, God is dying, I am dying. But how is it possible for God to die? Let us briefly return to the evangelical meaning of Christ's death. Theological, hermetic, and doctrinal accounts of the "mystery of redemption" are numerous, complex, and contradictory. While the analyst cannot accept them, he or she might try, by examining them, to discover the meaning of the text as it unfolds within his or her hearing.

There are words of Christ that foretell his violent death without referring to salvation; others, however, seem at once to be pointing to, hence serving, the Resurrection. "Serving," which in Luke's context refers to "serving at the table," shifts to "giving his life," a life that is a "ransom" *(lytron)* in Mark's gospel. Such a semantic shift clearly sheds light on the status of the Christly "sacrifice." He who provides food is the one who sacrifices himself and disappears so that others might live. His death is neither murder nor evacuation but a life-giving discontinuity, closer to nutrition than to the simple destruction of value or the abandonment of a fallen object. A change in the conception of sacrifice obviously takes place within those texts, one that claims to establish a link between men and God through the mediation of a donor. While it is true that giving implies deprivation on the part of the one who gives, who gives of *himself,* there is greater stress placed on the *bond,* on assimilation ("serving at the table"), and on the reconciliatory benefits of that process.

Nevertheless, one should not forget that a whole ascetic, martyrizing, and sacrificial Christian tradition has magnified the victimized aspect of that offering by eroticizing both pain and suffering, physical as well as mental, as much as possible. Is that tradition no more than a simple medieval deviation that betrayed the "true meaning" of the Gospels? That would be setting little store by the anguish expressed by Christ himself, according to the Evangelists. How can we understand it when it is so powerfully asserted alongside the oblatory assurance of an oblatory gift made to a father who is also oblatory, equally present in the Gospels' text?

The break, brief as it might have been, in the bond linking Christ to his Father and to life introduces into the mythical representation of the Subject a fundamental and psychically necessary discontinuity. Such a caesura, which some have called a "hiatus,"[2] provides an image, at the same time as a narrative, for many separations that build up the psychic life of individuals. It provides image and narrative for some psychic cataclysms that more or less frequently threaten the assumed balance of individuals. Thus, psychoanalysis identifies and relates as an indispensable condition for autonomy a series of splittings (Hegel spoke of a "work of the negative"): birth, weaning, separation, frustration, castration. Real, imaginary, or symbolic, those processes necessarily structure our individuation. Their nonexecution or repudiation leads to psychotic confusion; their dramatization is, on the contrary, a source of exorbitant and destructive anguish. Because Christianity set that rupture at the very heart of the absolute subject—Christ; because it represented it as a Passion that was the solidary lining of his Resurrection, his glory, and his eternity, it brought to consciousness the essential dramas that are internal to the becoming of each and every subject. It thus endows itself with a tremendous cathartic power.

In addition to displaying a dramatic diachrony, the death of Christ offers imaginary support to the nonrepresentable catastrophic anguish distinctive of melancholy persons. It is well known that the so-called "depressive" stage is essential to the child's access to the realm of symbols and linguistic signs. Such a depression—parting sadness as the necessary condition for the representation of any absent thing—reverts to and accompanies our symbolic activities unless exaltation, its opposite, reappropriates them. A suspension of meaning, a darkness without hope, a recession of perspective including that of life, then reawaken within the memory the recollection of traumatic partings and thrust us into a state of withdrawal. "Father, why have you deserted me?" Moreover, serious depression or paroxismal clinical melancholia represents a true hell for modern individuals, convinced as they are that they must and can realize all their desires of objects and values. The Christly dereliction presents that hell with an imaginary elaboration; it provides the subject with an echo of its unbearable moments when meaning was lost, when the meaning of life was lost.

The postulate according to which Christ died "for all of us" appears often in the texts. *Hyper, peri, anti:* the words mean not only "because of us" but "in favor of us," "in our stead." They go back to the "Songs of the Servant of Yahweh" (in the Book of the Consolation of Israel, a collection of prophecies included in the Book of Isaiah) and even earlier to the Hebraic notion of *ga'al:* "to free by purchasing back goods and people that have become alien property." Thus, *redemption* (repurchase, liberation) implies a substitution between the Savior and the faithful, which opened the way for many interpretations. One of these is a compelling one in the analyst's literal reading: the one that suggests an imaginary *identification*. Identification does not mean delegating sins or shifting their burden to the person of the Messiah. On the contrary, it calls for a total implication of the subjects in Christ's suffering, in the hiatus he experiences, and of course in his hope of salvation. On the basis of that identification, one that is admittedly too anthropological and psychological from the point of view of a strict theology, man is nevertheless provided with a powerful symbolic device that allows him to experience death and resurrection even in his physical body, thanks to the strength of imaginary identification—and of its actual effects—with the absolute Subject (Christ).

A true initiation is thus elaborated, at the very heart of Christian thought, which takes up again the deep intrapsychic meaning of initiatory rites that were anterior or alien to its domain, and gives them new meaning. Here as elsewhere, *death*—that of the old body making room for the new, death to oneself for the sake of glory, death of the old man for the sake of the spiritual body—lies at the center of the experience. But, if there be a Christian initiation, it belongs first and entirely within the imaginary realm. While opening up the entire gamut of complete identifications (real and symbolic), it allows for no ritualistic ordeal other than the words and signs of the Eucharist. From that standpoint, the paroxysmal and realistic manifestations of asceticism and "dolor" are indeed extreme positions. Beyond and above that, the implicitness of love and consequently of reconciliation and forgiveness completely transforms the scope of Christian initiation by giving it an aura of glory and unwavering hope for those who believe. Christian faith appears then as an antidote to hiatus and depression, along with hiatus and depression and starting from them.

Could it be superego voluntarism that maintains the image of an oblatory Father, or is it the commemoration of an archaic paternal figure arisen from the paradise of primary identifications? The forgiveness inherent in Redemption condenses *death and resurrection* and presents itself as one of the most interesting and innovative instances of trinitary logic. The key to the nexus seems to be primary identification: the oral and already symbolic oblatory gift exchanged between Father and Son.

For individual reasons, or else on account of the historical crushing of political or metaphysical authority, which is our social fatherhood, the dynamics of primary identification at the foundation of idealization can run into difficulty—it can appear as deprived of significance, illusory, false. The only thing then surviving is the meaning of the deeper workings represented by the cross: that of caesura, discontinuity, depression.

Did Holbein become the painter of such a Christian thought, stripped of its antidepressive carrier wave, and amounting to identification with a rewarding beyond? He leads us, at any rate, to the ultimate edge of belief, to the threshold of nonmeaning. The *form* (of art) alone gives back serenity to the waning of forgiveness, while love and salvation take refuge to the execution of the work. Redemption would simply be the discipline of a rigorous technique.

Representing "Severance"

Hegel brought to the fore the dual action of death in Christianity: on the one hand there is a natural death of the natural body; on the other, death is "infinite love," the "supreme renunciation of self for the sake of the Other." He sees in it a victory over the tomb, the *sheol*, a "death of death," and emphasizes the dialectic that is peculiar to such a logic. "This negative movement, which belongs to Spirit only as Spirit, is inner conversion and change . . . the end being resolved in splendor, in the feast honoring the reception of the human being into the divine Idea." [3] Hegel stresses the consequences of this action for representation. Since death is represented as being natural but realized only on condition that it be identified with its otherness, that is, divine Idea, one witnesses "a marvelous union of these absolute extremes," "a supreme alienation of the divine Idea. . . . 'God is dead, God himself is dead' is a marvelous, fearsome representation, which offers to representation the deepest abyss of severance."

Leading representation to the heart of that severance (natural death *and* divine love) is a wager that one could not make without slipping into one or the other of two tendencies: Gothic art, under Dominican influence, favored a pathetic representation of natural death; Italian art, under Franciscan influence, exalted, through the sexual beauty of luminous bodies and harmonious compositions, the glory of the beyond made visible through the glory of the sublime. Holbein's *Body of the Dead Christ in the Tomb* is one of the rare if not a unique realization located at the very place of the severance of representation of which Hegel spoke. The Gothic eroticism of paroxysmal pain is missing, just as the promise of the beyond or the renascent exaltation of nature are lacking. What remains is the tightrope—as the represented body—of an economical, sparing graphic rendition of pain held back within the solitary meditation of artist and viewer. To such a serene, disenchanted sadness, reading the limits of the insignificant, corresponds a painterly art of utmost sobriety and austerity. It presents no chromatic or compositional exultation but rather a mastery of harmony and measure.

Is it still possible to paint when the bonds that tie us to body and meaning are severed? Is it still possible to paint when *desire*, which is a bond, disintegrates? Is it still possible to paint when one identifies not with desire but with *severance*, which is the truth of human psychic life, a severance that is represented by death in the imagination and that melancholia conveys as symptom? Holbein's answer is affirmative. Between classicism and mannerism his minimalism is the metaphor of severance: between life and death, meaning and nonmeaning, it is an intimate, slender response of our melancholia.

Pascal confirmed, before Hegel and Freud, the sepulchre's invisibility. For him, the tomb would be Christ's hidden abode. Everyone looks at him on the cross but in the tomb he hides from his enemies' eyes, and the saints alone see him in order to keep him company in an agony that is peace.[4] Seeing the death of Christ is thus a way to give it meaning, to bring him back to life. But in the tomb at Basel Holbein's Christ is alone. Who sees him? There are no saints. There is of course the painter. And ourselves. To be swallowed up by death, or perhaps to see it in its slightest, dreadful beauty, as the limit inherent in life. *"Christ in grief . . . Christ being in agony and in the greatest sorrow, let us pray longer."*[5]

Painting as a substitute for prayer? Contemplating the painting might perhaps replace prayer at the critical place of its appearance—where the nonmeaning becomes significant, while death seems visible and livable.

Like Pascal's invisible tomb, death is not representable in Freud's unconscious. It is imprinted there, however, by spacings, blanks, discontinuities, or destruction of representation. Consequently, death reveals itself as such to the imaginative ability of the self in the isolation of signs or in their becoming commonplace to the point of disappearing: such is Holbein's minimalism. But as it grapples with the erotic vitality of the self and the jubilatory abundance of exalting or morbid signs conveying Eros's presence, death calls for a distant realism or, better, a grating irony: this brings forth the "danse macabre" and disenchanted profligacy inborn in the painter's style. The self eroticizes and signifies the obsessive presence of Death by stamping with isolation, emptiness, or absurd laughter its own imaginative assurance that keeps it alive, that is, anchored in the interplay of forms. To the contrary, images and identities—the carbon copies of that triumphant self—are imprinted with inaccessible sadness.

Our eyes having been filled with such a vision of the invisible, let us look once more at the people that Holbein has created: heroes of modern times, they stand strait-laced, sober, and upright. Secretive, too: as real as can be and yet indecipherable. Not a single impulse betraying jouissance. No exalted loftiness toward the beyond. Nothing but the sober difficulty of standing here below. They simply remain upright around a void that makes them strangely lonesome. Self confident. And close.

NOTES

1. See R. and M. Wittkower, *Born Under Saturn* (W. W. Norton, 1969).

2. See U. von Balthasar, *La Gloire et la Croix* (Aubier, 1975).

3. G. W. F. Hegel, *Lectures on the Philosophy of Religion*, E. B. Speirs (trans.). (Humanities Press, 1962), 3:93.

4. B. Pascal, "Thoughts: An Apology for Christianity," in Z. Tourneur (ed.), *Pensées de M. Pascal sur la religion* (Cluny, 1938), 2:101.

5. Ibid., "Le Mystere de Jesus," 2:12.

CHAPTER 28

Might Not Universality Be . . . Our Own Foreignness?

JULIA KRISTEVA

O ne cannot hope to understand Freud's contribution, in the specific field of psychiatry, outside of its humanistic and Romantic filiation. With the Freudian notion of the unconscious the involution of the strange in the psyche loses its pathological aspect and integrates within the assumed unity of human beings an *otherness* that is both biological *and* symbolic and becomes an integral part of the *same*. Henceforth the foreigner is neither a race nor a nation. The foreigner is neither glorified as a secret *Volksgeist* nor banished as disruptive of rationalist urbanity. Uncanny, foreignness is within us: we are our own foreigners, we are divided. Even though it shows a Romanticist filiation, such an intimist restoring of the foreigner's good name undoubtedly bears the biblical tones of a foreign God or of a Foreigner apt to reveal God.

Freud's personal life, a Jew wandering from Galicia to Vienna and London, with stopovers in Paris, Rome, and New York (to mention only a few of the key stages of his encounters with political and cultural foreignness), conditions his concern to face the other's discontent as ill-ease in the continuous presence of the "other scene" within us. My discontent in living with the other—my strangeness—rests on the perturbed logic that governs this strange bundle of drive and language, of nature and symbol, constituted by the unconscious, always already shaped by the other. It is through unraveling transference—the major dynamics of otherness, of love/hatred for the other, of the foreign component of our psyche—that, on the basis of the other, I become reconciled with my own otherness-foreignness, that I play on it and live by it. Psychoanalysis is then experienced as a journey into the strangeness of the other and of oneself, toward an ethics of respect for the irreconcilable. How could one tolerate a foreigner if one did not know one was a stranger to oneself? And to think that it has taken such a long time for that small truth, which transverses or even runs against religious uniformist tendencies, to enlighten the people of our time! Will it allow them to put up with one another as irreducible, because they are desiring, desirable, mortal, and death-bearing?

Explicitly given limited scope, as it was at first connected with esthetic problems and emphasized texts by E. T. A. Hoffmann, Freud's *Das Unhemliche* (1919) surreptitiously goes beyond that framework and the psychological phenomenon of "uncanny strangeness" as well, in order to acknowledge itself as an investigation into anguish generally speaking and, in a fashion that is even more universal, into the *dynamics of the unconscious*. Indeed, Freud wanted to demonstrate at the outset, on the basis of a semantic study of the German adjective *heimlich* and its antonym *unheimlich* that a negative meaning close to that of the antonym is already tied to the positive term *hiemlich* [friendly, intimate, homelike] which would also signify "concealed, kept from sight," "deceitful and malicious," "behind someone's back." Thus, in the very word *heimlich*, the familiar and intimate are reversed into their opposites, brought together with the contrary meaning of "uncanny strangeness" harbored in *unheimlich*. Such an immanence of the strange within the familiar is considered as an etymological proof of the psychoanalytic hypothesis according to which "the uncanny is that class of the frightening which leads back to what is known of old and long familiar,"[1] which, as far as Freud was concerned, was confirmed by Schelling who said that "everything is *unheimlich* that ought to have remained secret and hidden but has come to light" (p. 225).

Consequently therefore, that which is strangely uncanny would be that which *was* (the past tense is important) familiar and, under certain conditions (which ones?), emerges. A first step was taken that removed the uncanny strangeness from the outside, where fright had anchored it, to locate it inside, not inside the familiar considered as one's own and proper, but the familiar potentially tainted with strangeness and referred (beyond its imaginative origin) to an improper past. The other is my ("own and proper") unconscious.

What "familiar"? What "past"? In order to answer such questions, Freud's thought played a strange trick on the esthetic and psychological notion of "uncanny strangeness," which had been initially posited, and rediscovered the analytical notions of *anxiety, double, repetition,* and *unconscious*. The uncanny strangeness that is aroused in Nathaniel (in Hoffmann's tale, *The Sandman*) by the paternal figure and its substitutes, as well as references to the eyes, is related to the castration anxiety experienced by the child, which was repressed but surfaced again on the occasion of a state of love.

Furthermore, Freud noted that the archaic, narcissistic self, not yet demarcated by the outside world, projects out of itself what it experiences as dangerous or unpleasant in itself, making of it an alien *double*, uncanny and demoniacal. In this instance the strange appears as a defense put up by a distraught self: it protects itself by substituting for the image of a benevolent double that used to be enough to shelter it the image of a malevolent double into which it expels the share of destruction it cannot contain.

The repetition that often accompanies the feeling of uncanny strangeness relates it to the "compulsion to repeat" that is peculiar to the unconscious and emanating out of "drive impulses"—a compulsion "proceeding from the drive impulses and probably inherent in the very nature of the drives—a compulsion powerful enough to overrule the pleasure principle" (p. 238).

The reader is henceforth ready to accept the feeling of uncanny strangeness as an instance of anxiety in which "the frightening element can be shown to be something repressed which *recurs*" (p. 241). To the extent, however, that psychic situations evidencing an absolute repression are rare, such a return of the repressed in the guise of anxiety, and more specifically of uncanny strangeness, appears as a paroxystic metaphor of the psychic functioning itself. The latter is indeed elaborated by repression and one's necessarily going through it, with the result that the builder of the *other* and, in the final analysis, of the *strange* is indeed repression itself and its perviousness. "We can understand why linguistic usage has extended *das Heimliche* into its opposite, *das Unheimliche;* for this uncanny is in reality nothing new or alien, but something which is familiar and old-established in the mind and which has become alienated from it only through the process of repression" (p. 241).

Let us say that the psychic apparatus represses representative processes and contents that are no longer necessary for pleasure, self-preservation, and the adaptive growth of the speaking subject and the living organism. Under certain conditions, however, the repressed "that ought to have remained secret" shows up again and produces a feeling of uncanny strangeness.

While saying that he would henceforth tackle "one or two more examples of the uncanny," Freud in his text actually continues, by

means of a subtle, secret endeavor, to reveal the circumstances that
are favorable to going through repression and generating the uncanny
strangeness. The confrontation with *death* and its representation is
initially imperative, for our unconscious refuses the fatality of death:
"Our unconscious has as little use now as it ever had for the idea of its
own mortality." The fear of death dictates an ambivalent attitude: we
imagine ourselves surviving (religions promise immortality), but
death just the same remains the survivor's enemy, and it accompanies
him in his new existence. Apparitions and ghosts represent that ambiguity and fill with uncanny strangeness our confrontations with the
image of death.

The fantasy of being buried alive induces the feeling of uncanny
strangeness, accompanied by "a certain lasciviousness—the phantasy,
I mean, of intra-uterine existence" (p. 244). We are confronted with a
second source of the strange: "It often happens that neurotic men declare that they feel there is something uncanny about the female genital organs. This *unheimlich* place, however, is the entrance to the
former *Heim* of all human beings, to the place where each one of us
lived once upon a time and in the beginning." "There is a joking saying
that 'Love is homesickness' " (p. 245).

The *death* and the *feminine*, the end and the beginning that en-
gross and compose us only to frighten us when they break through—
to these one must add "the living person [. . .] when we ascribe evil
intentions to him [. . .] that are going to be carried out with the help of
special powers" (p. 243). Such malevolent *powers* would amount to a
weaving together of the symbolic and the organic—perhaps *drive* itself, on the border of the psyche and biology, overriding the breaking
imposed by organic homeostasis. A disturbing symptom of this may
be found in epilepsy and madness, and their presence in our fellow beings worries us the more as we dimly sense them in ourselves.

Are death, the feminine, and drives always a pretext for the uncanny strangeness? After having broadened the scope of his meditation, which might have led to seeing in uncanniness the description of
the working of the unconscious, which is itself dependent on repression, Freud marked its required limits by stressing a few particulari-
ties of the semiology within which it emerges. Magical practices,
animism, or, in more down-to-earth fashion, "intellectual uncertainty" and "disconcerted" logic (according to E. Jentsch) are all pro-
pitious to uncanniness. Now, what brings together these symbolic
processes, quite different for all that, lies in a weakening of the value
of signs as such and of their specific logic. The symbol ceases to be a

symbol and "takes over the full functions of the thing it symbolizes" (p. 244). In other words, the sign is not experienced as arbitrary but assumes a real importance. As a consequence, the material reality that the sign was commonly supposed to point to crumbles away to the benefit of imagination, which is no more than "the over-accentuation of psychical reality in comparison with material reality" (p. 244). We are here confronted with "the omnipotence of thought," which, in order to constitute itself invalidates the arbitrariness of signs and the autonomy of reality as well and places them both under the sway of fantasies expressing infantile desires or fears.

Obsessional neuroses, but also and differently psychoses, have the distinctive feature of "reifying" signs—of slipping from the domain of "speaking" to the domain of "doing." Such a particularity *also* evinces the fragility of repression and, without actually explaining it, allows the return of the repressed to be inscribed in the reification under the guise of the uncanny affect. While, in another semiological device, one might think that the return of the repressed would assume the shape of the somatic symptom or of the acting out, here the breakdown of the arbitrary signifier and its tendency to become reified as psychic contents that take the place of material reality would favor the experience of uncanniness. Conversely, our fleeting or more or less threatening encounter with uncanny strangeness would be a clue to our psychotic latencies and the fragility of our repression—at the same time as it is an indication of the weakness of language as a symbolic barrier that, in the final analysis, structures the repressed.

Strange indeed is the encounter with the other—whom we perceive by means of sight, hearing, smell, but do not "frame" within our consciousness. The other leaves us separate, incoherent; even more so, he can make us feel that we are not in touch with our own feelings, that we reject them or, on the contrary, that we refuse to judge them— we feel "stupid," we have "been had."

Also strange is the experience of the abyss separating me from the other who shocks me—I do not even perceive him, perhaps he crushes me because I negate him. Confronting the foreigner whom I reject and with whom at the same time I identify, I lose my boundaries, I no longer have a container, the memory of experiences when I had been abandoned overwhelm me, I lose my composure. I feel "lost," "indistinct," "hazy." The uncanny strangeness allows for many variations: they all repeat the difficulty I have in situating myself with respect to the other and keep going over the course of identification-projection that lies at the foundation of my reaching autonomy.

At this stage of the journey, one understands that Freud took pains
to separate the uncanniness provoked by esthetic experience from
that which is sustained in reality; he most particularly stressed those
works in which the uncanny effect is abolished because of the very
fact that the entire world of the narrative is fictitious. Such are fairy
tales, in which the generalized artifice spares us any possible comparison between sign, imagination, and material reality. As a consequence, artifice neutralizes uncanniness and makes all returns of the
repressed plausible, acceptable, and pleasurable. As if absolute en-
chantment—absolute sublimation—just as, on the other hand, absolute rationality—absolute repression—were our only defenses
against uncanny strangeness. Unless, depriving us of the dangers as
well as the pleasures of strangeness, they are the instruments of their
liquidation.

Linked to anguish, as we have been, the uncanny strangeness does
not, however, merge with it. Initially it is a shock, something unusual,
astonishment; and even if anguish comes close, uncanniness maintains that share of unease that leads the self, beyond anguish, toward
depersonalization. "The sense of strangeness belongs in the same category as depersonalization," Freud noted, and many analysts have
stressed the frequency of the *Unhemliche* affect in phobia, especially
when the contours of the self are overtaxed by the clash with something "too good" or "too bad." In short, if anguish revolves around an
object, uncanniness, on the other hand, is a *destructuration of the self*
that may either remain as a psychotic *symptom* or fit in as an *opening*
toward the new, as an attempt totally with the incongruous. While it
surely manifests the return of a familiar repressed, the *Unheimliche*
requires just the same the impetus of a new encounter with an unexpected outside element: arousing images of death, automatons, dou-
bles, or the female sex, uncanniness occurs when the boundaries
between *imagination* and *reality* are erased. This observation reinforces the concept— which arises out of Freud's text—of the *Unheimliche* as a crumbling of conscious defenses, resulting from the
conflicts the self experiences with an other—the "strange"—with
whom it maintains a conflictual bond, at the same time "a need for
identification and a fear of it" (Maurice Bouvet). The clash with the
other, the identification of the self with that good or bad other that
transgresses the fragile boundaries of the uncertain self, would thus
be at the source of an uncanny strangeness whose excessive features,
as represented in literature, cannot hide its permanent presence in
"normal" psychical dynamics.

The Strange within Us

In the fascinated rejection that the foreigner arouses in us, there is a share of uncanny strangeness in the sense of the depersonalization that Freud discovered in it, and which takes up again our infantile desires and fears of the other—the other of death, the other of woman, the other of uncontrollable drive. The foreigner is within us. And when we flee from or struggle against the foreigner, we are fighting our unconscious—that "improper" facet of our impossible "own and proper." Delicately, analytically, Freud does not speak of foreigners: he teaches us how to detect foreignness in ourselves. That is perhaps the only way not to hound it outside of us. After Stoic cosmopolitanism, after religious universalist integration, Freud brings us the courage to call ourselves disintegrated in order not to integrate foreigners and even less so to hunt them down, but rather to welcome them to that uncanny strangeness, which is as much theirs as it is ours.

In fact, such a Freudian distraction or discretion concerning the "problem of foreigners"—which appears only as an eclipse or, if one prefers, as a symptom, through the recall of the Greek word *xenoi*— might be interpreted as an invitation (a utopic or very modern one?) not to reify the foreigner, not to petrify him as such, not to petrify *us* as such. But to analyze it by analyzing us. To discover our disturbing otherness, for that indeed is what bursts in to confront that "demon," that threat, that apprehension generated by the projective apparition of the other at the heart of what we persist in maintaining as a proper, solid "us." By recognizing *our* uncanny strangeness we shall neither suffer from it nor enjoy it from the outside. The foreigner is within me, hence we are all foreigners. If I am a foreigner, there are no foreigners. Therefore Freud does talk about them. The ethics of psychoanalysis implies a politics: it would involve a cosmopolitanism of a new sort that, cutting across governments, economies, and markets, might work for a mankind whose solidarity is founded on the consciousness of its unconscious— desiring, destructive, fearful, empty, impossible. Here we are far removed from a call to brotherhood, about which one has already ironically pointed out its debt to paternal and divine authority—"In order to have brothers there must be a father," as Louis-François Veuillot did not fail to say when he sharply addressed humanists. On the basis of an erotic, death-bearing unconscious, the uncanny strangeness—a projection as well as a first working out of death drive— which adumbrates the work of the "second" Freud, the one of *Beyond the Pleasure Principle*, sets the difference within us in its most bewildering shape and presents it as the ultimate condition of our being *with* others.

NOTE

    1. S. Freud, "The 'Uncanny,' " in *The Standard Edition*, James Strachey (ed.), Vol. 17, p. 220.

CHAPTER 29

Reading the Bible

JULIA KRISTEVA

Two Approaches to the Sacred

T he idea of reading the Bible as we might read Marx's *Das Kapital* or Lautréamont's *Chants de Maldoror*, unraveling its contents as if it were one text among many, is without doubt an approach born out of structuralism and semiology. Although such an approach may seem reductive or even outrageous, we must not forget that any interpretation of a religious text or occurrence assumes that it can be made into an object of analysis, even if it means admitting that it conceals something that cannot be analyzed. Of course, we may question this interpretive obsession that tries so desperately to make the Holy Text say what it does not know it is saying, and I shall return to what I believe to be the motivation behind this eternal return to divinity, a return that may be glorious or profane.

When the "human sciences"—which rely upon a rationality that seeks to reveal the universal logic embedded in a myth, a hieratic text, or a poem—turn to the Bible, they are forced to limit themselves to the logic or rhetoric of the text. At first they disregard its sacred powers, although they hope that their positive and neutral analysis will guide them toward the mechanism—if not the enigma—of what is seen as "holy" and of what appears to function as such. Perhaps the Bible lends itself to semiological analysis more easily than do other forms of writing. Indeed, by paving the way for interpretations, the Talmudic and cabalistic traditions are always inviting us to make yet another one.

What is more, the Book dominates the Judaic religious experience. It overshadows and ultimately governs the ritual, which enables it to bypass the ritual in favor of the letter, or of its interpretive values and a Single yet Infinite Meaning that supports human desire in the face of God. Are reading and interpreting the Bible perhaps the dominant ritual, the very eruption of the Judaic ritual and sacrament into language and logic?

This paradigm of biblical interpretation has resulted in studies inspired by various schools of thought, but that are unified by their common goal of specifying the profound logic that has generated the sacred value of the biblical text. Let us take the example of Mary Douglas' functionalism. While working independently from specialists in religious studies like Jacob Neusner,[1] Douglas has shown that the Levitical food taboos obey the universal law of exclusion, which states that the impure is that which falls outside a symbolic order. The Bible's obsession with purity seems then to be a cornerstone of the sacred. Nevertheless, it is merely a semantic variant of the need for separation, which constitutes an identity or a group as such, contrasts nature with culture, and is glorified in all the purification rituals that have forged the immense catharsis of society and culture.[2]

J. Soler has proposed a reading of the Levitical abominations that is more "semiological" in approach. He has unearthed the way in which a taxonomy that bases itself on the separation and exclusion of food combinations has been transformed into a narrative and a ritual.[3] This taxonomy, which is initially dominated by the dichotomy between life and death, also corresponds to the God/Man dyad and provides a schematic version of the commandment "Thou shall not kill." In the end, the code of Levitical abominations becomes a veritable code of differences that seeks to eliminate ambiguity. In this sense, one might think of the food taboos that pertain to fish, birds, and insects, which are respectively associated to one of the three elements (water, sky, earth): any food product that mixes and blends with these elements is considered impure. According to this interpretation, the Levitical taboos would suggest that the fundamental confusion is incest—an inference that can be drawn from the well-known precept, "You shall not boil a kid in its mother's milk" (Exod. 23:19; Deut. 14:21).

Using a different approach, Evan Zuesse has delved into the hypostatized value of this exclusionary figure. He has noted that the Bible comprises a metonymic logic of taboos (which rely on displacement) that could be contrasted with the metaphorical nature of the sacrifice (which relies on deletion and substitution). This has led him to suggest that the Bible marks out the end of sacrificial religion and replaces it with a system of rules, prohibitions, and moral codes.[4]

That is all I shall say about these recent studies, which have helped clarify the inner workings of biblical thought in a way that can be distinguished from the historical or philosophical approach to religions, especially Judaism. I believe that the conclusions they have drawn are essential to any understanding of the Bible. These studies can be characterized, however, by an important omission: no attention is paid to the linguistic subject of the biblical utterance, nor by way of consequence, to its addressee. *Who is speaking in the Bible? For whom?*

This question is especially relevant for our purposes because it seems to suggest a subject who is not at all neutral and indifferent like the subject described by modern theories of interpretation, but who maintains a specific relationship of *crisis, trial,* or *process* with his God. If it is true that all texts considered "sacred" refer to borderline states of subjectivity, we have reason to reflect upon these states, especially since the biblical narrator is familiar with them. Such a reading would tend to focus on the intra- or infrasubjective dynamics of the sacred text. Yet even if these dynamics are manifested in the figure of the text itself, interpreting them would require that we recognize a *new space,* that of the speaking subject, who henceforth ceases to be an impenetrable point that guarantees the universality of logical operations, and who opens himself instead to analyzable spaces. If I am alluding to Freudian theory here, it is because Freud's theory is capable of using the results of the biblical analyses I have mentioned and of transporting them into subjective space. Were an interpretation to internalize these discoveries as devices proper to certain states of the subject of enunciation, it could go beyond a simply descriptive framework and account for the impact that the Bible has on its addressees.

To return to the characteristic figures of biblical food taboos, I have come to realize that the object excluded by these rules, whatever form it may take in biblical narrative, is ultimately the mother. I cannot review the logical process that has led me to this position, but I shall take the liberty of referring you to my *Powers of Horror.*[5] Let me simply state that it is not enough to study the logical processes of exclusion that underlie the institution of these taboos, for attention must also be paid to the semantic and pragmatic value of the excluded object. We notice, among other things, that separating oneself from the mother, rejecting her, and "abjecting" her; as well as using this negation to resume contact with her, to define oneself according to her, and to "rebuild" her, constitutes an essential movement in the biblical text's struggles against the maternal cults of previous and current forms of organism.

Now, the analyst is another person who sees such abjection as necessary for the advent of the subject as a speaking being. Studies on early childhood and on language acquisition have shown that the rejection of the mother causes her to be the originary object of need, desire, or speech. Yet she is also an ambiguous object who is, in fact, an *ab-ject*—a magnet of fascination and repulsion—before (in both the logical and chronological sense) she can be established as an object. This suggests an immersion in that which is not "one's own," as well as a dramatic distortion of the narcissistic dyad.

What is more, phobic and psychotic symptoms, which act out uncertainties about the limits of the subject (myself versus other people, inside versus outside), internalize this sort of aggressive fascination with the mother. In the discourse of adults, the mother becomes a locus of horror and adoration. She is ready for the entire procession of part-objects of *disgust* and *anality* that mobilize themselves to support the fragile whole of an ego in crisis.

Therefore, it could be said that a biblical text (the Book of Leviticus), which delineates the precise limits of abjection (from skin to food, sex, and moral codes), has developed a true archeology of the advent of the subject. Indeed, this Book recounts the subject's delicate and painful detachment—moment by moment, layer by layer, step by step—as well as his journey from narcissistic fusion to an autonomy that is never really "his own," never "clean," never complete, and never securely guaranteed in the Other.

I am suggesting, then, an interpretation that compares the Book of Leviticus to the preoedipal dynamic of the subject's separation. My interpretation is rooted in the fragile status of subjectivity, and it thus serves to explain, at least to some extent, the cathartic value of the biblical text. The Book of Leviticus speaks to me by locating me at the point where I lose my "clean self." It takes back what I dislike and acknowledges my bodily comfort, the ups and downs of my sexuality, and the compromises or harsh demands of my public life. It shapes the very borders of my defeats, *for it has probed into the ambivalent desire for the other,* for the mother as the first other, *which is at the base, that is, on the other side of that which makes me into a speaking being* (a separating, dividing, joining being). The Bible is a text that thrusts its words into my losses. By enabling me to speak about my disappointments, though, it lets me stand in full awareness of them.

This awareness is unconscious—so be it. Nevertheless, it causes me, as a reader of the Bible, to resemble someone who lives on the fringe, on the lines of demarcation within which my security and fragility are separated and merged. Perhaps that is where we might discover what is known as the sacred value of the text: a place that gives meaning to these crises of subjectivity, during which meaning, disturbed as it is by the object-abject of desire, eludes me and "I" run the risk of falling into the indifference of a narcissistic, lethal fusion.

Across the ages, sacred literature may never have done anything but use various forms of sacrifice to enunciate *murder* as a condition of Meaning. At the same time, this literature has emphasized the breathtaking threat that *fusion libido* inflicts upon meaning, which it can carry, destroy, or kill. The message of the biblical abominations, however, is particular and unique: you must be separated from your mother so that you do not kill anyone. Meaning is what guarantees desire and thus preserves the desire for death. You will displace your hatred into thought; you will devise a logic that defends you from murder and madness, a logic whose arbitrary nature shall be your coronation. The Bible offers the best description of this transformation of sacrifice into language, this displacement of murder into a system of meanings. In this way, this *system*, which counterbalances *murder*, becomes the place where all our crises can be exploded and assimilated. In my view, the fulcrum of this biblical process can be located in its particular conception of the *maternal:* the maternal is a promised land if you are willing to leave it, an object of desire if you are willing to renounce and forbid it; the maternal is delight as well as murder, an inescapable "abject" whose awareness haunts you, or which may very well be the constitutive double of your own awareness. "For your hands are defiled with blood and your fingers with iniquity" (Isa. 59:3).

Love That Cannot Be Represented

The Bible draws attention to the love that the Jewish people have for their God, and it demands or denounces this love when it is found to be insufficient. On the other hand, ancient texts have much less to say about God's love for Israel. Only two references to this love can be found:

> And David comforted his wife, Bathsheba, and went in unto her, and lay with her; and she bore a son, and he called his name Solomon; and the LORD loved him.
>
> And he sent by the hand of Nathan the prophet; and he called his name Jedidiah, because of the LORD (2 Sam. 12:24–25).

The queen of Sheba affirms that the Lord loves Israel:

> Blessed be the LORD thy God, which delighted in thee. (I Kings 10:9).

Christian agape was to turn the situation around and posit that Love falls from the heavens even before we know it as such. The love that the biblical God has for His people is expressed in another way. As direct as it may be, it demands neither worthiness nor justification, for it is interspersed with preferences and choices that immediately establish the loved one as a Subject. Ancient biblical texts do not make a great deal of this love, and when they do intimate it exists, they imply that it cannot be represented. For instance, note that Nathan is the one who says, though without any words, that Solomon is beloved. What is more, the name of Jedidiah the child ("Jedidiah" meaning loved by God) does not reappear in the narrative. As for the second passage, a foreign woman is the one who refers to God's love, and she speaks in riddles.

This brings us to the central problem of the biblical God: He cannot be seen, named, or represented. That these traits are particularly applicable to His *love*, as is shown by the passages I have cited, may give the analyst some insight into the infinitely complex question of the Bible's *prohibition of representation*.

When analysts listen to evocations of narcissistic wounds, or better yet, when they listen to subjects who are constituted by a narcissistic wound, they become aware of a ghostly yet secure presence of the father before they become aware of any oedipal hold on the father's love or on love for him. This archaic mirage of the paternal function, which is placed against the background of primary narcissism as the ultimate guarantee of identity, could very well be considered to be an imaginary Father. Although his actual existence may be hallucinatory, he appears to edify the keystone of the capacity to sublimate, especially through art. Freud characterized this particular Father, who is necessary for the Ego-Ideal, as a support for "primary identification." He referred to him as the "Father in personal prehistory" *(Vater der personlächen Vorzeit).*[6] Freud postulated that apprehension of this father is "direct and immediate" *(direkte und unmittelbare)*, and emphasized that he internalizes both parents and both genders. The immediacy of this absolute, which the young child of a Mother-Father in personal prehistory brings back to a mysterious and direct grasp, guarantees his ability to idealize.

This sheds some scandalous light on the theological or antitheological orientation of philosophy. We know, indeed, that philosophers from Hegel to Heidegger have tried to ascertain the meaning of Being by interpreting the absolute presence of Parousia. We are obliged to note that this two-sided and double-gendered figure of kinship, which is what creates the symbolic, limits the extent to which analysis may search for that which is not simply narcissistic in origin. This, however, does not guarantee symbolic autonomy (or the separation between subject and object that it presumes).

As the zero-degree of symbol formation, this imaginary Father, who is most likely the father desired by the mother (her own father?), is thus the focal point of the processes that lead not to the appearance of the object (along this path, we have found the *abject* and a separative obsession), but to the *position of subjectivity*, that is, a being for and by the Other. The early onset of this moment, as well as its mediation by the mother's desire, causes the subject to believe that this moment is resistant to representation, despite the array of signifiers brought about by the oedipal complex. Those who believe in the God of the Bible do not doubt His love. God—who is impossible to represent, fleeting, and always there though invisible—eludes me and invites me to let go of my narcissism, to venture forth, to inflict suffering and persecution upon myself in order to earn His love. Does He not force these roots into that ineradicable, archaic, and deeply felt conviction that occupies and protects those who accept Him? That is, the conviction that a preoedipal father exists, a *Vater der personlïchen Vorzeit*, an imaginary father?

Is Psychoanalysis a "Jewish Science"?

Interpreting the meaning of the sacred text as an elaboration of psychic conflicts that border on psychosis assumes, as I have made clear, that the psychoanalyst is attentive and even vulnerable to the biblical text. Why is it that ever since Freud, analytic attention has invariably focused on the sacred, and more specifically on the biblical sacred?

One might answer that such an orientation stems from the interpretive posture itself. I am made to use silence or speech to listen to and to interpret a discourse that no longer has any meaning for its subject, and that is consequently experienced as painful. I am struck, however, by the fact that analysands are privy to a meaning that is "already there," even if this meaning takes the form of the most dramatic explosions of subjective identity or of linguistic coherence. Does this stem from the conviction that there is an imaginary father? Whose father is it?

In like manner, the interpretive construction made by the analyst, who assimilates this speech through transference or counter-transference, also presents itself as a barrier to possible meaning (when I communicate an interpretation) or to a meaning that is arbitrary, if not eccentric (when I resort to silence). This interpretative construction, which can be as portentous as my own desire will allow, is nevertheless my only way—*the* only way?—to guide the analysand's speech from being completely eclipsed toward a state of relative autonomy. Interpretive constructions do not deny that crises occur, but they save us from getting trapped in them or reveling in them. I am proposing, then, an imaginary construction that can serve as an indefinite and infinite truth. As opposed to a positivist interpretation, which would delimit reality by giving itself the last word—the strongest word—analytic interpretation, as an imaginary discourse that serves as truth, makes no attempt to hide its status as fiction, as a *text*.

As a sacred text? This hypothesis is one which we should not be too quick to reject. Nevertheless, we can easily understand that the text of analytic interpretation defuses all beliefs: a psychoanalyst appears suspicious; he is banished from churches and temples. Why? By normalizing and understanding desire, psychoanalysis does not repudiate it, as commonly believed. It is true that analysis shapes and molds desire, but only as the wings of the Paragon of Faith, as the *subjection of desire to a fascinating object*, perhaps an unnameable one. The analyst remains fully aware that this object drapes itself in the attire of the mother Goddess, who extols our fantasies of origins and our desire for interpretation. Consequently, analysts are obliged to distance themselves from Faith in the Goddess of Reason as well as from religious Faith.

Hence, analysts find that the Bible offers a particular narration that suggests a treatment for the very symptoms that they are called on to interpret. Yet, this close relationship with biblical narration opens up the possibility of choice. Faced with the hypostatized Meaning of the Other, analysts maintain their interpretation by negating the intriguing power wielded by this Other, Father, or Law.

The analyst is not unaware that interpretive desire, which is abrasive and frustrating for the fantasy of the other, is tied to the fantasy of returning to the mother. It is true that under the demands of monotheism, such an attitude reveals the obsession with the pagan mother who has shaped it. Nevertheless, psychoanalysts can only avoid the trap of an archetypal Jungianism by admitting that their own sadomasochistic jubilation—which stems from approaching the source of that which is said—masks a certain hold on the unnameable Object (by way of the Law of the father as well as the fascination with the mother). What is more, analysts, as providers of meaning, should eventually saw off the branch, as well as the limb they are sitting on, for the driving force behind faith is the fantasy of returning to the mother, from whom biblical faith specifically distances us. The ensuing ambiguity causes Judaism, when it is completely internalized, to be the least religious of religions.

By laying bare the splendors of the Virgin Mary, Christianity, after having relied on a neo-testamentary discretion toward this subject, has unintentionally revealed what lies behind faith. In contrast to Freud, it could be maintained that the presence of the Virgin throughout Christianity is less a return to paganism than an acknowledgment of the hidden side of the sacred mechanism (of any sacred mechanism), which draws us into its soothing and grinding motion in order to leave us with a single path to salvation: having faith in the Father.

Psychoanalysis does not fall short of this, but goes even further: it is "post-Catholic" by X-raying *meaning as a fantasy,* and then going on to take various phantasmatic functions to be an original fantasy in the form of an adoration of the object-*abject of maternal love* and a cause of eternal return. Finally, it is "post-Catholic" in that it includes *its own process* within this same course of eternal return. Through this three-way loop, the experience of psychoanalysis results in a sort of combustion.

Let us say, then, that everything ends up as fire—the fire of Heraclitus, the fire of the burning bush, the fire that burned Isaiah's tongue, or the fire that bedazzled heads with Pentecostal tongues. The truth of the matter is that I envisage the fate of meaning during an analytic session in a similar fashion—as a meaning that is multifaceted, indefinable, set ablaze, yet One Meaning that exerts its influence everywhere. We can admit that this meaning requires the analyst to cling to the Bible's rigor, logic, and love, so that this fire might *be* and not die down right away. All the same, it must not blind us into thinking that this fire is the only thing that exists, for it need only state the truth at one point or another.

Neither biblical, rationalistic, religious, nor positivist, the place of the analyst is always elsewhere and deceptive, notable for the attention it gives to emptiness. This ambiguous position generates an ethics of construction if not of healing, and it bases itself not on hope but on the fire of tongues. This is enough to irritate believers, which amounts to almost everyone, in spite of what we might think. As Freud said, analysis "exasperates" human beings; it forces them to contradict themselves.

Nevertheless, the central focus (as well as the stumbling block) of this avoidance-through-profusion that constitutes the serene delicacy of the never-attained end of analysis is analogous to the logic of the Bible. Denying the extent of its impact, which means cleansing the Father in order to decipher the Mother or to decipher a walled-up desire, can easily lead to an anti-Semitism in good faith. In a clinical sense, this anti-Semitism may portray a patient caught in the maternal bosom of fantasy, hope, and dependent. The un-being of a chosen yet excluded being is extremely difficult to assimilate.

On the other hand, one could delight in a strict, "mathematical" reading of the biblical text, a reading that avoids all ambiguities, especially the pagan aspect coiled up beside the maternal body, which borders, as I have said, on the logical desire that serves as a foundation for monotheism. This sort of "scientific" reading would encourage us to make analytic practice into a preferred space for hysteria (in men as well as women), a space targeted by what Lacan would call a paranoid "lovehate" for the Other. Have we not seen a great deal of this recently in the various schools of thought and their schisms? What might be done about this? We should read the Bible one more time. To interpret it, of course, but also to let it carve out a space for our own fantasies and interpretive delirium.

NOTES

1. Jacob Neusner, *The Idea of Purity in Ancient Judaism* (Leiden: E. J. Brill, 1973).

2. See Mary Douglas, *Purity and Danger: An Analysis of Concepts of Pollution and Taboo* (London: Routledge and Kegan Paul, 1978).

3. J. Soler, "Sémiotique de la nourriture dans la Bible," *Annales* (July/August 1973): 93.

4. E. M. Zuesse, "Taboo and the Divine Order," *Journal of the American Academy of Religion* 42 (1974): 482–501.

5. Julia Kristeva, *Powers of Horror: Essay on Abjection*, trans. by Léon S. Roudiez. (New York: Columbia University Press, 1982).

6. Sigmund Freud, *The Ego and the Id* (1923), in *The Standard Edition of the Complete Psychological Works of Sigmund Freud*, vol. 19, James Strachey (ed.). (London: Hogarth Press, 1961), p. 31.

CHAPTER 30

The Wheel of Smiles

JULIA KRISTEVA

You creep into the orange light that splashes the eyelids of Saint Anne. Its brightness causes you to skim past the Virgin Mary's shoulder as well as the enigmatic smile of this dancing Mona Lisa. You make your way down her sensual and firm arm that takes Jesus from between her knees and places him on the ground, though she may also be drawing him nearer to her. You immerse yourself in a green the color of Venetian water, a green that flows along with the veil on these graceful thighs and legs. You pause for a moment on the chubby and already impish face of the child-God and of his extension, the lamb—his passion and his resurrection.

Now you make an about-turn, and while lingering in the dazzling movement of the reflected light, you are lured into the face of the mother-daughter double, of Anne and Mary. And you begin again, in an endless progression through these revolving reflections.

It seems that the petals of a mysterious rose of joy are unfolding, and you are soothed by a kaleidoscope of faces. By means of a circular reflection of gazes exchanged between a mother and her son, a very human story is about to be born beneath your eyes. *She* has a twofold grace, in memory of a past maternal caress. *He* is already engaged in an instinctive and erotic flight toward glory.

Modern man lacks the words and images needed to celebrate this imaginary prehistory of the individual. However this may be, the next time you go beyond the tenderness of a dream in which you are both he and she, the skin barely detached and the image barely unfolded, or the next time femininity acknowledges its maternal side, from one end to the other, from body to body, fold upon fold of an exquisite separation, all of which are silent when faced with the delicious torments of amatory or narcissistic uncertainty, go to the Louvre to see this Leonardo painting.

From a theological perspective, Leonardo condensed the Immaculate Conception and the Incarnation into the already accepted model of a "triple Saint Anne" (it is more clearly expressed in Italian and German: *santa Anna Metterza, heilige Anna Selbdritt).* Between the thirteenth and fifteenth centuries, this theme emerged as a double of and counterweight to the classical Trinity, which is composed of the Father, the Son, and the Holy Spirit. This required that a perspective for the Virgin Mary be created, and that Anne accept Mary's immaculate conception (in the form of *praeredemptio,* as Duns Scotus says), and, in the same vein, that both the ternary logic of Christianity and the treatment that it inflicts upon the consecration of a Goddess-mother be enhanced.

Leonardo, who was haunted by Dante's *Paradiso,* envisioned a female Trinity that was also a humanistic celebration of Jesus' body growing out of the iridescent flesh of an Anne lovingly coiled up beside her daughter, Mary. The Creator, like the creator of paintings, would be a man who possessed a glowing femininity that shone in the lamb's brow and guaranteed the Apocalypse as well as a universal smile. For a Renaissance man, then, Jesus had a sexuality. Was his sexuality sublime because he had a mother? We are right at the heart of the Western imaginary.

By grafting an autobiographical novel onto this canvas, Freud made it into a new object of meditation. In reality, no vulture and no kite seems to trace this mystic flight,[1] which nevertheless remains a cult of ideal maternity that the artist has absorbed. If there is a phallus, it may be elsewhere. Indeed, what are Jesus and the lamb actually doing? The animal leg extending the child's as if suggesting a continuity between baby and beast, those fists firmly encircling long, erect ears that resemble horns, this interlocking of the lamb between Christ's legs—is the autoeroticism of the child and the creator the guarantor of maternal exaltation?

Even if this were the case, I would wager that Leonardo's problem was most of all a *plastic* one: how might the *circle* be reconciled with the *triangle?* Mary's head is at a right angle to Anne's shoulder. Mary's legs could be Anne's and vice versa; they form two triangles that lean against each other like two pivots. The angle of Mary's knee points to the oval shape created by her arms. In the group of three feet, the one on the far left creates a mirror image of Mary's right foot. Finally, in the heart of the construction, the curves of Mary's body draw the angles toward an ellipse that points to Jesus, who completes the curve by turning his head. He is aided by the lamb, who reinforces this backward gaze.

Leonardo da Vinci quotes Dante: "If a triangle can be made in the semicircle so that it has no right angle" *(Paradiso,* 13.101). And he elaborates on this: "Any body placed within the luminous air emanates in a circular manner and fills the surrounding space with numberless enactments of the self. The whole appears within the whole, and within each part" *(Notebooks).*

The painter wrote in order to be deciphered in a mirror, perhaps in response to Plotinus. As opposed to the sketch from the National Gallery, in which Anne's index finger points to the heavenly origin of the group, the Louvre canvas depicts the source of the history of Christianity as mutual mirror-effects. "In the beginning" was the reflection of loving gazes. One child and two mothers: without beginning or end, a wheel of smiles.

NOTE

1. In his study on Leonardo da Vinci, Freud quotes the artist's *Notebooks:* "It seems I was always destined to be so deeply concerned with vultures; for I recall as one of my very earliest memories that while I was in my cradle a vulture came down to me and opened my mouth with its tail, and struck me many times with its tail against my lips." Freud perceived the form of this vulture within the drapes of the Virgin, who leans toward the Child. He analyzed what he believed to be less a memory than a fantasy, in an effort to account for Leonard da Vinci's childhood relationship with his mother as well as his subsequent homosexuality.

Original Sources and Permissions

CHAPTER 1: Sigmund Freud, "Obsessive Actions and Religious Practices" (1907), in vol. 9 of *The Standard Edition of the Complete Psychological Works of Sigmund Freud*, ed. James Strachey (London: Hogarth Press, 1959), 115–27. Reprinted by permission of A. W. Freud et al., by arrangement with Mark Paterson & Associates.

CHAPTER 2: Sigmund Freud, *Leonardo da Vinci and a Memory of His Childhood* (1910), in vol. 11 of *The Standard Edition of the Complete Psychological Works of Sigmund Freud*, ed. James Strachey (London: Hogarth Press, 1957), 57–137. Translated by Alan Tyson. Translation © 1957 by the Institute for Psycho-Analysis. Reprinted by permission of W. W. Norton & Company, Inc., Routledge, and A. W. Freud et al., by arrangement with Mark Paterson & Associates.

CHAPTER 3: Sigmund Freud, "The Moses of Michelangelo" (1914), in vol. 13 of *The Standard Edition of the Complete Psychological Works of Sigmund Freud*, ed. James Strachey (London: Hogarth Press, 1955), 211–38. Reprinted by permission of Alfred A. Knopf Inc. and A. W. Freud et al., by arrangement with Mark Paterson & Associates.

CHAPTER 4: Sigmund Freud, "A Seventeenth-Century Demonological Neurosis" (1923), in vol. 19 of *The Standard Edition of the Complete Psychological Works of Sigmund Freud*, ed. James Strachey (London: Hogarth Press, 1957), 69–105. Translated by James Strachey. Translation © 1961 by James Strachey, renewed 1989 by Alix Strachey. Reprinted by permission of A. W. Freud et al., by arrangement with Mark Paterson & Associates.

CHAPTER 5: Sigmund Freud, *The Future of Illusion* (1927), in vol. 21 of *The Standard Edition of the Complete Psychological Works of Sigmund Freud*, ed. James Strachey (London: Hogarth Press, 1961), 1–56. Translated by James Strachey. Translation © 1961 by James Strachey, renewed 1989 by

Alix Strachey. Reprinted by permission of W. W. Norton & Company, Inc., and A. W. Freud et al., by arrangement with Mark Paterson & Associates.

CHAPTER 6: Sigmund Freud, "A Religious Experience" (1928), in vol. 21 of *The Standard Edition of the Complete Psychological Works of Sigmund Freud*, ed. James Strachey (London: Hogarth Press, 1961), 167–72. Reprinted by permission of A. W. Freud et al., by arrangement with Mark Paterson & Associates.

CHAPTER 7: Sigmund Freud, *Civilization and Its Discontents* (1930), in vol. 21 of *The Standard Edition of the Complete Psychological Works of Sigmund Freud*, ed. James Strachey (London: Hogarth Press, 1961), 59–145. Translated by James Strachey. Translation © 1961 by James Strachey, renewed 1989 by Alix Strachey. Reprinted by permission of W. W. Norton & Company, Inc., and A. W. Freud et al., by arrangement with Mark Paterson & Associates.

CHAPTER 8: Sigmund Freud, *Moses and Monotheism: Three Essays* (1939), in vol. 23 of *The Standard Edition of the Complete Psychological Works of Sigmund Freud*, ed. James Strachey (London: Hogarth Press, 1964), 7–137. Reprinted by permission of Alfred A. Knopf Inc., and A. W. Freud et al., by arrangement with Mark Paterson & Associates.

CHAPTER 9: David Bakan, *Sigmund Freud and the Jewish Mystical Tradition* (Princeton: D. Van Nostrand, 1958), 214–18, 235–37. Reprinted by permission of the author.

CHAPTER 10: David Bakan, *The Duality of Human Existence: An Essay on Psychology of Religion* (Chicago: Rand-McNally, 1966), 202–7, 212–17. Reprinted by permission of the author.

CHAPTER 11: David Bakan, "Sacrifice and the Book of Job," in *Disease, Pain and Sacrifice: Toward a Psychology of Suffering* (Chicago: University of Chicago Press, 1968), 95–128. Reprinted by permission of the University of Chicago Press and the author.

CHAPTER 12: Erik H. Erikson, "Reflections on Dr. Borg's Life Cycle," *Daedalus* 105 (1976): 1–31. Reprinted by permission of *Daedalus*, Journal of the American Academy of Arts and Sciences, from the issue entitled "Adulthood."

CHAPTER 13: Erik H. Erikson, *Young Man Luther: A Study in Psychoanalysis and History* (New York: W. W. Norton, 1958), 69–70, 72–73, 115–24, 208, 263–66. © 1958, 1962, and renewed 1986, 1990 by Erik H. Erikson. Reprinted by permission of W. W. Norton & Company, Inc.

CHAPTER 14: Erik H. Erikson, *Toys and Reasons: Stages in the Ritualization of Experience* (New York: W. W. Norton, 1977), 78–92. © 1977 by W. W. Norton & Company, Inc. Reprinted by permission of W. W. Norton & Company, Inc.

CHAPTER 15: Erik H. Erikson, "Shared Visions," in *Toys and Reasons: Stages in the Ritualization of Experience* (New York: W. W. Norton, 1977), 121–34. © 1977 by W. W. Norton & Company, Inc. Reprinted by permission of W. W. Norton & Company, Inc.

CHAPTER 16: Erik H. Erikson, "The Galilean Sayings and the Sense of 'I'," *Yale Review* 70 (1981): 321–62. Reprinted by permission of the *Yale Review* and by Kai T. Erikson for the estate of E. H. Erikson.

CHAPTER 17: D. W. Winnicott, "Transitional Objects and Transitional Phenomena," *International Journal of Psycho-Analysis* 34 (1953): 89–97. Reprinted by permission of the *International Journal of Psycho-Analysis* and by Mark Paterson & Associates on behalf of the Winnicott Trust.

CHAPTER 18: W. W. Meissner, *Psychoanalysis and Religious Experience*, (New Haven: Yale University Press, 1984), 177–83. Reprinted by permission of Yale University Press.

CHAPTER 19: D. W. Winnicott, "The Use of an Object and Relating through Identifications," *International Journal of Psycho-Analysis* 50 (1969): 711–16. Reprinted by permission of the *International Journal of Psycho-Analysis,* and by Mark Paterson & Associates on behalf of the Winnicott Trust. © Institute of Psychoanalysis.

CHAPTER 20: Brooke Hopkins, "Jesus and Object Use: A Winnicottian Account of the Resurrection Myth," *International Review of Psychoanalysis* 16 (1989): 93–100. © Institute of Psychoanalysis. Reprinted by permission of *International Review of Psychoanalysis,* and by the author.

CHAPTER 21: Heinz Kohut and Ernest S. Wolf, "The Disorders of the Self and Their Treatment," *International Journal of Psycho-Analysis* 59 (1978): 413–25. © Institute of Psychoanalysis. Reprinted by permission of the *International Journal of Psycho-Analysis,* and by Ernest S. Wolf and Thomas A. Kohut.

CHAPTER 22: Heinz Kohut, "Forms and Transformations of Narcissism," *Journal of the American Psychoanalytic Association* 14 (1966): 243–72. Reprinted by permission of International Universities Press.

CHAPTER 23: Heinz Kohut, *The Restoration of the Self* (New York: International Universities Press, 1977), 199–219, 280–85. Reprinted by permission of International Universities Press.

CHAPTER 24: Heinz Kohut, "A Reexamination of Agoraphobia," in *How Does Analysis Cure,* ed. Arnold Goldberg (Chicago and London: University of Chicago Press, 1984), 28–33. © 1984 by the University of Chicago. Reprinted by permission of the University of Chicago Press.

CHAPTER 25: Heinz Kohut, "On Courage," in *Self Psychology and the Humanities: Reflections on a New Psychoanalytic Approach,* ed. Charles Strozier (New York: W. W. Norton, 1985), 5–50. © by Charles B. Strozier and Elizabeth Kohut. Reprinted by permission of W. W. Norton & Company, Inc.

CHAPTER 26: Julia Kristeva, "Credo in Unum Deum," in *In the Beginning Was Love: Psychoanalysis and Faith,* trans. Arthur Godhammer (New York: Columbia University Press, 1987), 37–44. Reproduced by permission of the publisher via Copyright Clearance Center, Inc.

CHAPTER 27: Julia Kristeva, *Black Sun: Depression and Melancholia,* trans. Leon S. Roudiez (New York: Columbia University Press, 1989), 110–15, 118–19, 126–38. Reproduced by permission of the publisher via Copyright Clearance Center, Inc.

CHAPTER 28: Julia Kristeva, *Strangers to Ourselves,* trans. Leon S. Roudiez (New York: Columbia University Press, 1991), 181–92. Reproduced by permission of the publisher via Copyright Clearance Center, Inc.

CHAPTER 29: Julia Kristeva, "Reading the Bible," in *New Maladies of the Soul,* trans. Ross Guberman (New York: Columbia University Press, 1995), 115–26. Reproduced by permission of the publisher via Copyright Clearance Center, Inc.

CHAPTER 30: Julia Kristeva, "Wheel of Smiles," in *New Maladies of the Soul,* trans. Ross Guberman. (New York: Columbia University Press, 1995), 154–58. Reproduced by permission of the publisher via Copyright Clearance Center, Inc.

Index

CPSIA information can be obtained
at www.ICGtesting.com
Printed in the USA
FSHW021559090820
72818FS